T0195306

FEEDING THE WORLD WELL

Feeding the World Well

World Well

A FRAMEWORK FOR ETHICAL FOOD SYSTEMS

Edited by Alan M. Goldberg

With Cara Wychgram, Associate Editor

JOHNS HOPKINS UNIVERSITY PRESS | *Baltimore*

Johns Hopkins University Press
2715 North Charles Street
Baltimore, Maryland 21218-4363
www.press.jhu.edu

Library of Congress Cataloging-in-Publication Data

Names: Goldberg, Alan M., editor.
Title: Feeding the world well : a framework for ethical food systems /
    Alan M. Goldberg.
Description: Baltimore, Maryland : Johns Hopkins University Press, 2020. |
    Includes bibliographical references and index.
Identifiers: LCCN 2020003383 | ISBN 9781421439341 (hardcover) |
    ISBN 9781421439358 (ebook)
Subjects: LCSH: Food supply—Moral and ethical aspects. | Sustainable agriculture. |
    Food—Safety measures. | Animal welfare.
Classification: LCC HD9000.5 .F3485 2020 | DDC 174/.963—dc23
LC record available at https://lccn.loc.gov/2020003383

A catalog record for this book is available from the British Library.

*Special discounts are available for bulk purchases of this book. For more informa-
tion, please contact Special Sales at specialsales@press.jhu.edu.*

Johns Hopkins University Press uses environmentally friendly book materials,
including recycled text paper that is composed of at least 30 percent post-consumer
waste, whenever possible.

CONTENTS

ANNE BARNHILL is a Research Scholar at the Johns Hopkins Berman Institute of Bioethics.

MARTIN W. BLOEM is the inaugural Robert S. Lawrence Professor and the Director of the Johns Hopkins Center for a Livable Future in the Department of Environmental Health and Engineering at the Johns Hopkins Bloomberg School of Public Health.

JONATHAN BLOOM is the author of *American Wasteland: How America Throws Away Nearly Half of Its Food (and What We Can Do About It)* and the creator of wastedfood.com.

NICOLE M. CIVITA is an Instructor and the Sustainable Food Systems Specialization Lead in the Masters of the Environment Graduate Program at the University of Colorado Boulder and Adjunct Faculty at the Johns Hopkins Berman Institute of Bioethics.

CLAIRE DAVIS is a Science Writer at the Johns Hopkins Berman Institute of Bioethics.

MICHIEL VAN DIJK is a Research Scholar at the International Institute for Applied Systems Analysis and a Senior Researcher at Wageningen Economic Research.

ADELE DOUGLASS is the Chief Executive Officer of Humane Farm Animal Care.

SHAUNA DOWNS is an Assistant Professor in the Department of Urban-Global Public Health at the Rutgers School of Public Health.

KEVIN ESVELT is an Assistant Professor and Leader of the Sculpting Evolution Group at the Massachusetts Institute of Technology's MIT Media Lab.

RUTH FADEN is the Founder of the Johns Hopkins Berman Institute of Bioethics and the inaugural Philip Franklin Wagley Professor of Biomedical Ethics.

JESSICA FANZO is the Bloomberg Distinguished Associate Professor of Global Food and Agricultural Policy and Ethics at the Johns Hopkins Nitze School of Advanced International Studies, the Johns Hopkins Berman Institute of Bioethics, and the Department of International Health at the Johns Hopkins Bloomberg School of Public Health. She is also the Director of the Johns Hopkins Global Food Ethics and Policy Program.

EVAN FRASER is a Professor in the Department of Geography, Environment, and Geomatics and the Director of the Arrell Food Institute at the University of Guelph.

MAISIE GANZLER is the Chief Strategy and Brand Officer at Bon Appétit Management Company.

TARA GARNETT is a researcher at the Environmental Change Institute at the University of Oxford, where she also leads the Food Climate Research Network. She is also a fellow of the Oxford Martin School.

SARA GLASS is a Research Program Manager at the Johns Hopkins Sidney Kimmel Comprehensive Cancer Center.

ALAN M. GOLDBERG is a Professor in the Department of Environmental Health and Engineering at the Johns Hopkins Bloomberg School of Public Health and the Founding Director (Emeritus) of the Johns Hopkins Center for Alternatives to Animal Testing. He is also Principal of the Global Food Ethics Project, a project of the Johns Hopkins Berman Institute of Bioethics, Bloomberg School of Public Health, and the Nitze School of Advanced International Studies.

CHRISTOPHER GOOD is the Director of Research at the Freshwater Institute.

MEREDITH KAUFMAN is a graduate of the LLM Program in Agricultural and Food Law at the University of Arkansas School of Law.

GILLIAN KELLEHER is Vice President of Food Safety and Quality Assurance at Wegmans Food Markets.

FREDERICK L. KIRSCHENMANN is a Distinguished Fellow at the Leopold Center for Sustainable Agriculture and a Professor in the Department of Religion and Philosophy at Iowa State University.

HERMAN B. W. M. KOËTER is the Founder and Managing Director of the Orange House Partnership.

JENNIFER KUZMA is the Goodnight-NCGSK Foundation Distinguished Professor in the School of Public and International Affairs and Co-Founder and Co-Director of the Genetic Engineering and Society Center at North Carolina State University.

KEES VAN LEEUWEN is Chief Science Officer and Principal Scientist at the KWR Watercycle Research Institute and a Professor in Water Management and Urban Development at the University of Utrecht.

ROBERT MARTIN is the Program Director of the Food System Policy Program at the Johns Hopkins Center for a Livable Future.

ANNE E. MCBRIDE is the Culinary Programs Director of the Strategic Initiatives Group at The Culinary Institute of America and the Deputy Director of the Torribera Mediterranean Center.

SUZANNE MCMILLAN is the Content Director of the Farm Animal Welfare Campaign at the American Society for the Prevention of Cruelty to Animals.

TOM MORLEY is a Researcher at Wageningen Economic Research.

MARION NESTLE is the Paulette Goddard Professor of Nutrition, Food Studies, and Public Health, Emerita, at New York University.

PETER O'DRISCOLL is Executive Director of the Equitable Food Initiative.

LANCE B. PRICE is a Professor in the Department of Environmental and Occupational Health and the Founding Director of the Antibiotic Resistance Action Center at the George Washington University Milken Institute School of Public Health.

MARIE LUISE RAU is a Researcher at Wageningen Economic Research.

BERNARD ROLLIN is a distinguished professor of philosophy, animal sciences, and biomedical sciences at Colorado State University.

YASHAR SAGHAI is an Assistant Professor in the Department of Philosophy at the University of Twente and an Associate Senior Scholar at the Millennium Project: Global Futures Studies and Research.

SUSAN A. SCHNEIDER is the William H. Enfield Professor of Law and the Director of the LL.M. Program in Agricultural & Food Law at the University of Arkansas School of Law.

ELLEN K. SILBERGELD is a Professor Emeritus in the Department of Environmental Health and Engineering at the Johns Hopkins Bloomberg School of Public Health. She is the author of *Chickenizing Farms and Food: How Industrial Meat Production Endangers Workers, Animals, and Consumers.*

PAUL B. THOMPSON is the W. K. Kellogg Chair in Agricultural, Food and Community Ethics and a Professor in the Departments of Philosophy, Community Sustainability, and Agricultural, Food and Resource Economics at Michigan State University.

PAUL WILLIS is a Farmer and Founder of the Niman Ranch Pork Company.

SYLVIA WULF is the former President of Stock Yards and Senior Vice President of Merchandising at US Foods. She is now Executive Director, President, and Chief Executive Officer of AquaBounty Technologies, Inc.

The Choose Food project would not have been possible without the generous support of the Stavros Niarchos Foundation (SNF). The entire Johns Hopkins team would like to acknowledge not only SNF's critical financial assistance but also the intellectual support and encouragement of Andreas Dracopoulos, Stelios Vasilakis, Jeannette Giorsetti, and Argero (Roula) Siklas. We cannot imagine a better program officer than Roula. We thank you.

I am grateful for all the help, support, freely shared ideas, and encouragement from my Johns Hopkins colleagues, the entire academic team, and project advisers—all of whom are identified in the book's introduction.

I am specifically grateful to Kelly Whalen and Cara Wychgram for their administrative support. The bulk of the editorial work was done by Cara Wychgram, and for this I have appropriately identified her as Associate Editor. Cara, nicely done.

I would also like to acknowledge the incredible support by my wife, Helene. She was there at every moment, soothed the feathers when they were ruffled by others, celebrated the successes, and always was available and encouraging. She never complained about the dirty and sometimes smelly clothes when I came back from a farm visit. And we always enjoyed the fresh foods that came with those visits.

To each and every one of you, THANK YOU.

FEEDING THE WORLD WELL

Introduction

ALAN M. GOLDBERG

IN THE UNITED STATES, we produce an abundance of food that is
cheap at the supermarket but loaded with hidden costs to the environment, human health, animal welfare, and the people who work in
our food systems. Our current food production systems lack diversity
in crops and animals and are intensified but not sustainable, inhumane
in the treatment of animals, and inconsiderate of labor. By 2050, the
world's population will have grown by about two billion people. In order to feed the world of 2050 and beyond with high-quality, ethically
produced food, we need to develop new food production systems. These
systems need to be genetically diverse and environmentally and nutritionally sustainable, and they must have internationally recognized animal welfare and labor considerations.

Just over 10 years ago, I was invited to be a commissioner on the Pew
Commission on Industrial Farm Animal Production. The purpose of the
commission was to investigate the impact of our current food animal
production systems on the environment, animal welfare, rural communities, and public health and to develop recommendations to improve
these systems. The commission's report, *Putting Meat on the Table: Industrial Farm Animal Production in America*, was cited by the press more
than 700 times in the week it was released. It is still considered to be the

defining report on this topic. Unfortunately, the report had virtually no regulatory or legislative impact. That was an important lesson for me and perhaps the first time I truly understood the power of industry to both effect and block change. Because it plays such an influential role, industry can contribute to both positive and negative outcomes.

I realized that in order to change our food systems, consumers need to be engaged and informed. What matters to consumers has direct implications for industry. That is why I approached Ruth Faden, the founding director of the Johns Hopkins Berman Institute of Bioethics, about developing a food ethics program. In 2012 we launched the Global Food Ethics Project, which evolved into the Global Food Ethics and Policy Program (GFEPP). The concept of informing consumers about the ethics of their food choices became the Choose Food project under GFEPP in 2016.

Over the past four years, the Choose Food project has focused on identifying ethical concerns in food production and consumption. Our initial work was to identify core areas of concern (i.e., environment, crops and horticulture, water, animal welfare, public health, food safety, and labor) and then commission experts to write white papers (also known as Moral Maps) laying out the ethical considerations in their respective areas. Drawing on these seven Moral Maps as well as workshop discussions, the project team developed a preliminary set of Core Ethical Commitments. Through continued analysis and refinement, the team finalized a set of 47 Core Ethical Commitments that cover 5 areas of concern: environment and resources; food chain labor; farmers, ranchers, and fishers; public health and community well-being; and animal welfare. The Core Ethical Commitments are intended to guide market-based shifts toward more ethical food systems. They provide a tool that consumers can use to inform their food choices, and a tool that producers can use to incorporate ethical considerations into their decision making and practices.

In November 2018, the project team presented the Moral Maps and Core Ethical Commitments at the Choose Food Symposium in Baltimore, Maryland. To provide valuable context and perspective to the team's work, leading food systems experts spoke on a wide range of topics, including climate change, antibiotic resistance, food waste, biotechnology, and historical and regulatory drivers in US agriculture. Representatives from industry and nonprofits were also invited to share how their organizations were responding to ethical challenges in the food system.

This volume, like the symposium that gave rise to it, serves to set up the Core Ethical Commitments framework developed by the Choose Food project. The topical chapters contributed by symposium presenters are not only interesting and informative on their own but also help build context and rationale for the framework. This volume is primarily intended as a textbook for undergraduate and graduate food studies courses, but it will appeal to anyone who is strongly interested in food, including conscious consumers, food industry leaders, researchers, and policy makers.

The first part of this volume, *The Big Picture*, sets up the challenge of feeding the world. The moral imperative underlying this challenge is that we need to produce enough nutritious food to feed the world's growing population.

In the second part, *Food Systems in Context*, some of the fundamental forces that have shaped, and will continue to shape, our food systems are discussed. It provides useful context for reading this volume's subsequent chapters on considerations and approaches for more ethical food systems.

The third part, *Contemporary Challenges and Complexities in Food Ethics*, explores the ethical challenges facing our food systems. The chapters are grouped into four sections: *Environment, Producers and Laborers, Public Health*, and *Animal Welfare*. Each section begins with the Moral Map chapters that are foundational works of the Choose Food project.

The fourth part, *Case Studies*, describes some of the approaches that food companies and nonprofit organizations are using to address ethical challenges in the food system.

The last part, *The Core Ethical Commitments: A Framework for Ethical Food Systems*, explains what the Core Ethical Commitments are (and what they are not), how they were developed, and how they might be used by food system actors.

Choose Food Project Team

Members of the Johns Hopkins Project Team were:

- Alan M. Goldberg, PhD, Principal Investigator, Professor, Johns Hopkins Bloomberg School of Public Health
- Ruth Faden, PhD, MPH, Founding Director, Johns Hopkins Berman Institute of Bioethics
- Jessica Fanzo, PhD, Director, Global Food Ethics and Policy Program, Johns Hopkins Berman Institute of Bioethics and School of Advanced International Studies
- Anne Barnhill, PhD, Associate Faculty, Research Scholar, Johns Hopkins Berman Institute of Bioethics
- Nicole M. Civita, JD, LLM, Adjunct Faculty, Johns Hopkins Berman Institute of Bioethics, Instructor and Sustainable Food Systems Specialization Lead, University of Colorado Boulder
- Claire Davis, MA, Science Writer, Johns Hopkins Berman Institute of Bioethics
- Cara Wychgram, MPP, Research Program Coordinator, Johns Hopkins Berman Institute of Bioethics
- Kelly Whalen, BS, Senior Administrative Coordinator, Johns Hopkins Berman Institute of Bioethics

The Core Academic Team/Moral Map authors were:

- Paul B. Thompson, Michigan State University
- Bernard Rollin, Colorado State University
- Kees van Leeuwen, University of Utrecht, KWR Watercycle Research Institute
- Anne Barnhill, Johns Hopkins Berman Institute of Bioethics
- Nicole M. Civita, Johns Hopkins Berman Institute of Bioethics, University of Colorado Boulder
- Tara Garnett, University of Oxford
- Herman B. W. M. Koëter, Orange House Partnership

Project Advisors were:

- Fedele Bauccio, Bon Appétit Management Company
- Maisie Ganzler, Bon Appétit Management Company
- Peter O'Driscoll, Equitable Food Initiative
- Steve Wearne, UK Food Standards Agency
- Adele Douglass, Humane Farm Animal Care
- Suzanne McMillan, American Society for the Prevention of Cruelty to Animals

Many chapters describe the weaknesses of the US food system prior to 2020. The COVID-19 pandemic made these weaknesses obvious to all. Hopefully, we will be able to change our food systems and incorporate the knowledge and wisdom shared in the volume.

PART I **THE BIG PICTURE**

ONE

Feeding the World (Well)

The Moral Imperative

JESSICA FANZO

O NE OF THE big-picture questions in food ethics is, How do we feed the world *well*? As we try to answer this question, we need to consider the state of our diets, the consequences of those diets, the actions we can take to shift our diets, those responsible for taking action, and the moral imperative of feeding the world well.

What Is the State of Our Diets?

The 2018 Global Nutrition Report (GNR) shows that a country's economic status does not necessarily indicate whether a population will consume healthy foods (figure 1.1). All income groups consume too much of sugar-sweetened beverages and salt and too little of fruits and vegetables on a daily basis. Even in high-income countries, populations are consuming too few of healthy food groups, including legumes, vegetables, whole grains, fruit, nuts, and seeds, and too much red meat, processed meats, and trans fats. Low- and lower-income countries' intake of legumes exceed that of upper-middle- and high-income countries.[1] Subregionally, or even at a household or individual level, there are, of course, people who are consuming healthy diets, but overall the global dietary pattern is falling short.

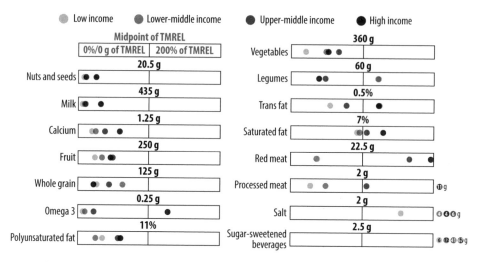

Figure 1.1. Consumption of Food Groups and Components across Income Groups, 2016.

Notes: Men and women aged 25 and older. Chart ordered by mean. TMREL: theoretical minimum risk exposure level. *Source:* Jessica Fanzo and Corinna Hawkes, Development Initiatives, "2018 Global Nutrition Report: Shining a Light to Spur Action on Nutrition" (Bristol, UK: Development Initiatives, 2018). Data from Global Burden of Disease, the Institute for Health Metrics and Evaluation.

Our diets not only are unhealthy but also have repercussions on the environment. As incomes rise, people consume more animal-source foods. Beef has a particularly large greenhouse gas footprint compared to other animal-source and plant-based foods.[2] However, when we look across a suite of environmental indicators beyond just greenhouse gases, such as cropland use, blue water use, biodiversity, and nitrogen and phosphorus application, different foods have different environmental footprints. Although beef is an outlier in terms of the high extent of its effect on greenhouse gases, other foods can also have significant environmental footprints.

Different food groups and their present (2010) and projected (2050) environmental pressures are shown in figure 1.2. For example, animal-source foods currently have a large greenhouse gas footprint, which is expected to continue. However, staple crops have a significant land use impact, and many of the staple crops we grow are fed to the animals we consume.

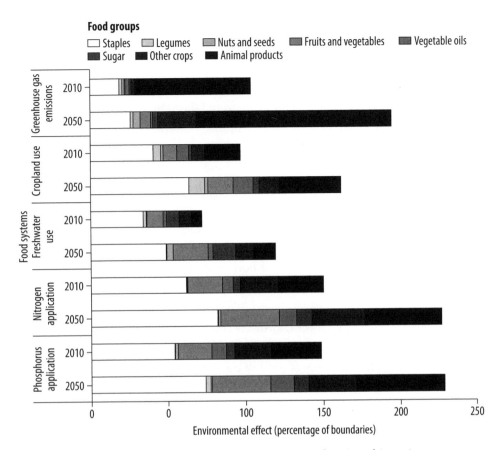

Figure 1.2. Food Groups and Their Present (2010) and Projected (2050) Environmental Pressures.

Source: Walter Willett, Johan Rockström, Brent Loken, Marco Springmann, Tim Lang, Sonja Vermeulen, Tara Garnett, et al. "Food in the Anthropocene: The EAT-Lancet Commission on Healthy Diets from Sustainable Food Systems," *Lancet* 393, no. 10170 (February 2, 2019): 447-92.

In 1992 world scientists issued a "Warning to Humanity" about the worsening destruction of environmental resources. Twenty-five years later, scientists renewed that warning by publishing data showing that almost every environmental issue identified in the 1992 warning has been exacerbated in the time since. In 25 years, the planet has experienced further loss of forests, freshwater resources, and vertebrate species and further increases in ocean dead zones, carbon emissions, and temperatures.[3] Food systems are both a contributor to and a victim of environmental degradation, and diets feed into that.

In many countries undergoing a "nutrition transition,"[4] diets are transforming in inequitable ways. With urbanization, globalization, and economic growth, we see a shift away from labor-intensive lifestyles and low-variety diets (stage 3 of the transition) to more sedentary lifestyles and diets abundant in highly processed convenience foods high in salt, sugar, and unhealthy fats and in street foods (stage 4). It is a shift from undernutrition to overweight and obesity. There are still nearly one billion people in stage 3 who go to bed hungry every night.[5] Probably an equal number of people in stage 5 purposefully eat healthily and exercise. But most people on this planet—around five billion—are in stage 4, where there is a double burden of both undernutrition and obesity and a shift from communicable diseases to diet-related noncommunicable diseases.

Stage 4 of the nutrition transition represents an often-overlooked population that we need to pay attention to because otherwise the societal costs will be quite profound. We are seeing a shift toward obesity even in low-income countries. The *New York Times* has an ongoing series called "Planet Fat,"[6] which shows that rapidly transforming food environments are everywhere. Fast-food chains and other unhealthy food outlets are moving into places like Accra, Ghana, and Brazil's Amazon. The infiltration of cheap and convenient food outlets could have enormous consequences for obesity rates around the world.

What Are the Consequences of Suboptimal Diets?

Diets are the second-leading risk factor for disease (measured as DALYs, or disability-adjusted life years), especially cardiovascular disease (figure 1.3). Suboptimal diets—those high in unhealthy fats, sugar, salt, and red meat and low in fiber, fruit and vegetables, whole grains, and legumes—are a greater risk factor for disease than tobacco, air pollution, alcohol and drug use, and occupational risks.

According to the 2018 Global Nutrition Report, the burden of malnutrition "remains unacceptably high." One hundred fifty-one million

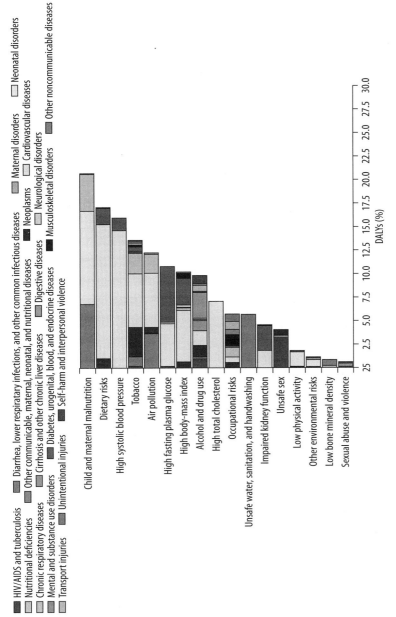

Figure 1.3. Global DALYs Attributed to Risk Factors in 2016.

Source: Emmanuela Gakidou, Ashkan Afshin, Amanuel Alemu Abajobir; Kalkidan Hassen Abate, Cristiana Abbafati, Kaja M. Abbas, Foad Abd-Allah, et al., "Global, Regional, and National Comparative Risk Assessment of 84 Behavioural, Environmental and Occupational, and Metabolic Risks or Clusters of Risks, 1990–2016: A Systematic Analysis for the Global Burden of Disease Study 2016," *Lancet* 390, no. 10100 (September 16, 2017): 1345–1422, doi: 10.1016/S0140-6736(17)32366-8. This figure is reproduced here under the terms of the Creative Commons 4.0 license.

children (or 22% of the world's children) under five years of age are stunted, 51 million children are wasted or acutely malnourished, 38 million children are overweight, and over 2 billion adults are overweight or obese. We also see double and triple burdens of malnutrition, where more than one form of malnutrition can be found in the same individual, household, or country.[7] A child can be stunted, obese, and deficient in micronutrients such as vitamin A and iron.

Lastly, diets are not accessible to all. Food remains incredibly expensive in many parts of the world. In low-income countries, consumers tend to spend a large percentage of their income on food. In Kenya and Cameroon, consumers spend nearly half of their income on food, and in Nigeria they spend even more. Conversely, in high-income countries, consumers tend to spend very little of their income on food. In the United States, the average consumer spends only about 6% of income on food.[8]

What Actions Can We Take to Achieve Sustainable, Nutritious Diets by 2050?

To successfully shift diets on a global, national, or even individual scale, we need various approaches that target different people and at different scales. There are many ways to effect change, including fiscal measures, regulatory and trade interventions, voluntary and industry approaches, interventions focusing on the context and social norms of dietary consumption, and behavior change communication approaches.

Food systems are complex and encompass food supply chains, the food environment, personal filters, and nutrition and health outcomes (figure 1.4). Our diets are born from these food systems, which determine the types of food produced and the nature of their journey from farm to fork. With increasing globalization, urbanization, and income growth, the length and efficiency of food supply chains overall have increased, and food environments in which consumers make decisions about what to buy or order have become more complex and nuanced with multiple actors shaping their transformation. Currently, commercial food systems are designed to sustain a diverse range of private-sector actors ranging from small businesses to multinational corporations.

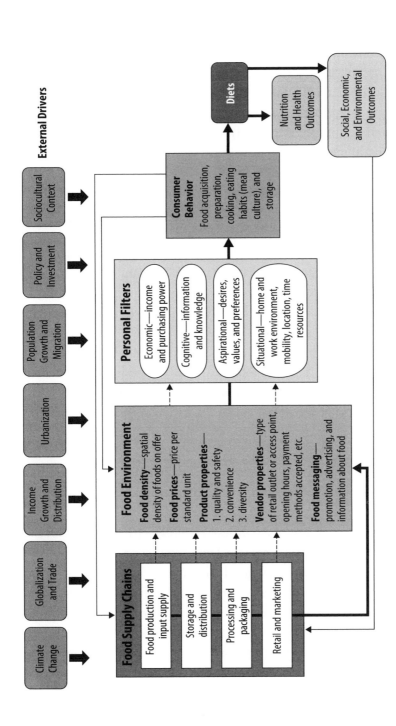

Figure 1.4. A Conceptual Framework of Food Systems.

Source: Adapted from HLPE. "Nutrition and Food Systems. A Report by the High Level Panel of Experts on Food Security and Nutrition of the Committee on World Food Security," Rome, 2017.

The globalized food system is not optimal and contributes to the high burden of malnutrition in all its forms and environmental degradation. This failure to ensure that food systems deliver better diets while minimizing environmental impacts is costly. We must ensure food systems are reshifted to provide a sufficient quality and quantity of food that is healthy, affordable, safe, culturally acceptable, and produced in an environmentally sustainable way. Because food systems are complex, this will require multifaceted solutions.

First, we need to care. We need to care about diets. We especially need to care about the climate. This means governments, too. In 2018 the Intergovernmental Panel on Climate Change (IPPC) released a special report that emphasized that the challenge of avoiding catastrophic climate breakdown requires "rapid, far-reaching and unprecedented changes in all aspects of society,"[9] including changes in our food systems. Without these changes, our ability to produce enough food will be threatened and the situation will get much worse.

Second, we need to commit to the 17 global Sustainable Development Goals (SDGs). They are lofty goals, but they matter. They matter because they provide us with a roadmap for how to move forward without leaving anyone behind. We also need to anticipate the trade-offs between these goals. Achieving one goal may have negative impacts on another. For example, the zero hunger goal (SDG 2) converges with many other goals in ways that are synergistic but also has negative impacts on other goals. Therefore, we need to consider our approaches to these goals very carefully.

Third, we need to institute policies that work across food system entry points. World Cancer Research Fund International developed the NOURISHING framework, which looks at policy interventions across three domains: the food environment, the food system, and behavior change communication.[10] There is already evidence that these policy areas can improve nutrition and health. School-based interventions, for example, have shown promising health results.[11] All of these interventions are important, and we need all of them happening at once. However, policies like these are not being scaled.

Fourth, we need to maximize entry points and minimize exit points for nutrition along the value chain. Food value chain approaches can provide useful frameworks to examine the food system and the potential to achieve improved nutritional outcomes by leveraging market-based systems. One of the main uses of value chain analysis is to help identify points in the chain—from inputs to production to processing, marketing, and consumption—that can be "leveraged for change."[12] Understanding the links between value chains, the overall environment in which they operate, and nutrition among targeted populations is complex. Policymakers need to understand the possible leverage points, invest in them, and scale them up.

Fifth, we need to consider options for keeping the food system within environmental limits. Dietary changes, technological changes in food production, and reductions in food loss and waste are all critical to reducing the environmental impacts of our food system. Dietary changes toward more plant-based foods can have a significant impact on greenhouse gas emissions. Technological changes on farms can reduce cropland use, blue water use, and nitrogen and phosphorous application.[13]

Lastly, we need to ensure that no one is left behind. There are still many people living in extreme poverty.[14] These are the people who are the most vulnerable to malnutrition as well as climate change. We need to ensure that the most vulnerable have enough food and that this food is safe, nutritious, and culturally appropriate so they can rise up and have an equal footing and equal voice.

Who Should Take Action?

Governments need to play a key role in creating innovative partnerships and a supportive political environment. Donors need to invest in food systems; they need to care about diets and food systems and understand the implications of not investing. Civil society organizations can cultivate movements, coalitions, and networks among individuals and communities and put pressure on governments and the private sector. Private-sector actors must share power across food systems and prioritize health and the environment. Academia and research need to govern conflicts of interest and build the evidence base of what works, where, and why.

We cannot leave it all to the individual. We cannot simply say that it is the individual's responsibility to become informed enough and to have enough willpower to choose the right foods. Public understanding of the health and environmental impacts of food is low. We also cannot leave it all to industry goodwill. Some in the food industry are acting, but their efforts alone are not enough. We need governments to actually govern the food system. Policy makers need to create a strong regulatory and fiscal framework and start making informed decisions that promote sustainable healthy diets.

Is Feeding the World Well a Moral Imperative?

We assume that all people, now and in the future, should have access to affordable, safe, sufficient, and nutritious food, as well as the conditions necessary to benefit from that food, for adequate health across the life span. But is it our moral imperative to feed the world well? Most people would argue that we do have a moral obligation.

Food is ethically significant because of its critical impact on what we must value. We must value human life, and eating is a daily necessity, and making choices about what to eat is a daily part of life. We must value cultures, and food encompasses many aspects, including cooking know-how, culinary traditions, eating practices, rural ways of life, agricultural landscapes, and sociocultural organization. We must value labor, and the food system is one of the world's largest employers. We must value the environment and the lives of nonhuman animals, and the food system is tied to the diversity and health of our ecosystems and natural resources as well as the species and varieties within those landscapes.

According to Wendell Berry, "eating is an agricultural act,"[15] yet we could argue that "eating is an ethical act" as well. Through the act of eating, we are more than just consumers. Eating evokes emotion. It can be mundane or sublime, but either way eating involves moral decision making rooted within traditions, cultures, and structures surrounding human nourishment.

Conclusion

Our diets not only contribute to the massive burden of malnutrition but also have significant impacts on the environment. We need significant action across food systems now to ensure that people can eat and that they can eat *well*. There are many policy actions that we can take, from committing to the global Sustainable Development Goals to enacting national food policies that span value chains, food environments, and consumer demand. No one approach can do everything, so we need to apply a mix of regulatory, fiscal, voluntary, and other approaches. Importantly, our approaches need to consider the whole food system so that we can recognize health and environmental win-wins as well as trade-offs.

REFERENCES

1. Development Initiatives, "2018 Global Nutrition Report: Shining a Light to Spur Action on Nutrition" (Bristol, UK: Development Initiatives, 2018).

2. J. Poore and T. Nemecek, "Reducing Food's Environmental Impacts through Producers and Consumers," *Science* 360, no. 6392 (June 2018): 987–92.

3. William J. Ripple et al., "World Scientists' Warning to Humanity: A Second Notice," *Bioscience* 67, no. 12 (December 2017): 1026–28.

4. Barry M. Popkin, "An Overview of the Nutrition Transition and Its Health Implications: The Bellagio Meeting," *Public Health Nutrition* 5, no. 1A (February 2002): 93–103.

5. Food and Agriculture Organization of the United Nations et al., *The State of Food Security and Nutrition in the World 2018: Building Climate Resilience for Food Security and Nutrition* (Rome: FAO, 2018).

6. "Planet Fat," *New York Times*, https://www.nytimes.com/series/obesity-epidemic.

7. Development Initiatives, "2018 Global Nutrition Report."

8. HLPE, "Nutrition and Food Systems. A Report by the High Level Panel of Experts on Food Security and Nutrition of the Committee on World Food Security" (Rome, 2017).

9. Intergovernmental Panel on Climate Change, "Summary for Policymakers of IPCC Special Report on Global Warming of 1.5°C approved by governments,"

news release, October 8, 2018, https://www.ipcc.ch/site/assets/uploads/2018/11/pr_181008_P48_spm_en.pdf.

10. "Our Policy Framework to Promote Healthy Diets & Reduce Obesity," World Cancer Research Fund International, https://www.wcrf.org/int/policy/nourishing/our-policy-framework-promote-healthy-diets-reduce-obesity.

11. Tara Garnett and Jess Finch, "What Can Be Done to Shift Eating Patterns in Healthier, More Sustainable Directions?," in *Foodsource*, ed. Food Climate Research Network (Oxford: University of Oxford, 2016).

12. Corinna Hawkes, "Identifying Innovative Interventions to Promote Healthy Eating Using Consumption-Oriented Food Supply Chain Analysis," *Journal of Hunger & Environmental Nutrition* 4, nos. 3–4 (July 2009): 336–56.

13. Marco Springmann et al., "Options for Keeping the Food System within Environmental Limits," *Nature* 562, no. 7728 (October 2018): 519–25.

14. "Number of People Living in Extreme Poverty," Development Initiatives, http://data.devinit.org/global-picture/poverty.

15. Wendell Berry, *What Are People For?* (New York: North Point Press, 1990).

[TWO]

Malnutrition, Food Systems, and Climate Action

MARTIN W. BLOEM

IN SEPTEMBER 2015, almost all of the world's leaders signed the declaration of the Sustainable Development Goals (SDGs). After years of preparation and technical meetings, the United Nations established 16 goals and recognized that partnerships (Goal 17) are essential to accomplishing these goals. The SDGs are fundamentally different from the previous Millennium Development Goals, which were designed and implemented for low- and middle-income countries (LMICs). The SDGs are goals for all of us. We cannot expect only a subset of countries to address climate change and malnutrition, and we need to leave behind our traditional notions of domestic versus international work. Wherever we work in the field of food systems, all of our actions are interlinked and interdependent. It is critical that we adhere to goals that are important for all of us in the world.

Lessons from UNAIDS

The SDGs are complex, wicked problems that cannot be solved with a single solution. We can learn from how the HIV/AIDS problem has been tackled in the past 50 years under the leadership of the Joint United Nations Programme on HIV/AIDS (UNAIDS). UNAIDS is the only UN program in which *all* stakeholders have had a role. Most importantly, people living with HIV have been at the core of the program. We could not even define the disease in the early 1980s, but today, with the private sector's help, we can test and treat people living with HIV almost immediately.

Human rights are at the heart of UNAIDS. One example of how the program has encouraged respect for human rights is by developing an appropriate language for discussing HIV/AIDS. For example, the terms "sex workers," "people living with HIV," and "drug users," have replaced the terms "prostitutes," "HIV patients," and "drug addicts." This language is intended to change the discourse around HIV/AIDS and avoid stigma and discrimination.

UNAIDS has 11 Cosponsors, and the division of labor among Cosponsors helps address the multidimensional nature of the HIV/AIDS problem and contributes to a more effective response. The World Food Programme (WFP), for example, integrates food and nutrition security in the HIV/AIDS response in humanitarian settings.

A final important lesson from UNAIDS is that the program moved ahead using incomplete information, while simultaneously conducting essential research to fill the knowledge gaps in various fields (e.g., treatment, testing, legislation, and nutrition). Compared to the body of knowledge available when UNAIDS started, we have more knowledge now about the issues in the food system. We need to take action now. The framework developed by the Institute of Medicine and the National Research Council in 2015 is a great tool to develop strategies along the value chain with the following perspectives: markets, policies, biophysical environment, science and technology, and social organization.[1]

The Global Problem of Malnutrition in All Its Forms

The Global Nutrition Report shows that the world must cope with all forms of malnutrition: hunger, undernutrition (wasting and stunting), overnutrition (overweight/obesity), and micronutrient deficiencies. Although we have seen a reduction in hunger and undernutrition in LMICs, the rise in overnutrition and obesity is substantial.[2] What is behind this shift? Ruel and Alderman show that a 10% increase in GDP is correlated with a 6% decrease in stunting and a 7% increase in maternal obesity.[3] Economic growth is clearly a strong driver behind the shift in type of malnutrition in many LMICs. The poor spend a large percentage of their income on food, and their diet consists mainly of staple foods such as rice, maize, or wheat. However, these plant-based diets are not the same nutrient-adequate plant-based diets consumed by vegans or vegetarians in the United States or Europe. These diets are determined by poverty, and they lack many essential nutrients.

Since the first *Lancet* nutrition series came out in 2008, we have understood much more about the etiology and consequences of stunting. Stunting is a proxy for poor development in the first 1,000 days of life (from conception to the child's second birthday). Stunting is indicated by a low height-for-age or less than −2 standard deviations from the World Health Organization reference population. The effects of stunting are irreversible by the age of two. Stunted children have increased mortality risk and decreased cognitive development. They are also less productive as adults, which has negative economic consequences.

In Bangladesh, the prevalence of stunting was higher than 70% in 1989. That number has dropped by almost 50% over the past 30 years, but the current prevalence remains high (36%).[4] And despite that drop, 70% of Bangladeshis in their early 30s are at risk of chronic heart diseases, lower cognitive development, and obesity because of malnutrition when they were children. When those adults are in their early 50s, 20 years from now, they will still be affected by those same risks. The Global Nutrition Report shows that there are currently 155 million stunted children,[5] but if we factor in the lifetime effects of stunting, then billions of people are affected by the long-term epigenetic consequences of stunting. Tackling the problem of stunting is the first step in preventing obesity in most LMICs.

A good understanding of how poverty leads to stunting and eventually obesity is very important. The poor will increase the nutrient content of their diets as their access to more nutritious and animal-source foods increases with GDP growth. Most LMICs do not produce enough of the right food to feed their citizens a nutrient-adequate diet.[6] Micronutrient deficiencies remain highly prevalent. The World Food Programme's "Fill the Nutrient Gap" research confirmed that, because the poor cannot afford to buy a local diet with the right amount of nutrients,[7] the effectiveness of behavior change programs is seriously limited. The impacts of stunting are so dramatic that we cannot wait until the food systems in LMICs have improved; we cannot wait until the poor are able to afford nutrient-adequate diets. Again, we need to act now. Micronutrient supplementation and fortification programs have proven to be effective and need to be scaled-up.

Food-Based Strategies to Fight Stunting

Many reports argue that the increase in consumption of animal-source foods in LMICs is a result of food industry marketing. Marketing of sugar-sweetened beverages is indeed effective even among the poor. However, marketing is not the critical factor. Studies in Indonesia and Bangladesh showed that the nonstaple food component of food expenditure determines nutritional status.[8] When the poor can afford to buy more nonstaple foods, their nutritional status improves. Our task, therefore, is to understand at which point the marketing of ultra-processed food interferes with the natural improvement of diets as income increases. Education and social marketing programs promoting healthy foods among young children need to be central to this task.

An interesting and promising food-based strategy to prevent stunting in LMICs is the promotion of egg consumption in children 6–23 months of age. One egg a day in a breastfed child of 9 months provides almost all recommended daily nutrients. However, consumption and availability of eggs remain low in countries with a high prevalence of stunting. It is, therefore, important to consider the possibilities of poultry production in LMICs. This issue is complicated because industrial food animal production (also known as factory farming) in other countries has had many unintended negative impacts on public health, animal welfare, and the environment. In recent decades, we have come to understand with great detail where, how, and even why the poultry production industry has made mistakes. We should use this understanding to support LMICs and help them prevent these mistakes. But while factory farming is a problem, the solution is not as simple as having free-range chickens live near residential areas. Research shows that when children in the developing world live in close proximity to animals, they have a higher prevalence of environmental enteric dysfunction.[9] Therefore, although an egg a day could solve the problem of stunting, we would not want to give households in LMICs chickens to raise in their backyards.

How can we avoid unintentional negative health consequences when improving the food system? Let us return to the lessons from UNAIDS. The HIV/AIDS community realized that if it really wanted to make changes, then UNAIDS needed to be inclusive and bridge many groups that did not agree on certain policies. For example, stakeholders included sex workers, drug users, and gay populations. Certain countries did not and still do not accept these populations, but these countries were never removed from the discussions and negotiations. Otherwise, UNAIDS would have never made so much progress and been so successful. Translating this to food systems work, we must identify populations that may not be welcome at the table, and then we must invite them and listen to them, regardless of any discomfort or ideological disapproval.

The EAT-Lancet Commission Report

In January 2019, the *Lancet* published the EAT-Lancet Commission report, which proposes a sustainable diet that operates within planetary boundaries.[10] The report is a milestone in the field of health, food, and climate, but it has some limitations. The commission states that the report does not provide a strategy or design for how its recommendations can be translated at country or subnational levels. The proposed diet is based on the availability and affordability of food and agricultural production within various cultural contexts, as opposed to what would be a nutritionally adequate diet for those various cultures. The Johns Hopkins Center for a Livable Future recently published an analysis of the greenhouse gas (GHG) and water footprints of various increasingly plant-forward diets (e.g., low and no red meat, pescetarian, vegetarian, and vegan), specific to 140 countries.[11] This and further research will help countries develop dietary guidelines that can support efforts against both undernutrition and overnutrition, while also operating within planetary boundaries.

Conclusion

There is a great need for improving our food systems against the background of a growing population and climate change. It is, therefore, of utmost importance that we work together, and that we include and convene those partners with whom we disagree or disapprove. It is also critical that we move forward despite not having all the facts or data that we might like to have. Proceeding this way may make us uncomfortable, but we will have to make the best decisions we can with the information available to us, while continuing to build the body of knowledge. There is no time for ideology or certainty. The urgency of climate change and food systems dysfunction requires us to be inclusive, pragmatic, and solution oriented.

REFERENCES

1. Institute of Medicine and National Research Council, *A Framework for Assessing Effects of the Food System* (Washington, DC: National Academies Press, 2015).

2. Development Initiatives, "2018 Global Nutrition Report: Shining a Light to Spur Action on Nutrition" (Bristol, UK: Development Initiatives, 2018).

3. Marie T. Ruel, Harold Alderman, and Maternal and Child Nutrition Study Group, "Nutrition-Sensitive Interventions and Programmes: How Can They Help to Accelerate Progress in Improving Maternal and Child Nutrition?," *Lancet* 382, no. 9891 (August 2013): 536–51.

4. "Prevalence of Stunting, Height for Age (% of Children under 5)," World Bank, https://data.worldbank.org/indicator/SH.STA.STNT.ZS?end=2014&locations=BD&start=1986&view=chart.

5. Development Initiatives, "2018 Global Nutrition Report."

6. Yukyan Lam et al., "Industrial Food Animal Production in Low-and Middle-Income Countries: A Landscape Assessment," Johns Hopkins Center for a Livable Future, 2016, https://www.jhsph.edu/research/centers-and-institutes/johns-hopkins-center-for-a-livable-future/_pdf/projects/IFAP/IFAPLowmid_income_countriesWeb1.pdf.

7. "Fill the Nutrient Gap," World Food Programme, November 9, 2017, https://www1.wfp.org/publications/2017-fill-nutrient-gap.

8. See, for example, Ashley A. Campbell et al., "Household Rice Expenditure and Maternal and Child Nutritional Status in Bangladesh," *Journal of Nutrition* 140, no. 1 (January 2010): 189S-94S; and Mayang Sari et al., "Higher Household Expenditure on Animal-Source and Nongrain Foods Lowers the Risk of Stunting among Children 0–59 Months Old in Indonesia: Implications of Rising Food Prices," *Journal of Nutrition* 140, no. 1 (January 2010): 195S-200S.

9. See, for example, Sophie Budge et al., "Environmental Enteric Dysfunction and Child Stunting," *Nutrition Reviews* 77, no. 4 (April 2019): 240–53.

10. Walter Willett et al., "Food in the Anthropocene: The EAT-Lancet Commission on Healthy Diets from Sustainable Food Systems," *Lancet* 393, no. 10170 (February 2019): 447–92.

11. Brent F. Kim et al., "Country-Specific Dietary Shifts to Mitigate Climate and Water Crises," *Global Environmental Change* (August 2019): 101926.

PART II FOOD SYSTEMS IN CONTEXT

This section discusses some of the fundamental forces that have shaped, and will continue to shape, our food systems. These forces include the industrialization of agriculture and the accompanying failure to regulate agriculture as an industry, as well as the food industry's powerful role in shaping consumers' food choices and health. They also include the increase in food demand, due to population and income growth, and the uncertainty in food supply, due to climate change and promising but controversial technologies. The chapters in this section focus generally, but not exclusively, on the United States. They provide useful context for reading this volume's subsequent chapters on considerations and approaches for more ethical food systems.

[THREE]

The Agriculture We Deserve

ELLEN K. SILBERGELD

W E LIVE in an era of contradiction about food. In many countries
there is abundant food at the same time as there is hunger; we
have undernourishment and obesity, often within the same societies. Although the goal of universal food access and food security remains
unfulfilled in every country, both the extent to which food is available
and accessible in market-based systems and the largesse of programs of
national and international food aid would have been incomprehensible
to an era as recent as 80 years ago. This volume reminds us that these
advances have come with gross inequities and collateral damage that
demand ethical analysis and response. We have the agriculture we deserve, and we deserve the agriculture we have gotten. This chapter focuses on food derived from animals, but much of the same contradic-
tions and inequities pertain to plant-based food, which is intermingled
with food animal production.

Our agriculture is the consequence of millennia of transitions in agricultural technology, diets, and socioeconomic organization that began
in the Neolithic era and continue to the present day. The history of agriculture is essentially a discourse between expanding human settlement
and the response of agriculturists to increase food production and food
security. Increased food enabled increases in the size of human settlements.

These expansions in turn generated the need for further increases in food production and changes in social organization to enable reliable food production.[1,2,3] Larger settlements took on the structure of cities with social castes and recognizably urbane tastes for food diversity as revealed through the archaeological excavations at Çatalhöyük in Anatolia.[4]

These drivers—population growth and urbanization—have shaped agricultural transitions from the beginnings of human societies. They persist to the present as mainsprings for the spread of our current models of agricultural production.[5,6]

While agriculture has shaped the growth of cities, urbanization has exerted pressure on rural society. For most of human history, this pressure was extreme with the work of food production done by slaves, prisoners, serfs, or their modern counterparts of indentured sharecroppers. This reality did not stop the Greek and Roman poets—such as Hesiod, Virgil, and Horace—from romanticizing rural life and the virtues of farmers. This idealization continues to this day and in many ways obscures our recognition of the extent to which agriculture has changed and causes us to privilege the experience of landowners and so-called "gentleman farmers" over that of agricultural workers.

Over history, during times of shortages, landowners continued to profit, and urban populations received some sustenance often to forestall revolution.[7] The agrarian workforce suffered the brunt of these cycles of crop failures and poverty. It is therefore not surprising that the history of agriculture is one of farming populations leaving the land for the city. The hard conditions of farming—whether based on enslavement or even the difficult conditions of independent or "yeoman" farmers—has meant that food production has been frequently insufficient to provide a living. The economic and other attractions of cities still operate to drive migration from rural to urban settlements. Policies requiring farmers to stay in the country, such as the forced collectivization of farmers of kulaks in early Soviet Russia[8,9] and policies forcing city dwellers back to the countryside in China,[10] have never succeeded in maintaining agricultural production or reversing the demographic flow to cities. At present, accelerated by the most recent technological and organizational transformations of agriculture in the 20th century, this rural-to-urban trend is almost complete in the highest-income countries, and it is increasing both in middle- and in higher low-income countries.

The Industrialization of Agriculture:
The Last Agricultural Transition

According to Mazoyer and Roudart, six distinct transitions can be defined in agriculture; these began slowly and required centuries to take effect. Starting in the 19th century in northern Europe, the speed of agricultural transitions in technology accelerated and deepened in concert with the Industrial Revolution. Transitions followed rapidly with the adaptation of coal- and gas-powered machines that replaced human energy, the invention of synthetic chemicals that augmented soil fertility and controlled plant pests, and the introduction of biotechnology and synthetic biology, which supplanted the traditional evolutionary processes of selective breeding. The last transition to date, in the 20th century, involved not only technological innovation but also the adoption of new organizational models and practices in terms of ownership, finance, and management.[11] This radical reorganization of ownership and work in the 20th century fundamentally severed agriculture from the persistence of traditional methods in many important ways, including the end of the entrepreneurial model of the family farm, the disruption of mutuality between farmers and their animals, and the end of the rule of nature in terms of favorable soils and climate. In many ways we are still adjusting to these shocks, not without resistance.[12,13,14]

For the production of food from animals, this most recent revolution began in the poultry sector in the United States in the 1920s. It was enabled by several unconnected events: investments in chicken breeding, successful industrialization for producing other goods, mechanization, transportation, and refrigeration. These advances involved government as well as private industry support: the US Department of Agriculture (USDA) funded research through the land-grant university system that improved both the poultry breed and its nutrition; the private sector built the railways while the US government funded the first interstate highway network; and a scientist at DuPont invented Freon, the chlorofluorocarbon refrigerant that made it possible to distribute safe and fresh food, including chicken, over long distances.[15]

Coincidentally, all these technological advances were first exploited in a small region of the United States relatively distant from major cities, in the Delmarva Peninsula of Delaware, Maryland, and Virginia. A remarkable innovator, Arthur Perdue, was the first to fully understand the potential for change leveraged by these events. True to the modern model of disruptive change brought about by outsiders from traditional practice,[16] he was not a farmer or involved in agriculture aside from dabbling in egg layers. From the outside, Perdue established a model of poultry production that disrupted traditional food animal production and agriculture in general. In the 21st century, we are used to disruptive technologies, but very few transitions have displaced traditional production methods so rapidly. As shown in table 3.1, the growth in poultry production and consumption spurred by his innovative methods was more than 100-fold in less than 10 years, a pace matched only by global sales of iPhones from 2007 to 2017.[17] In recognition of the importance of Perdue's innovations to agriculture, the USDA coined the term "chickenization" to refer to the industrial transformation of any area of agriculture.

Perdue was the first to respond to the opportunities of new technologies to transcend the limits of traditional chicken raising. He was the first to import key aspects of industrial production that had first been employed by the textile industry in the 19th century and reinvented by Henry Ford in the early 20th century. Perdue built a business based on the critical importance of the factory rather than the generation of raw inputs. His system of supply chain management used vertical integration to include all aspects of production that added value and to exclude those activities that reduced profits. These strategies of internalizing profits and externalizing more risky parts of production had long been employed in industry, starting with the textile industry in England. Henry Ford did not make steel or sell cars; the English textile owners did not grow cotton or sell dresses.

Table 3.1. Broiler Poultry Production from 1920 to Present, in Delmarva, Pocomoke Watershed, and US Totals

Date	Delmarva Poultry Production	Worcester/Somerset Production	US Total
1920	No broiler production		
1925	~50,000 estimated		
1934	7,000,000		34.03 million
1941	48,000,000		191.50 million
1942	77,000,000		228.19 million
1943	102,000,000		285.29 million
1944		10,363,658/3,602,573	
1949		12,150,568/4,347,273	513.30 million
1954	248,000,000		1.05 billion
1957	180,000,000		1.45 billion
1965	260,000,000		2.06 billion
1967	280,378,000		2.32 billion
1970	330,000,000		2.77 billion
1973	346,000,000		2.91 billion
1977	380,000,000		3.33 billion
1978	397,000,000	55,031,424/33,008,941	3.52 billion
1980	418,000,000		3.93 billion
1982	471,000,000	57,407,808/48,523,355	4.13 billion
1983	468,000,000		4.07 billion
1987	490,000,000	67,860,514/45,671,603	4.97 billion
1990	517,300,000		5.84 billion
1992	548,500,000		6.43 billion
1995	603,000,000		7.37 billion
1997	609,000,000	56,651,265/42,167,603	7.74 billion
2002	455,454,274	64,117,468/63,884,924	8.40 billion
2004	561,000,000		8.75 billion
2011	563,000,000		8.54 billion

Sources: William Williams, *Delmarva's Chicken Industry: 75 Years of Progress* (Georgetown, DE: Delmarva Poultry Industry), 1998; "DPI Facts & Figures," Delmarva Poultry Industry, https://www.dpichicken.org/facts/facts-figures.cfm; and "Statistics by Subject"; USDA National Agricultural Statistics Service. https://www.nass.usda.gov/Statistics_by_Subject/.

From the beginning of industrial agriculture, producers developed new technologies and revised organizational structures to maximize profits by controlling most of the food chain in food animal production while excluding or externalizing costs. The most important technological change in the early years of industrialized poultry production was the implementation of confinement methods for raising animals. Introducing this "premanufacture" step in poultry production consigned both farmers and animals to an artificial and highly controllable environment that is a main source of collateral damage to human and animal health and welfare as well as to the integrity of the environment. The costs of this damage are of course externalized.

This business model is defined as vertical integration always with limits. These limits of vertical integration were designed to externalize cost centers that had higher risks or that reduced profits, such as the actual raising of poultry and the construction and maintenance of growing houses (assigned to growers), the management of animal wastes (assigned to growers and public entities), and worker health (assigned to public entities). Integration by itself is a means for externalizing costs, with implications for transferring these costs, particularly those related to health and the environment, to the public.[18] This is not unique to agriculture and characterizes the history of industrialization in general, but in agriculture the practice of externalizing costs has continued to avoid regulation and reform. For this reason, the owners of food industries are often referred to as "integrators."

The second strategy utilized by industrial agriculture also drew on practices by earlier industries. Owners focused on reducing labor costs and avoiding revolts against contracts by explicitly locating their operations in regions with surplus labor, depressed labor costs, and hostility to labor unions. They also forced political entities from localities to nations to relax regulations and to provide tax incentives and preferential zoning, as exemplified by the recent competition encouraged by Amazon for locating new business hubs. This economic model of food production, operating at a regional or national level, has now gained further power by evolving into a global system of flexible accumulation involving transnational value chains that have supplanted governmental institutions in controlling national and international markets.[19,20]

In summary, the importance of the industrial model is twofold: controlling the supply chain and outsourcing or avoiding the less profitable and more risky aspects of production.[21] In agriculture, the owner of the enterprise is the producer, not the farmer; the factory is not the farm but the slaughter and processing operation; and farmers are now contracted labor, an arrangement that repeats the pattern of industrialization in textiles and car production, where traditional weavers became employees in textile factories and skilled coach makers worked on Henry Ford's production line. Like these earlier industries, the integrated model in food animal production radically eliminated the skills and autonomy of entrepreneurial farming that often included and supported whole families. As in all industrial production, the transition from entrepreneurial to contract labor models was essential for food animal production so that producers could ensure a reliable system of timely inputs of raw materials into the factory production line. In agriculture, these requirements were met by the contract system that bound farmers to exclusive relationships with producers and ended the tradition of self-employment in agriculture. As consumer demand for broiler chickens exploded in the United States, the need for increased production of crops for poultry feed also grew. In Maryland, market gardens were converted to soybean and corn production; similarly, almost 100 years later in Brazil much of the central Amazon has been deforested for the same goal.[22] In this way, food animal production now largely controls crop production.

Karl Marx was among the first to discern that social disruption is a characteristic of industrialization when the independence and autonomy of work disappear.[23] In agriculture, this disruption has resulted in the erosion of rural communities as well as the disruption of animal communities through current practices in housing and management, exemplified by breeding crates for sows and cages for egg-laying hens.[24] Industrialization began within capitalist systems through earlier transformations of production.[25] Capitalism was part of the agricultural transition in ownership that began in the 17th century in England and France.[26] Capitalist systems strive for profit for owners by wresting control over production from workers, who are left with the weak and often self-damaging tactic of withdrawing their labor by going on strike. Resistance to these changes was weak in agriculture for political, economic, and personal reasons: farmers have never been able to control the market for food, and the profit margin for farmers in traditional agriculture was always subject to natural disasters and pressure from consumers. For this reason, agricultural industrialization spread rapidly and with little effective opposition.

The industrial food animal production system began in the United States within a capitalist economy that had already incorporated transitions to industrial models of production for many goods on the basis of the Fordist model of production. This economic model has now evolved to a global system of flexible accumulation.[27] For food, this system involves intensive competition not only limited to competition among firms or within national markets but also used more widely among transnational supermarket chains for national and international markets.[28]

The Benefits and Risks of the Agriculture We Have

All agricultural transitions have responded to the needs and desires of humans as individuals, communities, and populations. These transitions have generated indisputable benefits to human health: increases in agricultural productivity, decreases in hungry populations, and opportunities for improved nutrition. With the advent of the latest agricultural transitions, populations in developing countries have increased access to nutritional food such as eggs, milk, and other animal sources.[29] Notwithstanding these benefits, there is a critical discussion about the effects of the agricultural transition as a driver of the nutritional transition in human diets toward a "triple burden" through enabling and promoting unhealthy changes in diet in countries with increasing affluence and growing cities.[30] This trend towards the "Western diet" has resulted in increased consumption of meat-based protein, sugars, and saturated fats, all of which contribute to poor nutrition and obesity, as well as diabetes and cardiovascular diseases.[31,32]

New diets and production conditions have not benefited the nutrition and health of animals. Their health is compromised by replacing traditional grazing and forage with artificial feeds consisting of finely ground mixtures of corn, soybeans, drugs, and other components, including slaughterhouse renderings and even industrial waste.[33] Fish species are raised with feeds containing unnatural constituents such as animal blood and bird feathers.[34] Salmon raised in confinement with restricted movement fail to develop muscle tissue.[35] Cattle and pigs suffer digestive impacts from these feeds, and an increasing growth rate in chickens results in leg bone fractures during the last weeks of their lives.

The industrial transition in agriculture has reduced the cost of food for consumers, but this has been associated with collateral harms and impacts associated with the unceasing search for lowering costs in the interest of increased profit. Some of the most harmful impacts have fallen on food animals, whose lives and welfare have been deeply compromised by confinement. Over their increasingly short lives, they are entirely segregated from the natural world and access to natural foods through foraging and grazing. Natural behaviors are now impossible within the confined spaces of buildings, nets, and impoundments that in some regions are now being built to hold more than 300,000 chickens, 10,000 hogs, and 60,000 salmon. Within these new nonnatural settings, human and animal welfare have been affected by the conditions they share.

Animal welfare policies do not extend to animals raised for food. Worker protection has been compromised in large part by the strategies deployed by the industry to reduce costs. Many locate in regions hostile to regulation and unionization where occupational safety and health rules are assigned to the US Department of Agriculture, whose regulatory actions have been supportive of agribusiness, not workers. Not surprisingly, injury rates are the highest in animal slaughter and processing.[36] Food animal production presents the strongest case for a One Health perspective on recognizing the commonality of disease risks shared between animals and humans. Because both humans and animals share these living and working conditions, they share exposures and risks.[37] These common health hazards are well described for workers and animals exposed to dusts and bioaerosols in animal confinement houses. These chronic exposures can affect respiratory function in humans, including asthma-like syndromes, bronchitis, asthma exacerbation, and hypersensitivity pneumonitis.[38] These conditions and diseases are shared by animals in confinement.[39] In addition, novel as well as known epizoonoses originate and spread more readily among and within herds and flocks as a consequence of the adaptations in food animal production.[40] Animals live in dense populations within confinement houses and impoundments, and these facilities are run with minimal or no sanitation requirements for animal husbandry or waste management. In the United States, poultry houses in Delmarva are now large enough to house between 250,000 and 300,000 birds. In China, hogs are raised in so-called multistory hog hotels in which as many as 1,000 animals are confined to each floor.[41] The crowded conditions of food animal production favor the transmission of these diseases, and the proximity of poultry and pig production in some cases contributes to genetic reassortments that enable avian influenza strains to evolve into viruses that have caused continuing outbreaks of highly pathogenic avian influenza strains and cases of illness and deaths in human populations. These "premanufacture" facilities produce enormous waste loadings, far in excess of beneficial usage as fertilizer, and the costs of this excess are also externalized to farmers and the public.

A New and Unnecessary Risk

All these conditions impact the health and welfare of animals and humans. However, the use of antimicrobial drugs in food animal production is the innovation that has most profoundly, and dangerously, transformed human health at the global level. It has also elevated the global risks to food safety related to the presence of antimicrobial resistant pathogens in the food supply.[42,43,44]

The story of how antibiotic drugs came to be used for increasing growth to reduce costs in food animal production is a confusing and contradictory narrative as promulgated by its first advocates, Robert Stokstad and Thomas Jukes at Lederle Laboratories.[45] It stretches from the work of nutritionists decades before the isolation of antimicrobial molecules to the first approvals for agricultural use granted by the FDA starting in 1947.[46] The first drugs were rapidly approved by the USDA starting in 1947, within a very short period of time after the development of mass fermentation processes that took these new molecules out of the lab and into medicine (table 3.2). Despite the fact that the most recent studies by industry have questioned the economic and production benefits of using drugs in animals in the absence of disease,[47,48]

Table 3.2. Dates for FDA Approval of Drugs as Growth-Promoting Additives to Poultry Feeds

Drug	Date of Approval	Approved Use	Drug Class
Penicillin	1946	Growth promotion	β lactam
Streptomycin and aureomycin	1947	Growth promotion	Aminoglycosides
Arsanilic acid	1947	Growth promotion, coccidiostat	Metal
Chlortetracycline	1949	Growth promotion	Aminoglycoside
Bacitracin	1951	Growth promotion/ coccidiostat	Polypeptide
Erythromycin	1952	Growth promotion	Macrolide
Oxytetracycline	1953	Growth promotion	Aminoglycoside
Bambermycin	1955	Growth promotion	Glycolipid
Gentamicin	c1964*	Growth promotion	Aminoglycoside
Roxarsone	1964	Growth promotion/ coccidiostat	Metal
Lincomycin	1970	Growth promotion	Lincosamide
Virginiamycin	1981	Growth promotion	Streptogramin
Enrofloxacin	1995	Growth promotion	Fluoroquinolone

Source: Thomas H. Jukes and William L. Williams, "Nutritional Effects of Antibiotics," *Pharmacological Reviews* 5, no. 4 (December 1953): 381–420; William Boyd, "Making Meat: Science, Technology, and American Poultry Production," *Technology and Culture* 42, no. 4 (2001): 631–64; Margaret G. Mellon, Charles Benbrook, and Karen Lutz Benbrook, *Hogging It: Estimates of Antimicrobial Abuse in Livestock* (Cambridge, MA: Union of Concerned Scientists, 2001); US Food and Drug Administration, "2011 Summary Report on Antimicrobials Sold or Distributed for Use in Food-Producing Animals," Washington, DC: US Food and Drug Administration, 2012; and George Haibel (US Food and Drug Administration), personal communication, May 3, 2013.
*No precise information was found on approval of gentamicin.

global adoption of the industrial model of food animal production continues to increase along with uses of antimicrobials in animal feeds.

There are new global drivers of diets and agriculture that are more intensive and effective in propagating the industrialization of food animal production. This latest transition with its benefits and harms has spread from the United States and been rapidly propagated globally in the context of modern communications technology, which has influenced adoption of new diets as well as the proliferation of global food markets.

Conclusions

The latest agricultural transition began in the early 1930s in the United States as a result of the same drivers that have operated throughout the history of agriculture: growing populations, sociocultural influences on diet, and the importance of reducing the costs of food. Part of this bargain has been fulfilled: the productivity of current food animal and crop production is extraordinary, and the costs of meat-based protein have enabled millions to change diets to include animal sources. For this reason, the ethical response to the ills of postmodern agriculture must be tempered by the ethical importance of high-production methods to feed the world. Returning to traditional preindustrial methods has never been able to generate increased food for expanding human populations. Traditional farming proved insufficient to support the livelihoods of farmers and contributed to the movement of rural populations to cities. The solution to the adversities of industrial agriculture is not to go backward, either in agriculture or in diets, compelling populations (usually in lesser developed countries) to forego their desires for diets of richer cultures or to force returns to the land and resumption of the hard work of inefficient agriculture. We have a useful roadmap to go forward, but it requires us to acknowledge the reality of agriculture as an industry. Starting in the late 19th century, the industrialized countries started to reject the bargain implicit in industrialization—the availability of desirable goods in exchange for externalization of costs. Slowly, and then more rapidly, these countries imposed rules on industrial behavior in terms of worker health and safety, releases of wastes and contaminants, product safety, and healthy environments. Externalization tactics by industry can be controlled, and when regulations are equitably imposed, firms and markets respond. By calling agriculture by its proper name— an industry—we can use these tools to end some of the unacceptable practices imbedded in modern agriculture, starting with enforceable standards for animal and human health and welfare, ownership of wastes, product safety, and environmental stewardship.

REFERENCES

1. Marcel Mazoyer and Laurence Roudart, *A History of World Agriculture: From the Neolithic Age to the Current Crisis* (London: Earthscan, 2006).

2. Immanuel Wallerstein, *The Modern World-System I: Capitalist Agriculture and the Origins of the European World-Economy in the Sixteenth Century*, vol. 1 (Berkeley: University of California Press, 2011).

3. George J. Armelagos and Mark Nathan Cohen, eds., *Paleopathology at the Origins of Agriculture* (Orlando, FL: Academic Press, 1984).

4. Sonya Atalay and Christine A. Hastorf, "Food, Meals, and Daily Activities: Food Habitus at Neolithic Çatalhöyük," *American Antiquity* 71, no. 2 (2006): 283–319.

5. David Satterthwaite, "Urbanization and Its Implications for Food and Farming," *Philosophical Transactions of the Royal Society B: Biological Sciences* 365, no. 1554 (2010): 2809–20.

6. H. Charles J. Godfray et al., "Food Security: The Challenge of Feeding 9 Billion People," *Science* 327, no. 5967 (February 2010): 812–18.

7. Andrew Rimas and Evan Fraser, *Empires of Food: Feast, Famine, and the Rise and Fall of Civilizations* (New York: Free Press, 2010).

8. Robert Conquest, *The Harvest of Sorrow: Soviet Collectivization and the Terror-Famine* (Oxford: Oxford University Press, 1987).

9. Mark Tauger, "Soviet Peasants and Collectivization, 1930–39: Resistance and Adaptation," *Journal of Peasant Studies* 31, no. 3–4 (2004): 427–56.

10. Pan Yihong, "An Examination of the Goals of the Rustication Program in the People's Republic of China," *Journal of Contemporary China* 11, no. 31 (2002): 361–79.

11. Mazoyer and Roudart, *A History of World Agriculture*.

12. Peter Jackson, N. Ward, and P. Russell, "Moral Economies of Food and Geographies of Responsibility," *Transactions of the Institute of British Geographers* 34, no.1 (2009): 12–24.

13. Peter Laslett, *The World We Have Lost: Further Explored* (New York: Routledge, 2015).

14. Wendell Berry, *Another Turn of the Crank* (Washington, DC: Counterpoint Press, 1995).

15. Ellen Silbergeld, *Chickenizing Farms and Food* (Baltimore: Johns Hopkins University Press, 2016).

16. Clayton Christensen, *The Innovator's Dilemma: When New Technologies Cause Great Firms to Fail* (Boston: Harvard Business Review Press, 2013).

17. "Cell Phone Sales Worldwide, 2007–2017," Statista, https://www.statista.com/statistics/263437/global-smartphone-sales-to-end-users-since-2007.

18. Oliver E. Williamson, "The Vertical Integration of Production: Market Failure Considerations," *American Economic Review* 61, no. 2 (1971): 112–23.

19. David Harvey, *The Condition of Postmodernity*, vol. 14 (Oxford: Blackwell, 1989).

20. Jason Konefal, Michael Mascarenhas, and Maki Hatanaka, "Governance in the Global Agro-food System: Backlighting the Role of Transnational Supermarket Chains," *Agriculture and Human Values* 22 (2005): 291–302.

21. William Boyd, "Making Meat: Science, Technology, and American Poultry Production," *Technology and Culture* 42, no. 4 (2001): 631–64.

22. Elizabeth Barona et al., "The Role of Pasture and Soybean in Deforestation of the Brazilian Amazon," *Environmental Research Letters* 5, no. 2 (2010): 024002.

23. Karl Marx, *Capital*, vol. 1, *A Critique of Political Economy* (Mineola, NY: Dover Publications, 2011).

24. Harold W. Gonyou, "Why the Study of Animal Behavior Is Associated with the Animal Welfare Issue," *Journal of Animal Science* 72, no. 8 (1994): 2121–77.

25. Harvey, *The Condition of Postmodernity*.

26. Wallerstein, *The Modern World-System I*.

27. Harvey, *The Condition of Postmodernity*.

28. Konefal, Mascarenhas, and Hatanaka, "Governance in the Global Agro-food System."

29. Andrew W. Speedy, "Global Production and Consumption of Animal Source Foods," *Journal of Nutrition* 133, no. 11 (2003): 4048S–4053S.

30. Jessica L. Johnston, Jessica C. Fanzo, and Bruce Cogill, "Understanding Sustainable Diets: A Descriptive Analysis of the Determinants and Processes That Influence Diets and Their Impact on Health, Food Security, and Environmental Sustainability," *Advances in Nutrition* 5, no. 4 (2014): 418–29.

31. Polly Walker et al., "Public Health Implications of Meat Production and Consumption," *Public Health Nutrition* 8, no. 4 (2005): 348–56.

32. Barry M. Popkin, Linda S. Adair, and Shu Wen Ng, "Global Nutrition Transition and the Pandemic of Obesity in Developing Countries," *Nutrition Reviews* 70, no. 1 (2012): 3–21.

33. Amy R. Sapkota et al., "What Do We Feed to Food-Production Animals? A Review of Animal Feed Ingredients and Their Potential Impacts on Human Health," *Environmental Health Perspectives* 115, no. 5 (2007): 663.

34. Brett D. Glencross, M. Booth, and G. L. Allan, "A Feed Is Only as Good as Its Ingredients: A Review of Ingredient Evaluation Strategies for Aquaculture Feeds," *Aquaculture Nutrition* 13, no.1 (2007): 17–34.

35. David W. Cole et al., "Aquaculture: Environmental, Toxicological, and Health Issues," *International Journal of Hygiene and Environmental Health* 212, no. 4 (2009): 369–77.

36. Emmanuel Kyeremateng-Amoah et al., "Laceration Injuries and Infections among Workers in the Poultry Processing and Pork Meatpacking Industries," *American Journal of Industrial Medicine* 57, no. 6 (2014): 669–82.

37. Jay P. Graham et al., "The Animal-Human Interface and Infectious Disease in Industrial Food Animal Production: Rethinking Biosecurity and Biocontainment," *Public Health Reports* 123, no. 3 (2008): 282–99.

38. Susanna Von Essen and Kelley Donham, "Illness and Injury in Animal Confinement Workers," *Occupational Medicine* 14, no. 2 (1999): 337–50.

39. John Pickrell, "Hazards in Confinement Housing—Gases and Dusts in Confined Animal Houses for Swine, Poultry, Horses and Humans," *Veterinary and Human Toxicology* 33, no. 1 (1991): 32–39.

40. Jessica H. Leibler et al., "Epizootics in Industrial Livestock Production: Preventable Gaps in Biosecurity and Biocontainment," *Zoonoses and Public Health* 64, no. 2 (2017):137–45.

41. Dominique Patton, "China's Multi-story Hog Hotels Elevate Industrial Farms to New Levels," *Reuters Business News*, May 18, 2018, https://www

.reuters.com/article/us-china-pigs-hotels-insight/chinas-multi-story-hog-hotels-elevate-industrial-farms-to-new-levels-idUSKBN1IB362.

42. Patrick F. McDermott et al., "The Food Safety Perspective of Antibiotic Resistance," *Animal Biotechnology* 13, no. 1 (2002): 71–84.

43. Ellen Silbergeld, Awa Aidara-Kane, and Jennifer Dailey, "Agriculture and Food Production as Drivers of the Global Emergence and Dissemination of Antimicrobial Resistance," *AMR Control*, 2017, http://resistancecontrol.info/2017/agriculture-and-food-production-as-drivers-of-the-global-emergence-and-dissemination-of-antimicrobial-resistance/.

44. Ellen Silbergeld, Jay Graham, and Lance B. Price, "Industrial Food Animal Production, Antimicrobial Resistance, and Human Health." *Annual Review of Public Health* 29 (2008): 151–69.

45. Thomas H. Jukes, "Antibiotics in Animal Feeds and Animal Production," *Bioscience* 22, no. 9 (1972): 526–34.

46. Silbergeld, *Chickenizing*.

47. H. M. Engster, D. Marvil, and B. Stewart-Brown, "The Effect of Withdrawing Growth Promoting Antibiotics from Broiler Chickens: A Long-Term Commercial Industry Study" *Journal of Applied Poultry Research* 11, no. 4 (2002): 431–36.

48. Jay P. Graham et al., "The Animal-Human Interface and Infectious Disease in Industrial Food Animal Production: Rethinking Biosecurity and Biocontainment," *Public Health Reports* 123, no. 3 (2008): 282–99.

FOUR

The Pew Commission on Industrial Farm Animal Production in America

Lessons Learned

ROBERT MARTIN

IN RECENT DECADES, the production of farm animals for food in the United States is characterized by an industrial system that concentrates power in the hands of a few large companies. This system is dominated by concentrated animal feeding operations (CAFOs) that confine large numbers of the same species in relatively small areas, generally in enclosed facilities that restrict natural movement.

The Pew Commission on Industrial Farm Animal Production was established in 2005 by a grant from the Pew Charitable Trusts to the Johns Hopkins Bloomberg School of Public Health. The commission was charged to investigate the problems associated with industrial farm animal production and to make recommendations to solve them. The 15 commissioners were from diverse fields, including veterinary medicine, public health, agribusiness, animal welfare, government, and rural advocacy.[1] Over two and a half years, the commissioners met regularly and traveled across the country to conduct site visits to production facilities, consult with industry stakeholders, and hold public meetings. In April 2008, the commission published its findings and recommendations. Broadly, it found that industrial farm animal production is not sustainable and presents an unacceptable threat to public health and the environment, as well as unnecessary harm to the animals we raise for food. It made 24 consensus recommendations, the following six of which were designated as priority recommendations:

1. Phase out and then ban the nontherapeutic use of antimicrobials.
2. Improve disease monitoring and tracking.
3. Improve industrial farm animal production regulation.
4. Phase out intensive confinement.
5. Increase competition in the livestock market.
6. Improve research in animal agriculture.[2]

Environmental Concerns

CAFOs generate more than 500 million tons of animal waste annually.[3] In dairy and swine operations, liquid waste is typically stored in open pit lagoons. In poultry and beef cattle operations, solid waste is typically stored in compost heaps and later applied to nearby fields. Hog waste is 75 times more concentrated than untreated human sewage and 500 times more concentrated than treated sewage.[4] One hog produces as much waste as four people,[5] so a 10,000-hog CAFO produces as much waste as a town of 40,000. Unlike human waste, there is no requirement to treat animal waste before it is released in the environment, which can result in contamination of nearby waters.

Water use is another main concern. To produce one pound of broiler chicken, 420 gallons of water are required.[6] In 2017, 42.2 billion pounds of chicken were produced in the United States,[7] which equates to 17.7 trillion gallons of water used. Feedlot beef requires about four to six times the amount of water as chicken.[8]

Lastly, an estimated 18% of anthropogenic greenhouse gas emissions are attributable to livestock operations. Greenhouse gases, primarily methane, carbon dioxide, and nitrous oxide, mainly come from feed production and processing (including land use changes), enteric fermentation in ruminant animals, and waste management practices.[9]

CAFOs are regulated through the US Environmental Protection Agency's (EPA) Clean Water Act (CWA), specifically the CWA's National Pollution Discharge Elimination System (NPDES) permit program. One of the commission's main recommendations was to require permitting of more operations. At the time of the commission, less than 30% of CAFOs had NPDES permits.[10] Since then, hundreds of new CAFOs have been established, many of them in already saturated areas. In 2008 the EPA published a final rule that revised the NPDES permitting requirements and required CAFOs that discharge or propose to discharge to apply for a permit. This rule was loosened in 2012 to cover only those operations that actually discharge. In 2012, after protests from industry, the EPA withdrew a proposed reporting rule that would have allowed the agency to obtain basic operational information about CAFOs. CAFOs were also exempted in 2008 from the Comprehensive Environmental Response, Compensation, and Liability Act (CERCLA) and Emergency Planning and Community Right-to-Know Act (EPCRA) reporting requirements for air releases of hazardous substances.[11] Overall, since the commission released its report, federal oversight of food animal production has been weakened.

Public Health Concerns

CAFOs also raise many public health concerns. In 2011, 29.9 million pounds of antimicrobials were sold for use in food animal production, representing 80% of all antimicrobials sold in the United States for any purpose. It is commonplace in CAFOs for animals to be administered antimicrobials for purposes other than disease treatment and control. Nontherapeutic uses include growth promotion, feed efficiency, weight gain, and routine disease prevention. Chronic overuse of antimicrobials in food animal production contributes to the evolution of antimicrobial-resistant bacteria, which can diminish the effectiveness of antimicrobials in both animal and human medicine.[12] The US Centers for Disease Control and Prevention (CDC) estimates that more than 2 million illnesses and 23,000 deaths from resistant infections occur every year. Antimicrobial resistance is estimated to cost the US health care system in excess of $20 billion every year.[13]

One of the commission's primary recommendations was to phase out and then ban nontherapeutic uses of medically important antimicrobials, but limited progress has been made on this front. In 2013 the FDA issued voluntary guidance for industry to restrict antimicrobial use to treatment, control, and prevention. However, allowing use for disease prevention creates a loophole, because at some point in the production cycle every animal is going to be exposed to bacteria that can cause disease.

Air quality is another major public health concern. Hydrogen sulfide, ammonia, carbon dioxide, and carbon monoxide are among the 160 gases released by CAFOs. Workers and nearby communities are at risk of developing adverse respiratory and neurobehavioral symptoms.[14]

Lastly, the scale and methods common to industrial food animal production pose risks to food safety. The CDC estimates that 48 million people get sick, 128,000 are hospitalized, and 3,000 die from foodborne infections each year in the United States.[15]

Animal Welfare Concerns

The commission found that intensive confinement systems, such as gestation crates, restrictive veal crates, and battery cages are inhumane because they restrict animals' movement and natural behaviors. It recommended phasing out these systems within a decade. It also recommended phasing out tail docking of dairy cattle, a practice commonly done without anesthetic. Tail docking is not only inhumane, but it also has a concurrent health impact. When cows are not in the milking parlor, their tails are very important for keeping flies off them and surrounding cows. Their tails also help reduce the spread of bacteria and other pathogens.

While there have been no federal regulatory efforts to phase out intensive confinement since the commission's report, there have been successful state-level efforts. For example, California, in the 2018 election, passed the strongest animal welfare measure in the country. Prop 12 builds on Prop 2, an earlier measure that banned intensive confinement of pregnant pigs, calves raised for veal, and egg-laying hens. It sets minimum space requirements and bans the sale of products from animals that do not have the minimum space required.[16] There have also been some voluntary industry efforts to phase out intensive confinement. For example, Smithfield Farms made a commitment in 2007 to phase out gestation crates and convert to group housing systems, which it fulfilled by 2018 for all of its US company-owned sow farms.[17] This is progress that should be acknowledged and commended, but the company is still a long way from eliminating gestation crates.

Lessons Learned

Although the commission's recommendations have had limited regulatory and legislative impact, its report remains significant today for its documentation of the problems associated with industrial food animal production. In addition, lessons have been learned from the commission's experience. Building trust among the commissioners was crucial, and meeting quarterly for a few days at a time really helped build that trust. The commissioners' diverse backgrounds and perspectives were also necessary for fostering a balanced, unbiased approach. In the beginning, it was important for the commission to be science-based, and primarily it was. But eventually that was expanded to evidence-based, because all it takes is a walk through a hog CAFO to know that what goes on in there is wrong. Both science and evidence are important in decision making. It is also important not to make assumptions. Don't assume that industry isn't open to dialogue. Industry may not have liked the final report, but it was crucial to talk to companies, hear their points of view, and have their help in getting access to CAFOs. Don't assume that civil society organizations are open to dialogue. Of all the civil society organizations in the country, only one was willing to talk to the commission. And don't assume that policy makers or the media understand the issues. Lastly, the most important lesson is that industrial food animal production is still in need of significant change.

REFERENCES
    1. The commissioners were John Carlin, Michael Blackwell, Brother David Andrews, Fedele Bauccio, Tom Dempster, Dan Glickman; Alan Goldberg, John Hatch, Dan Jackson, Frederick Kirschenmann, James Merchant, Marion Nestle, Bill Niman, Bernard Rollin, and Mary Wilson.
    2. Pew Commission on Industrial Farm Animal Production, "Putting Meat on the Table: Industrial Farm Animal Production in America," 2008, https://www

.pewtrusts.org/-/media/legacy/uploadedfiles/phg/content_level_pages/reports/pcifapfinalpdf.pdf.

3. US Environmental Protection Agency, FY08–FY10 Compliance and Enforcement National Priority: Clean Water Act, Wet Weather, Concentrated Animal Feeding Operations (CAFOs), 2007, http://citeseerx.ist.psu.edu/viewdoc/download?doi=10.1.1.164.5187&rep=rep1&type=pdf.

4. Pew Commission, "Putting Meat on the Table."

5. Polly Walker et al., "Public Health Implications of Meat Production and Consumption," *Public Health Nutrition* 8, no. 4 (June 2005): 348–56.

6. David Pimentel et al., "Water Resources: Agriculture, the Environment, and Society," *Bioscience* 47, no. 2 (1997): 97–106.

7. "The United States Meat Industry at a Glance," North American Meat Institute, https://www.meatinstitute.org/index.php?ht=d/sp/i/47465/pid/47465.

8. "Health & Environmental Implications of U.S. Meat Consumption & Production," Johns Hopkins Center for a Livable Future, 2014, https://www.jhsph.edu/research/centers-and-institutes/johns-hopkins-center-for-a-livable-future/projects/meatless_monday/resources/meat_consumption.html.

9. Henning Steinfeld et al., *Livestock's Long Shadow: Environmental Issues and Options* (Rome: Food & Agriculture Organization, 2006).

10. Claudia Copeland, "Animal Waste and Water Quality: EPA Regulation of Concentrated Animal Feeding Operations (CAFOs)" (Congressional Research Service, 2006), http://www.pcifapia.org/_images/CRS_Animal_Waste_and_Water_Quality_EPA_CAFOs_Sept_2006.pdf.

11. Johns Hopkins Center for a Livable Future, "Industrial Food Animal Production in America: Examining the Impact of the Pew Commission's Priority Recommendations," 2013, https://www.jhsph.edu/research/centers-and-institutes/johns-hopkins-center-for-a-livable-future/_pdf/research/clf_reports/CLF-PEW-for%20Web.pdf.

12. Johns Hopkins Center for a Livable Future, "Industrial Food Animal Production in America."

13. US Centers for Disease Control and Prevention, Antibiotic Resistance Threats in the US, 2013, https://www.cdc.gov/drugresistance/threat-report-2013/pdf/ar-threats-2013-508.pdf.

14. Pew Commission, "Putting Meat on the Table."

15. "Burden of Foodborne Illness: Findings," US Centers for Disease Control and Prevention, https://www.cdc.gov/foodborneburden/2011-foodborne-estimates.html.

16. "California to Only Sell Cage-Free Eggs by 2022," Hunter College New York City Food Policy Center, November 27, 2018, https://www.nycfoodpolicy.org/california-to-only-sell-cage-free-eggs-by-2022/.

17. Smithfield Foods, "Smithfield Foods Achieves Industry-Leading Animal Care Commitment, Unveils New Virtual Reality Video of Its Group Housing Systems," news release, January 8, 2018, https://www.smithfieldfoods.com/newsroom/press-releases-and-news/smithfield-foods-achieves-industry-leading-animal-care-commitment-unveils-new-virtual-reality-video-of-its-group-housing-systems.

FIVE

Agriculture in Transition

FREDERICK L. KIRSCHENMANN

M OST PEOPLE still think about sustainable agriculture in terms of making the current system a little less bad, but that kind of thinking is not going to prepare us for the future. Humanity has never been very good at predicting the future. However, we can learn an important lesson from Jared Diamond's study of past civilizations. He found that civilizations that anticipated oncoming changes and got a head start on preparing for them tended to thrive. Those that failed in that exercise tended to collapse.[1,2] We don't need to be able to predict the future, but we do need to be aware of possible changes and start preparing for them.

In his 1989 book *Culture and Agriculture*, Ernest Schusky tries to do this by looking at how the human species has fed itself ever since emerging on the planet some 200,000 years ago. Schusky points out that for most of this time, we fed ourselves as hunter-gatherers. It wasn't until about 12,000 years ago that we started to transition from food collectors to food producers. We began to select the kinds of plants and animals that we liked and to domesticate them. Our early food production was based on slash-and-burn agriculture. A common practice was to burn off the perennials (trees or grasses) on a particular plot of land we had settled and then proceed to grow crops there. The natural soil fertility plus the nutrients from the ash enabled us to produce good yields there for some time, and once the nutrients were depleted we found a new plot to slash and burn. After allowing the first plot to lay fallow for about 20 years, we could usually return and grow food there again.[3] This is how we fed ourselves for much of the past 12,000 years.

Schusky writes that around the beginning of the 20th century, we entered into a third era of feeding ourselves, which he calls the "neo-caloric era" because it is based on "old calories" from fossil fuels and other nonrenewable resources. He argues that this era will be very short, because at some point we will have used up all of the resources that support our input-intensive food system.[4] Indeed, we are now just starting to leave this neo-caloric era and enter into the post-neo-caloric era. That is why simply trying to make the current system a little less bad is going to leave us ill-prepared for the future.

In 1828, Carl Sprengel developed a concept called the law of the minimum.[5] This was a time in our history when we were starting to use technologies more, and Sprengel figured out that it was really important to be efficient. In 1840 Justus von Liebig applied Sprengel's concept to food and agriculture. In his book *Organic Chemistry and Its Application to Agriculture and Physiology*, Liebig demonstrates that applying nitrogen, phosphorus, and potassium to soil in the right quantities results in the maximum output for the minimum input.[6] Liebig's law of the minimum did not really take root until after World War II when munitions factories, having lost their market at the end of the war, discovered that they could manufacture synthetic fertilizers for agriculture and sell them cheaply to farmers. Many farmers were attracted to the idea of cheap and readily available fertilizer and began to turn their farms into input-intensive farms. Ironically, Liebig published another book in 1863 that contradicts his own concept of the law of the minimum and argues that simply adding inputs to the soil is not a sustainable way of maintaining soil health.[7] However, by that time the law of the minimum had become so popular that no one paid any attention to Liebig's new advice.

While this industrialized culture of food production was emerging after World War II, an alternative culture had been emerging since the early 1900s. Liberty Hyde Bailey, who was one of the first deans of a college of agriculture, published *The Holy Earth* in 1915. In his book he argues that, rather than forcing nature to do whatever we want, we should learn from nature how we should be farming.[8] This was such a strange idea at the time that the book did not become any kind of adoptive literature. In the 1920s, Rudolf Steiner developed the concept of biodynamic farming, which says that a farm should be managed like an organism without the use of outside inputs like fertilizers.[9] Biodynamic farming became attractive to a few farmers at the time (and is, interestingly enough, becoming somewhat more popular today), but by no means was it accepted in the mainstream.

In the 1930s and 1940s, Aldo Leopold inspired a rethinking of our food and agriculture system as well as our relationship with nature. According to his land ethic, humans are plain members and citizens, not conquerors, of the land community, the interdependent biological system of which we are all a part. In his 1945 essay "The Outlook for Farm Wildlife," Leopold writes: "It was inevitable and no doubt desirable that the tremendous momentum of industrialization should have spread to farm life. It is clear to me, however, that it has overshot the mark, in the sense that it is generating new insecurities, economic and ecological, in place of those it was meant to abolish. In its extreme form, it is humanly desolate and economically unstable. These extremes will some day die of their own too-much, not because they are bad for wildlife, but because they are bad for farmers."[10]

We are beginning to recognize how insightful Leopold was back then and consider the possibility that we are now on the cusp of making a major transition—not because we have decided that we need to make one but because the neo-caloric era is coming to a close.

This transition is already happening on some farms. In 2017 David Montgomery published an inspiring book called *Growing a Revolution: Bringing Our Soil Back to Life*. The book features different farms that Montgomery visited, many of them fairly sizable conventional farms located in the heartland of the United States. Each of the farmers had discovered that by using an input-intensive system, they were beginning to lose money. And all of them have made essentially the same three changes as a result: they have reduced their tillage, which disturbs the soil less; have added cover crops, which play a significant role in restoring soil health; and have increased the biological biodiversity of their operations. According to Montgomery, each of the farmers is now making a profit, and not a single farmer is interested in getting bigger, because size is not the solution to the problem. Rather, it is the enhancing of the biological dynamics that makes their farms more self-renewing and self-regulating, and therefore more profitable.[11] This is the beginning of farmers discovering for themselves that an input-intensive system is just not working for them anymore. This is the beginning of the post-neo-caloric era.

In their book *Journey of the Universe*, Brian Swimme and Mary Evelyn Tucker point out that we humans are on this tiny planet Earth, which is part of a tiny universe, which is part of a much larger cosmos that has been evolving for billions of years and that we are only just beginning to understand. If we as humans still think that we're in charge, then we are really kidding ourselves.[12] What we need to do is start focusing on learning from nature and the environment—in other words, learning from (and adapting to) what Aldo Leopold called the interdependent land community, of which we are simply members and citizens.

REFERENCES

1. Jared M. Diamond, *Guns, Germs, and Steel: The Fates of Human Societies* (New York: W. W. Norton, 1997).

2. Jared M. Diamond, *Collapse: How Societies Choose to Fail or Succeed* (New York: Viking, 2005).

3. Ernest Lester Schusky, *Culture and Agriculture: An Ecological Introduction to Traditional and Modern Farming Systems* (New York: Bergin & Garvey, 1989).

4. Schusky, *Culture and Agriculture.*

5. Carl Sprengel, "Von den Substanzen der Ackerkrume und des Untergrundes," *Journal für Technische und Ökonomische Chemie* 2 (1828): 423–74.

6. Justus Liebig and Lyon Playfair, *Organic Chemistry in Its Applications to Agriculture and Physiology* (London: Taylor and Walton, 1840).

7. Justus Liebig and John Blyth, *The Natural Laws of Husbandry* (New York: D. Appleton, 1863).

8. Liberty Hyde Bailey, *The Holy Earth* (New York: Charles Scribner's and Sons, 1915).

9. Rudolf Steiner and Malcolm Gardner, *Spiritual Foundations for the Renewal of Agriculture: A Course of Lectures Held at Koberwitz, Silesia, June 7 to June 16, 1924* (Kimberton, PA.: Bio-Dynamic Farming and Gardening Association, 1993).

10. Aldo Leopold, J. Baird Callicott, and Eric T. Freyfogle, *For the Health of the Land: Previously Unpublished Essays and Other Writings* (Washington, DC: Island Press for Shearwater Books, 1999).

11. David R. Montgomery, *Growing a Revolution: Bringing Our Soil Back to Life* (New York: W. W. Norton, 2017).

12. Brian Swimme and Mary Evelyn Tucker, *Journey of the Universe* (New Haven: Yale University Press, 2011).

SIX

Agricultural Exceptionalism and the US Regulatory Landscape

SUSAN A. SCHNEIDER AND MEREDITH KAUFMAN

A GRICULTURAL EXCEPTIONALISM—that is, excepting agriculture from many of the regulatory burdens that apply to other industries—has been criticized for its societal impact, most notably allowing environmental harm and permitting harsh labor conditions. Exceptionalism has been justified by the unique aspects of agricultural production, thin profit margins, and the overall need to "feed the world." After exploring the concept of exceptionalism, we propose a new paradigm for agricultural regulation and support.

History of Agricultural Exceptionalism

The notion that agriculture should be regulated less rigorously and treated more favorably under the law as compared to other industries is a commonly held view. As agricultural law scholarship reveals, agricultural exceptionalism is firmly embedded in the historical fabric of the US legal system.[1] Indeed, although many in the agricultural community sincerely believe that they are overregulated, objective analysis confirms that agriculture is regulated far less than other industries and afforded many legal advantages.

Some of the most obvious instances of agricultural exceptionalism are found in federal labor law. Agricultural laborers are excluded from the protections provided under the National Labor Relations Act,[2] and they are excepted from some of the worker protections created by the Fair Labor Standards Act.[3] Under federal law, farmworkers have no right to collective bargaining,[4] no right to overtime pay,[5] and limited protection under the minimum-wage standards.[6] Children who are hired to work on farms and in farm fields have less protection than they do in any other industry,[7] even though farming is recognized as one of the most hazardous industries.[8]

Agricultural exceptionalism is also apparent in environmental law. As noted legal scholar J. B. Ruhl has documented, agriculture receives special treatment under almost all environmental laws, often avoiding regulation completely.[9] For example, under the Clean Water Act (CWA),[10] the primary US federal water protection law, most agricultural activities are exempted from regulation. With few exceptions, crop production, a major US industry with more than $100 billion in annual sales, is largely unregulated under the CWA.

An EPA Memorandum confirms that "we respect and support the underlying purposes of the Clean Water Act regarding the exemption from Section 404 permitting requirements for 'normal farming' activities. The exemptions (at Section 404(f) of the Act) recognize that American agriculture fulfills the vitally important public need for supplying abundant and affordable food and fiber and it is our intent to assure that the exemptions are appropriately implemented."[11]

Agriculture's special status under the CWA is not because farming practices are environmentally insignificant: the largest source of water pollution in the country is nonpoint source pollution, and agriculture is the largest nonpoint source polluter.[12] Various pollutants including fertilizers, pesticides, and animal manure embedded with pathogens make their way to waterways via irrigation return flow, storm water flow, and general agricultural runoff without federal regulation.[13]

A recent example from the Midwest concerns the Des Moines Municipal Water Works, the entity tasked with providing safe drinking water to area residents. Agricultural runoff carrying nitrate and pesticides from farm fields flows through drainage ditches and drainage tile systems into surface water streams that flow into the Raccoon River, one of the primary sources of drinking water for Des Moines.[14] In 2015 the Water Works spent $1.5 million to remove nitrate from the drinking water obtained from the river, and it sued the drainage districts in three adjacent agricultural counties. The lawsuit was unsuccessful, largely because there is no legal framework holding farmers or their drainage districts liable for this type of pollution.[15]

Concentrated Animal Feeding Operations, or CAFOs, are the only form of agriculture that receives direct regulatory attention under the CWA. It is estimated that more than 10 billion animals are slaughtered in the United States annually, and most are raised in highly productive but controversial CAFOs. CAFOs are defined under the CWA regulations as Animal Feeding Operations (AFOs) in which livestock are kept and raised in confinement and in which the livestock exceed a set regulatory number of animals.[16] For example, a large CAFO is defined as one that contains more than 125,000 chickens, 10,000 swine, or 1,000 cattle.[17] As a point of reference, the midpoint size for broiler production in 2012 was 680,000 birds.[18] Large CAFOs that apply the manure waste to farmland must meet nutrient planning requirements. However, only CAFOs that directly discharge manure to a US water source are required to have a permit.[19] Of the 20,000 CAFOs identified by the EPA, fewer than 6,600 have permits.[20]

Given the amount of waste generated, even facilities that are permitted have regulatory burdens that are far below that of other waste facilities. Many CAFOs address waste accumulation by creating large open-air storage lagoons and eventually spraying the waste on nearby farm fields. As noted in a report produced by the National Association of Local Boards of Health, the lack of regulation of CAFOs and the manure produced by them can be the source of significant public health problems.

The most pressing public health issue associated with CAFOs stems from the amount of manure they produce. CAFO manure contains a variety of potential contaminants. It can contain plant nutrients such as nitrogen and phosphorus, pathogens such as *E. coli*, growth hormones, antibiotics, chemicals used as additives to the manure or to clean equipment, animal blood, silage leachate from corn feed, or copper sulfate used in footbaths for cows. Depending on the type and number of animals in the farm, manure production can range between 2,800 tons and 1.6 million tons a year. Large farms can produce more waste than some U.S. cities—a feeding operation with 800,000 pigs could produce over 1.6 million tons of waste a year. That amount is one and a half times more than the annual sanitary waste produced by the city of Philadelphia, Pennsylvania. Annually, it is estimated that livestock animals in the U.S. produce each year somewhere between 3 and 20 times more manure than people in the U.S. produce, or as much as 1.2–1.37 billion tons of waste. Though sewage treatment plants are required for human waste, no such treatment facility exists for livestock waste.[21]

The primary US air quality statute, the Clean Air Act (CAA), provides another example of agricultural exceptionalism. Admittedly, when the CAA was passed in 1970, widely dispersed family farms were not a major source of air pollution. As livestock operations have become larger and more concentrated, however, workers and communities living near CAFOs complain of air pollution causing serious health problems.[22] CAFOs can release several different air pollutants, including ammonia, hydrogen sulfide, particulate matter (PM), volatile organic compounds (VOCs), and hazardous air pollutants. Emissions come from lagoons, barns, other farm buildings, and manure spread on fields.[23] According to the EPA review of public health literature, health effects can include a variety of respiratory diseases; eye, nose, and throat irritation; cancer risk; and even damage to liver, kidney, and the central nervous system.[24] Nevertheless, there is no federal regulation of CAFO emissions.

The CAA authorizes the EPA "to establish a greater threshold quantity for, or to exempt entirely, any substance that is a nutrient used in agriculture when held by a farmer."[25] Since the late 1990s, and despite mounting complaints, the EPA has delayed taking action on air pollution from CAFOs, claiming that it did not have sufficient data to determine whether individual facilities were posing problems that warranted federal action under the CAA or under two related statutes: the Comprehensive Environmental Response, Compensation, and Liability Act (CERCLA) and the Emergency Planning and Community Right-to-Know Act (EPCRA). CAA permitting requirements and CERCLA/EPCRA release reporting requirements are triggered only if a facility emits certain pollutants at or above specific regulatory thresholds, and the EPA has continually delayed setting those thresholds for CAFO pollutants.

It is unlikely that CAFOs will be subject to increased regulation under the CAA in the near future. In late 2017, the EPA denied a petition for rulemaking requesting more stringent regulation of CAFOs under the CAA. In the denial letter, the former EPA administrator, Scott Pruitt, wrote that the agency was conducting ongoing studies of CAFO emissions, but that it was not a regulatory priority for the agency in light of limited resources and budgetary uncertainties.[26] Despite compelling testimony from residents who live near CAFOs, Congress advanced the Fair Agricultural Reporting Method (FARM) Act (S. 2421), a bill exempting farmers from reporting air emissions to federal agencies. The bill was enacted when it was attached to an omnibus federal appropriations bill.[27]

Justifications for Agricultural Exceptionalism

For many, these examples of agricultural exceptionalism point to the need for increased regulation. As farms have become larger and production methods more industrialized, it can be argued that exceptionalism has outlived its usefulness—that agriculture should be regulated just as other industries.

In sharp contrast, there is perhaps no group in American society that is more concerned about the dangers of regulation than farmers and ranchers. Many within the agricultural industry argue that our reliance on agriculture for global food security necessitates increasing support for the industry and decreased regulation, encouraging more and more production. They allege that any additional regulation will impose costs on individual farmers that they cannot afford, micromanage farm decision making, and intrude on farmers' autonomy. They argue for even less regulation, particularly with regard to environmental protections.

For example, a recent Heritage Foundation report argues:

> Regulations, in particular, make agricultural production and innovation more difficult by limiting farmers' and ranchers' ability to address agricultural risk, work their land, and meet market needs. . . . For regulated entities, such as farmers and ranchers, these unnecessary regulations can impose major compliance costs and other significant burdens. They can also discourage a party from taking an action (e.g., using land for ordinary business activities) due to fear of being out of compliance or because the regulation prohibits the action or makes it cost prohibitive. Regulatory costs are borne not merely by those parties who are regulated, but also by third parties such as consumers who may have to pay higher prices for goods and services.

The American Farm Bureau (AFB), the self-described "voice of agriculture,"[28] promotes this view, often warning farmers of regulatory dangers. Echoing a common refrain, an AFB rally cautioned that addressing "efforts by the federal government to regulate agriculture is one of the biggest challenges facing farmers and ranchers."[29] Farmers are encouraged to "defend their land" from regulatory intrusion.[30] These warnings of overregulation have heightened concerns within the farming community, even when the warnings are misplaced or misleading.[31]

To best evaluate these competing views on agricultural regulation, it is first instructive to consider the original justifications for exceptionalism. From this basis, the current utility can be determined.

Agricultural exceptionalism in the United States has its historical roots in Jeffersonian theories of democracy and agrarianism, with family farmers holding a special place in the fabric of the developing American society.[32] Agrarianism, often referred to alternatively as either the agrarian ideal or the agrarian myth, elevates family farming above other occupations. It emphasizes the "political value of the family farm, a farm owned and worked by members of one family," and it observes that "such a farm conferred independence, since the people on it worked for themselves not others, and it required self-reliance and hard work."[33]

Support for these idealized family farmers has always been a useful rationale for agricultural exceptionalism, even when it was used by other models of farming to the detriment of family farming.

Although some true agrarians remain within US agriculture, and farm families still own most farming operations, US agriculture as a whole represents an industrialized model of specialized monocultural production on an increasingly large scale.[34]

Beyond the narrative of the family farm, historically, there have been other justifications given for the special treatment provided to agriculture. The atomistic nature of the agricultural sector, "with many producers, few of whom have any real control over prices paid for inputs or prices received for commodities," is one additional justification. Similarly, there are the "periodic boom and bust cycles" recognized in the industry that make farmers particularly vulnerable.[35]

Today, most farmers are still "price-takers" in the marketplace, for while they have increased in size, market consolidation has dramatically increased the power of the industries that they buy from and sell to. Unfortunately for farmers, agricultural exceptionalism has tended to encourage this consolidation as any effort to regulate markets has been discouraged.

Although agrarianism and the vulnerability of individual farmers may have provided the justification for agricultural exceptionalism, such an extensive system of support could have been effectuated only as a result of significant political clout. Indeed, some have persuasively argued that it was likely the economic and political power of the agricultural industry as far back as colonial times that set the stage for the exceptionalism that continues today.[36] The original Constitution allowed slavery, essential to Southern plantation agriculture,[37] and it was not until 1865 that the Thirteenth Amendment abolishing slavery was ratified.[38] In addition, the Constitution was drafted in a manner that assured political power to rural states by allocating two senators, regardless of population to each state.[39]

In 1935, there were 6.8 million farms in the United States representing a significant percentage of the population. This gave agriculture a powerful democratic voice. Today, there are just over 2.1 million farms, with the number continuing to decline.[40] Although this has diminished the political power of farmers at the voting box, it has not resulted in less political power for the industry as a whole. As the number of farms has declined, their assets have been purchased by other farms, concentrating production on large farms.

> U.S. agricultural production has become more concentrated over time, with a smaller number of larger farms producing most of the value. This is a continuation of a longstanding trend. In 2002, farms with more than $1 million in sales produced 47 percent of all production; in 2007, they produced 59 percent of U.S. agricultural sales. In 2012, farms with more than $1 million in sales produced 66 percent of total farm sales. In 2012, farms with agricultural sales of more than $5 million produced 32 percent of the total value.[41]

These larger, asset-rich farms have significant political power. Individual producers and their respective trade associations spend millions of dollars annually lobbying and supporting politicians in state and federal elections. In 2017 agribusinesses spent more than $132 million on lobbying and more than $41 million on contributions to congressional candidates and incumbents.[42]

In addition to the increased political power of larger farms, agricultural exceptionalism has been claimed by industries throughout the food and agricultural industries. Where once exceptionalism was thought to benefit family farms buffeted by economic forces beyond their control, in more recent times multinational corporations have jumped on the farm bandwagon. Everyone is eager to be part of agriculture in the hopes of gaining special treatment.

- So called "ag-gag" laws have been enacted in numerous states, providing special protection for slaughterhouses and meat-processing facilities whose practices might be disclosed by undercover videos.[43]
- State antidisparagement laws have been enacted, providing extensive protection for food and agricultural industries within the state. A high-profile example is South Dakota's Agricultural

Food Products Disparagement Act, with its potential for triple damages. This act created a cause of action allowing Beef Products, Inc., a South Dakota meat processor, to sue ABC News, two USDA employees, and others for referring to their product as "pink slime." The suit was settled for $1.9 billion.[44]

- Multinational poultry processors have attempted to use agricultural laborer exemptions under federal labor law to prevent chicken catchers, workers who catch chickens and transport them to slaughter and processing plants, from organizing.[45]
- "Right to Farm" laws that limit nuisance litigation have been strengthened to provide increased protection for large concentrated operations where farmers care for animals that are owned by vertically integrated multinational meat and poultry companies. After neighbors won lawsuits against CAFO hog operations in North Carolina, the North Carolina legislature strengthened its protections for CAFOs and limited the rights of others to sue for damages.[46]

This dramatically expanded use of agricultural exceptionalism is instructive in isolating what it is that truly makes agriculture unique. There are in fact several valid justifications for treating farming operations differently than other industries, and these justifications survive even in today's transformed agricultural system. These special attributes of farming were first listed in the article, "A Reconsideration of Agricultural Law: A Call for the Law of Food, Farming, and Sustainability":

First, agricultural production is the primary way that we obtain food—a product that is essential to human health and survival. . . .

Second, agricultural production involves the production of living things, evoking ecological and moral issues that are completely different from the production of inanimate products. That these products are the food we eat accentuates this imperative.

Third, agricultural production is heavily dependent upon the natural world and its resources—in particular, land and water, and it has been both a significant consumer of natural resources and a significant source of environmental degradation. . . . Each of these attributes makes agriculture a unique industry, and each reflects an important societal concern.[47]

But, how should these special attributes impact public policy and affect regulation? Whereas agricultural exceptionalism has been linked to deregulation, these attributes actually support specialized regulation.

The first attribute, assuring food security, is a fundamental goal for government. The agricultural industry's essential role in providing food is a valid justification for government support and is a role that differentiates agriculture from most other industries.

The second attribute, that agriculture is in the business of raising of living products, also raises practical risks that justify support to the industry. Similarly, the involvement of living products also raises public policy issues such as animal welfare, biosecurity, and extended environmental impacts, each of which justifies treating agriculture differently than other industries that produce inanimate objects.

The third attribute, agriculture's dependency on the natural environment and its associated vulnerability to weather, pest, drought, and disease, is also a valid justification for industry support and differentiation. Support can help to minimize the special risks presented. However, this dependency on the natural environment also places agriculture as the most significant consumer of our natural resources, with important public policy implications.

Although these attributes justify different policies, including support for agriculture, differentiating it from other industries, none justify an exception to regulation. Indeed, each unique attribute supports a *greater* need for regulation, albeit regulation that is carefully crafted and tailored to the specific characteristics of the industry.

Consider each of these attributes in the context of excepting the industry from regulation.

- Agriculture is the industry that we depend on for producing our entire domestic food supply. Therefore, we should not regulate it.
- Agricultural production involves the production of living things, evoking ecological and moral issues; therefore, no regulation is needed.

- Agriculture uses natural resources upon which we all depend as incidents of production; therefore, we will not regulate their use.

Thus, these unique attributes justify support to the industry but also justify society's interest in regulating the industry. They do not justify excepting agriculture from regulation.

A New Paradigm for Regulation

As has been shown, agriculture is both an essential industry and a unique one. Current policies that except agriculture from regulation and support protective legislation for the overall food industry have advanced the economic interests of the most powerful in the industry, often to the detriment of others. The portrayal of regulation as the enemy of agriculture is shallow in its analysis and misleading in its conclusion. In many instances, lax regulation has rewarded those who seek to behave badly, lowering the industry bar and forcing other farmers to lower their standards in order to compete.

In this regard, agricultural exceptionalism when viewed as a free-market deregulatory model has played a significant role in promoting consolidation, industrialization, and concentration of wealth within our food system. While it is acknowledged that this has provided an abundant food supply, it has also produced significant societal costs that have not been factored into either the economics of the industry or the public policy debate.

Moreover, while allegedly based on support for family farming, agricultural exceptionalism has promoted the loss of many diversified, family-sized farming operations. These operations have been unable to compete with larger operations that are not required to consider the external costs of their production in an unregulated environment.

Regulation is certainly not appropriate in all instances, and the burden of regulation must always be weighed in the regulatory analysis. However, given the significant environmental challenges presented, it is time to replace agricultural exceptionalism with a new paradigm that links well-designed regulations to promote the public welfare and the long-term sustainability of the industry with government support that reflects societal interests in promoting the sustainable production of healthy foods. This paradigm calls for agricultural policies that benefit society as a whole, including farmers, rather than policies that serve to benefit the direct economic interests of the most powerful within our food and agricultural sector.

Climate change makes this paradigm shift all the more urgent. Its impact on future food production is well documented. Scientists predict that climate change will reduce the amount of food produced globally and increase the problem of crop pests. Weather disruptions will have devastating results in different regions at different times.[48]

Not as well known but of serious concern are studies indicating that the food produced will be nutritionally inferior due to the impact of increased levels of carbon dioxide in the atmosphere. Testing has confirmed that crops grown with increased levels of carbon dioxide have lower levels of protein, zinc, and iron.[49]

Given the importance of the issues presented—we all depend on our food system for survival—policies must be carefully thought out and regulations carefully drafted so as not to impose undue burdens on food production or cause unanticipated and unwelcome consequences. Agriculture should no longer be excepted from regulation; rather, it should be guided and supported by regulation, providing financial incentives when necessary to achieve societal goals.

The following broad-based guidelines should be reflected in our creation of this new approach to agriculture and the new paradigm for guiding and supporting our food system.

The Protection of Natural Resources

The protection of natural resources essential for human survival, including water, air, and soil, should be articulated as a national priority and embodied in all governmental policies as a matter of national security. Embedded within that policy should be a recognition of the dangers of climate change and an expression of will to combat it. Although such a broad priority statement will not provide easy answers to the balancing of interests that it requires, it is an essential first step in recognizing that our days of unlimited consumption of our natural resources are at an end.

Within this guideline, specific attention must be given to the interconnectedness of groundwater, surface water, wetlands, and land use. Scientific analysis should be incorporated into the regulation of water pollution, prompting congressional action to strengthen and expand the reach of the Clean Water Act. Water depletion concerns only heighten the need to protect the integrity of water bodies, above and below ground. Where regulation is unwieldy or too difficult to enforce, incentive-based systems that tie farm program subsidies to environmental compliance should be adopted.

The Production of Sufficient and Healthful Food to Feed the Population

The production of sufficient and healthful food to feed the population is a related and equally vital goal. This goal, however, must be achieved in a way that maximizes resilience in the face of climate disruption, drought, and increased pestilence. Government must be willing to provide support to achieve this goal, but the focus of this support should no longer be on the maximum annual production of commodity crops, many of which are used for nonfood purposes. Rather, societal interests should determine government support to agriculture, with the primary goal of the sustainable production of food that meets the health needs of the population and that does not jeopardize other life essentials, now or for future generations.

These two goals must work in tandem. For example, producing food while contaminating drinking water supplies is not an acceptable trade-off no matter how economically valuable that production is. Both food and water are basic societal needs. One should not be sacrificed for the other. Policies should support agricultural systems that are in line with sustainable practices and the associated resource protection goals.

An Accurate Assessment of Agricultural Externalities

Just as current efforts toward deregulation stress an economic cost-benefit analysis of the restrictions imposed by regulations, the long-term costs of not regulating activities must also be considered. Externalities that are often not addressed in current economic analysis, such as the environmental costs and public health costs, must be included in this analysis. For example, the true environmental and social costs of CAFOs must be honestly assessed and factored into the cost of production. Regulations that restrict environmental harm and require remediation of natural resources that are damaged provide the only way to effectively accomplish this.

Support for Diversification and Cropping Systems
That Protect Soil Health and Promote Resilience

Multiyear crop rotation is widely accepted as the most beneficial cropping system for maintaining soil health and minimizing damage from crop pests. Incentives should be provided to farmers who diversify their farming operations and who rotate their crops on a multiyear basis. Other conservation practices including organic agriculture should be incentivized as well. For a generation, taxpayers have financially rewarded farmers for maximizing the short-term production of commodity crops without regard to the health of our nation's soil. This incentive system must be changed to reward farmers for practices that build back soil that is capable of withstanding disruptive weather events and feeding future generations.

Support for Farming Systems That Protect Animal Welfare

In perhaps the most extensive application of agricultural exceptionalism, there are no federal laws that regulate the care of livestock or poultry that are raised on farms, AFOs or CAFOs. Extensive research on animal sentience and intelligence as well as the ability of farm animals to experience pain, fear, and other stresses suggests that it is time for federal standards that provide basic protections for the animals we raise for food. A model to consider for adoption would be that adopted by the European Union as well as some large US food retailers. This model is based on the European Convention for the Protection of Animals Kept for Farming Purposes. The model is more commonly known as the Five Freedoms: freedom from hunger and thirst; freedom from discomfort; freedom from pain, injury, and disease; freedom to express normal behavior; and freedom from fear and distress.

Support for Family-Sized Farming Operations

Although some elements of the agrarian ideal may be exaggerated—farmers are not really any more "virtuous" than any other occupation—the model of the family-sized farm is one that has enduring strengths, contributing to a wide range of societal goals. While government has paid lip-service to its support for family farming, this support has morphed into a system of incentives that encourages greater and greater consolidation of land, larger farming operations, and increasing wealth disparities within the sector. Farm families continue to own most farm operations, yet many of these farms are more akin to the plantation model of agriculture than to the family farms of the agrarian ideal. A landed gentry now limits access to the profession, discouraging young farmers who are not directly related to a land-owning farmer.

Smaller farming operations may not produce all the efficiencies of scale in the short term, but many farming methods that are the most beneficial and productive in the long term are best accomplished on small to mid-size operations. Smaller farm equipment, the greater use of multiple cropping systems, innovative techniques, and conservation practices produce the greatest resilience. These are all the hallmarks of family-sized farms, and they are most often lost in the quest for larger and larger operations. Moreover, family-sized farms help to maintain and promote economically healthy rural communities and are the building block for a regenerated regional food system.

While regulation cannot ensure farm size, in recent decades the lack of environmental regulation coupled with government incentives has incentivized the increase in farm size and created the economic climate for consolidation. These incentives must be reversed in favor of policies that support and reward the family-sized farm as the centerpiece of a revitalization of rural America. Such a program should actively welcome a new diverse generation of young farmers.

Recognition of the Diversity within Agriculture: S ize and Location Matter

Perhaps the only legitimate argument against the regulation of agriculture is a practical one. With more than two million farms operating in diverse environments, it is difficult to craft regulations that will apply reasonably to the seemingly infinite variations found on the farms scattered across the country.

The pragmatic answer is that size truly does matter, and regulations must reflect this. The "transformation" of agriculture that has occurred in the livestock industry necessitates the strict regulation of concentrated facilities. These are industrial-scale facilities that should be regulated as such by environmental regulators. As with the existing regulatory scheme, either no regulations or perhaps a lighter regulatory touch may be more appropriate for smaller operations.

Similarly cropping activities that are appropriate in one setting (e.g., a flat terrain with little access to surface water or wetland) will not be appropriate in another, such as a field that is hilly or near water. Specific conservation plans that address the unique characteristics of a farm or field must guide any regulatory effort and continue to serve as a condition of participation in federal farm program support. Enforcement is best accomplished through the network of USDA offices in each state and most counties.

Regulations Must Be Practical

Many farmers will have at least one story of someone from Washington, DC, or even the state capital who failed to understand the reality of life on the farm. Many will tell of a regulatory agency that proposed something that was either unworkable or simply stupid. Agricultural regulations must be written by those who understand farming, with direct input from farmers, soil scientists, animal scientists, and horticulturists. Regulations must be practical and pragmatic, recognizing the realities of rural life.

Conclusion

At its best, agricultural exceptionalism recognizes the unique aspects of agriculture and seeks to provide special support for an industry on which we all depend. At its worst, it rewards a sector for activities that are harmful to society and creates an expectation of entitlement and a disdain for following the rules that apply to other sectors. Because more and more American consumers are seeking information about their food system and environmental concerns are heightened, it is time to reconsider agricultural exceptionalism. Agriculture is a unique industry, and farmers are deserving of governmental support. However, that support must be delivered in ways that further legitimate societal goals. And farming activities, when they impact others or the environment beyond their border, should also be subject to practical regulation.

REFERENCES
1. See Susan A. Schneider, *Food, Farming, and Sustainability: Readings in Agricultural Law* (Durham, NC: Carolina Academic Press, 2016), 14–18.
2. 29 U.S.C. §§ 151–69.
3. 29 U.S.C. §§ 201–19.
4. 29 U.S.C. §152(3).
5. 21 U.S.C. § 213(b).
6. 21 U.S.C. § 213(a)(6).
7. 21 U.S.C.§ 212.
8. "Agricultural Safety," US Centers for Disease Control and Prevention, April 12, 2018, https://www.cdc.gov/niosh/topics/aginjury/default.html.
9. See, for example, James B. Ruhl, "Farms, Their Environmental Harms, and Environmental Law," *Ecology L.Q.* 27, no. 2 (June 2000): 263.
10. 33 U.S.C. §§1251–1387.
11. "Memorandum: Clean Water Act Section 404 Regulatory Program and Agricultural Activities," US Environmental Protection Agency and US Department of the Army, May 3, 1990, https://www.epa.gov/cwa-404/memorandum -clean-water-act-section-404-regulatory-program-and-agricultural-activities.

12. David Zaring, "Agriculture, Nonpoint Source Pollution, and Regulatory Control: The Clean Water Act's Bleak Present and Future," *Harvard Environmental Law Review* 20, no. 2 (1996): 515–46.

13. Ruhl, "Farms."

14. Kai Olson-Sawyer, "Controversial Des Moines Water Works Lawsuit Calls for Farmers to Clean Up Drinking Water," *Civil Eats*, July 29, 2016, https://civileats.com/2016/07/29/controversial-des-moines-water-works-lawsuit -calls-for-farmers-to-clean-up-drinking-water/.

15. Daniel C. Vock, "Iowa Farmers Won a Water Pollution Lawsuit, but at What Cost?" *Governing the States and Localities*, May 3, 2017, http://www .governing.com/topics/transportation-infrastructure/gov-des-moines-water -utility-lawsuit-farmers.html.

16. According to the regulations, AFOs confine livestock in a facility without crops, vegetation, forage growth, or post-harvest residues for a total of 45 days or more in any 12-month period. 40 C.F.R. § 122.23(b).

17. 40 C.F.R. § 122.23(b).

18. James M. Macdonald, Robert A. Hoppe, and Doris Newton, "Three Decades of Consolidation in U.S. Agriculture," *USDA, ERS, Econ. Inf. Bulletin*, no. 189 (March 2018), https://ageconsearch.umn.edu/record/276247/.

19. A 2005 Second Circuit Court of Appeals held, among other issues, that the EPA cannot regulate a CAFO if it only has the potential to discharge pollutants; the facility must actually discharge pollutants to come within the regulatory scope of the permitting scheme. Waterkeeper Alliance et al. v. EPA, 399 F.3d 486 (2005). See also, Nat'l Pork Producers' Council v. U.S. EPA, 399 F.3rd 486 (2005).

20. "NPDES CAFO Permitting Status Report—National Summary, End-Year 2017, Completed 12/31/17 (as Reported by EPA Regions)," December 31, 2017, https://www.epa.gov/sites/production/files/2018-05/documents/tracksum_endyear _2017.pdf.

21. Carrie Hribar, "Understanding Concentrated Animal Feeding Operations and Their Impact on Communities" (Bowling Green, OH: National Association of Local Boards of Health, 2010), https://www.cdc.gov/nceh/ehs/docs/understanding _cafos_nalboh.pdf.

22. Thomas Nelson, "Family Says CAFOs Making Them Sick," *Courier*, August 26, 2018, https://wcfcourier.com/news/local/state-and-regional/family -says-cafos-making-them-sick/article_a742ed1b-51f2-53f8-a317-965387776fbc .html.

23. "Eleven Years after Agreement, EPA Has Not Developed Reliable Emission Estimation Methods to Determine Whether Animal Feeding Operations Comply with Clean Air Act and Other Statutes," EPA Office of Inspector General, Rep. No. 17-P-0396, September 19, 2017.

24. "Eleven Years."

25. 42 U.S.C. §7412(r)(5).

26. Letter from Scott Pruit to Tom Franz, Association of Irritated Citizens, denying 2009 petition to list CAFOs as a source category under the CAA,

December 15, 2017, https://www.regulations.gov/document?D=EPA-HQ-OAR
-2017-0638-0003.

27. Britt E. Erickson, "Livestock Emissions Still Up in the Air: Congress
Exempts Farms from Reporting Air Pollutants to Federal Agencies, Leaving
States to Deal with Animal Waste Releases," *Chemical and Engineering News*
96, no. 14 (2018): 28–32.

28. See Farm Bureau website, bearing trademarked claim as the "Voice of
Agriculture," https://www.fb.org/.

29. Christopher Doering, "AFBF: Federal Regulations Are the Biggest Threat to
Farmers," *Des Moines Register*, January 10, 2016, https://www.desmoinesregister
.com/story/money/agriculture/2016/01/10/federal-regulations-biggest-threat
-farmers/78131422/.

30. Indeed, opposition to regulation is often linked to the importance of
private property rights to the farming community. Farmland ownership and
autonomy are often portrayed as central components of American agriculture,
despite the fact that approximately 50% of farmland is owned by someone
other than the farmer who is working the land. Similarly, much of the grazing
land in the American West is owned by the government and leased to ranchers.

31. See, for example, Neil D. Hamilton, "High Hopes Meet Hard Truths:
Facing the Reality of Iowa's Water Quality Policy," September 21, 2017,
http://aglawcenter.wp.drake.edu/wp-content/uploads/sites/99/2018/01/High
-Hopes-meet-Hard-Truths-Iowa-Water.pdf.

32. Susan A. Schneider, "A Reconsideration of Agricultural Law: A Call for
the Law of Food, Farming, and Sustainability," *William & Mary Environmental
Law and Policy Review* 34, no. 3 (2010): 935.

33. Richard S. Kirkendall, "Up to Now: A History of American Agriculture
from Jefferson to Revolution to Crisis," *Agriculture and Human Values* 4, no. 1
(December 1, 1987): 4–26.

34. Macdonald, Hoppe, and Newton, "Three Decades."

35. Donald B. Pedersen, "Introduction," *U.C. Davis Law Review* 23, no. 3
(1990): 401–14.

36. Jim Chen, "Of Agriculture's First Disobedience and Its Fruit," *Vanderbilt
Law Review* 48, no. 5 (October 1995): 1261–1333.

37. Article I, Section 2, Clause 3 of the original Constitution, the Three-fifths
Compromise, allocated congressional representation based "on the whole
Number of free Persons" and "three fifths of all other Persons." According to
Article IV, Section 2, Clause 3, the Fugitive Slave Clause, "No person held to
Service or Labour in one State" would be freed by escaping to another.

38. The adoption of the Thirteenth Amendment to the United States Constitution abolishing slavery was declared by Secretary of State William H. Seward
on December 18, 1865.

39. "The Senate of the United States shall be composed of two Senators from
each State." US Constitution, Article I, Section 3, Clause 1.

40. USDA National Agricultural Statistics Service, https://www.nass.usda.gov/.

41. Schneider, *Food, Farming, and Sustainability*, 56.

42. "Agribusiness: Money to Congress," OpenSecrets.org, https://www
.opensecrets.org/industries/summary.php?cycle=2018&ind=A.

43. See Meredith Kaufman, "The Clash of Agricultural Exceptionalism and
the First Amendment: A Discussion of Kansas' Ag-Gag Law," *Journal of Food
Law & Policy* 15, no. 1 (Spring 2019): 49–73.

44. Dan Flynn, "BPI Settles with ABC over $1.9 Billion Defamation Claim,"
Food Safety News, June 28, 2017, https://www.foodsafetynews.com/2017/06
/bpi-settles-with-abc-over-1-9-billion-defamation-claim/.

45. See, for example, Holly Farms v. National Labor Relations Board, 517
U.S. 392 (1996); Heath v. Perdue Farms, Inc., 87 F. Supp. 2d 452 (D. MD.
2000).

46. Anne Blythe, "Hog Farmers Win New Protections as Lawmakers
Override Roy Cooper's Veto," *News & Observer*, June 27, 2018, https://www
.newsobserver.com/news/politics-government/article213914154.html.

47. Schneider, "A Reconsideration," 935, 947.

48. "Fourth National Climate Assessment, Volume II: Impacts, Risks, and
Adaptation in the United States," US Global Change Research Program, 2018.

49. Helena Bottemiller Evich, "The Great Nutrient Collapse," *Politico*,
September 13, 2017, https://www.politico.com/agenda/story/2017/09/13/food
-nutrients-carbon-dioxide-000511; see also Sara G. Miller, "Climate Change Is
Transforming the World's Food Supply," *Live Science*, February 16, 2017,
https://www.livescience.com/57921-climate-change-is-transforming-global-food
-supply.html.

[SEVEN]

US Oversight of GM Crops

JENNIFER KUZMA

The Past

The first generation of genetically modified (GM) crops was produced in the mid-1980s and was largely limited to two introduced traits: pest resistance (Bt) and herbicide tolerance (Ht). Commercialization of Bt and Ht crops began in the mid-1990s and benefited primarily the biotech industry in patenting and selling the seeds but also farmers who could reduce pesticide use in some cases. GM crops led to pesticide reductions in some areas of the country because they were engineered to produce pesticidal proteins (from the bacterium *Bacillus thuringiensis*, or Bt). Herbicide-tolerant (or Roundup-ready) genes were also engineered into crops so that farmers could spray herbicides to kill weeds without killing the crops. Bt and Ht crops permeated the US market to near saturation—close to 90% of corn, cotton, and soybean crops. Many crops were engineered with stacked Bt and Ht traits so that farmers could control a broad range of pests and weeds.

The history of the oversight system for this first generation of GM crops is important for informing the future of how we deal with new types of genetic engineering (GE) and different traits in a wider variety of crops and other organisms. It can be demarcated by four phases according

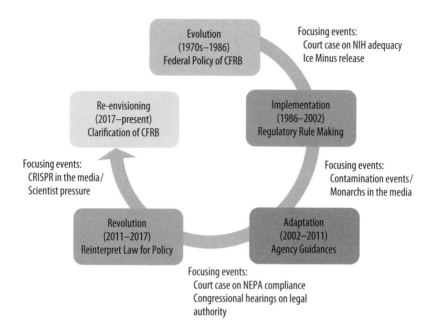

Figure 7.1. Oversight of GM Crops: Phases, Policy Tools, and Focusing Events.
Source: Jennifer Kuzma, "Properly Paced? Examining the Past and Present Governance of GMOs in the United States," in *Innovative Governance Models for Emerging Technologies*, ed. Gary E. Marchant, Kenneth W. Abbott, and Braden Allenby (Cheltenham, UK: Edward Elgar, 2013), 176-97.

to the policy tools used to keep pace with the emerging field of biotechnology and the growing number of products.[1] Each transition to a different phase was sparked by what we call in policy process studies "focusing events," which had the potential to cause policy changes to the system. These events for GM crops consisted of both court cases from environmental or consumer advocacy organizations in federal courts that brought challenges to the adequacy of oversight and reports in the news media about contamination events, risk studies, or new technologies (figure 7.1).

The first phase started with the laboratory development of recombinant DNA (rDNA) methods—the origins of modern biotechnology—in the 1970s. During the early work with biotech, National Institutes of Health (NIH) guidelines were formulated to govern good practices in minimizing risk in the laboratory. However, when it was proposed that they also be the only oversight for the environmental release of frost-preventing GM bacteria (Ice Minus) in the early 1980s, court challenges brought on by environmental activists ensued. These legal challenges led to congressional hearings, which in turn sparked national policy setting emanating from the White House. The evolution phase ended in 1986, when the Office of Science and Technology Policy developed the Coordinated Framework for the Regulation of Biotechnology (CFRB). Principles of the Coordinated Framework were that the risks of biotechnology products were the "same in kind" as conventionally bred crops and that it was the product that should be the focus of regulation, not the process by which it was made.[2] Therefore, the CFRB suggested that no new laws were needed and existing product categories could be used to regulate biotechnology products. As such, products were divided among the federal agencies according to type. Thus, the main policy tool used in this phase was interagency, national policy making expressed in a guidance document stemming from the White House's science arm.

Then in the implementation phase, from 1986 to approximately 2002, the different agencies put forth formal regulations and rules. The US Department of Agriculture (USDA) passed rules to regulate GE plants as "plant pests" under the Federal Plant Pest Act (of 1957) in 1987 for field trials and in 1993 for interstate movement of GE products (called "deregulation"). At that time, rDNA methods used engineered sequences from viruses and bacteria that caused plant disease (e.g., *Agrobacterium*) in order to deliver genes into plants and express them. Thus, the DNA fragments from these plant pests provided a regulatory hook for the USDA, even if the gene of interest for a desired trait had nothing to do with a plant pest. In a similar fashion, the EPA loosely interpreted its authorities under the CFRB: GE plants engineered with pesticidal-like proteins were to be regulated under the Federal Insecticide, Fungicide, and Rodenticide Act as pesticides (plant-incorporated protectants), and GE microorganisms were to be regulated as "toxic chemicals" under the Toxic Substances Control Act. The FDA, however, took a different approach and assumed that conventionally bred products were, as a whole, substantially equivalent to GE products; therefore, a mandatory regulatory process was not required. In 1992, FDA published guidance for a voluntary consultation process under the Federal Food, Drug, and Cosmetic Act (FFDCA), asking GE developers to consult with the agency about the safety of their plant-based GE foods. To this day, FDA's process does not involve a determination of safety. The agency reviews data voluntarily submitted by GE-food companies and then writes a letter indicating that the agency has no safety concerns about the product at this time. These new rules and procedures were the primary policy tool up until around 2002. These rules for GM crops have essentially constituted the oversight system we still have today.

The next phase, adaptation, was marked by public controversies over the use of GM crops. Several mishaps occurred in the system: with Star-Link, Bt corn, which was approved only for animal feed, was found in the human food supply; Mexican maize was cross-contaminated with Bt genes; pharmaceuticals in plants were co-mingled with food; and, according to published studies, Monarch butterflies were harmed by Bt corn. These mishaps also prompted legal challenges by NGOs and subsequent changes to the oversight system.[3,4,5] The policy tool of subagency guidance documents was introduced to minimize risk of contamination and increase the rigor of safety studies. For example, in 2003 the USDA published more stringent confinement measures for field trials of GE plants designed to produce pharmaceutical and industrial proteins so they would not contaminate human food crops. Then, in 2006, the FDA published a guidance document to improve the safety evaluation of GE crops. Toward the end of the adaptation phase in 2009, the FDA also published a guidance document that proposed to oversee GE animals as "investigational" new animal drugs under the FFDCA. Oversight for GE animals was not specified in the original CFRB. Shortly after, FDA approved use of a transgenic goat engineered to produce the human drug anti-thrombin in its milk for medicinal use, though not for food use.[6,7,8,9]

The end of the adaptation phase was marked by key court challenges to the adequacy of USDA's assessment of GM crops under the National Environmental Policy Act (NEPA). Lawsuits against industry and the USDA were introduced, claiming that the agency did not comply with NEPA because it used the less rigorous environmental assessments rather than using a full-scale Environmental Impact Statement (EIS) process. In 2007, USDA's Animal and Plant Health Inspection Service lost two federal district court cases because of inadequate data to support its decision to allow deregulation of GE alfalfa and for ignoring evidence of environmental harm in field trials of GE bentgrass. The case over GE alfalfa was appealed to the US Supreme Court. The court upheld the claim that USDA needed to conduct a full EIS, and the USDA was forced to complete its first-ever EIS document for GE-crop deregulation in 2010, and with continuing legal challenges, it appeared that it would be forced to use a more intensive EIS process for future GE crops.[10,11] The decision about this case marked the end of the adaptation phase and the beginning of significant changes in US oversight policies.

Around the time of the Supreme Court challenges, a new method for making GM crops, called gene editing, emerged. USDA, faced with potentially more legal challenges and increasing congressional pressure against its authority to regulate GM crops at all,[12] had a choice to make about these gene-edited crops. Ultimately, this "revolution phase," from around 2011 to 2017, prompted a shift to a more antiregulatory climate nationally, including in the area of biotechnology, specifically for these new gene-edited crops.

To implement the CFRB, the USDA had used the Plant Pest Act as the regulatory hook to capture GM plants for oversight. GM plants were considered "plant pests" because they were made by using DNA sequences from plant pests, such as *Agrobacterium*, to insert genes of interest. However, with newer gene-editing methods, those plant pest sequences were no longer needed. All that was needed was knowledge about a specific sequence to target, a nuclease system like CRISPR-Cas9, and a DNA template to introduce any changes. At the start of this revolution phase, the USDA made decisions outside of the realm of public debate, between the GM crop developer and the agency, to exempt these gene-edited plants and any GM plant without plant-pest sequences from regulation.[13] The USDA made a political choice, as its legal authority was flexible enough to capture GM plants without plant pest sequences into the Plant Protection Act of 2000 by considering them as noxious weeds or by a USDA administrator categorizing the whole plant as a plant pest. Hence the new biotech revolution of gene editing was accompanied by a similar revolution phase in our US oversight system. This revolution returned to the policy tool of national policy making, but this time, unlike the CFRB, it was behind closed doors and captured only in letters between GM crop developers and agency staff. It involved the reinterpretation of the CFRB and laws on which USDA regulations were based. It wasn't until 2018 that the USDA stated publicly that this exemption for gene editing would be its formal policy (final phase in figure 7.1 of "Re-envisioning" and resetting policy).

From a policy standpoint, the GMO oversight story is defined by contention and conflict. Court challenges separated the phases of oversight marked by different policy tools—the ones of the mid-1980s over GM bacteria, the ones around the year 2000 over StarLink, and the Supreme Court challenges to USDA assessment practices. These changes, in combination with press and public pressure, were focusing events that prompted policy change.[14]

Procedural Ethics: Who Has a Voice?

Why is there controversy if GMOs are really the "same in kind" and there are no new risks compared to conventional breeding? One way to view the oversight system comes from the lens of policy analysis. In one study, we used a multicriteria assessment approach to evaluate the oversight system for genetically engineered crops.[15] We found US oversight of GMOs to be highly flexible with a weak legal grounding that allows for shifts based on the current political climate. Little transparency, a low level of informed consent, few opportunities for public input, and a low-resource capacity all contributed to public mistrust and contention.

Another way to view US oversight of GMOs is more philosophical. One of the core claims of the oversight system is its adherence to "sound science." But we know that science, especially as applied to safety and risk, is not value-free.[16,17] For example, even if scientists know the dose-response curve for a product, how do we determine an acceptable level of risk? More often, scientists do not know the dose-response curve well because the data concern only high doses. This uncertainty leads to studies being interpreted according to the worldviews of those doing the interpreting. A lot of industry-funded studies are not trusted in the GM crop policy domain, and peer-reviewed studies showing risk are often picked apart and discredited through highly coordinated campaigns initiated by biotechnology developers. The reality is that there will always be uncertainty and risk. Science can and should inform decisions and be a guide, but it cannot tell us what is "safe."

Making regulatory decisions based solely on "sound science" marginalizes values and other worldviews. Keeping decisions about gene editing closed from the public process and confined to "sound science" privileges the values of scientists at federal agencies who have a mandate to promote innovation and technology developers who are conflicted.[18] Even these experts bring their worldviews and values to bear on interpreting risk and uncertainty; for example, those that lean toward more of an egalitarian-communitarian worldview may perceive a higher risk for emerging technologies and desire more precaution than those who lean toward a more hierarchical-individualist worldview.[19]

Thus, federal oversight of this first generation of GM crops offered different policy tools to govern GM crops, but phase changes were prompted by public controversy and legal challenges, indicating a public failure with regard to US oversight for GMOs.[20] It was a contested system in which changes to increase regulation happened only by increasing public pressure against GMOs. There was little transparency and few opportunities for meaningful dialogue and input. The system operated in a low-knowledge and a low-choice environment.

The Present

Gene-edited crops, such as those made with CRISPR-Cas9, entered the food market in 2019. In prior interviews with developers of gene-edited crops, most agreed that mistakes were made with the first generation of GM crops and acknowledged that stakeholders and citizens should be informed.[21] They also feared that gene-edited crops would turn out to be as controversial as the first generation of GM crops, especially given the increasing consumer demand for non-GM food products.

However, to date, they are arguing for policies that are likely to lead to lower public trust and confidence in gene-edited food products because of four ethical shortcomings: lack of transparency, of integrity, of oversight, and of procedural justice.[22]

The lack of transparency is shown in new labeling policies. The National Bioengineered Food Disclosure Law, which was passed by Congress in July 2016, directed the USDA to implement a mandatory standard for disclosing GM foods. After failing to meet the July 2018 deadline set by Congress, the USDA published a final rule in December 2018.[23] The standard goes into effect for large food manufacturers in January 2020, with mandatory compliance by January 2022. This mandatory disclosure policy undercuts transparency in two key ways. First, it allows manufacturers to identify their products as "bioengineered" rather than "genetically modified or GM" to avoid the negative connotations with GM foods. Second, it gives manufacturers several disclosure options. Either they can place a label on their product consisting of a sunny landscape surrounded by the words "bioengineered" or "derived from bioengineering," or they can use text, an electronic or digital link disclosure (e.g., a QR code), or a text message. Some of these options are more transparent than the others, and none use the familiar term "GM." Many food producers are expected to use the QR code (with a telephone number to call for more information) and altogether avoid the term "bioengineered" on the package. This is the least transparent option, and it will be difficult for consumers to know that the product does include genetically modified ingredients.[24]

The lack of integrity is demonstrated by the dishonest communication around gene editing. In recent meetings and publications, biotech developers are turning to different ways to describe gene editing, such as "new plant breeding," "precision breeding," "accelerated breeding," or "new mutagenesis." Some of this language is not accurate and is misleading. Although many gene-edited crops will contain no foreign genetic material in the final crop, some might. There are differences in gene-editing methods, some of which involve the addition of foreign genes (transgenes) or parts of them, or synthetic DNA sequences coding for genes not found at all in nature. Trying to mask what gene-edited products are or how they are derived is ultimately likely to lead to public mistrust of them.

Due to the USDA's exemption of gene-edited and other GM crops not engineered with plant pest sequences from its regulations, there is no mandatory authority to test gene-edited products in the field prior to market entry. Furthermore, FDA's review for food safety is currently voluntary, and the agency has not yet released a guidance for gene-edited foods. As a result, we are likely to see gene-edited crops enter the market without having undergone safety testing. Is this problematic from an ethical standpoint? An argument could be made that the government is failing to protect the health of the environment and consumers by not regulating gene-edited crops. Plant biotechnologists disagree, calling the desire to regulate gene-edited crops unscientific because the same risks may be present with conventionally bred crops. They argue that because conventional crops and foods are not regulated, gene-edited crops and foods should also not be regulated.[25] However, arguments about what to capture under regulations that are strictly based on "sound science" lead to only two logical conclusions: regulate everything, regardless of genetic modification method, or regulate nothing. And which one of these options you choose is based on your worldview; therefore, it is impossible to decide what to capture in a regulatory system without inserting some value judgements.

Finally, there is a lack of procedural justice in terms of power and control and whose values count. As mentioned earlier, values are implicit in every regulatory and scientific assessment. With this second generation of GM crops, we are still counting only the values of product developers and regulatory reviewers in choosing not to regulate them without any public discussion or consultation. We are using "sound science" as an exclusionary tactic to privilege those in power and marginalize the values of people without "expertise." This is especially hypocritical now given the "product not process" case that developers made with the first generation of GM crops. Before they argued that genetically engineered crops were the same as conventionally bred crops and thus should be regulated no differently. Now they are arguing that the process of gene editing is different from the process of genetic engineering in the first generation and that should determine exemption from regulation. They seem to be using science to mask their worldview that regulation impedes innovation. This is a perfectly valid worldview, but it is not the only one that should count. Most consumers prefer mandatory regulation for GM crops, and deferring to the views of only the developers of these crops seems unjust.

Ways Forward

Where do we go from here? Given the rapid pace of agricultural biotechnology development, there is a need for better governance of GM crops. Although it is likely unwise to unduly stifle innovation in this area, regulatory decision making needs to incorporate more than just the values of developers. There are plenty of governance models that one could describe as taking a "middle-ground,"[26] that is, ones where science informs the choices but diverse public values are also taken into account. For example, post-normal science (PNS) says that when the decision stakes and systems uncertainties are high, open dialogue between "extended peer communities" is needed.[27] More recently, responsible research and innovation (RRI) has been advanced as a "transparent, interactive process by which societal actors and innovators become mutually responsive to each other with a view to the (ethical) acceptability, sustainability and societal desirability of the innovation process and its marketable products (in order to allow a proper embedding of scientific and technological advances in our society)."[28] A recent National Academies of Sciences study suggests that for highly unfamiliar, complex, and novel products, the decision-making process should include an external, expert advisory panel and also consultation with interested publics and affected parties.[29] Although we cannot expect such a rigorous process to occur for every single gene-edited crop, it would have seemed wise to take this course for the first batch of gene-edited crops before they went to market and for ones that significantly differ from this first batch in the future. But while there is no shortage of better governance models available to us, we first need the political and social will to change so that the second generation of GM crops is not plagued with the public failures of the first.

REFERENCES

1. Jennifer Kuzma, "Properly Paced? Examining the Past and Present Governance of GMOs in the United States," in *Innovative Governance Models for Emerging Technologies*, ed. Gary E. Marchant, Kenneth W. Abbott, and Braden Allenby (Cheltenham, UK: Edward Elgar, 2013), 176–97.

2. Office of Science and Technology Policy, "Coordinated Framework for the Regulation of Biotechnology," *Federal Register* 51, no. 123 (1986): 23302–50.

3. Jeffrey L. Fox, "Puzzling Industry Response to ProdiGene Fiasco," *Nature Biotechnology* 21, no. 1 (January 2003): 3–4.

4. David Quist and Ignacio H. Chapela, "Transgenic DNA Introgressed into Traditional Maize Landraces in Oaxaca, Mexico," *Nature* 414, no. 6863 (November 29, 2001): 541–43.

5. Alejando E. Segarra and Jean M. Rawson, "StarLink Corn Controversy: Background," CRS Report for Congress No. RS20732. Washington, DC: Congressional Research Service, January 10, 2001.

6. Kuzma, "Properly Paced?"

7. US Department of Agriculture, "Field Testing of Plants Engineered to Produce Pharmaceutical and Industrial Compounds," *Federal Register* 68, no. 46 (2003): 11337–40.

8. "Guidance for Industry. Recommendations for the Early Food Safety Evaluation of New Non-pesticidal Proteins Produced by New Plant Varieties Intended for Food Use," US Food and Drug Administration, June 2006, https://www.fda.gov/Food/GuidanceRegulation/GuidanceDocumentsRegulatory Information/Biotechnology/ucm096156.htm.

9. "Guidance for Industry: Regulation of Genetically Engineered Animals Containing Heritable Recombinant DNA Constructs," US Food and Drug Administration, June 2015, https://www.fda.gov/downloads/AnimalVeterinary /GuidanceComplianceEnforcement/GuidanceforIndustry/ucm113903.pdf.

10. Tadlock Cowan and Kristina Alexander, "Deregulating Genetically Engineered Alfalfa and Sugar Beets: Legal and Administrative Responses," CRS Report for Congress No. R41395. Washington, DC: Congressional Research Service, May 22, 2013.

11. "Glyphosate-Tolerant Alfalfa Events J101 and J163: Request for Nonregulated Status," Final Environmental Impact Statement, US Department of Agriculture, December 2010, https://www.aphis.usda.gov/biotechnology /downloads/alfalfa/gt_alfalfa%20_feis.pdf.

12. Committee on Agriculture, US House of Representatives, *Forum to Review the Biotechnology Product Regulatory Approval Process: A Forum before the Committee on Agriculture, U.S. House of Representatives, One Hundred Twelfth Congress, First Session, January 20, 2011* (Washington, DC: U.S. G.P.O., 2011).

13. Jennifer Kuzma, "Policy: Reboot the Debate on Genetic Engineering," *Nature News* 531, no. 7593 (March 10, 2016): 165.

14. Paul Cairney and Tanya Heikkila, "A Comparison of Theories of the Policy Process," in *Theories of the Policy Process*, ed. Paul A. Sabatier and Christopher M. Weible (Boulder, CO: Westview Press, 2014).

15. Jennifer Kuzma, Pouya Najmaie, and Joel Larson, "Evaluating Oversight Systems for Emerging Technologies: A Case Study of Genetically Engineered Organisms," *Journal of Law, Medicine & Ethics* 37, no. 4 (December 1, 2009): 546–86.

16. Paul B. Thompson, *Food Biotechnology in Ethical Perspective* (Dordrecht: Springer, 2007).

17. Jennifer Kuzma, "Regulating Gene-Edited Crops," *Issues in Science and Technology* 35, no. 1 (2018): 80–85.

18. Zahra Meghani and Jennifer Kuzma, "The 'Revolving Door' between Regulatory Agencies and Industry: A Problem That Requires Reconceptualizing Objectivity," *Journal of Agricultural & Environmental Ethics* 24, no. 6 (December 1, 2011): 575–99.

19. Dan M. Kahan, "Fear of Democracy: A Cultural Evaluation of Sunstein on Risk," *Faculty Scholarship Series*, Paper 104, 2006, http://digitalcommons .law.yale.edu/fss_papers/104.

20. Barry Bozeman and Daniel Sarewitz, "Public Values and Public Failure in US Science Policy," *Science & Public Policy* 32, no. 2 (April 1, 2005): 119–36.

21. Jennifer Kuzma, Adam Kokotovich, and Aliya Kuzhabekova, "Attitudes towards Governance of Gene Editing," *Biotechnology and Development Monitor* 18, no. 1 (2016): 69–92.

22. Kuzma, "Regulating Gene-Edited Crops."

23. US Department of Agriculture, "National Bioengineered Food Disclosure Standard," *Federal Register* 83, no. 245 (2018): 65814–76.

24. Deloitte, "Study of Electronic or Digital Link Disclosure: A Third-Party Evaluation of Challenges Impacting Access to Bioengineered Food Disclosure," July 2017.

25. Kuzma, "Regulating Gene-Edited Crops."

26. Jennifer Kuzma, "Risk, Environmental Governance, and Emerging Biotechnology," in *Environmental Governance Reconsidered: Challenges, Choices, and Opportunities*, 2nd ed., ed. Robert F. Durant, Daniel J. Fiorino, and Rosemary O'Leary (Cambridge, MA: MIT Press, 2017).

27. Silvio O. Funtowicz and Jerome R. Ravetz, "A New Scientific Methodology for Global Environmental Issues," in *Ecological Economics: The Science and Management of Sustainability*, ed. Robert Costanza (New York: Columbia University Press, 1991), 137–52.

28. René Von Schomberg, "A Vision of Responsible Innovation," in *Responsible Innovation: Managing the Responsible Emergence of Science and Innovation in Society*, ed. Richard Owen, John Bessant, and Maggy Heintz (Chichester, UK: John Wiley & Sons, 2013), 51–74.

29. National Academies of Sciences, Engineering, and Medicine et al., *Preparing for Future Products of Biotechnology* (Washington, DC: National Academies Press, 2017).

EIGHT

Conflicts of Interest in Food and Nutrition Research

MARION NESTLE

IN RECENT YEARS, the *Journal of the American Medical Association* (*JAMA*), *Science*, and other major scientific and medical journals have devoted entire issues to discussing conflicts of interest in research.[1,2] According to *JAMA,* "a conflict of interest exists when professional judgment concerning a primary interest (such as patients' welfare or the validity of research) may be influenced by a secondary interest (such as financial gain)."[3] My most recent book, *Unsavory Truth: How Food Companies Skew the Science of What We Eat,*[4] deals with conflicts of interest caused by funding of research by companies that make foods, beverages, and supplements or by their trade associations.

One frequently asked question in the field of food studies is whether it is ethical for food and beverage companies to fund research with the potential to promote their marketing interests. The *New York Times* recently published an exceptionally egregious example of such practices. It reported that five large alcoholic beverage companies had given more than $67 million to the National Institutes of Health (NIH) to conduct a study demonstrating the effects of one daily drink of alcohol on the risk of coronary artery disease. The reporter had obtained documents demonstrating that the alcohol industry had influenced the development of this trial and that NIH personnel had essentially promised the funders that the trial would produce the desired outcome and not demonstrate harm. They would not run the trial long enough to demonstrate a greater risk for breast cancer, for example. NIH administrators, presumably embarrassed by these revelations, ordered an investigation and halted enrollment in the trial. The scathing results of the investigative report caused NIH to stop the study altogether,[5] after having spent $4 million in taxpayer money.[6] The moral: industry funding of research has consequences—especially if it's caught.

When I write about food industry funding of research, I am calling attention to the makers of all the different brands of food and beverages that we love and buy by the billions every year. Most of these brands are owned by one of ten global food giants.[7] Food companies would like us to believe that food choices are solely a matter of personal responsibility, and it is true that companies are not forcing us to buy their products. But what I find fascinating about the personal-responsibility argument is how it completely ignores food industry marketing actions. One of the reasons why I first wrote *Food Politics* in 2002 was that I was tired of attending meetings about childhood obesity in which the principal topic addressed was how to get mothers to do a better job of feeding their children[8]—as if the food industry were entirely uninvolved in directly and indirectly selling to children. We are not supposed to notice marketing. As advertising industry executives have told me, when they do their job well, the advertising slips below the radar of critical thinking and is invisible.

As for what we are supposed to eat: healthy diets are so easy to explain that the journalist Michael Pollan can do it in seven words: "Eat food, not too much, mostly plants."[9] But if everyone followed Pollan's advice, the makers of ultraprocessed "junk" foods would go out of business. Such foods are the most profitable items in supermarkets. Food companies are up against a highly competitive food environment in part because we have so much food available. The United States has 4,000 calories available per day per capita,[10] whereas the population needs only about half that number. With so great a surplus of calories, food companies must compete for sales. At the same time, they are under pressure from advocates like me who want them to stop selling unhealthful products, regulators who want to tax them, lawyers who want to sue them, and Wall Street, which simply wants them to report higher profits every quarter.[11]

At first, food companies responded to such pressures by doing nothing. Then, they denied responsibility for contributing to the obesity problem. They also reformulated some products to make them appear healthier. But now, they are fighting back, most obviously through marketing. It is not easy to find marketing figures for specific products, but every now and then *Advertising Age* publishes a few of them. In 2016, for example, Coca-Cola spent $254 million just to advertise classic Coke, and Pepsi spent $127 million just to advertise Gatorade—just in the United States and just through advertising agencies.[12] Altogether, food, beverage, alcohol, and restaurant chain companies spend about $30 billion on advertising as well as more subtle activities such as trade shows and grocery store slotting fees.[13] Under US tax laws, every penny of those expenditures are deductible as a business expense.

Another way to sell more food is to increase portion sizes. Many food and drink items have increased two- to fivefold since the early 1980s, as have the sizes of restaurant meals.[14] To state the obvious, larger portions have more calories. And, as a result of industry lobbying and government policies, the relative price of fruits and vegetables has increased much more than the relative price of sugars, fats, and soft drinks.[15] Altogether, it appears as if the government and the food industry are collaborating to support a food environment that encourages people to eat more food than they need.

Advertising and large portions are visible to anyone who notices them. Less visible is the way the food industry supports marketing objectives by funding research. During the time I was preparing to write *Soda Politics*,[16] I frequently came across industry-funded studies with results that favored the sponsors' commercial interests and began posting them, five at a time, on my website (foodpolitics.com). I did this for a year, from March 2015 until March 2016. At the end of that year, I had posted 168 industry-funded studies; 156 of them had results predictable from knowing the sponsor. This was a convenience sample, and the only scientific conclusion that can be drawn is that it is easier to find industry-sponsored studies with favorable results than it is to find studies with unfavorable results. One observation: food company sponsorship of research is widespread. I had posted studies sponsored by more than 50 companies and trade associations for products such as sugar-sweetened beverages and snack foods but also for just about any fruit, vegetable, or nut you can think of that might be able to be marketed as a superfood. All these companies and associations were paying for research that might produce results useful for marketing purposes.

The key event that led to my writing *Unsavory Truth* was an investigative report published by the *New York Times* in August 2015. It focused on Coca-Cola's funding of the Global Energy Balance Network, a now defunct group of university investigators who argued that lack of physical activity is responsible for obesity—not diet—but neglected to mention its sponsorship by Coca-Cola.[17] I was quoted in the article and in the week following its publication, I was called by about thirty reporters surprised by its findings. They found it hard to believe that Coca-Cola would fund such a group, that university researchers would accept funding from Coca-Cola, and that universities would permit their faculty to do so. If reporters were surprised by these practices, I had another book to write. Hence: *Unsavory Truth*.

The *Times* article had consequences. The CEO of Coca-Cola wrote an op-ed promising that the company would do a better job of being transparent and would post the names of the individuals and groups funded by the company on its website.[18] It fulfilled that promise. On its Transparency website, the company states that from 2010 to 2018, it spent more than $146 million on "well-being related scientific research, partnership and health professional activities."[19]

Unfortunately for Coca-Cola, transparency allows analysis, and investigators can now compare studies funded by Coca-Cola to those funded by independent sources. In one such study, "Do Sugar-Sweetened Beverages Cause Obesity and Diabetes? Industry and the Manufacture of Scientific Controversy," investigators identified 60 studies examining the association between sugary drink consumption and obesity and diabetes. Of the 26 studies that found no association, 25 were industry funded. In contrast, of the 34 studies that did find an association, only

1 was industry-funded.[20] This tendency of industry-funded research outcomes to favor the sponsors' interests has its own name: the "funding effect."

The scientific literature on funding effects in the tobacco, chemical, and pharmaceutical drug industries is enormous. Research on the influence of drug-industry funding, for example, dates back to the 1970s and could fill a library.[21] Studies that have examined the influence of gifts—for example, a gift from a drug industry representative to a physician—repeatedly demonstrate that this influence operates at an unconscious level. The influence is unintentional and unrecognized. Large gifts are more influential, but even small gifts—a pen or a pad of paper—can influence physicians' prescription practices. Research on funding effects also finds that justifications for accepting industry funding are largely, although not entirely, invalid, and disclosure of industry connections is necessary but not sufficient to prevent industry influence.

Studying the results of drug-industry funding became easier with the passage of the Affordable Care Act of 2010, which required drug companies to publicly disclose the amounts of the payments contributed to physicians and hospitals and to post the information on the US Centers for Medicare & Medicaid Services Open Payments website (OpenPay mentsData.CMS.gov). A glance at this site reveals that in 2017, for example, 1,525 drug companies gave $8.4 billion to 628,000 doctors at 1,158 teaching hospitals. Investigators can and do correlate these payments to physicians' prescription practices, advisory committee decisions, and research outcomes and then measure the degree of influence.

In contrast, research on the effects of industry funding on food and nutrition research is in its infancy. I was able to identify precisely 11 studies of funding effects that appeared between 2003 and 2018; these are summarized in *Unsavory Truth*. These few studies varied in the food products examined (although half dealt with sugary drinks), the health effects measured, the methods of analysis used, and the outcomes of their analysis. Nevertheless, some general conclusions can be made, even from this small sample. Industry-funded studies generally favor the sponsor, skew the research question, and put a positive spin on the results. Food companies can bias studies at every stage of the research process, but as Lisa Bero and her collaborators have shown, this bias shows up most prominently in the development of the research question.[22] There is a significant difference between studies designed to ask how a product *benefits* health and those asking how a product *affects* health.

Industry funding has consequences. It creates scientific risks in that it biases the research agenda, results, and interpretations. It can lead to distorted dietary advice and loss of public trust in the entire scientific process. It also creates personal risks for researchers. Researchers who accept industry funding may be disqualified from membership on prestigious committees and run the risk of being exposed in the press and appearing "sold out."[23] Industry funding also creates personal risks for public health advocates. From emails leaked during the 2016 election, I learned that Coca-Cola had been monitoring my activities in Australia when I was a visiting scholar in Lisa Bero's group at the University of Sydney. The company also was planning to monitor Professor Bero's activities.[24]

Whether researchers should accept industry funding is a matter of intense debate in the medical and scientific literature.[25] Some scientists believe that it is appropriate to take money from food companies, while others insist that doing so risks "derailing public health nutrition."[26] Researchers who accept industry funding use many rationales, some of which are better supported by data than others. One of the more convincing arguments is the declining level of federal spending for research at a time when universities are requiring researchers to bring in more grant money. Federal funding indeed has leveled off, while corporate funding is increasing.[27]

Other arguments, however, are less well substantiated. One such argument is that industry funding is only one among many other sources of bias. Other sources include career goals, scientific beliefs, and dietary practices. Lisa Bero's group has also investigated this claim and argues that industry funding biases research in ways that differ from those other types of bias.[28] Career and scientific beliefs are intrinsic to research; science cannot be done without them. In contrast, industry funding is extrinsic to the process, is discretionary, and produces results that almost invariably favor the sponsors' interests.

Is disclosure sufficient to address conflicts of interest? Since the 1980s, scientific journals in the United States have required authors to disclose their sources of funding as well as their financial ties to the funders. Whether or not authors fully disclose is also a matter of research. Disclosure can be embarrassing, and researchers often fail to acknowledge their ties to sponsors. This failure also can have consequences. In 2018, for example, José Baselga, then chief medical officer at Memorial Sloan Kettering Cancer Center, landed on the front page of the *New York Times* because he had omitted disclosure of financial ties to numerous drug companies in research articles about their products.[29] Baselga resigned, but not before arguing that his industry contacts were public knowledge and in no way compromised his integrity as a researcher.

The appearance of a conflict of interest, however, is enough to undermine credibility. In recent years, disclosures in nutrition research have come under particular scrutiny from scientists who argue that "advocacy or activist work as well as their dietary preferences" should also be disclosed. If researchers are writing about dietary practices, they should disclose if they themselves follow a vegan, Atkins, or gluten-free diet or use any specific supplements.[30] Although nondisclosure is a problem, this level of personal disclosure seems inappropriate in comparison to the evident value of disclosing industry funding.

Conflicts of interest in food and nutrition research need to be recognized as an ethical problem. Because the influence of food industry funding can occur unconsciously, disclosure alone is not enough to solve the problem. In theory, the solution to the problems caused by conflicts of interest is simple: do not accept industry funding in the first place. For researchers under intense pressure to bring in grant funding, this solution may not appear realistic. In practice, addressing conflicts of interests requires much thought and work on the part of researchers, food companies, journalists who report on food studies, and eaters. At the very least, everyone should recognize that industry funding leads to conflicted interests and be skeptical of industry-funded studies. And all of us should be seeking ways to make sure that food and nutrition research is funded independently.

REFERENCES

1. Harvey V. Fineberg, "Conflict of Interest: Why Does It Matter?," *JAMA* 317, no. 17 (May 2017): 1717–18.

2. Charles Piller, "Hidden Conflicts?," *Science* 361, no. 6397 (July 2018): 16–20.

3. Phil Fontanarosa and Howard Bauchner, "Conflict of Interest and Medical Journals," *JAMA* 317, no. 17 (May 2017): 1768–71.

4. Marion Nestle, *Unsavory Truth: How Food Companies Skew the Science of What We Eat* (New York: Basic Books, 2018).

5. NIH Advisory Committee to the Director (ACD), *ACD Working Group for Review of the Moderate Alcohol and Cardiovascular Health Trial*, June 2018.

6. Roni Caryn Rabin, "Federal Agency Courted Alcohol Industry to Fund Study on Benefits of Moderate Drinking," *New York Times*, March 17, 2018.

7. Beth Hoffman, *Behind the Brands: Food Justice and the "Big 10" Food and Beverage Companies* (Oxford: Oxfam, 2013).

8. Marion Nestle, *Food Politics: How the Food Industry Influences Nutrition and Health* (Berkeley: University of California Press, 2013).

9. Michael Pollan, *In Defense of Food: An Eater's Manifesto* (New York: Penguin, 2008).

10. US Department of Agriculture Economic Research Service, "Food Availability (Per Capita) Data System," October 29, 2018, https://www.ers.usda.gov/data-products/food-availability-per-capita-data-system/food-availability-per-capita-data-system/.

11. Michele R. Simon, *Appetite for Profit: How the Food Industry Undermines Our Health and How to Fight Back* (New York: Nation Books, 2006).

12. Ad Age, *2017 Edition Marketing Fact Pack*, 2016.

13. "Ad Age Datacenter," Ad Age, https://adage.com/datacenter/.

14. Lisa R. Young and Marion Nestle, "Reducing Portion Sizes to Prevent Obesity: A Call to Action," *American Journal of Preventive Medicine* 43, no. 5 (November 2012): 565–68.

15. US Bureau of Labor Statistics, "Consumer Price Index," https://www.bls.gov/cpi/.

16. Marion Nestle, *Soda Politics: Taking on Big Soda (and Winning)* (New York: Oxford University Press, 2015).

17. Anahad O'Connor, "Coca-Cola Funds Scientists Who Shift Blame for Obesity Away from Bad Diets," *New York Times*, August 9, 2015.

18. Muhtar Kent, "'We'll Do Better': Coca-Cola Vows to Improve Transparency," *Wall Street Journal*, August 20, 2015.

19. Journey Staff, "Frequently Asked Questions," Coca-Cola Company, December 18, 2018, https://www.coca-colacompany.com/transparency/transparency-faq.

20. Dean Schillinger et al., "Do Sugar-Sweetened Beverages Cause Obesity and Diabetes? Industry and the Manufacture of Scientific Controversy," *Annals of Internal Medicine* 165, no. 12 (December 2016): 895–97.

21. See, for example, Milton Silverman and Philip Randolph Lee, *Pills, Profits, and Politics* (Berkeley: University of California Press, 1976); Marc A. Rodwin, *Medicine, Money, and Morals: Physicians' Conflicts of Interest* (Oxford: Oxford University Press, 1995); Marilyn J. Field and Bernard Lo, eds., *Conflict of Interest in Medical Research, Education, and Practice* (Washington, DC: National Academies Press, 2009); Jerome P. Kassirer, *On the Take: How Medicine's Complicity with Big Business Can Endanger Your Health* (Oxford: Oxford University Press, 2004); Sheldon Krimsky, *Science in the Private Interest: Has the Lure of Profits Corrupted Biomedical Research?* (Lanham, MD: Rowman & Littlefield, 2004); and Piller, "Hidden Conflicts?"

22. Alice Fabbri, Taylor J. Holland, and Lisa A. Bero, "Food Industry Sponsorship of Academic Research: Investigating Commercial Bias in the Research Agenda," *Public Health Nutrition* 21, no. 18 (December 2018): 3422–30.

23. Fiona Gillison, "Reflections from a Casualty of the Food Industry Research Funding Debate," *BMJ* 365 (May 2019): l2034.

24. Marcus Strom, "Coca-Cola's Secret Plan to Monitor Sydney University Academic Lisa Bero," *Sydney Morning Herald*, October 21, 2016, https://www.smh.com.au/technology/cocacolas-secret-plan-to-monitor-sydney-university-academic-lisa-bero-20161020-gs6m4a.html.

25. See, for example, Yoni Freedhoff and Paul C. Hébert, "Partnerships between Health Organizations and the Food Industry Risk Derailing Public Health Nutrition," *Canadian Medical Association Journal* 183, no. 3 (February 2011): 291–92; Paul Aveyard et al., "Should We Welcome Food Industry Funding of Public Health Research?," *BMJ* 353 (April 2016): i2161; and Jeffrey Zachwieja et al., "Public-Private Partnerships: The Evolving Role of Industry Funding in Nutrition Research," *Advances in Nutrition* 4, no. 5 (September 2013): 570–72.

26. Freedhoff and Héber, "Partnerships."

27. Jeffrey Mervis, "Data Check: US Government Share of Basic Research Funding Falls below 50%," *Science* 355, no. 6329 (March 2017): 1005.

28. Lisa A. Bero and Quinn Grundy, "Not All Influences on Science Are Conflicts of Interest," *American Journal of Public Health* 108, no. 5 (May 2018): 632–33.

29. Charles Ornstein and Katie Thomas, "Top Cancer Researcher Fails to Disclose Corporate Financial Ties in Major Research Journals," *New York Times*, September 8, 2018, https://www.nytimes.com/2018/09/08/health/jose-baselga-cancer-memorial-sloan-kettering.html.

30. John P. A. Ioannidis and John F. Trepanowski, "Disclosures in Nutrition Research: Why It Is Different," *JAMA* 319, no. 6 (February 2018): 547–48.

NINE

Global Food Demand Projections

A Review

MICHIEL VAN DIJK, YASHAR SAGHAI, MARIE LUISE RAU, AND TOM MORLEY

SINCE THE 1960s, the world population has increased from about three billion to more than seven billion people.[1] At the same time, although inequality remains large, global average gross domestic product (GDP) per capita worldwide has increased almost threefold from around US$3,700 per capita to more than US$10,000 per capita measured in constant 2010 dollars.[2] Most of the growth can be attributed to the emerging economies such as China and India, but notable progress has also occurred in African countries. Population and income growth have led to an increasing demand for food. At least until the end of the past century, modernization of farming systems, technological change, and increase in trade ensured that food supply kept pace with the increasing demand for food, illustrated by the trend in decreasing food prices.[3] Nonetheless, the food price spikes in 2007–8 indicated that the balance between food demand and food supply is becoming fragile.

The latest population projections show that the world population will reach 9.8 billion in 2050 and 11.2 billion in 2100, resulting in an increase in the demand for food. At the same time, climate change is expected to have negative effects on agricultural yields, and crops such as maize and sugar are increasingly used for the production of biofuels, putting additional pressure on the food demand-and-supply equation. An important question that arises is what this all means for future food demand. Will food consumption continue to grow in the future? And by how much would the production of food need to increase in order to satisfy food demand?

The aim of our study is to review and compare existing scenarios of world food demand up to 2050. These explorative scenarios present trends on contrasting but plausible developments of food demand in the future and, hence, provide information on the required increase in the food production that is necessary to feed the world population by 2050. This latter issue is a key question for policy makers and scientists. In general, it requires an assessment of the earth's capacity to produce sufficient food and/or an analysis of population dynamics and diets. Note that our analysis does not cover the question, By how much *should* food demand and production change in the future to feed the world population? This normative question requires different types of scenario studies that we do not cover in our review.

Drivers of (Future) Food Demand

The global demand for food, now and in the future, is strongly influenced by several key driving forces. The most obvious factor is population growth. A second important determinant of global food consumption constitutes the changes in dietary patterns. In particular, lower- and middle-income countries are experiencing a rapid "nutrition transition"[4,5,6] from a traditional diet of grains rich in fiber toward a "Western diet" that is high in saturated fats (especially from animal products), sugar, and processed foods.[7,8,9] The most important drivers of the nutrient transition are economic growth, urbanization, technical change, and culture.[10] In this section, we first discuss the three main drivers of global food demand and reflect on how their development may affect the change in food demand in the future. Factors like culture, beliefs and religion also play a very important role in determining diet. These are, however, very idiosyncratic factors that often differ from country to country and are therefore very difficult to incorporate into global food demand projections. For this reason, we do not discuss them here.

Population Growth

According to the medium variant in the United Nations World Population Projections (figure 9.1), the global population will increase from 7.4 billion in 2015 to 9.8 billion in 2050. If we assume that average global food consumption remains constant at 2,897 kcal/cap/day,[11] a simple back-of-the-envelope calculation reveals that total food demand (measured as food availability) will increase by 32%. If we also consider the low and high variants of the population projections, the demand for food will increase by between 19% and 47% over the coming four decades.

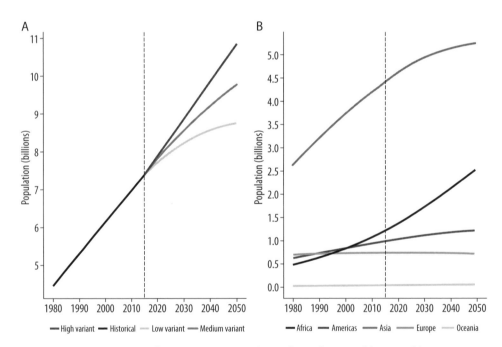

Figure 9.1. UN Population Projections. (A) High, medium, and low world population projections; (B) Medium world population projections by region.
Source: Data from "2017 Revision of World Population Prospects," United Nations Department of Economic and Social Affairs, 2018, https://population.un.org/wpp/.

FOOD AVAILABILITY AS PROXY FOR FOOD DEMAND

There are several sources of information that can be used to make international comparisons of the demand for food. Probably the most accurate sources are household budget surveys and individual dietary surveys, which provide detailed information on the consumption pattern at the individual and household level. Unfortunately, this type of information is difficult to compare across countries due to differences in methodology, definitions, and country coverage. For this reason, all global analyses of (future) food demand, including those in this chapter, use food availability from the FAOSTAT Food and Balance Sheets as an indicator of food consumption.

See John Kearney, "Food Consumption Trends and Drivers," *Philosophical Transactions of the Royal Society of London. Series B, Biological Sciences* 365, no. 1554 (September 2010): 2793–2807, and Sophie Hawkesworth et al., "Feeding the World Healthily: The Challenge of Measuring the Effects of Agriculture on Health," *Philosophical Transactions of the Royal Society of London. Series B, Biological Sciences* 365, no. 1554 (September 2010): 3083–97.

Most of the population growth will occur in Africa, where the total population is expected to more than double from 1.2 to 2.5 billion over the period 2015–50. At the same time, with 2,597 kcal/cap/day, Africa is also the region with the lowest average food consumption. Hence, the combination of rapid population growth and the expected nutrient transition toward diets that are higher in energy content will have a disproportional effect on total global food demand. The impact on other regions will be much smaller because of lower projected population growth and higher average food consumption levels.

The FAOSTAT Food and Balance Sheets (FBS) provide country-level annual breakdowns of the food that is available for human consumption. Food availability is calculated as total food produced in and imported into the country, minus exports of food, minus food used for other purposes (e.g., livestock feed, seed use, and losses along the supply chain), divided by population size. All food items are expressed in "primary commodity equivalent" (the amount of primary commodity input that would be required to produce a given amount of derived product output). This means that, for example, quantities of bread are expressed as wheat equivalents, using a product-specific technical coefficient, and then added to other wheat (equivalent) availability measures. Food availability is expressed in terms of both quantity and raw energy equivalent (kcal/cap/day), which can easily be aggregated and compared across countries.

The FBS Food availability indicator has to be regarded as a proxy for the actual food that is consumed. Comparison with household budget surveys has shown that it tends to overestimate actual food consumption. The main reason for this is that the availability indicator does not account for food waste and food fed to animals at the household and retail levels.[12,13]

Economic Development and Income Change

Income change is one of the main drivers of food demand and diet shifts. Two well-known empirical relationships describe distinct aspects of the connection between income and food demand. The first is Engel's law, named after the German statistician Ernst Engel (1821–96), which states that the proportion of food expenditure to total expenditure declines as income increases.[14] The second law is Bennett's law, named after M. K. Bennett,[15] who presented a pioneering study in which the diet composition of 40 countries is related to per capita income for the period 1934–39. Bennett's law shows that as people become wealthier, the share of starchy staples (e.g., cereals, potatoes, and plantain) in the diet will decrease, while the share of animal-related products, sugars, fruits, and vegetables will increase. The main explanation for this observation is that consumers tend to improve the variety of their diet as soon as they can afford it. As we discuss later, the empirical relationships described by Engels's and Bennett's laws are a key for the modeling of future food demand.

Bennett's law is illustrated by plotting the share of meat consumption in the diet against economic development at the country level (figure 9.2). The figure clearly shows a positive relationship between meat consumption and income per capita. In most developing countries, in particular those located in Africa and Asia, the share of meat consump-

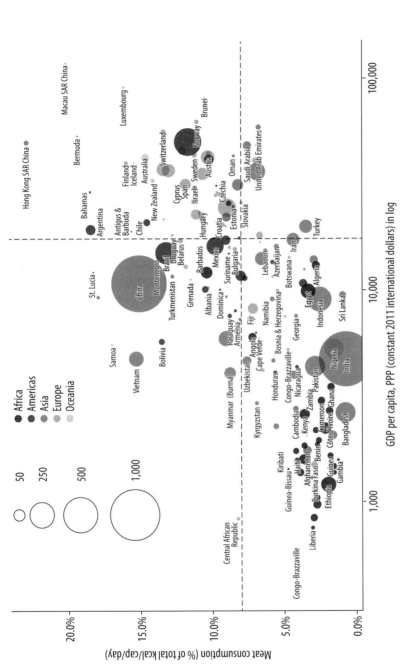

Figure 9.2. Meat Consumption and GDP per Capita, 2010–2015. Meat consumption includes bovine, mutton on goat, pig, poultry, and other meat groups.

Notes: Values are averages for the period 2010-15. The dashed lines indicate global averages, and the size of the circles measure population size. PPP = purchasing power parity. *Source:* Data on meat consumption: "FAOSTAT," Food and Agriculture Organization, http://www.fao.org/faostat/en/. Data on GDP per capita and population data: "World Development Indicators," World Bank, 2018, https://datacatalog.worldbank.org/dataset/world -development-indicators.

tion in the total diet is below the world average of 8%, while countries with a high income per capita exhibit a meat consumption of up to 23%. Bennett's law has important implications for the projection of future food demand. The OECD long-term global growth prospects expect that GDP per capita in the poorest economies will more than quadruple in the period from 2011 to 2060.[16] Combining these projections implies a dramatic increase in meat consumption for many African and Asian countries.

Urbanization

Apart from changes in income and population growth, urbanization, defined as the proportion of the urban residents in the total population, is considered a key driver of future food demand. Although urbanization is strongly linked to and interacts with economic development, it also has an independent effect on the pattern and structure of diets.[17] Several studies show a clear difference in food consumption patterns between urban and rural populations.[18] Overall, the diet of urban residents is characterized by consumption of superior grains (e.g., rice and wheat instead of corn and millet), foods higher in fat, more animal products, more sugar, and more processed food that is often prepared outside the home. This is illustrated by comparing the diets of households in urban and rural areas in Vietnam (figure 9.3).

There are various causes that explain this finding.[19] First, work done by urban residents is mainly sedentary and therefore requires less calorie-rich food than more physical demanding activities, which are often related to agriculture in rural areas. Second, food availability and income differ between urban and rural areas. In rural areas, most consumers are farm households that produce most of their own food, which means that the diet is often restricted to a relatively small number of crops that are regionally produced (e.g., starchy roots and tubers). This pattern contrasts with urban areas, where households generally do not grow their own food and have access to a broader selection of food products. The rapid increase in the number of supermarkets in African, Latin American, and Asian cities,[20] as well as the spread of "fast-food" res-

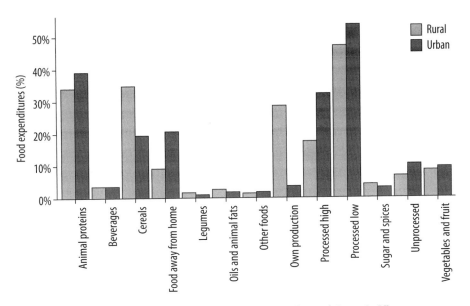

Figure 9.3. Comparison in Diets between Urban and Rural Areas in Vietnam.
Source: Data from Thomas Reardon, David Tschirley, Michael Dolislager, Jason Snyder, Chaoran Hu, and Stephanie White, "Urbanization, Diet Change, and Transformation of Food Supply Chains in Asia," Michigan State University, May 2014.

taurants, has made it easier for urban residents to purchase preprocessed products and "Western-style" food. Finally, urbanization is associated with greater participation of women in the workforce. The increased opportunity costs of time for women in combination with higher wages has shifted demand toward more processed foods with shorter preparation times and away from traditional food products.[21]

By far most of future population growth depicted in figure 9.1 will take place in urban areas. The urban population of the world has grown rapidly from 751 million in 1950 to 4 billion in 2015. According to the 2018 Revision of World Urbanization Prospects of the United Nations, the overall growth of the world population would add more than 2.5 billion people to urban areas by 2050.[22] A large part of this growth will take place in populous developing countries, such as China, India, and Nigeria and will therefore have a dramatic impact on the growth in global food demand.

The Prevailing View: Food Demand Will Increase by 70% (or 60%) in 2050

If one searched the Internet for an answer to the question, By how much will global food demand increase by 2050?, there is a large chance one would find 70%. This figure, which was downscaled to 60% in a revision,[23] has been (and still is) frequently cited in the media. It is evident that this figure (hereafter referred to as the 70% figure) has had considerable impact on the political, public, and scientific debate about global hunger, food price trends, and the capacity of the planet to feed the global population. In this section, we briefly describe its origins, summarize the methodology that was used to derive the figure, and outline several reasons why the 70% figure should be interpreted with care.

Its Origins: The Food and Agriculture Organization "World Agriculture: Towards" Studies

The 70% figure was first reported in a Food and Agriculture Organization (FAO) briefing paper that was released on 23 September 2009, as part of the High-Level Expert Forum on "How to Feed the World in 2050." The paper stated that, "in order to feed this larger, more urban and richer population, food production (net of food used for biofuels) must increase by 70 percent."[24] It is part of a series of FAO reports that assesses future world agriculture and food, the "World Agriculture: Towards . . ." (or FAO WAT) studies (figure 9.4).[25]

The basis of the 70% figure is the fourth report in the series, titled "World agriculture: Towards 2030/2050 Interim Report." Using UN global projections for population growth and FAO historical statistics on global diet change, agricultural production, and crop and livestock yield, the report presents a baseline scenario on future development of agricultural production and world food demand and supply until 2050. One of the main findings is that global agricultural production will need to increase by 87% between the base year 1999/2001 and 2050.[26,27,28] The 70% figure is essentially based on the analysis presented in the 2006 report with a minor update in terms of data and, most importantly, a

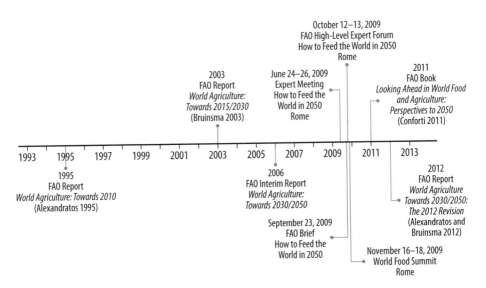

Figure 9.4. Timeline of FAO WAT (Related) Reports and Events.
Notes: The figure does not depict the *World Agriculture: Toward 2000* study, published in 1988. *Source:* Adapted from Harald Grethe, Assa Dembélé, and Nuray Duman. *How to Feed the World's Growing Billions: Understanding FAO World Food Projections and Their Implications* (Berlin: Heinrich-Böll-Stiftung, 2011).

more recent base year of 2005/7. The shorter projection period (44 years versus 50 years) is the main reason for the lower estimate of the required increase in world agricultural production.

Methodology

The 70% figure (and subsequent 60% revision) reflects an increase in value terms using constant 1989/91 international dollar prices: "The figures we use refer to the aggregate volume of demand and production of the crop and livestock sectors. They are obtained by multiplying physical quantities of demand or production times price for each commodity and summing up over all commodities (each commodity is valued at the same average international price in all countries in all years)."[29]

It is based on a single baseline scenario that describes trends in agricultural production and food demand and supply for a range of commodities and major regions. The scenario represents the "most likely" future change in world agriculture and food,[30] and does not explicitly refer to what is "required to feed the projected world population or to meet some other normative target."[31] For this reason, hunger is not completely eliminated in the FAO projections, and 4% of the developing countries' populations is still undernourished in 2050. The basis of the projections is the FAO Supply-Utilization Accounts (SUAs), which are part of an accounting framework that annually harmonizes the sources and uses of agricultural commodities. The first step is the preparation of food demand projections by commodity and country using Engel demand functions and exogenous assumptions on population and GDP per capita growth. The results are then "inspected by the commodity and nutrition specialists and adjusted taking into account any relevant knowledge and information, in particular the historical evolution of per caput demand and the nutritional patterns in the country examined."[32] In subsequent steps, food supply is projected and demand and supply are reconciled, which involves "several rounds of iterations and adjustments in consultation with specialists."[33]

The projections for future food demand rely on the 2002 UN medium population projections and (extrapolated) World Bank GDP growth projections as key inputs. World population is assumed to increase by around 40% between 2005/7 and 2050, reaching 8.8 billion in 2050. GDP per capita is assumed to increase by 2.1% in 2030 and by 2.7% in 2050. Although GDP per capita and population growth are the main drivers of the 70% projection, the FAO WAT methodology also incorporates other drivers of the demand for food and other agricultural products, including changes in income distribution (through the GDP projections), sociocultural factors (by means of country specific adjustments), food loss and waste, and the demand for biofuels. However, the reports present only very limited and often not specific information on how these factors have affected the food demand projections.[34]

The revised 60% figure is presented by Alexandratos and Bruinsma,[35] who apply the same basic methodology and reference year (2005/7) but use updated information on agricultural statistics and projections for population and GDP per capita growth. The main reason for the lower estimate is not a change in the food demand projections for 2050 but higher values for 2005/7 world production in comparison to the provisional figures that were used in the 2009 FAO briefing paper. They also indicate that the baseline scenario should be regarded as a "limited biofuels" scenario, as projections for biofuel demand apply only to the medium term.

Why the FAO WAT Results Must Be Interpreted with Care

For a number of reasons, the 70% (and 60%) increase in food demand should be interpreted with care.[36] First, the reference year that is used to calculate the 70% figure (2005/7) is more than 10 years old. As total agricultural production has increased since 2005/7, the actual increase estimated when using the present as the base year for the projection will be surely lower. Second, FAO uses a price-weighted index to measure aggregate food demand and production. A price-based index will grow faster than an index that uses calorie content as weights when there is a shift in the diet from low-priced staples toward higher-value products (e.g., processed foods and animal products).[37] Interestingly, the FAO WAT reports also present projections for the global change in kcal/cap/day, which makes it possible to calculate a calorie-based index of food demand that can be compared to other projections (see the next section). Third, the FAO WAT studies are largely based on expert knowledge (with limited documentation), which makes it very difficult to validate the assumptions and methodology.[38] Fourth, the FAO WAT projections do not take into account climate change, which is not realistic in view of the current evidence on the (mostly) negative impact of climate change on agricultural production.[39] Finally, and most importantly, the FAO WAT studies present only one baseline scenario. While the studies claim to represent the "most likely" future, there are, in fact, many other plausible futures and hence projections of food demand. Alternative projections of future population growth and income change will result in different food demand trajectories. It can hence be argued that assessing only one scenario is potentially misleading as it suggests only a limited degree of uncertainty.

Review of Recent Scenario-Based Food Demand Projections

As described earlier, global food demand depends on the complex inter-action of several drivers whose future trajectory is far from clear. This means that future food demand is subject to a high level of uncertainty and might consequently diverge from the historical trend. A common approach to deal with high levels of complexity and uncertainty is the use of scenario analysis, which envisages several contrasting futures. A scenario is defined as a "plausible and often simplified description of how the future may develop, based on a coherent and internally consis-tent set of assumptions about key driving forces (e.g., rate of technology change, prices) and relationships."[40] To ensure consistency, scenario analysis often combines the development of storylines, which present the key features of potential future worlds (e.g., rate of technical change, population growth, and economic development), with quantitative mod-eling in order to assess the structural relationship between drivers and scenario outputs (e.g., agricultural production, food demand and supply, and number of people at risk of hunger).[41] Scenario analyses have been frequently used to asses major global issues, such as climate change,[42] ecosystem change,[43] and environmental and sustainability challenges.[44] They emerged only recently as a tool to assess global food security.[45]

In this section, we summarize the results of a systematic literature review to evaluate all major and recent global food demand scenario exercises.[46] Among the 61 that are included in the review, 23 use the "Shared Socio-economic Pathways (SSPs)" to quantify global food demand and supply.[47] In this section, we start by providing background information on the SSPs, followed by a brief description on the quanti-tative modeling approaches that have been used to quantify global food demand in a scenario setting. In the next two parts, we show the band-width of total food and commodity demand projections under different SSPs and provide an illustration of regional level results.

Shared Socioeconomic Pathways

The Shared Socio-economic Pathways (SSPs) are a recently developed scenario framework, prepared by the climate change research community in order to assess the impact of climate change.[48,49] They consist of two elements: narratives that describe five alternative but potential future socioeconomic developments[50] and a database with projections for key driving forces, in particular population and GDP growth.[51,52] The SSPs can be combined with assumptions on climate outcomes, the so-called representative concentration pathways (RCPs), to derive a matrix that reflects an elaborate scenario framework to assess the impact of climate change and its mitigation under a variety of socioeconomic conditions, such as the degree of inequality within and between societies, types of technology development, economic development, consumption patterns, and international integration or fragmentation between nations and regions.[53]

The five SSPs represent a variety of often contrasting worlds that are intended to span a wide range of plausible futures (table 9.1). They include a world with sustainable growth and equality (SSP1); a "middle-of-the-road" world in which future trends are comparable to historical patterns (SSP2); a fragmented world, characterized by nationalism and regional conflict (SSP3); a world with persistent and growing global inequality (SSP4); and a world dominated by rapid fossil-fueled economic growth (SSP5).

Methodologies to Assess Future Food Demand

As described earlier, the FAO WAT studies heavily rely on expert opinion to prepare the food demand projections. This approach is not very transparent and therefore difficult to validate and replicate. The systematic literature review by Van Dijk et al. shows that most recent studies use quantitative modeling approaches to assess future food demand. In these approaches, the structural relationship between drivers and the demand for food (following Engel's and Bennett's laws) is made explicit and analyzed in a consistent framework. Most of the studies that were

Table 9.1. Summary of SSP Narratives

SSP1   Sustainability

The world shifts gradually, but pervasively, toward a more sustainable path, emphasizing more inclusive development that respects perceived environmental boundaries. Management of the global commons slowly improves, educational and health investments accelerate the demographic transition, and the emphasis on economic growth shifts toward a broader emphasis on human well-being. Driven by an increasing commitment to achieving development goals, inequality is reduced both across and within countries. Consumption is oriented toward low material growth and lower resource and energy intensity.

SSP2   Middle of the Road

The world follows a path in which social, economic, and technological trends do not shift markedly from historical patterns. Development and income growth proceeds unevenly, with some countries making relatively good progress while others fall short of expectations. Global and national institutions work toward but make slow progress in achieving sustainable development goals. Environmental systems experience degradation, although there are some improvements and overall the intensity of resource and energy use declines. Global population growth is moderate and levels off in the second half of the century. Income inequality persists or improves only slowly and challenges to reducing vulnerability to societal and environmental changes remain

SSP3   Regional Rivalry

A resurgent nationalism, concerns about competitiveness and security, and regional conflicts push countries to increasingly focus on domestic or, at most, regional issues. Policies shift over time to become increasingly oriented toward national and regional security issues. Countries focus on achieving energy and food security goals within their own regions at the expense of broader-based development. Investments in education and technological development decline. Economic development is slow, consumption is material-intensive, and inequalities persist or worsen over time. Population growth is low in industrialized and high in developing countries. A low international priority for addressing environmental concerns leads to strong environmental degradation in some regions

SSP4   Inequality

Highly unequal investments in human capital, combined with increasing disparities in economic opportunity and political power, lead to increasing inequalities and stratification both across and within countries. Over time, a gap widens between an internationally-connected society that contributes to knowledge- and capital-intensive sectors of the global economy, and a fragmented collection of lower-income, poorly educated societies that work in a labor intensive, low-tech economy. Social cohesion degrades and conflict and unrest become increasingly common. Technology development is high in the high-tech economy and sectors. The globally connected energy sector diversifies, with investments in both carbon-intensive fuels like coal and unconventional oil, but also low-carbon energy sources. Environmental policies focus on local issues around middle and high income areas

SSP5   Fossil-fueled Development

This world places increasing faith in competitive markets, innovation and participatory societies to produce rapid technological progress and development of human capital as the path to sustainable development. Global markets are increasingly integrated. There are also strong investments in health, education, and institutions to enhance human and social capital. At the same time, the push for economic and social development is coupled with the exploitation of abundant fossil fuel resources and the adoption of resource and energy intensive lifestyles around the world. All these factors lead to rapid growth of the global economy, while global population peaks and declines in the 21st century. Local environmental problems like air pollution are successfully managed. There is faith in the ability to effectively manage social and ecological systems, including by geo-engineering if necessary.

Source: Keywan Riahi, Detlef P. van Vuuren, Elmar Kriegler, Jae Edmonds, Brian C. O'Neill, Shinichiro Fujimori, Nico Bauer, et al. "The Shared Socioeconomic Pathways and Their Energy, Land Use, and Greenhouse Gas Emissions Implications: An Overview," *Global Environmental Change: Human and Policy Dimensions* 42 (January 1, 2017): 153-68, doi://doi.org/10.1016/j.gloenvcha.2016.05.009. This table is reproduced here under the terms of the Creative Commons 4.0 license.

published after 2013 combine modeling with the SSP scenario framework in order to account for the large uncertainty in socioeconomic drivers and climate change.[54]

Taking a step back from the SSP scenarios, studies on future food demand can be divided into three broad approaches (figure 9.5).[55] The most popular is the use of global simulation models. Out of the 58 studies that assessed future food demand, 49 used a global simulation model. Two types of models have mostly been used for the modeling of the food system: partial equilibrium (PE) models and computable general equilibrium (CGE) models.[56] Both PE and CGE models are economic simulation models in which trade, price development, and the clearing of markets are key in determining global food demand and supply. The main difference is that PE models cover only the agriculture and food sector, whereas CGE models represent the total economy, including agriculture, energy, and manufacturing, but with less detail.

A second approach, which was used by eight studies included in the systematic literature review, comprises statistical extrapolation in order to project food demand.[57] In this approach, calorie consumption per capita per day (total or per major food group) is regressed on explanatory

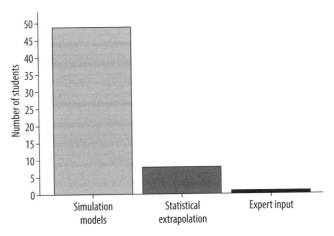

Figure 9.5. Frequency of Approaches Used to Assess Future Food Demand.
Notes: The figure shows the results of 58 studies published between 2004 and 2018.
Source: Data from Michiel van Dijk et al., "Systematic Review of Global Food Security Projections," Presentation, 3rd International Conference on Global Food Security, December 2017.

factors, in most cases GDP per capita. The estimated relationship is subsequently combined with income per capita and population scenarios to extrapolate total food demand into the future. Godfray and Robinson compare the strengths and weaknesses of simulation models and statistical extrapolation. The advantage of simulation models is that they explicitly capture the underlying dynamics that determine food demand, including the impact of food supply and prices. The statistical approaches do not capture this effect and therefore might generate biased results—for example, if prices change dramatically in the future. A drawback of the simulation models is that they require a large amount of information, which is often not easily available. This may affect their performance when used in scenario analysis to project future trends.[58] The final category is made up by the FAO WAT study, which mainly relies on expert opinion to generate food demand projections.

SSP-Based Global Food Demand Projections

In this section, we use the global food demand projections from the studies identified by the systematic literature review to calculate by how much global food production needs to be increased to fulfill demand in 2050 under different but plausible futures as described by the five SSPs. As such, they provide an alternative for the 60/70% figure presented in the FAO WAT and take into account the high level of uncertainty in socioeconomic drivers that is expected to affect the change in the future food demand.

For 5 out of the aforementioned 58 studies, we are able to extract comparable information on food demand projections. To calculate the increase in food demand, we start by extracting information on global food demand projections expressed in kcal/cap/day—the preferred measure of aggregate food demand as opposed to the price-weighted figure presented in the FAO WAT—for each of the five SSPs. Next, we multiply these values with the population growth projections, which differ between SSPs, to obtain the total global food demand in kcal. Finally, the increase in food demand in 2050 is calculated relative to 2010, the base year for most of the model studies.

There are three steps for the SSPs as well as the FAO WAT projection (figure 9.6). If we use the information on kcal/cap/day development up to 2050 in Alexandratos and Bruinsma's article and use 2010 (instead of 2005/7) as a base year, food demand is projected to increase by 44% if one assumes no climate change. This figure is similar to that of Hunter et al.,[59] who also present an update of Alexandratos and Bruinsma's article but limit their analysis to total cereal consumption and a base year of 2014. If we assume no climate change, food demand in SSP3, the scenario with the highest population growth but the lowest kcal/cap/day consumption, increases with on average 51% in 2050. In contrast, under SSP1, which describes a sustainable future with relative low population growth and medium calorie consumption per capita, and again with no climate change, food demand expands on average 37%. Food demand projections for SSP2, SSP4, and SSP5 are in between those of SSP1 and SSP3, which represent the most extreme scenarios.

Apart from the average SSP projections (in bold), figure 9.6b–c also depicts all individual scenario projections, which show much larger bandwidth, in particular for the kcal/cap/day projections. The wide range in results is caused by a combination of factors. Several studies assess future food demand under a range of climate change scenarios (i.e., RCPs combined with SSPs), which (often negatively) affect food consumption.[60] Other factors that contribute to the variety in scenario results include differences in model design and reporting.[61]

Global Demand Projections at the Food Group Level

The previous section reviewed global projections on total demand of food, adding together a broad range of food items that among others include animal-based products, fruits and vegetables, and cereals. Due to the high level of aggregation, such projections do not provide insights into the different patterns of dietary change, which, in addition to population growth, are one of the main reasons why total food demand projections differ between the SSPs.

The future dietary pattern will have a large influence on global health. At present, unhealthy diets, characterized by high consumption of red

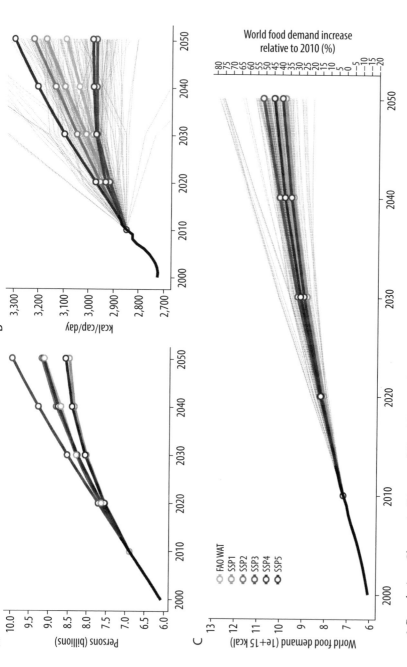

Figure 9.6. Population, Change in Diets, and Food Demand up to 2050. (A) SSP global population projections; (B) Average global food demand in kcal/cap/day; and (C) Total food demand in kcal (left axis) and percent increase relative to 2010 (right axis).

Notes: The solid black line illustrates the historical trend. The other solid lines show the average of the no climate change SSP baseline scenarios. The thin dashed lines show variations of the SSP scenarios under different climate change scenarios. Total number of scenarios is 211. *Source:* Data from Michiel van Dijk et al., "Systematic Review of Global Food Security Projections," Presentation, 3rd International Conference on Global Food Security, December 2017.

and processed meat and low consumption of fruits and vegetables, are already responsible for the greatest health burden worldwide.[62] The situation is expected to get worse in the future if the observed nutrient transition toward Western diets continues, resulting in an increase in nutrient-related noncommunicable diseases (NR-NCDs) that are associated with overweight and obesity.[63] The change in diets will also have a large influence on climate change. A growing demand for meat can be expected to push the expansion of the livestock sector, which makes up for the largest share of agricultural greenhouse gas emissions.[64] A recent study assessed the health and climate impact of a shift toward "sustainable" diets and found that the transition toward more plant-based diets could reduce global mortality by 6–10% and food-related greenhouse gas emissions by 29–70% in 2050.[65]

Reviewing the projections for future demand for meat and other food groups would have been interesting. Unfortunately, only a few of the studies, for which results are presented in figure 9.5, present detailed information on the shifts in diet. In most cases, the results are not comparable due to differences in the composition of food groups and cover only a subset of the SSPs. One recent study presents changes in the composition of the diet for the world and China for three SSPs between 2010 and 2050 (figure 9.7).

Differences in diet trends between the three scenarios are clearly revealed in figure 9.7. In SSP1, as a consequence of a move toward a more sustainable lifestyle and a shift toward lower meat consumption, the share of meat in the diet decreases by around 19%. At the same time, the consumption of fruits and vegetables increases by more than 100%. SSP5, which is characterized by high growth and resource-intensive lifestyles, shows the opposite trend. Meat consumption increases by 69–74%, while fruit and vegetable consumption decreases by 5%. The SSP2 scenario shows a pattern that lies between the change in diets projected by SSP1 and SSP2 (32–37% increase in meat and 19% increase in fruits and vegetables consumption). The pattern for China is similar, but the increase in meat consumption is much larger in SSP5 as a consequence of a change in diets induced by income growth, which illustrates important differences across regions.

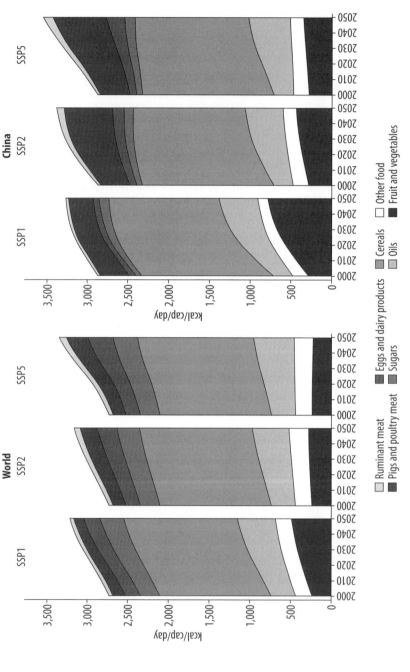

Figure 9.7. SSP Diet Projections for the World and China.

Source: Unpublished data from Oliver Fricko, Petr Havlik, Joeri Rogelj, Zbigniew Klimont, Mykola Gusti, Nils Johnson, Peter Kolp, et al. "The Marker Quantification of the Shared Socioeconomic Pathway 2: A Middle-of-the-Road Scenario for the 21st Century," *Global Environmental Change: Human and Policy Dimensions* 42 (2017): 251–67.

Discussion and Conclusion

The most cited figure on future global food demand originates from an FAO study that projects that food production needs to be increased by 70% (later downscaled to 60%) to fulfill demand in 2050. However, we have shown that this figure is not a satisfactory indicator of future global food demand. Unlike the FAO 70% figure, which presents only a single baseline projection of the "most likely" future, recent studies explore multiple plausible futures using a combination of scenario narratives and model simulations. Many studies use the Shared Socioeconomic Pathways (SSPs), which are the main scenarios used in climate change research, to capture the high level of uncertainty in socioeconomic factors (e.g., technical change, income development, and population growth) that drive future trends in global food demand. Comparing a large number of food demand projections from a systematic literature review in Van Dijk et al., we find an average increase in future food demand between 37% and 51%, under the assumption of no climate change, which is much lower than the 60–70% suggested by the FAO study. The main reasons for the difference are (1) the use of simulation models that account for feedback effects to project future food demand (as opposed to expert opinion), (2) the adoption of a more recent base year as reference (2010 instead of 2005/7), and (3) the use of a raw energy equivalent measure (i.e., kcal/cap/day instead of a price-weighted index) to measure food demand.

Despite the improvements in methodology, the 37–51% range still needs to be interpreted with care as it represents the range only in average SSP projections. The real uncertainty in food demand projections is expected to be much larger as the individual scenario projections show a much wider bandwidth. The large spread can be attributed to a combination of factors, including the impact of climate change and other policy assumptions, differences in model design, and differences in the reporting of results. A meta-analysis that statistically compares the results of all scenarios is required to determine the confidence interval of global food demand projections.

Naturally, the latest SSP-based studies also have their limitations.[66] Many studies model a limited number of socioeconomic drivers and focus predominantly on future projections of food availability, which is only one of the three dimensions of food security.[67] Designing more complex global food futures studies requires the creation of new indicators and the reliable collection and analysis of accurate data. For example, future studies need to better account for the impact of food loss and waste (see chapter 12 for more on this topic). Already there is considerable effort to create global databases for food and nutrient consumption,[68,69] which are used by the latest studies to quantify the impact of healthy and sustainable diets on climate change and the environment.[70]

REFERENCES

1. "2017 Revision of World Population Prospects," United Nations Department of Economic and Social Affairs, 2018, https://population.un.org/wpp/.

2. "World Development Indicators," World Bank, 2018, https://datacatalog .worldbank.org/dataset/world-development-indicators.

3. Uris Lantz C. Baldos and Thomas W. Hertel, "Debunking the 'New Normal': Why World Food Prices Are Expected to Resume Their Long Run Downward Trend," *Global Food Security* 8 (March 2016): 27–38, http://dx.doi .org/10.1016/j.gfs.2016.03.002.

4. Barry M. Popkin, "Nutritional Patterns and Transitions," *Population and Development Review* 19, no. 1 (March 1993): 138–57.

5. Adam Drewnowski and Barry M. Popkin, "The Nutrition Transition: New Trends in the Global Diet," *Nutrition Reviews* 55, no. 2 (February 1997): 31–43.

6. Barry M. Popkin, "The Nutrition Transition: An Overview of World Patterns of Change," *Nutrition Reviews* 62, no. suppl. 2 (July 2004): S140–43.

7. Barry M. Popkin, "The Shift in Stages of the Nutrition Transition in the Developing World Differs from Past Experiences!," *Public Health Nutrition* 5, no. 1A (February 2002): 205–14.

8. Barry M. Popkin, "The Nutrition Transition in the Developing World," *Development Policy Review: The Journal of the Overseas Development Institute* 21, nos. 5–6 (September 2003): 581–97.

9. The nutrition transition model offers a much broader framework than what is presented here. It describes and explains changes in global dietary patterns, their health effects and nutritional outcomes, and how they are affected by economic, social, and demographic factors.

10. Popkin, "The Nutrition Transition in the Developing World."

11. "Food Security Statistics," Food and Agriculture Organization, 2018, http://www.fao.org/economic/ess/ess-fs/en/.

12. John Kearney, "Food Consumption Trends and Drivers," *Philosophical Transactions of the Royal Society of London. Series B, Biological Sciences* 365, no. 1554 (September 2010): 2793–2807.

13. Sophie Hawkesworth et al., "Feeding the World Healthily: The Challenge of Measuring the Effects of Agriculture on Health," *Philosophical Transactions of the Royal Society of London. Series B, Biological Sciences* 365, no. 1554 (September 2010): 3083–97.

14. C. Peter Timmer et al., *Food Policy Analysis* (Baltimore: Johns Hopkins University Press, 1983).

15. See M. K. Bennett, *The World's Food* (New York: Harper & Brothers, 1954).

16. Åsa Johansson et al., "Looking to 2060: Long-Term Global Growth Prospects," OECD Economic Policy Papers, No. 3 (Paris: OECD Publishing, 2012), https://doi.org/10.1787/5k8zxpjsggfo-en.

17. Barry M. Popkin, "Urbanization, Lifestyle Changes and the Nutrition Transition," *World Development* 27, no. 11 (November 1999): 1905–16.

18. See Anita Regmi and John Dyck, "Effects of Urbanization on Global Food Demand," in *Changing Structure of Global Food Consumption and Trade,* ed. Anita Regmi (Washington, DC: ERS-USDA, 2001), 23–30, and Popkin, "Urbanization."

19. Regmi and Dyck, "Effects of Urbanization."

20. Thomas Reardon et al., "The Rise of Supermarkets in Africa, Asia, and Latin America," *American Journal of Agricultural Economics* 85, no. 5 (December 2003): 1140–46.

21. Thomas Reardon et al., "Urbanization, Diet Change, and Transformation of Food Supply Chains in Asia" (Michigan State University, May 2014), http://www.fao.org/fileadmin/templates/ags/docs/MUFN/DOCUMENTS/MUS_Reardon_2014.pdf.

22. "2018 Revision of World Urbanization Prospects," United Nations Department of Economic and Social Affairs, 2018, https://population.un.org/wup/.

23. Nikos Alexandratos and Jelle Bruinsma, "World Agriculture towards 2030/2050: The 2012 Revision," ESA Working Paper (Rome, 2012), doi:10.1016/S0264-8377(03)00047-4.

24. FAO, "How to Feed the World in 2050" (Rome: High-Level Expert Forum; Food and Agricultural Organisation, 2009).

25. See Nikos Alexandratos, ed., *World Agriculture: Toward 2000* (London: Belhaven Press, 1988); Nikos Alexandratos, ed., *World Agriculture: Toward 2010* (Chichester, UK: John Wiley & Sons, 1995); Jelle Bruinsma, ed., *World Agriculture: Towards 2015/2030; An FAO Perspective* (London: Earthscan, 2003); FAO, "World Agriculture: Towards 2030/2050 Interim Report" (Rome: Food; Agriculture Organization of the United Nations, 2006); FAO, "How to Feed the World"; Jelle Bruinsma, "The Resource Outlook to 2050: By How Much Do Land, Water and Crop Yields Need to Increase by 2050," in *Expert Meeting on How to Feed the World in 2050* (Rome: Food and Agriculture

Organization, 2009); and Alexandratos and Bruinsma, "World Agriculture towards 2030/2050."

26. Estimation by Harald Grethe, Assa Dembélé, and Nuray Duman, *How to Feed the World's Growing Billions: Understanding FAO World Food Projections and Their Implications* (Berlin: Heinrich-Böll-Stiftung, 2011).

27. FAO, "World Agriculture: Towards 2030/2050."

28. Note that the FAO 2006 report, the Bruinsma 2009 paper, and the Alexandratos and Bruinsma 2012 paper refer to an increase in world "agricultural" production, whereas the FAO 2009 report refers to "food production (net of food used for biofuels)." Both refer to the same aggregate.

29. FAO, "World Agriculture: Towards 2030/2050."

30. Bruinsma, *World Agriculture: Towards 2015/2030.*

31. Alexandratos and Bruinsma, "World Agriculture towards 2030/2050."

32. Alexandratos, *World Agriculture: Toward 2010.*

33. Alexandratos and Bruinsma, "World Agriculture towards 2030/2050."

34. Grethe, Dembélé, and Duman, *How to Feed the World's Growing Billions.*

35. Alexandratos and Bruinsma, "World Agriculture towards 2030/2050."

36. See also Mitchell C. Hunter et al., "Agriculture in 2050: Recalibrating Targets for Sustainable Intensification," *Bioscience* 67, no. 4 (April 2017): 386–91.

37. FAO, "World Agriculture: Towards 2030/2050.

38. Grethe, Dembélé, and Duman, *How to Feed the World's Growing Billions.*

39. Cynthia Rosenzweig et al., "Assessing Agricultural Risks of Climate Change in the 21st Century in a Global Gridded Crop Model Intercomparison," *Proceedings of the National Academy of Sciences of the United States of America* 111, no. 9 (March 2014): 3268–73.

40. Millennium Ecosystem Assessment, *Ecosystems and Human Well-Being: Our Human Planet,* vol. 2, *Scenarios (*Washington, DC: Island Press, 2005).

41. Joseph Alcamo, "The SAS Approach: Combining Qualitative and Quantitative Knowledge in Environmental Scenarios," in *Developments in Integrated Environmental Assessment,* ed. Joseph Alcamo (Amsterdam: Elsevier, 2008): 123–50.

42. Nebojsa Nakicenovic et al., *Special Report on Emissions Scenarios (SRES), A Special Report of Working Group III of the Intergovernmental Panel on Climate Change* (Cambridge: Cambridge University Press, 2000).

43. Millennium Ecosystem Assessment, *Ecosystems.*

44. United Nations Environment Programme, *GEO-4 Global Environment Outlook: Environment for Development* (Valetta: Progress Press, 2007).

45. International Assessment of Agricultural Knowledge, Science and Technology for Development, *Agriculture at a Crossroad, Global Report* (Washington, DC: Island Press, 2009).

46. See Michiel van Dijk et al., "Systematic Review of Global Food Security Projections," Presentation, 3rd International Conference on Global Food Security, December 2017.

47. Tomoko Hasegawa et al., "Scenarios for the Risk of Hunger in the Twenty-First Century Using Shared Socioeconomic Pathways," *Environmental Research Letters* 10, no. 1 (January 2015): 014010.

48. Elmar Kriegler et al., "The Need for and Use of Socio-economic Scenarios for Climate Change Analysis: A New Approach Based on Shared Socioeconomic Pathways," *Global Environmental Change: Human and Policy Dimensions* 22, no. 4 (October 2012): 807–22.

49. Keywan Riahi et al., "The Shared Socioeconomic Pathways and Their Energy, Land Use, and Greenhouse Gas Emissions Implications: An Overview," *Global Environmental Change: Human and Policy Dimensions* 42 (January 2017): 153–68.

50. Brian C. O'Neill et al., "The Roads Ahead: Narratives for Shared Socioeconomic Pathways Describing World Futures in the 21st Century," *Global Environmental Change: Human and Policy Dimensions* 42 (January 2017): 169–80.

51. Samir KC and Wolfgang Lutz, "The Human Core of the Shared Socioeconomic Pathways: Population Scenarios by Age, Sex and Level of Education for All Countries to 2100," *Global Environmental Change: Human and Policy Dimensions* 42 (January 2017): 181–92.

52. Rob Dellink et al., "Long-Term Economic Growth Projections in the Shared Socioeconomic Pathways," *Global Environmental Change: Human and Policy Dimensions* 42 (January 2017): 200–214.

53. Detlef P. van Vuuren et al., "A New Scenario Framework for Climate Change Research: Scenario Matrix Architecture," *Climatic Change* 122, no. 3 (February 2014): 373–86.

54. Van Dijk et al., "Systematic Review."

55. H. Charles, J. Godfray, and Sherman Robinson, "Contrasting Approaches to Projecting Long-Run Global Food Security," *Oxford Review of Economic Policy* 31, no. 1 (March 2015): 26–44.

56. Hugo Valin et al., "The Future of Food Demand: Understanding Differences in Global Economic Models," *Agricultural Economics* 45, no. 1 (January 2014): 51–67.

57. See David Tilman et al., "Global Food Demand and the Sustainable Intensification of Agriculture," *Proceedings of the National Academy of Sciences of the United States of America* 108, no. 50 (December 2011): 20260–64; Benjamin Leon Bodirsky et al., "Global Food Demand Scenarios for the 21st Century," *PloS One* 10, no. 11 (November 2015): e0139201; David L. Bijl et al., "A Physically-Based Model of Long-Term Food Demand," *Global Environmental Change: Human and Policy Dimensions* 45 (July 2017): 47–62; and Christophe Gouel and Houssein Guimbard, "Nutrition Transition and the Structure of Global Food Demand," *American Journal of Agricultural Economics* 101, no. 2 (March 2019): 383–403.

58. Godfray and Robinson, "Contrasting Approaches."

59. Hunter et al., "Agriculture in 2050."

60. See, for example, Alexander Popp et al., "Land-Use Futures in the Shared Socio-economic Pathways," *Global Environmental Change: Human and Policy Dimensions* 42 (January 2017): 331–45.

61. Michiel van Dijk and Gerdien W. Meijerink, "A Review of Global Food Security Scenario and Assessment Studies: Results, Gaps and Research Priorities," *Global Food Security* 3, nos. 3–4 (November 2014): 227–38.

62. GBD 2013 Risk Factors Collaborators et al., "Global, Regional, and National Comparative Risk Assessment of 79 Behavioural, Environmental and Occupational, and Metabolic Risks or Clusters of Risks in 188 Countries, 1990–2013: A Systematic Analysis for the Global Burden of Disease Study 2013," *Lancet* 386, no. 10010 (December 2015): 2287–2323.

63. Barry M. Popkin, "Global Nutrition Dynamics: The World Is Shifting Rapidly toward a Diet Linked with Noncommunicable Diseases," *American Journal of Clinical Nutrition* 84, no. 2 (2006): 289–98.

64. Sonja J. Vermeulen, Bruce M. Campbell, and John S. I. Ingram, "Climate Change and Food Systems," *Annual Review of Environment and Resources* 37, no. 1 (November 2012): 195–222.

65. Marco Springmann et al., "Analysis and Valuation of the Health and Climate Change Cobenefits of Dietary Change," *Proceedings of the National Academy of Sciences of the United States of America* 113, no. 15 (April 2016): 4146–51.

66. Van Dijk et al., "Systematic Review."

67. FAO, *Rome Declaration on World Food Security and World Food Summit Plan of Action* (Rome: FAO, 1996).

68. Shahab Khatibzadeh et al., "A Global Database of Food and Nutrient Consumption," *Bulletin of the World Health Organization* 94, no. 12 (December 2016): 931–34.

69. Matthew R. Smith et al., "Global Expanded Nutrient Supply (GENuS) Model: A New Method for Estimating the Global Dietary Supply of Nutrients," *PloS One* 11, no. 1 (January 2016): e0146976.

70. See Marco Springmann et al., "Global and Regional Health Effects of Future Food Production under Climate Change: A Modelling Study," *Lancet* 387, no. 10031 (May 2016): 1937–46; Marco Springmann et al., "Options for Keeping the Food System within Environmental Limits," *Nature* 562, no. 7728 (October 2018): 519–25; and Walter Willett et al., "Food in the Anthropocene: The EAT-Lancet Commission on Healthy Diets from Sustainable Food Systems," *Lancet* 393, no. 10170 (February 2019): 447–92.

PART III CONTEMPORARY CHALLENGES AND COMPLEXITIES IN FOOD ETHICS

This section explores the ethical challenges facing our food systems. The chapters are organized into four subsections (Environment, Producers and Laborers, Public Health, and Animal Welfare), similar to how the Core Ethical Commitments are presented by major area of concern in chapters 30 and 31. Each subsection begins with a Moral Map chapter written by members of the Choose Food project's core academic team. The seven Moral Maps are foundational works of the Choose Food project because they helped the team determine which ethical considerations should be included in the Core Ethical Commitments. Additional chapters in this section complement the Moral Maps by providing further analysis of specific ethical issues (e.g., food waste, antibiotic resistance) or highlighting programs that are addressing major ethical challenges.

Food, Environment, and Ethics

TARA GARNETT

FOOD SYSTEMS today have a very major and generally negative impact upon the environment. The way we produce and consume food gives rise to some 20-30% of global-climate-changing greenhouse gas (GHG) emissions, uses around 70% of irrigation water use, and acts as a major source of water pollution. Occupying nearly 40% of the earth's land surface, agriculture has historically been—and continues to be— the main driver of land use change (including deforestation) and is directly and indirectly responsible for about 80% of associated biodiversity loss. In addition, unsustainable fishing practices (in combination with water pollution—often from terrestrial agriculture) lead to the collapse of many fish stocks—around 90% of fish stocks are now fully or overexploited—and major disruption to marine and freshwater ecosystems.[1]

The ethical relevance of these impacts is as follows:

- Environmental damage may affect the well-being of current generations. Well-being is here defined to include factors such as food security and adequate nutrition; other health effects arising from pollution, heat stress, and changes in the spread of diseases; extreme weather events; dwindling resource availability and associated developmental prospects; stability of life; livelihoods and habitats; and spiritual well-being. This erosion of well-being through environmental damage is also most likely to affect those who are already among the most poor and vulnerable.

- Environmental damage may affect the well-being of future generations.
- Many also believe that the environment has intrinsic value—that is, value of itself over and above any utility to us.

Ethical questions also arise when trade-offs develop between the preceding points—that is, between the needs of present and future generations, or between the well-being of "nature" and immediate human needs or wants.

The environmental impacts of food systems are a consequence of *how* and *what kind* of food is produced and distributed, with what *inputs* and what *outputs*. They also arise from *how much* food is produced and ultimately consumed—the difference between the two being the amount that is lost between these two stages.

Ethical challenges arise when it comes to actions to address environmental concerns. For example, measures to address one particular environmental impact (e.g., GHG emissions) may have negative consequences for another impact raising ethical questions about how different environmental issues should be prioritized—and who should be doing the ranking. Pro-environmental actions may also negatively affect non-environmental areas of concern (e.g., nutrition and food security, workers' well-being, animal welfare), raising similar questions around trade-offs.

This chapter begins by considering one overarching question for the food system: How should we best use land—the ultimately finite resource—and how do our decisions about how much and what kind of food we need and want affect our options and decisions about land use? The issues that arise from consideration of that question should be seen as cross cutting. In addition, the chapter considers some of the specific questions that arise at different stages in the food supply chain.

Overarching Issue: Demand Trajectories on a Finite Planet

The food system is responsible for most of the transformations humans have made to the surface of the planet. Because most of these transformations have been negative (e.g., species extinctions, soil degradation, deforestation), it is increasingly recognized that, to avoid further damage, future food production needs to be limited to the current agricultural area. This means that either overall food output needs to stay the same despite a growing global population (implying changes in diets and a reduction in food losses and waste) or else agricultural productivity needs to increase.

There are disputes about which approach is more desirable and most feasible. Advocates of the "more food" arguments tend to be mainstream policy makers and the food industry. Notwithstanding some debate about how much more food needs to be produced—with increases of 60%, 70%, and 100% suggested[2]—their general contention is that more food is certainly needed and that current trajectories of demand are inevitable. They may additionally argue that low- and middle-income countries have a "right" to enjoy the lifestyles and consumption patterns traditionally found in the affluent West. Moreover, there is a need to achieve this increase in food production not only without incurring any further land use change but while also avoiding the environmental damage caused by Green Revolution–style inputs and technologies. At heart, agriculture needs to be as intensive as possible in order to "spare" land for nature—but also "green." The concept developed to encapsulate this need for both greater productivity and avoidance of further environmental cost has been termed "sustainable intensification"—although other phrases such as "climate smart agriculture" have similar connotations.

On the other hand, critics of this view—mainly drawn from the alternative food movement, animal welfare organizations, and environmental organizations, as well as some public-health-oriented stakeholders—argue that this win-win-win is impossible and that more food is also unnecessary. Instead, they posit that through a combination of waste reductions and dietary shift away from animal-source foods, populations of 9 to 10 billion or more can be adequately sustained. This would allow for food to be produced using less chemical intensive approaches (such as organic)—that is, for agriculture to be more wildlife friendly and "share" land with nature. These stakeholders often use the term "agroecology" to describe their approach. Agroecology denotes principles of "working with" nature but may also encompass broader social and cultural goals, such as supporting smallholder agriculture and traditional crops, dietary patterns, and lifestyles.

Supporters may also argue that a shift in diets can also help address the growing burden of obesity and diet-related noncommunicable diseases, so yielding a double gain.

This is not simply a technical dispute to be resolved by more comprehensive and accurate modeling studies. At the heart of the "land sparing versus land sharing" dispute lie ethical questions about how much and what kind of food is needed and whether we can or should be persuaded to change our diets; the legitimacy or otherwise of technologies and inputs aimed at increasing production; power structures within the agricultural sector; and moral hazard arising from the Jevon's Paradox effect. In more detail, ethical questions embedded in this debate include:

- Inputs: The extent to which research and development (R&D) can deliver a truly green next generation of crop protection and fertilizer applications; if not, the legitimacy or otherwise of using agrichemicals to achieve a certain level of intensity even when these inputs cause environmental damage; the environmental, health, and moral risks of new(ish) and emerging technologies such as GM.
- The role of food systems in addressing climate change: How much responsibility should the food system take in addressing climate change given that food is arguably more essential than any other human-made good or service?
- Power: Power imbalances in the food system, the risk that sustainable intensification simply legitimates the business-as-usual existing practices of major corporations; alternatively, the

fear that access to cleaner sustainably intensive technologies may be affordable only to larger corporations.

- Needs versus wants: The question of what sort of food is being produced, its nutritional value, and the relationship between our desires and our needs.
- Culture and tradition: The extent to which modern intensive systems undermine traditional food production practices and food cultures—and whether just because something is traditional it is "good" in itself.
- Individual versus collective rights: The right of the individual to consume what he or she wants versus the right of the state to do what is best for the environment or for future generations.
- Ranking among trade-offs: The extent to which the environment trumps human food security, nutrition, and pleasure; the extent to which environmental efficiencies trump other concerns, such as animal welfare or smallholder agriculture.
- The morality of risk: The moral risk of relying on the potential of greater food output on the one hand to address hunger and food security (without contributing to the obesity crisis) versus the moral risk of relying on effective public policies to shift diets, reduce food losses and waste, and redistribute food away from those that consume too much toward those that consume too little.
- Moral hazard: The danger that greater productivity lowers costs, which can then drive down prices and stimulate demand, such that greater consumption overcompensates for higher unit environmental efficiencies.

These cross-cutting issues are touched on in different ways in a later section that is structured loosely according to the stages in the food supply chain. However, this supply chain approach has been modified slightly to bring in ideas about a "food system"—this being a concept that encompasses also the actors and institutions that make the value chain happen, or that are affected by its functioning, and the power relations among them.

Specific Issues
Agriculture

Chemical Inputs

One way of avoiding further land use change is to ensure that any required increases in food output are achieved through increases in agricultural productivity rather than in land area. The principle of sustainable intensification says that this should be achieved without causing further environmental damage. Ways of squaring this circle include the production of cleaner, more targeted agrichemicals; smarter ways of applying inputs; and the development of nonchemical dependent techniques such as "push pull" crop protection.

Nevertheless, if the pace of technological progress does not keep up with the rise in demand for food, higher yields may well require the use of synthetic fertilizers, irrigation, and agrichemicals. Ethical issues associated with their use include the environmental damage they cause both on farm and off farm (through runoff)—causing damage to ecosystems, other life forms, and potentially undermining the food security and ecosystem services provision of future generations.

An alternative is to decide that use of these inputs is unacceptable and that lower yielding, more wildlife friendly agriculture (e.g., organic) is to be preferred. The ethical concern arising from this approach is that if demand trajectories continue as they are today, and waste is not curbed, then further land clearance may be needed.

Questions:

- What chemicals are used and what harms to nontarget species do they cause?
- What application methods are followed?
- Are impacts on soil quality, emissions, water, and other factors measured and processes in place to minimize damage?
- What efforts are made to avoid their use (e.g., via integrated pest management)?

Impacts on Land Use

Agriculture is the major global user of land and the main cause of biodiversity loss because it is implicated in one or more of the identified drivers of this loss: habitat destruction, climate change, invasive species, pollution, human overpopulation and overharvesting. Land use change generally causes CO_2 release (through deforestation, destruction of organic soils, plowing up of grasslands) and is the main driver of biodiversity loss. Ethical considerations include:

- Does production directly or indirectly cause land use change and/or deforestation? Note that in some cases this is a difficult question to answer as it could be argued that organic agriculture, by using more land per given volume of output, indirectly causes land use change.
- Does a particular production system in a particular area contribute to one or more of the main identified drivers of biodiversity loss?
- Could an alternative area of land be found for production that is less critical as regards its biodiversity or conservation value?
- What steps are being taken to build and improve soil quality?

Impacts on Climate Change

Mitigation

Food systems are a major contributor to climate change. Impacts arise from the use of fossil fuels at all stages in the food value chain (CO_2), the rearing of livestock (causing methane and nitrous oxide emissions), the cultivation of rice (methane), and the production and use of synthetic fertilizers (CO_2 from energy use and nitrous oxide from application). Ethical considerations include:

- All human activities generate emissions, but arguably food is more essential than any other human activity. Is food then deserving of special treatment, meaning that the requirement to achieve radical cuts in emissions is less for food than for other human activities? If yes, then this means that other activities may have to make even deeper cuts than they already do, potentially at a cost to human development or well-being.

- Certain mitigation activities lead to "gas swapping." For example, methane emissions from animal agriculture can be reduced but often through the use of improved feed or confined housing, which may in turn increase dependence on fossil fuels. While methane has a higher global warming potential than CO_2, it has a shorter life span, whereas that of CO_2 is effectively permanent. Action to address methane emissions may help avoid overshooting the 2°C temperature limit (so buying us time), but if this is achieved via greater dependence on fossil fuels, the effect may be counterproductive, by committing us to future irreversible warming. The ethics of buying time now versus future commitment needs to be considered.

A major area of interest is in the potential of soils to sequester carbon. This can be achieved through measures such as improved grazing management, planting of deep-rooted grasses, avoiding tillage above ground, and sequestering carbon through afforestation. However:

- All these measures are time limited—after a period of decades soils become saturated and no longer take up carbon. The ethical risk is that we may be committed to certain forms of activity (e.g., animal agriculture) but can no longer rely on this approach to achieve negative emissions.
- There may be trade-offs with other environmental concerns (e.g., methane from grazing animals needs to be weighed up against the carbon sequestering effects of good grazing management; N_2O emissions from fertilizing soils needs to be weighed against the carbon sequestering effects of better plant growth) and other nonenvironmental concerns (e.g., tree planting versus food production).
- Measures are reversible—for example, trees can be cut down and soils allowed to degrade, meaning that it is hard to bank on these

approaches as a permanent mitigation measure and thus potentially irresponsible as regards our obligations to future generations.

- Where sequestration is linked to carbon markets, there will be practical and ethical challenges as to how actions can be attributed to a certain actor, or how additionality can be proved (i.e., that the measure would not have been undertaken anyway), or how to ensure that the gains continue even if the financial reward is removed.
- All sectors of human activity are interested in having a slice of the carbon sequestration pie. For example, the transport sector is keen to use afforestation and soil carbon sequestration as a means of offsetting its emissions. This means that there is a risk of overselling the potential or double-counting benefits.

Adaptation
Agriculture will need to adapt to climate and other forms of environmental change. Adaptation can go hand in hand with mitigation and with human well-being but not always. For example, ethical considerations arise if:

- Adaptation entails the use of technologies that make the problem of climate worse or that affect other environmental concerns—e.g., where irrigation is used to adapt to water scarcity. How should present needs (for food) be ranked against future harms (to the environment and for future generations)?
- Adaptation entails the abandonment of certain forms of traditional food production or diversification into new livelihoods. It may be hard for some people—particularly the poor and marginalized—to adapt.

Use of Farm Animals

Animal agriculture takes up about two-thirds of total agricultural land; directly and indirectly (via feed production) drives deforestation and biodiversity loss; accounts for 14.5% of global GHG emissions;[3] and is a major user and polluter of water. Ethical considerations with respect to animals and the environment include:

- Is the company's main business the production, processing, or sale of animal products? Leaving aside fundamental ethical concerns about rearing animals for slaughter, the ethical concern arises from the fact that animal production generates major environmental costs, causing harm to present and future generations. On the other hand, these are nutrient-rich foods that, if eaten in moderation, can enhance the diet—this is especially the case for the world's poorest, whose diets may lack diversity and be critically short in the essential micronutrients that are readily available in animal source foods.
- What do animals eat? About 30-40% of the global grain harvest is fed to animals.[4] It has been argued that these grains could be more environmentally and efficiently consumed directly by people. It could be argued therefore that production systems that depend upon use of feed grains are less ethical than those that do not. On the other hand, many of the grains fed to livestock are less liked (e.g., sorghum and millet) or of lower quality (e.g., feed wheat versus bread-quality wheat), and animal source foods contain nutrients in forms that are more bioavailable than in grains.
- What is the production system—what combination of breed, feed, and housing is used? There is a possible trade-off between certain aspects of environmental improvement and animal welfare. Animals that fatten more quickly or that produce more milk are lower in their GHG intensity, expressed in terms of tons CO_2 eq/tons food output. Higher productivity may be achieved through improved veterinary care and improved feed, but it may be also occur at the expense of animal welfare.
- It has been argued that grass-fed livestock production offers a "win-win" because well-managed grazing systems can help contribute to soil carbon sequestration and the animals do not consume feed grains. However, the evidence here is mixed, the

benefits extremely context specific, and the available grassland would simply not support levels of production sufficient to meet current levels of affluent world consumption or the growing demands of those in the developing world. Issues of price and equity, discussed later, also come into it.

- There is also the moral hazard issue to consider. Measures to reduce the carbon intensity of animal production through increasing animal productivity may also reduce production costs. These lower costs can be passed onto the consumer and overall demand may increase, thus offsetting or overcompensating for the GHG savings.

Transport, Trade, and Globalization

Food systems are increasingly becoming globalized. Whether this is a good or bad thing is the subject of fierce debate. Are globalized systems more or less resilient? Do they foster or undermine power relations across countries and within populations? As regards the environment, ethical considerations raise the following questions:

- Does trade offer "ecological comparative advantage" over self-sufficiency? Some products may be produced at lower environmental cost further afield (e.g., New Zealand lamb sold in the United Kingdom has a lower carbon footprint than British lamb even when the transport stage is taken into account). A commodity may be produced in a water-abundant country and exported to one that is water scarce. From an ecological comparative advantage point of view, foods should be produced where they are optimally suited to be produced.
- To what extent does this approach undermine local producers and traditional production systems?
- How does this approach affect power relations between countries and within countries?
- To what extent does a global perspective make it impossible to make locally appropriate decisions because the knock-on global

effects need to be thought through—and in the absence of a fully comprehensive model, this is impossible?

- To what extent does the principle of "ecological comparative advantage" lead to the moral hazard of consumption pattern lock-in? For example, if tomatoes from Spain carry a lower environmental cost than British out-of-season tomatoes, to what extent does this lead to people thereby concluding that consuming Spanish tomatoes is ok rather than questioning the norm of consuming tomatoes out of season?

Food Processing, Refrigeration, and Waste

Food processing encompasses activities such as chopping and refining, heating, cooking, and cooling. Additives to the main component may also be included (e.g., sugars, salts, fats, preservatives) to increase palatability or extend shelf life. Ethical concerns include:

- Processing and refrigeration require the use of energy, and usually the source is fossil fuels, although renewables and cleaner technologies such as combined heat and power may be used. However, there may be environmental benefits arising from food processing; for example, food processing may make use of less desirable parts of the food and so reduce food waste (e.g., processed meat).
- Additives may make food more stable, so extending their shelf life or enabling them to be stored without energy-using refrigeration. On the other hand, their inclusion may reduce the nutritional quality of the food.
- Processing may extend the commercial value of the raw ingredient in ways that increase environmental impacts elsewhere (e.g., the by-products from grain refining produce a by-product that can be used for animal feed, which drives animal production and its associated environmental impacts).
- Conversely "clean label" or more healthy foods may often be those that are refrigeration dependent.

- Food refrigeration can in principle help reduce food waste. However, the ubiquity of the chill-chain (at least in the developed world) means that new products are developed that are predicated on the availability of refrigeration and that are inherently perishable (e.g., ready meals, chilled deserts, salad bags). Furthermore, in high-income countries food waste occurs despite or even because of the availability of the fridge because of the relatively low cost of food, demographic and lifestyle changes, and the fact that the fridge can sometimes function as a "black hole"—people put food in the fridge and then forget to eat it.
- Measures to encourage more fresh "unprocessed" product consumption may increase dependence on energy-using refrigeration and may lead to food waste.

Marketing and Pricing

There is already considerable scrutiny focused on the public health impacts of advertising and marketing strategies. However, how food is marketed, advertised, and priced also has environmental implications.

Marketing and Advertising
Ethical considerations here include:

- The extent to which companies market foods that have inherently high environmental impacts (air freighted produce, animal products).
- Related to this, the extent to which companies promote foods that may be healthy but that nevertheless have high environmental impacts.
- The extent to which companies run price or other promotions that encourage overpurchasing, leading to food waste or excessive consumption (which both represent a "waste" of food production and associated impacts).

Pricing

There is a general line of thinking that food prices should be higher to reflect their "environmental externalities." There are several difficulties with this approach.

- Some impacts "translate" better into cost than others. For example, it is relatively easy to assign an economic value to carbon or avoided carbon. The same applies to water. This is less easy to do with biodiversity, where values strongly affect judgments. The danger of "if you can measure it, you can manage it . . . and therefore monetize it" is its corollary—"if you can't measure it, it isn't worth talking about"—the consequence being that some issues are simply ignored.
- Leaving aside the difficulties of coming up with a price that describes or embeds the cost of all the environmental concerns highlighted thus far, the effects are likely to be socially regressive— that is, it may make food less affordable to people on low incomes. Several consequences—with ethical implications—may follow. The first is that poor people may become (more) food insecure. The second is that governments, fearing food riots or other forms of social unrest, may simply respond by allocating more land for food production (causing land use change).
- Who is responsible for altering the price? Is it governments or should companies voluntarily take action? If so, it may be hard for either to act unilaterally—but if they act together, they may be accused of price fixing.

Power Relations in the Food Systems

Power within the food system is heavily imbalanced. Ten food companies collectively generate daily revenues of more than $1.1 billion while more than a billion people who rely upon agriculture for their livelihoods live below the poverty line of US$1.25 a day.[5]

The question arises whether approaches such as "sustainable intensification" simply perpetuate existing unequal power structures. It could be argued that the focus on increased production lends itself well to a philosophy of maximizing profits, while intensification is inherently linked to the development and use of chemicals and other inputs whose production and sale profit large corporations at the expense of the environment.

On the other hand, supporters of sustainable intensification may argue that this concept is scale and power neutral; they may also argue that rejection of chemicals or novel techniques such as GM is a luxury affordable only to the rich in the affluent West. As such the ethical debate centers around the development and control of technologies and new knowledge. For example:

- New and useful "precision technologies" for agriculture are being developed that improve the environmental performance of agriculture. Examples include drip irrigation and the use of Global Navigation Satellite Systems (e.g., GPS) to analyze soil and crop conditions and identify areas where targeted fertilizer or water applications may be needed. This optimizes use of inputs. However, these technologies are very expensive and as such are affordable only to larger producers. A focus on the improved environmental performance of products may mean that these larger producers are favored over smaller ones.

- The breeding and use of GM crops hold potential to address some environmental concerns. For example, crops could be developed to retain more of the nitrogen in soils (so as to reduce leaching or N_2O emissions) or that are resistant to drought or flooding. The environmental and health concerns—and the validity or otherwise of those concerns—have been widely discussed. In addition, other ethical concerns voiced by critics of GM approaches include the following:

  ○ The extent to which GM R&D is in the hands of large corporations, which get to decide which crops are to be the focus of attention or not. For example, it has been argued that companies favor commercially profitable crops such as maize, soy, and rapeseed (canola) rather than "orphan crops" that may have higher nutritional value or be more widely grown and consumed by the poor.

- ○ Biofortification. By increasing the presence of certain key nutrients in a crop, provides higher nutritional gain per unit of environmental impact. On the other hand, investment in this route to nutritional enhancement may divert attention and resources away from supporting true dietary diversification and the development of a nutrition enhancing food system.
- ○ The extent to which governments support and fund R&D in gene technologies. While this solves the problem of corporations dictating the agenda, the anti-GM movement may argue that this is an immoral or irresponsible use of taxpayers' money.
- Ultimately questions about the role of agriculture in human development are also a subject of ethical disagreement. Some stakeholders argue that that smallholder farming is central to a fair and sustainable future. Others contend that the ongoing shift toward diversification out of farming and a shift to urban centers—with production left in the hands of fewer larger farmers—is the route to human progress.

Consumption and Diets

There is increasing interest in the concept of "healthy and sustainable diets" as a route to addressing some of the environmental problems generated by the food system. The thinking behind this is that our consumption patterns drive our unsustainable production systems, and they are therefore responsible for the food system's negative impacts. It is argued that there are many synergies between diets that have lower environmental impacts and those that are healthier for us, with a shift toward reduced animal product consumption core to this. At the same time, the evidence suggests there can also be trade-offs. For example:

- Diets that are lower in animal source foods may be deficient in certain key micronutrients and may be higher in sugars (because carbohydrates are a relatively low GHG food). Where these exist, how do we prioritize? Put another way, does the dietary health of an individual today trump the environment and, linked to that, the health of an individual tomorrow who may be negatively affected (e.g., by climate change) by the consumption patterns of the individual today?
- Are arguments for a wholesale shift to sustainable and healthy diets a new form of cultural imperialism—that is, telling the developing world how to eat now that we have realized the "error of our ways"?
- There may be trade-offs between environmental or between environmental and other nonenvironmental concerns. For example, diets that carry lower GHG impacts may also require greater water use, may be poorer for animal welfare, or may be more expensive.
- Do governments have a right to influence the diets of individuals, and, if so, to what extent—through information and education, or by regulation and taxation? Where is the divide between individual and state responsibility?
- Where meat is central to food cultures, is this an important consideration? Is culture a good in and of itself?
- There is a huge focus on meat since it has the highest environmental footprint. However, less attention is paid to "unnecessary" foods, such as sweets, chocolates, alcohol, tea, and coffee. These are important sources of pleasure and indeed can have addictive qualities (e.g., caffeine). They are also huge employers of people (cocoa, tea, coffee, sugar production). Why is this? Can the massive attention paid to animal products be partly explained by the fact that many in the environmental movement are sympathetic to the causes of animal welfare and vegetarianism but on the other hand would find it hard to give up tea, coffee, and so forth? In other words, do many nonenvironmental values implicitly influence the research and

advocacy agenda even when the debate is ostensibly just about the environment? And if so, is this a problem—are arguments being mixed up—or is it proof that multiple different problems stem from the same cause (e.g., an exploitative approach to the natural world)?

REFERENCES

1. Tara Garnett, "Planting up Solutions: Knowledge for Better Food Systems," Women's Environmental Network, August 1, 2017, https://www.wen.org.uk/blog/2017/8/plating-up-solutions-knowledge-for-better-food-systems.

2. Tara Garnett and Charles Godfray, "Sustainable Intensification in Agriculture. Navigating a Course through Competing Food System Priorities," Food Climate Research Network and the Oxford Martin Programme on the Future of Food, University of Oxford, UK 51 (2012), https://www.fcrn.org.uk/sites/default/files/SI_report_final_0.pdf.

3. FAO, "Tackling Climate Change through Livestock: A Global Assessment of Emissions and Mitigation Opportunities" (Rome: Food and Agriculture Organization, 2013).

4. FAO, *Food Outlook, 2015* (Rome: Food and Agriculture Organization of the United Nations, 2015).

5. Tara Garnett, "Policy Briefing: Sustainable and Healthy Eating Patterns?," Discover Society, September 6, 2016, https://discoversociety.org/2016/09/06/policy-briefing-sustainable-and-healthy-eating-patterns/.

ELEVEN

Water Utilization and Food

KEES VAN LEEUWEN

Population Growth

The world's population is projected to increase by more than 1 billion people within the next 15 years, reaching 8.5 billion by 2030, and to increase further to 9.7 billion by 2050 and 11.2 billion by 2100. Approximately 60% of the global population lives in Asia (4.4 billion), 16% in Africa (1.2 billion), 10% in Europe (738 million), 9% in Latin America and the Caribbean (634 million), and the remaining 5% in Northern America (358 million) and Oceania (39 million).[1] Recent population growth patterns are different across the globe (Figure 11.1).

Many countries in Africa are still growing exponentially. This implies that their claims on resources are also increasing rapidly. In Western Europe and India+ (India, Bangladesh, Nepal, Sri Lanka, Bhutan, Pakistan, Afghanistan, and Maldives), population growth is gradually leveling off (logistic growth),[2] while in China growth will soon decline due to the one-child family policy. This policy was introduced in 1979 to halt the rapid growth in the Chinese population. As well as the restriction on family size to just one child per family with high penalties for infringement, it recommended delaying marriage and childbearing (delaying the start of reproduction).[3] In fact, the maximum population

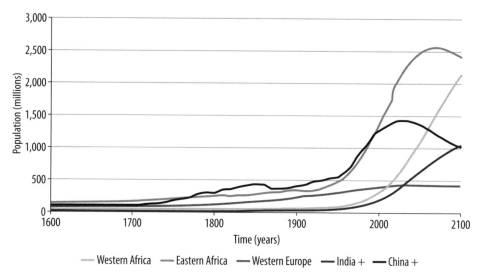

Figure 11.1. Total Population Estimations of India+ (India, Bangladesh, Nepal, Sri Lanka, Bhutan, Pakistan, Afghanistan, and Maldives), China+ (China, Hong Kong, Macao, and Mongolia), Eastern Africa, Western Africa, and Western Europa Based on the HYDE 3.1 Database and the UN Medium Variant of the World Population Predictions.

Source: S. H. A. Koop, and C. J. van Leeuwen. "The Challenges of Water, Waste and Climate Change in Cities," *Environment, Development and Sustainability* 19, no. 2 (April 1, 2017): 385-418. doi: 10.1007/s10668-016-9760-4. This figure is reproduced here under the terms of the Creative Commons 4.0 license.

densities in China+ (China, Hong Kong, Macao, and Mongolia), Western Europe, and India+ are expected to be reached in the year 2026 (1428 million), 2045 (424 million), and 2069 (2554 million), respectively.[4]

Urbanization will continue in both the more developed and the less developed regions so that, by 2050, urban dwellers will likely account for 86% of the population in the more-developed regions and for 64% of that in the less-developed regions. Overall, the world population is expected to be 67% urban in 2050.[5] Thus, urban areas of the world are expected to absorb all the population growth over the next decades.

Water Use

Drinking water consumption in cities makes up a small fraction of the total water footprint. For example, people in the Netherlands use about 2,300 m^3 of water per person per year of which 67% is for agriculture and 31% is used in industry, while only 2% makes up household water.[6] This means that water challenges in cities need to be solved predominantly by actors outside the traditional water sector. In fact, half of all cities with populations greater than 100,000 are located in water-scarce basins. In these basins, agricultural water consumption accounts for more than 90% of all freshwater depletions.[7,8] In a critical analysis, Richter et al. point out that nearly all water used for domestic and industrial purposes is eventually returned to a water body. For instance, toilets are flushed, and purified wastewater, as well as cooling water, in power plants is often returned to rivers. Because much of this water is not consumed, efforts to reduce urban water use or to recycle water, with the aim of alleviating water scarcity per se, hardly makes any difference.[9] In total, the domestic, industrial, and energy sectors account for less than 10% of global water consumption.[10,11] Of course, proper urban use and reuse of water, along with adequate sanitation, contribute significantly to pollution reduction and local water stress, as well as to energy and nutrient recovery.

Water and Food
Water Footprints

According to the Water Footprint Network:

> The water footprint has three components: green, blue and grey. Together, these components provide a comprehensive picture of water use by delineating the source of water consumed, either as rainfall/soil moisture or surface/groundwater, and the volume of fresh water required for assimilation of pollutants. The green water footprint is water from precipitation that is stored in the root zone of the soil and evaporated, transpired or incorporated by plants. It is particularly relevant for

agricultural, horticultural and forestry products. The blue water footprint is water that has been sourced from surface or groundwater resources and is either evaporated, incorporated into a product or taken from one body of water and returned to another, or returned at a different time. Irrigated agriculture, industry and domestic water use can each have a blue water footprint. The grey water footprint is the amount of fresh water required to assimilate pollutants to meet specific water quality standards. The grey water footprint considers point-source pollution discharged to a freshwater resource directly through a pipe or indirectly through runoff or leaching from the soil, impervious surfaces, or other diffuse sources.[12]

Water and Food Security

Hoekstra et al. estimate that agriculture accounts for 92% of the global blue water footprint.[13] Land, energy, and climate studies have shown that the livestock sector plays a substantial role in deforestation, biodiversity loss, and climate change. Livestock also significantly contributes to humanity's water footprint, water pollution, and water scarcity.[14,15] Furthermore, "nearly half of our food comes from the warm, dry parts of the planet, where excessive groundwater pumping to irrigate crops is rapidly shrinking the porous underground reservoirs called aquifers. Vast swaths of India, Pakistan, southern Europe, and the western United States could face depleted aquifers by midcentury—taking a bite out of the food supply and leaving as many as 1.8 billion people without access to this crucial source of fresh water."[16]

Wasting Food

Furthermore, the Food and Agriculture Organization of the United Nations (FAO) estimates that 32% of all food produced in the world was lost or wasted in 2009.[17,18] Therefore, consumers (i.e., citizens) can play a major role in the reduction of the global water footprint by both reducing the fraction of animal products in their diets and curbing their food waste.

Examples of Water Use for Food Products

Useful information has been provided by the Water Footprint Network on the amount of water needed to produce various food items. This information is available as an interactive tool. Meat production is very water intensive. The global average water footprint of chicken meat, for example, is about 4,330 liter/kg. The water footprint of chicken meat is smaller than the footprints of meat from beef cattle (15,400 liter/kg), sheep (10,400 liter/kg), pig (6,000 liter/kg) or goat (5,500 liter/kg).[19]

Implications

The implications are summarized in the following excerpt:[20]

> According to Steinfeld et al., livestock takes 70% of all agricultural land and 30% of the planet's land surface. They argue that livestock is an important factor in global biodiversity loss: livestock accounts for 20% of total terrestrial animal biomass, and the 30% of the Earth's land surface now claimed by farm animals was once habitat for wildlife. Furthermore, they estimate that livestock is responsible for 18% of anthropogenic greenhouse gas emissions (in terms of CO_2 equivalents). Compared to crop products, animal products do not only require more land to obtain a certain nutritional value, but also more energy and water.[21] Pimentel and Pimentel estimate that an average of 25 kcal of fossil energy is required to produce 1 kcal of animal protein, which is ten times greater than in the case of plant protein.[22] Mekonnen and Hoekstra show that the water footprint (WF) of any animal product is larger than the WF of a crop alternative with equivalent nutritional value. For example, the average WF per calorie for beef (10 L kcal^{-1}) is 20 times larger than for cereals and starchy roots (0.5 L kcal^{-1}). The WF per gram of protein for milk, eggs and chicken meat (around 30 L g^{-1} protein) is 1.5 times larger than for pulses (20 L g^{-1} protein).[23] Jalava et al. find that a global shift from current diets (period 2007-2009) to recommended diets (following the dietary guidelines of the World Health Organization) and a replacement of animal products by nutritionally equivalent local

crop products will reduce the food-related global green WF by 23% and the global blue WF by 16%.[24] Earlier, Hoekstra estimated a potential overall WF reduction of 36% in the industrialized world and 15% in the developing world.[25] Vanham et al. found a possible WF reduction of 41% for Southern and Western Europe and possible reductions of 27% and 32% for Eastern and Northern Europe, respectively.[26] Unlike Jalava et al., the previous studies considered the effect of a replacement of meat only, leaving the consumption of dairy products.

About 92% of humanity's WF relates to agriculture,[27] thus food production is a key factor in freshwater scarcity. Animal products are responsible for nearly thirty per cent of the WF of the global agricultural sector.[28] Jalava et al. point at a number of nuances to be brought into the discussion when proposing diet changes as a partial solution to water scarcity. First of all, the possible impact differs per country, depending on current dominant diets in a country. Obviously, countries where current meat consumption per capita is relatively high, like in the US and Australia, WF reductions through diet change can be most substantial. Second, we should distinguish between green and blue WF reductions.[29] Jalava et al. did not study this, but obviously we should also look at grey WF reductions specifically. Third, they point at the importance to look at where WF reductions are achieved: the immediate environmental benefit is greatest when WF reductions take place in water-scarce areas.[30] However, I would add here that it matters less where precisely the saving takes place than one may think at first instance, because the key is that total global demand for land and water to produce food diminishes. Making sure that the world's food is produced in the best places—where environmental impacts of land and water allocation for food production are smallest—is a separate concern. Fourth, Jalava et al. show that human health and environmental protection partly go together: following dietary guidelines will reduce the WF of our diet.[31] This comes out more pronounced in Vanham et al.[32] Fifth, they point at the possible water saving by reducing waste, which was quantified for example by Liu et al.[33] for China. Sixth, they argue for a careful consideration of what crop substitutes for animal products to select in order to remain within dietary guidelines and stay close to typical local diets so that shifting becomes more realistic.[34] A final point that should be added is the need to look more comprehensively at the livestock sector. Eating animal products is inefficient from the perspective of land, water and energy and undesirable from a biodiversity, climate change and animal welfare point of view.[35] The relatively high demand on our limited freshwater resources is just one specific entry point when talking about the need to rethink the consumption of animal products.

Changing Consumption Patterns

Worldwide, per capita meat consumption is increasing. People in the industrial world on average eat 80 kg of meat per year, while those in the developing world eat 32 kg.[36] The rising demand for meat is associated with rising incomes and greater urbanization.[37] In the developing world, where almost all world population increases take place, consumption of meat and dairy products has been growing at 4-6% per annum in the past few decades.[38] In sub-Saharan Africa and South Asia, the number of kilocalories consumed from livestock products will double from 200 kilocalories per person per day in 2000 to some 400 kilocalories in 2050.[39] The relevance of consumption patterns on water use, together with the City Blueprints of about 45 cities, is included in the Urban Water Atlas for Europe.[40]

Conclusion

In conclusion, water quantity and quality are affected by food production, meat consumption, food waste, and changing consumption patterns, all of which are major issues that deserve our attention. The World Economic Forum, FAO, and OECD all consider water, which is used most extensively in agricultural production, as a top priority and source of future conflicts if not managed appropriately.

This chapter is adapted from S. H. A. Koop and C. J. van Leeuwen, "The Challenges of Water, Waste and Climate Change in Cities," *Environment, Development and Sustainability* 19, no. 2 (April 2017): 385-418, https://doi.org/10.1007/s10668-016-9760-4, under the terms of the Creative Commons 4.0 license.

REFERENCES

1. UN, "World Urbanization Prospects: The 2015 Revision" (New York: United Nations, 2015).

2. Logistic growth is population growth in which the growth rate decreases with increasing number of individuals until it becomes zero when the population reaches a maximum. This maximum is the carrying capacity (i.e., the maximum number of individuals in a population that the environment can support).

3. Therese Hesketh, Li Lu, and Zhu Wei Xing, "The Effect of China's One-Child Family Policy after 25 Years," *New England Journal of Medicine* 353, no. 11 (September 2005): 1171-76, https://doi.org/10.1056/NEJMhpro 51833.

4. UN, "World Urbanization Prospects."

5. UN, "World Urbanization Prospects: The 2011 Revision" (New York: United Nations, 2012).

6. P. R. van Oel, M. M. Mekonnen, and A. Y. Hoekstra, "The External Water Footprint of the Netherlands: Geographically-Explicit Quantification and Impact Assessment," *Ecological Economics*, 2009, https://doi.org/10.1016/j .ecolecon.2009.07.014.

7. Martin Hunger and Petra Döll, "Value of River Discharge Data for Global-Scale Hydrological Modeling," *Hydrology and Earth System Sciences Discussions* 4, no. 6 (2007): 4125-73, https://hal.archives-ouvertes.fr/hal -00298912/.

8. Brian D. Richter et al., "Tapped Out: How Can Cities Secure Their Water Future?," *Water Policy* 15, no. 3 (2013): 335-63, https://iwaponline.com/wp /article-abstract/15/3/335/31209.

9. Richter et al., "Tapped Out."

10. Richter et al., "Tapped Out."

11. Arjen Y. Hoekstra et al., "Global Monthly Water Scarcity: Blue Water Footprints versus Blue Water Availability," *PloS One* 7, no. 2 (February 2012): e32688, https://doi.org/10.1371/journal.pone.0032688.

12. "What Is a Water Footprint?," Water Footprint Network, n.d., https:// waterfootprint.org/en/water-footprint/what-is-water-footprint/.

13. Hoekstra et al., "Global Monthly Water Scarcity."

14. M. Jalava et al., "Diet Change—a Solution to Reduce Water Use?" *Environmental Research Letters* 9, no. 7 (July 2014): 074016, https://doi.org/10 .1088/1748-9326/9/7/074016.

15. Arjen Y. Hoekstra, "Water for Animal Products: A Blind Spot in Water Policy," *Environmental Research Letters* 9, no. 9 (September 2014): 091003, https://doi.org/10.1088/1748-9326/9/9/091003.

16. Cheryl Katz, "As Groundwater Dwindles, a Global Food Shock Looms," *National Geographic*, December 22, 2016, https://news.nationalgeographic.com /2016/12/groundwater-depletion-global-food-supply/.

17. Brian Lipinski et al., "Reducing Food Loss and Waste. Working Paper, Installment 2 of Creating a Sustainable Food Future" (Washington, DC: World Resources Institute, 2013).

18. Jenny Gustavsson, *Global Food Losses and Food Waste: Extent, Causes and Prevention; Study Conducted for the International Congress "Save Food!" at Interpack 2011 Düsseldorf, Germany* (Rome: Food and Agriculture Organization, 2011), http://www.fao.org/3/a-i2697e.pdf.

19. "What Is a Water Footprint?"

20. This excerpt originally appeared in Arjen Y. Hoekstra, "Water for Animal Products: A Blind Spot in Water Policy," *Environmental Research Letters* 9, no. 9 (September 2014): 091003, https://doi.org/10.1088/1748-9326/9/9/091003, and is reproduced in this chapter (with reformatted citations) under the Creative Commons 3.0 license.

21. Henning Steinfeld et al., *Livestock's Long Shadow: Environmental Issues and Options* (Rome: Food and Agriculture Organization, 2006), http://www.fao.org/3/a0701e/a0701e.pdf.

22. David Pimentel and Marcia H. Pimentel, *Food, Energy, and Society* (Boca Raton, FL: CRC press, 2007).

23. Mesfin M. Mekonnen and Arjen Y. Hoekstra, "A Global Assessment of the Water Footprint of Farm Animal Products," *Ecosystems* 15, no. 3 (April 2012): 401-15, https://doi.org/10.1007/s10021-011-9517-8.

24. Jalava et al., "Diet Change."

25. Arjen Y. Hoekstra, "The Water Footprint of Animal Products," in *The Meat Crisis: Developing More Sustainable Production and Consumption*, ed. Joyce D'Silva and John Webster (London: Eartscan, 2010), 22-33.

26. D. Vanham, A. Y. Hoekstra, and G. Bidoglio, "Potential Water Saving through Changes in European Diets," *Environment International* 61 (November 2013): 45–56, https://doi.org/10.1016/j.envint.2013.09.011.

27. Arjen Y. Hoekstra and Mesfin M. Mekonnen, "The Water Footprint of Humanity," *Proceedings of the National Academy of Sciences of the United States of America* 109, no. 9 (February 2012): 3232-37, https://doi.org/10.1073/pnas.1109936109.

28. Mekonnen and Hoekstra, "A Global Assessment of the Water Footprint of Farm Animal Products."

29. Jalava et al., "Diet Change."

30. Jalava et al., "Diet Change."

31. Jalava et al., "Diet Change."

32. Vanham, Hoekstra, and Bidoglio, "Potential Water Saving through Changes in European Diets."

33. Junguo Liu et al., "Food Losses and Waste in China and Their Implication for Water and Land," *Environmental Science & Technology* 47, no. 18 (September 2013): 10137-44, https://doi.org/10.1021/es401426b.

34. Jalava et al., "Diet Change."

35. Vaclav Smil, *Should We Eat Meat? Evolution and Consequences of Modern Carnivory* (Hoboken, NJ: John Wiley & Sons, 2013).

36. Worldwatch Institute, "Global Meat Production and Consumption Continue to Rise," n.d., http://www.worldwatch.org/global-meat-production-and-consumption-continue-rise.

37. Organisation for Economic Co-operation and Development, "Meat Consumption," n.d., https://data.oecd.org/agroutput/meat-consumption.htm.

38. Jelle Bruinsma, ed., *World Agriculture: Towards 2015/2030; An FAO Perspective* (London: Earthscan, 2003), http://www.fao.org/3/a-y4252e.pdf.

39. Worldwatch Institute, "Global Meat Production and Consumption Continue to Rise."

40. Bernd Manfred Gawlik et al., eds., *Urban Water Atlas for Europe* (Luxembourg: European Commission, Publications Office of the European Union, 2017).

TWELVE

The Impact and Opportunity of Wasted Food

JONATHAN BLOOM

THE WASTING OF FOOD is a needless, global catastrophe unfolding daily before our eyes. Despite food being wasted at all points of the food chain, our actions also make it a hyperlocal problem. When noticed at all, wasted food is usually categorized as an unfortunate but unavoidable byproduct of our food system. Yet there is no larger social or environmental challenge that we can significantly tackle with as little effort or as few structural changes. The strategies to minimize wasted food are approachable, feasible, and effective. In considering global solutions for climate change, Project Drawdown found that reducing food waste was the third most effective option.[1]

In this chapter, after discussing how much food we are wasting, what causes so much food to be wasted, and why it is important to minimize wasted food, I suggest remedies for both individuals and our culture at large. I hope that by the end of this chapter, you will believe that wasted food is a problem that demands not only our attention but also our action.

Globally, about a third of all the food available for consumption is not consumed. Domestically, the best estimate is that 40% of available calories are not eaten.[2] That certainly adds up—to 160 billion pounds of food worth roughly $218 billion annually.[3] Those are ballpark estimates, but to provide a sense of scale on those findings, let's turn to a ballpark: every day America wastes enough food to fill the Rose Bowl, a 90,000-seat stadium in Southern California. In fact, we could likely fill the stadium twice daily with all the food wasted from sea to shining sea.[4]

In a word: *What?!* Why are we wasting so much food? Why are we squandering two Rose Bowls of food every day? There are many root causes, but the primary reason is sheer abundance. The American food system produces about twice the amount of food needed. This has a triple impact. It enables our squandering, encourages our overeating, and desensitizes us to waste. This abundance leads to a cheapening of the food, both literally—which will be discussed later—and psychologically.

Additionally, this abundance has changed our food ecosystem. We now encounter food almost everywhere we go. Food is sold not just at supermarkets but also at convenience stores, gas stations, airports, and other locations. The near-constant exposure to food creates a mindset of excess that influences our behavior. We simply do not value our food as much as we once did.

One of the clearest illustrations of our edible abundance happens during gleaning outings. These events set enthusiastic, yet untrained volunteer harvesters to work in a field of unwanted crops. At least once a year, I participate in one of these food recovery outings in my home state of North Carolina. Sweet potatoes are often the object of excess being gleaned, especially during the annual "Yam Jam." But that fun nomenclature belies the sad truth that for every field being gleaned, there are countless others where crops are plowed under because the price of that good may not justify the expenditure of labor. And, symbolizing our epic abundance, many gleaning outings recover only a fraction of the available, excess food.

The second instance of abundance is the massive portion sizes that have become commonplace. The average number of calories served to us at restaurants has steadily increased, and portions are two to three times larger than they were 20 years ago.[5] Unfortunately, consumers are often left with two bad choices when dining out: overeat or waste food. There is a third option of taking leftovers home, but you may not be going straight home, or you may be one of those strange people who doesn't like leftovers! The common restaurant strategy of conveying value through abundance prompts two problems: obesity and food waste. Additionally, those massive portions influence how we eat at home by changing our perceptions of reasonable amounts of food to serve and eat.

Despite rising food prices, the actual cost of our food expenditures is particularly cheap. It is near all-time lows in the United States, and no other nation spends as little on food.[6] That impacts how we value (or, in most cases, devalue) our food. It is worth noting here that the cheapness of food is artificially created by agricultural subsidies. As with gasoline, food is perhaps cheaper than it otherwise would be, and there is a complex conversation to be had on how best to move forward at the intersection of food abundance, cost, and waste.

The third illustration of abundance is superficiality, the result of which is wasted food. We want our food to look both perfect and homogeneous. Anything blemished or the wrong shape, size, or color will be cast aside at some point from farm to fork. In other words, the cost of having that immaculate supermarket display of apples is wasted food at every step of the food chain. With many varieties of produce, a sizable portion of the crop is never harvested (and usually goes ungleaned). After harvest, grading standards also weed out a good portion of crops that do not have the desired appearance.

To be clear, this need for perfection stems from us—from consumer preferences. We actively avoid unusual produce in our shopping. Our choices inform how supermarkets stock their shelves, which in turn influences behaviors at the wholesale and farm levels. The topic of ugly or quirky produce has been quite popular in social and traditional media and has even prompted several retailers to create lines of "ugly produce." But unless these items sell well—and so far they haven't—odd produce will be a novelty instead of a paradigm shift. Packaging also plays a harmful role here. Many fruits are packed by size to ensure a certain number per box. As a result, an apple with a diameter that is too small or too large may be deemed useless, and green beans of only a certain length may fit the plastic bag in which they are sold. Those literal and figurative structural restrictions doom perfectly good food to an unnecessary demise.

Finally, this abundance has led to a general loss of food knowledge. We as a country and a culture have essentially stepped out of the kitchen. Several generations of Americans have not learned the traditional food-ways of their parents and grandparents, as convenience has and does prompt fewer Americans to cook. As a result, many Americans lack the knowledge on how to store food properly, stretch their food supply, or even determine how long a food will stay good. Wasted food is the result.

Date labels have bloomed in the wake of that cultural blind spot. What began as a way to assert freshness and reassure consumers has morphed into a ubiquitous business practice. Date labels now dot not just bottles of milk, but also individual eggs and bottles of water. Yet misconceptions abound here. First, the variety of terminology prompts confusion. Most of the date label terms are meant to speak to food quality—texture and taste—not food safety. Still, many people think that they should not eat any food past the day of its date label. Second, most date labels are cautious estimates, so if consumers treat those dates as the gospel truth on when a food will go bad, they will be throwing away perfectly edible food. Finally, the only food item required by federal law to have a date label is infant formula. Food companies are voluntarily adding dates to their packages, prompting a lot of wasted food. Unfortunately, "when in doubt, throw it out" is the prevailing mindset, and most consumers trust a near-arbitrary date stamped on a package before their own senses of smell, sight, and taste.

Who Cares?

Why should we care if we're wasting a lot of food? As earlier mentioned, we have a lot of food. So what's the big deal? First, in a world where nearly a billion people do not get enough to eat, squandering food is viscerally reprehensible. Food waste matters even more in light of the impact our food system has on the environment. Additionally, wasted food comes at a significant economic impact. If we frame those factors positively, addressing wasted food will make our planet healthier ethically, environmentally, and economically.

Starting with the ethical aspect, there is a saying that is applicable here. As a child, you may have heard your parents or grandparents say something like, "Clean your plate because there are children starving in Africa." Perhaps they were more geographically specific or mentioned another part of the world. Nonetheless, that kind of saying is fairly common, despite two flaws. First, it is logistically inaccurate, as the food on your plate cannot affect what anyone outside of your home can eat. It is more important to think about what ends up on your plate before you take, serve, or prepare too much food. Second, it employs guilt as the motivating factor—never a good idea with food. Yet, there is a reason why this expression has persisted for generations: there is a kernel of truth in that saying. The coexistence of hunger and waste is incongruous and ludicrous.

Wasting roughly 40% of our food supply while 12% of American households are food insecure is morally callous.[7] In the words of Pope Francis, "Throwing away food is like stealing from the table of the poor and the hungry."[8] The juxtaposition of hunger and waste must change. That paradox exists globally, but it is far worse in the United States. That is strange, considering the United States is among the wealthiest countries in the world. If we truly had the social and political will to end hunger, we could do so. Of course, hunger is tied to poverty, and so it is not quite as simple as one or the other. Then again, maybe it is. Redistributing a small percentage of the food that is currently wasted would be enough to lift all the food-insecure Americans into food security. That finding is the essence of why we should focus on eliminating or at least reducing the amount of wasted food in America.

Squandering 40% of our food also represents a real waste of money. It is a poor use of financial resources, resulting in a loss of $218 billion annually in the United States.[9] The social and environmental impacts of wasted food also have financial implications. Globally, the UN Food and Agriculture Organization (FAO) found that wasted food had a grand impact of $2.6 trillion, after considering the social, environmental, and food costs.[10] There is a significant per household cost, too. The average American family of four loses roughly $2,000 annually through the food that it does not eat.[11] That squandered money should provide a significant disincentive to wasting, but people don't often attach a dollar amount to their wasted food.

In terms of the environmental impact of wasted food, there are several factors to unpack. Wasting food squanders the vast amount of water embedded in our food. Our food system is incredibly reliant upon irrigation. Agriculture sucks up approximately 80% of all the precious fresh water used in the United States.[12] Given that we waste nearly 40% of our food, a tremendous amount of water is used in vain: About one-fourth of fresh water usage is embedded in the food that we throw away.[13] Certain foods have larger water footprints, notably beef, pork, and cheese. To give a sense of perspective, wasting a quarter-pound hamburger is equivalent to taking a 90-minute shower![14] As the planet becomes warmer, water will become an increasingly precious commodity.

Making matters worse, landfilling food creates harmful greenhouse gas emissions. When food is buried in a landfill, anaerobic decomposition creates methane that slowly seeps out of the landfill. Those emissions aid climate change because methane is more than 34 times as potent as carbon dioxide in trapping heat.[15] A conservative estimate is that landfill food waste produces emissions equivalent to 3.4 million vehicles.[16] Given that, we are essentially aiding climate change from our kitchen waste bins.

Most importantly, wasted food has a hefty carbon footprint. Nearly 3% of all US greenhouse gas emissions stem from wasted food.[17] Every step of our food chain is powered by petroleum, from planting to fertilizing to harvesting, cooling, shipping, cooking, and—after we're done with the food—hauling it off to the landfill. At least 2% of all US energy consumption is embedded in food that is not used, equating to 350 million barrels of oil annually.[18] While those two data points represent the massive scale of wasted food, they do not exactly jump off the page. Here is another way of looking at it: every year we squander 100 times the amount of oil lost in the Deepwater Horizon spill through the food we waste.[19]

Also conveying that scale is Project Drawdown, mentioned earlier. This initiative and book by Paul Hawken found that reducing global food waste 50% by 2050 would be the third-most-effective solution toward minimizing climate change.[20] Project Drawdown's finding is so empowering because it conveys that wasted food is not just a problem but also an opportunity. While that is promising, the key question is how to realize that reduction.

What Now?

In finding solutions, the EPA's venerable "reduce, reuse, recycle" mantra provides a solid starting point. There is a reason "reduce" is mentioned first. All too often, the energy, attention, and funding go toward recycling or composting food waste. The EPA created a helpful hierarchy that applies that "reduce, reuse, recycle" mantra to the topic of food waste. Not surprisingly, the EPA prioritizes "source reduction." In other words, stop creating excess food at all levels of the food chain. The second priority is channeling the excess food to feed hungry people. If that isn't possible—and much wasted food is inedible, for various reasons— feeding livestock is the next best option. Subsequently, the EPA recommends creating energy from wasted food through anaerobic digestion, followed by composting. Only if we cannot do any of the above should we be landfilling or incinerating food. Unfortunately, in practice, the exact opposite occurs—94% of available food waste is thrown away or incinerated.[21] We have some work to do.

Fortunately, we as individuals can have a major impact on wasted food. Some estimates pin as much as 43% of the food waste problem on households.[22] That may be a bit high, as farm-level loss and waste are consistently underestimated. Nonetheless, that estimate provides good and bad news. On the negative side, we as individuals are quite wasteful. Framed positively, though, we the people have the potential to make a real change. We have agency! Then again, behavior change does not occur easily. We will need both cultural and policy shifts to nudge us toward wasting less food. Let us now delve into selected solutions.

On the topic of superficial perfection, it is time to expand what kind of food we consider acceptable. If appearance currently trumps taste, the end goal should be prioritizing taste and nutrition over homogeneity, especially with produce. In the past few years, several supermarket chains have marketed lines of ugly produce with branded names like Misfits or Incredibly Ugly. Those initiatives may mark an interesting transitional phase, but the ultimate goal should be to become more accepting of food with varying shapes and sizes—to avoid establishing divisions dictating that five-inch green beans are marketable but six-inch ones are trash. Instead of distinguishing between a curved carrot and a straight one, we should just classify both as—and I know this is radical—carrots!

We will have lasting change only when food is judged not by its appearance but by the content of its character (in other words, its nutritional value). When a curved cucumber is treated no different from a straight one, or vice versa with bananas. And, yes, there's an intentional parallel with not judging people by their race, gender, creed, or orientation. Both must happen!

Although awareness on the food waste problem has progressed, that communication must increase. The imaginative Save the Food campaign, created by the Ad Council in coordination with the Natural Resources Defense Council, is effective, but it exists only in select markets. We should extend and expand that valuable campaign to make it a truly national phenomenon. We can think back to a couple of other public service campaigns that really had a national impact. Wouldn't it be great if Save the Food were the next Smokey the Bear or Woodsy the Owl? It is encouraging that the New Jersey legislature recently passed a bill directing the state Department of Agriculture to create a public awareness campaign on food waste.

On the policy level, the most significant impact would come from a national ban on landfilling food. Several states, including Massachusetts, Vermont, Connecticut, Rhode Island, and California, have passed bills making it illegal to send food to the landfill. Further landfill food waste bans would prevent much of our food from reaching a landfill, where it creates harmful methane. This intervention is counterintuitive, as focusing on the end of the food chain—the landfill—dramatically affects what happens throughout earlier parts of the food chain. Yet, it is effective. State-level bans have already boosted food recovery and food recycling infrastructures. Were it not so easy or inexpensive to throw away food, actors at all parts of the food chain would focus on right-sizing the amount of food that they grow, buy, or cook. For example, it would prompt restaurants to serve more reasonable portion sizes or at least provide more choice on amounts. If a national ban is not feasible, passing additional state bills would achieve the same goal.

Separately and in concert, Congress and the food industry have discussed fixing date labels. Yet, nothing has changed. Whether by the carrot or the stick, we must find a way around the status quo of date-label confusion. The variety of terms used—"Best by," "Use by," "Use or freeze by," and "Sell by"—are mystifying. They are also unnecessary, given that they all essentially speak to the same thing: a food's quality will not be optimal after that date. Because none of the terms indicates a hard date after which food safety will definitely be an issue, there is even more reason to streamline the terminology. Both industry and regulatory discussions proposed a single term, "Best if used by." Now it is just a question of determining whether that standardization can happen voluntarily or whether Congress must act.

Next, a reckoning on portion size is long overdue. It is time to curtail the massive quantities of food served at restaurants through a waste-ban nudge or, more likely, a cultural shift. The latter will likely require redefining value in our food system. Thanks to the cheapness of food, restaurants have long equated value with quantity. Because of that artificial, subsidy-assisted inexpensiveness, most restaurants are happy to entice customers by serving more food than is generally needed for most appetites. It is time for a rethink. Focusing on quality instead of quantity will lead us to a better place.

Lastly, it is imperative to teach kids that throwing away food is not okay. Most US schools serve mediocre meals due to limited budgets, offer limited choice, and do not have compost bins. As a result, our kids are learning that food is trash, just like any other commodity in our throwaway culture. We must teach them the opposite—that food is special and much needed by many. At the very least, landfilling food cannot continue to be the norm.

To reverse that trend, there are many potential remedies, as evidenced by Minneapolis Public Schools' recent food waste prevention plan, True Food, No Waste.[23] For example, schools can prevent plate waste by establishing a share table. Any horizontal surface will do, as long as it enables students to leave unwanted foods to be claimed by their peers. This redistribution mechanism can also enable cafeteria workers to reserve excess food at the next lunch. The USDA, which oversees the National School Lunch Program, recommends this action (as long as food is re-served only once). Additionally, schools should establish compost bins for food that cannot be shared. If given the choice, though, share tables should take priority. As we saw with the EPA hierarchy, reducing food waste is more important than recycling it. Students (and plenty of adults!) often misunderstand those priorities and see composting a once-bitten apple as a success.

Finally, on a holistic level, it is vital that we connect with our food. We must do better at knowing our food. That may mean growing your own or buying from a local producer. It may just mean cooking some or all of your own food. Although many of us feel too busy to cook—and the food industry has pushed convenience to the top of the food agenda—preparing our own meals does not have to be time-consuming. With a little planning and strategizing, most of us can cook at least some of our meals and do so with young people. We tend not to waste food that we have helped bring to the table, whether via the garden, the market, or the kitchen. The closer we are to our food, the harder it is to throw it away.

When we reflect on the stakes for minimizing wasted food, we should consider the number of people on this growing planet. The latest estimates predict that there will be 10 billion people on Earth in 2050. That's a lot of zeroes and a lot of mouths to feed. When food thinkers hear those numbers, they jump to some conclusions: we must create more arable land, even if it means cutting down forests, turn to GMO crops on a widespread basis, and maybe even switch to genetically engineered proteins. Those changes may or may not be necessary and are discussions for other chapters of this volume. Before we turn to those irreversible processes, though, let's focus on efficiency. It is imperative that we find the political and social will to tackle wasted food in a serious manner. That does not mean simply setting ambitious goals but rather dedicating the resources and, yes, possibly the time and effort to reach them. Only after pursuing comprehensive efficiency should we turn toward other, drastic solutions. We have more than enough food on this planet to feed everyone; it's just a matter of distributing it effectively.

REFERENCES

1. "Reduced Food Waste," Project Drawdown, 2016, https://www.drawdown .org/solutions/food/reduced-food-waste.

2. Kevin D. Hall et al., "The Progressive Increase of Food Waste in America and Its Environmental Impact," *PloS One* 4, no. 11 (November 2009): e7940.

3. Rethink Food Waste through Economics and Data (ReFED), "A Roadmap to Reduce US Food Waste by 20 Percent," 2016, www.refed.com.

4. Jonathan Bloom, *American Wasteland: How America Throws Away Nearly Half of Its Food (and What We Can Do about It)* (Cambridge, MA: Da Capo, 2011).

5. Wendy Scinta, "How Portion Sizes Have Changed throughout History," Your Weight Matters, April 28, 2016, https://www.yourweightmatters.org /portion-sizes-changed-time/.

6. Brad Plumer, "Map: Here's How Much Each Country Spends on Food," Vox, July 6, 2014, https://www.vox.com/2014/7/6/5874499/map-heres-how -much-every-country-spends-on-food.

7. Alisha Coleman-Jensen et al., "Household Food Security in the United States in 2016," Economic Research Report Number 237, U.S. Department of Agriculture, September 2017, https://www.ers.usda.gov/webdocs/publications /84973/err-237.pdf.

8. Pope Francis' comments were made during his weekly address in St. Peter's Square on June 5, 2013.

9. ReFED, "A Roadmap."

10. FAO, "Food Wastage Footprint: Full-Cost Accounting" (Rome: FAO, 2014), http://www.fao.org/3/a-i3991e.pdf.

11. ReFED, "A Roadmap."

12. "Irrigation & Water Use," U.S. Department of Agriculture, Economic Research Service, https://www.ers.usda.gov/topics/farm-practices-management /irrigation-water-use/.

13. M. Kummu et al., "Lost Food, Wasted Resources: Global Food Supply Chain Losses and Their Impacts on Freshwater, Cropland, and Fertiliser Use," *Science of the Total Environment* 438 (November 2012): 477-89.

14. Dana Gunders and Jonathan Bloom, "Wasted: How America Is Losing up to 40 Percent of Its Food from Farm to Fork to Landfill," Natural Resources Defense Council, August 2017, https://www.nrdc.org/sites/default/files/wasted-2017-report.pdf.

15. Intergovernmental Panel on Climate Change. *Climate Change 2013— The Physical Science Basis: Working Group I Contribution to the Fifth Assessment Report of the Intergovernmental Panel on Climate Change* (Cambridge: Cambridge University Press, 2014), doi:10.1017/CBO9781107415324.

16. Gunders and Bloom, "Wasted."

17. Martin C. Heller and Gregory A. Keoleian, "Greenhouse Gas Emission Estimates of US Dietary Choices and Food Loss," *Journal of Industrial Ecology* 19, no. 3 (2015): 391-401.

18. Amanda D. Cuéllar and Michael E. Webber, "Wasted Food, Wasted Energy: The Embedded Energy in Food Waste in the United States," *Environmental Science & Technology* 44, no. 16 (August 2010): 6464-69.

19. Author's calcuations. 350 million barrels of oil compared to 3.19 million from Deepwater Horizon spill, https://ocean.si.edu/conservation/pollution/gulf-oil-spill.

20. "Reduced Food Waste."

21. "Reducing Wasted Food at Home," U.S. Environmental Protection Agency, https://www.epa.gov/recycle/reducing-wasted-food-home.

22. ReFED, "A Roadmap."

23. Jonathan Bloom, "A Food Waste Action Plan for Minneapolis Public Schools," Natural Resources Defense Council, January 2019, https://www.nrdc.org/sites/default/files/minneapolis-k-12-food-waste-action-plan-201901.pdf.

THIRTEEN

Climate Change and Food Production

Big Worries, Uncertain Impacts

EVAN FRASER

IN 2009, Professor John Beddington, chief scientific advisor to the UK government, warned of a "perfect storm" of food, water, and energy shortages that would trigger public unrest and mass migration by 2030.[1] His warning came at a dramatic time in the history of the world's food system. Flat, stable food prices throughout the 1990s and early 2000s had given way to a bit of a roller coaster. Prices soared in 2008, crashed shortly thereafter, and then skyrocketed again in 2011 (see figure 13.1).[2]

Many scientists worry that we will face a massive food crisis driven by a combination of climate change and population growth and that we will need to produce more food at a time when food is harder than ever to produce. According to the *Economist*, "In the next 40 years, humans will need to produce more food than they did in the previous 10,000 put together."[3]

This crisis will have significant political effects as well. Between 2008 and 2011, there were serious food riots in parts of Asia and Africa.[4] Food riots are people taking to the streets in violent protest, outraged over the price of their daily bread. During the Arab Spring, protestors raised baguettes into the air as an international sign of protest and outrage over an unfair food system that allows some to eat while others starve.[5]

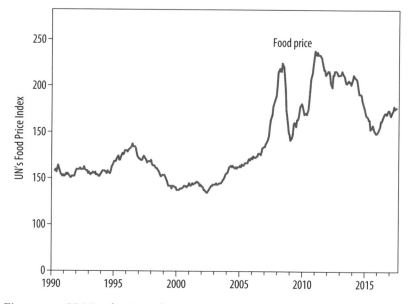

Figure 13.1. UN Food Price Index, 1990-2018.
Source: Data from "FAO Food Price Index," Food and Agriculture Organization of the United Nations, http://www.fao.org/worldfoodsituation/foodpricesindex/en/.

The latest *State of Food Security and Nutrition in the World* report from the UN's Food and Agriculture Organization adds further evidence that the world is tipping toward a food crisis. Even though world hunger had been falling for decades, in the past few years it has risen. The report suggests that a combination of economic upheaval, conflict, and climate change are to blame.[6]

Climate Change's Large but Uncertain Threats to Global Food Production

When the narrative around global food security and climate change is framed this way, it seems like a production problem. In fact, food security and food production are only loosely related. Instead of concluding from the high, volatile prices of the past ten years that this is a production problem and we need to produce more food, let's frame the problem as a question: Will producing more food have any measurable effect on

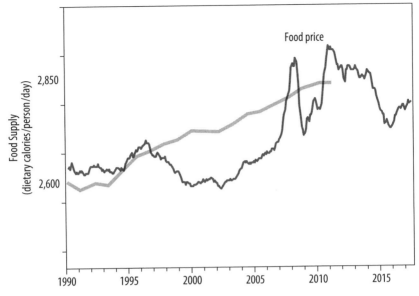

Figure 13.2. Global Food Supply and Food Prices, 1990-2018.
  Source: Data on supply: "Food Balance Sheets," Food and Agriculture Organization of the United Nations, http://www.fao.org/faostat/en/#data/FBS. Data on price: "FAO Food Price Index," Food and Agriculture Organization of the United Nations, http://www.fao.org/worldfoodsituation/foodpricesindex/en/.

food security? When we frame the problem as a question, we can collect data. In Figure 13.2, global food supply data, measured in dietary calories available per person per day, are superimposed on food price data.

There are three points to take note of in figure 13.2. First, the supply trend is positive. Over the past 20 years, every year farmers have produced more food per person per day than the previous year. Second, there are 2,850 dietary calories available each day for every man, woman, and child on the planet. There is more than enough food to feed everyone. Third, there is no correlation between food prices and food supply, at least at the global level. Nothing about the figure indicates that producing more food will measurably improve food security. This suggests that food security has more to do with other issues, such as equitable food distribution. Discussions about climate change and food security often focus on production and yields, but this may overlook the root causes of food insecurity.

There have been many attempts to model how climate change will affect crop yields in the future. Despite the scientific sophistication that goes into these kinds of models, there is still tremendous uncertainty. We could jump out to 2050 and not necessarily see the changes in crop yields projected by these models. Even sophisticated models struggle to capture one of the most important parts of the food production equation: the farmer.

A crop-climate model from a study that simulated the effect of climate change on China's winter wheat crop shows the percentage of harvests likely to fail over the 21st century due to climate change (figure 13.3). The projected failure of between 20% and 30% of crops would be a terrible scenario. The study then simulated different adaptation strategies by conducting a series of thought experiments. For example, what if farmers had access to heat-tolerant cultivars of winter wheat? When that assumption was put into the model, the percentage of harvests failing decreased. When it was assumed that farmers would have access

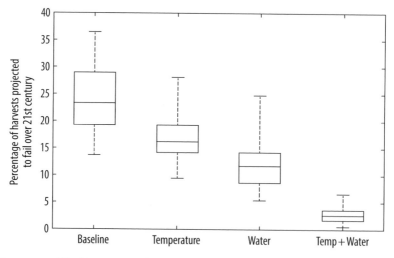

Figure 13.3. The Percentage of Harvests Failing under Different Adaptation Strategies.

Source: Adapted from Andrew J. Challinor, Elisabeth S. Simelton, Evan D. G. Fraser, Debbie Hemming, and Mathew Collins, "Increased Crop Failure Due to Climate Change: Assessing Adaptation Options Using Models and Socio-Economic Data for Wheat in China," *Environmental Research Letters* 5, no. 3 (September 29, 2010): 034012.

to drought-tolerant cultivars or better irrigation, the percentage also decreased. Finally, when the study simulated a so-called perfect adaptation scenario, the effect of climate change essentially disappeared. Although climate change seems scary from a production perspective—and it may indeed be scary—much hinges on farmers' ability to adapt, which in turn hinges on socioeconomic decisions.[7]

New Opportunities for Food Production

Recent work that I have been involved in has looked at opportunities for agriculture in our northern frontiers. Climate change is expected to increase agricultural potential in the North due to a longer growing season that may make land currently unsuitable for cultivation amenable to farming. The first step of our analysis was to overlay crop suitability maps with climate change projections to identify lands that could become suitable for farming. We then analyzed the potential of these lands to boost global food production. If Canadian or Russian wheat yields are average, cultivating these lands could increase global wheat production by about 2% per year. Finally, we considered the possible environmental impact of this new cultivation. We estimated that if all these lands were cultivated, the amount of carbon dioxide that might be released would be equivalent to over a century of current US emissions. Of course, it is unrealistic to think that all these lands could be cultivated or that they would be suitable for farming. Nevertheless, our work shows some of the potential challenges associated with expanding agriculture in the North.[8]

The Need for Interdisciplinary, Participatory, and Multi-Stakeholder Work

Regardless of what is possible, from a climate perspective, in the North, we must consider First Nations governance. If the agricultural industry starts looking to expand in the North without adequate engagement and consultation with First Nations communities, it will run into massive resistance. Climate change may create new agricultural frontiers, but to avoid unintended negative trade-offs, we must embark on multistakeholder and participatory processes that include environmental governance and indigenous representation.

The Role of Consumers in Choosing Lower-Impact Diets for Themselves and the Planet

Consumers can play a role in developing healthy and sustainable diets. A recent study compared nutritional recommendations (figure 13.4, *left*) to actual global food production (figure 13.4, *right*). Fruits and vegetables should make up about half of our diet, yet we are producing only a fraction of what we need. By contrast, the grains and starches that should make up 20% of our diet are about half of the global food supply. There is a significant mismatch between what we produce and what we should be producing if we all wanted to eat a healthy diet.

The same study then explored the greenhouse gas implications of healthier diets now and in the future using a life-cycle approach. Not surprisingly, a significant portion of our emissions comes from animal protein systems. The study found that a shift to a nutritionally optimal diet would result in an increase in total emissions now and in the future as we ramp up production for the global population. This would be driven mostly by increased production of animal protein.[9] This study is evidence that we, as a global society, need to be thinking about less resource-intensive protein systems.

There are many options for alternative proteins, such as plant, fungal, algal, and insect proteins. Each of them seems to offer several environmental benefits. For example, crickets require 12 times less feed and 12 times less water compared to cattle. Compared to mealworms, pigs produce somewhere between 10 and 100 times more greenhouse gas emissions per edible kilogram.[10] Quorn products reportedly use 5 times less greenhouse gas emissions than beef and 1.5 times less than chicken.[11] Does this mean that we will all be eating cheddar cheese larvae instead of beef jerky at future Super Bowl parties? The answer may actually be yes. Industry and food science innovation are driving a revolution that will bring us an increasingly wide range of novel protein products.

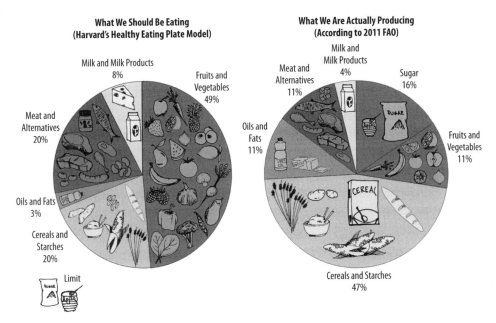

What We Should Be Eating
(Harvard's Healthy Eating Plate Model)

Milk and Milk Products 8%
Fruits and Vegetables 49%
Meat and Alternatives 20%
Oils and Fats 3%
Cereals and Starches 20%
Limit

What We Are Actually Producing
(According to 2011 FAO)

Milk and Milk Products 4%
Meat and Alternatives 11%
Sugar 16%
Oils and Fats 11%
Fruits and Vegetables 11%
Cereals and Starches 47%

Figure 13.4. Global Food Production vs. Recommended Consumption.
Source: Adapted from Krishna Bahadur KC, Goretty M. Dias, Anastasia Veeramani, Clarence J. Swanton, David Fraser, Dirk Steinke, Elizabeth Lee, et al. "When Too Much Isn't Enough: Does Current Food Production Meet Global Nutritional Needs?," *PloS One* 13, no. 10 (October 23, 2018): e0205683.

Feeding the world's growing population while dealing with climate change is a grand challenge, but I am not pessimistic about our future. There is so much innovation among industry, adaptive capacity latent within the farm community, and excitement about utilizing the earth's resources in a sustainable way. I believe that when the history books of the 21st century are written, there will be a significant chapter about how we, as a species, came to grips with the challenge of sustainably feeding us all.

REFERENCES

1. Ian Sample, "Beddington: World Faces 'Perfect Storm' of Problems by 2030," *Guardian*, March 18, 2009, http://www.theguardian.com/science/2009/mar/18/perfect-storm-john-beddington-energy-food-climate.

2. "FAO Food Price Index," Food and Agriculture Organization of the United Nations, http://www.fao.org/worldfoodsituation/foodpricesindex/en/.

3. "Barbarians at the Farm Gate," *Economist*, December 30, 2014, https:// www.economist.com/finance-and-economics/2014/12/30/barbarians-at-the-farm -gate.

4. Gwynne Dyer, "The Future of Food Riots," CRISISBOOM, January 12, 2011, http://crisisboom.com/2011/01/12/the-future-of-food-riots/.

5. Maria Godoy, "Can Riots Be Predicted? Experts Watch Food Prices," *NPR*, October 2, 2012, https://www.npr.org/sections/thesalt/2012/09/20/161501075 /high-food-prices-forcast-more-global-riots-ahead-researchers-say.

6. Food and Agriculture Organization of the United Nations et al., *The State of Food Security and Nutrition in the World 2018: Building Climate Resilience for Food Security and Nutrition* (Rome: FAO, 2018).

7. Andrew J. Challinor et al., "Increased Crop Failure Due to Climate Change: Assessing Adaptation Options Using Models and Socio-economic Data for Wheat in China," *Environmental Research Letters* 5, no. 3 (September 29, 2010): 034012.

8. Lee Hannah et al., "The Environmental Consequences of Climate-Driven Agricultural Frontiers," *PloS One* 15, no. 2 (February 2020): e0228305.

9. Krishna Bahadur KC et al., "When Too Much Isn't Enough: Does Current Food Production Meet Global Nutritional Needs?," *PloS One* 13, no. 10 (October 23, 2018): e0205683.

10. "Bug Bites," University of British Columbia, September 25, 2014, http:// news.ubc.ca/2014/09/25/bug-bites/.

11. "Sustainable Development Report, 2014," Quorn Foods, Ltd, 2014, https://web.archive.org/web/20140717071449/http://www.quorn.co.uk/~/media /Quorn/Downloads/SustainabilityReport.ashx.

FOURTEEN

Primary Agricultural Production

Crops and Farmers

PAUL B. THOMPSON

P LANT PRODUCTION can be considered as the base for contemporary food systems, a generalization that becomes more literally true as systems tend more toward industrial organization. Although global food systems still rely on grazing of uncultivated pasture, on wild caught fish from oceans as well as lakes and rivers, and on hunting or foraging from uncultivated areas such as forests or grasslands, industrialized animal production systems tend to rely heavily on feeds produced through plant agriculture. Thus, whether for food or feed production, the cultivation of plant species is the basis for food availability within industrialized economies of the world. As a consequence, the ethical dimensions of plant agriculture can be characterized broadly into two large categories. On the one hand, there are ethical imperatives to maintain a certain level of total productivity for plant agriculture, simply to meet basic food needs. This is not to say that specifying that level is easy or unambiguous. On the other hand, all plant production systems have unintended side effects that can be regarded as ethically problematic. Again, there are uncertainties, ambiguities, and value-based differences of opinion that arise in specifying what these side effects are. However, this two-pronged approach to classifying the ethical dimensions of plant production can serve as an organizational framework for listing the ethical issues that arise in connection with plant production.

The table of contents for this volume will tell you what the main side effects are. Crop production has significant impacts on the environment, while the way in which we feed these crops to livestock has created a host of problems in animal welfare. Crops do not grow without water, and agriculture has a dominating impact on both the quality of water and its availability for other uses. Planting and harvesting crops require a human workforce, and those who work for wages are frequently among the most poorly paid and the most frequently exploited workers in the world. Finally, there are impacts on public health that are associated with eating what our food system produces and that result from pollutants that are released in the production process. All these topics are given a detailed treatment elsewhere.

The first point to stress here is that the side effects from plant production that will be discussed by others are appropriately the main focus of food ethics. These are the front-of-mind concerns that have been the target of efforts to develop certification schemes that would allow people to make food consumption choices that are more consistent with their ethical values. But because these concerns are addressed systematically in other contributions to this volume, my focus is on the component of the food system that may tend to get overlooked in a survey of side effects. That is the person who makes the primary, ground-level decisions about how crops will be produced: the farmer. Because much of what will be said about farmers is also true of people who manage livestock or who harvest food from the sea, my subject extends to ranchers and fishers—in short, to primary producers in the food system.

Primary Producers as Subjects of Moral Concern: The Past

If side effects are now the main focus of food ethics, it is worth noting that it has not always been thus. Until relatively recently, the ethics of crop production has had two very different points of focus. First, there has been the obvious imperative of sufficiency: it has always been morally important to produce enough to meet people's needs. This was not a side effect of crop production; it was the intended purpose. If it is no longer the main reason for crop production, that is a point worth calling out and thinking about. Second, after sufficiency of production, the perspective of the past has seen farmers and other primary producers as themselves the primary subject of moral concern. I begin my discussion with this focus on farmers, before returning to the topic of sufficiency.

Two quotations from Thomas Jefferson will resonate with many. In his *Notes on the State of Virginia*, Jefferson refers to "those who labour in the earth" as the chosen people of God: "Corruption of morals in the mass of cultivators is a phaenomenon of which no age nor nation has furnished an example."[1] Perhaps even more famously Jefferson elsewhere describes farmers as "the most valuable citizens," and goes on to say, "They are the most vigorous, the most independent, [and] the most virtuous."[2] The alleged virtue of cultivators has been the basis of government programs intended to improve the lot of primary producers and to shield them from the vagaries of capricious nature and economic forces. This has not changed. On January 8, 2018, US President Donald J. Trump addressed the Farm Bureau, praising young farmers as "the future of our country" and promising that they would not bear the brunt of his administration's trade policy.[3]

Although many will regard recent statements from politicians with some degree of cynicism, Jefferson was serious. His views on farmers as appropriate subjects of moral concern were shared by Abraham Lincoln, who created programs to make land available to farmers, established publicly funded agricultural research efforts, and established the US Department of Agriculture, which he referred to as "the people's department." Farmers were viewed as appropriate targets of concern for a complex set of reasons. First, in Lincoln's and Jefferson's day, most of them were poor. Second, they were vulnerable to many forces beyond their ability to control or even anticipate. These included not only crop-destroying droughts or storms but also rapid shifts in supply and demand for the products of agriculture. Third, they were numerous, making up perhaps 80% of the US population in Jefferson's day and about 40% well into the 20th century.

Finally, food producers were seen to occupy a social position that was, as Jefferson asserted, linked to 18th- and 19th-century virtues. These links are not easy to perceive from the standpoint of the 21st century. One virtue is self-reliance. All these primary producers, including fishers, were notably less dependent on others for their basic sustenance. They could feed themselves, and they had survival skills that gave them an ability to persist even in highly isolated social environments. They were also viewed as being more fit for citizenship. As landowners and decision makers, the primary producer had a deep interest in the sustainability and the future of the polity. Unlike those with portable assets, farmers could not readily pick up and move when times got tough. It was this feature that made them valuable *as citizens,* difficult as it might be for us to include ownership of land as a criterion for becoming a citizen. The moral point was that far from simply looking for someone to create a job for them, they took a deeper interest in the way their country was actually being run because of the way that this particular form of property made their personal interests dependent on the survival of the state.

This is not to say that these elements contributing to the farmer's moral status were uncontroversial, even in the time of Jefferson and Lincoln. The operators of 18th- and 19th-century plantations were deeply embroiled in international trade and were practicing forms of agriculture that made them dependent on slavery. In the US context, this created a rift between the self-reliant New England farmers celebrated by Ralph Waldo Emerson and Southern planters, who became increasingly dependent on their ability to exploit field labor. It is this dark side of agrarianism that is most evident today. Jefferson has become at best an outdated figure whose notion of democracy has failed to keep pace with the times. In Lin-Manuel Miranda's *Hamilton,* Jefferson is still singing the blues when everyone else has moved on to rap. More darkly, he is seen as a misogynous racist who demanded sexual favors from his enslaved servant Sally Hemmings, while maintaining his lavish Monticello lifestyle by continuing to profit from the sale of slaves.

In fact, the moral reputation of farmers has fallen almost as far as Jefferson's own. Many if not all of the side effects that will be discussed throughout the rest of this volume can be laid directly on the doorstep of the primary producer. Although there is some perception that farmers' ability to do otherwise is constrained, it is farmers who use the chemicals, who abuse the animals, who pump the water, and who grow the food that creates public health problems. And most of all, it is farmers who employ the fieldworkers who suffer from forms of poverty and exploitation that, in the worst cases, are the moral equivalent of the enslavement practiced by Jefferson and his contemporaries. In the meantime, American farmers are themselves no longer poor. Now thoroughly embroiled in capitalistic profit seeking, industrial farmers are seen as dependent on government handouts and unable to exert the strength needed to address the host of moral problems that beset the 21st-century food system. Hence efforts like the Choose Food project seem necessary to save them from their own excess.

Primary Producers as Subjects of Moral Concern: The Present

Are there any words that today can be advanced on behalf of the farmer? It is important to consider this question before moving on to a more detailed accounting of the problems that need fixing. One place to start is to note that even if they are no longer poor or particularly numerous, even industrial-scale farmers are undertaking an economically precarious activity. Economies of scale that are associated with both farm equipment and labor utilization have tended to place traditional household production farms of the past into an uncompetitive position with respect to larger farms. Even where technology does not yield an advantage to larger producers, buyers of farm commodities often prefer to deal with larger-sized producers as a way to manage transaction costs. The net effect has been to fuel a two-centuries-long shift in the farm-size distribution. Although small family farms continue to exist, the bulk of food production in industrialized farm economies is contributed by only 5%–20% of farms. Farms are thus still quite vulnerable, and analysts predict that current losses to the farm sector will predict a wave of farm bankruptcies comparable to what was seen in the late 1980s.

It is not just the farmers who suffer when things go south for farming. Loss of farm population is in turn a key source of poverty, unemployment, and decline in service-sector business, schools, churches, and other institutions for rural areas. Farmers are described as "price-takers," not price-setters. Even if employment conditions for farm labor remain a moral issue, it is nevertheless crucial to put this issue into a context that recognizes the way in which most farmers cannot pass an increase in production cost on to the buyers of their products. Thus, even if many of the factors that made Lincoln describe the USDA as "the people's department" no longer hold, primary production is still vulnerable to the vicissitudes of weather and the market. And if farmers are now less than 2% of the population in many industrialized countries (including the United States), this is not to say that farm operators are the only ones who are hurt when things go badly.

We must also remind ourselves that on a global basis many of Lincoln's reasons for regarding farmers as moral subjects still hold. Globally, primary producers still make up 80% of the population in much of Africa, and 40% of the population even in much of South America and the rapidly industrializing countries of Asia and the Indian subcontinent. More importantly from an ethics perspective, farmers constitute between one-half and three-quarters of those who live at or below the World Bank standard for extreme poverty, earning less than $2 per day. Thus, even if this is not the picture we see in North America, farmers still are poor, numerous, and highly vulnerable when viewed across the full range of today's planet-wide food system.[4]

There are also factors of structural inequality that are more evident today than they might have been in Lincoln's time. When viewed from a global basis, many—perhaps more than half—of the world's farmers are women. As such they have suffered not only from the prejudices of colonizing governance strategies, which tended to presume that men were the key decision makers, but they continue to face legal and financial systems that do not give them standing or recognize their full status as property owners or economic agents eligible for credit. Racial and ethnic inequalities also track with poverty and as such fall disproportionately on primary producers in many parts of the world.[5]

What is more, it is these primary producers who also bear the brunt of climate change, experiencing increased variance in weather that can take the form of drought, on the one hand, or damaging events like hail and flooding, on the other. Again, because they make up a disproportionate share of the poor and vulnerable outside the industrialized nations, the people who are growing crops, raising animals, and fishing in treacherous waters are the ones most exposed to the risks of rising sea levels, increased temperatures, and greater unpredictability in weather events. These producers face the challenges of climate change on a day-to-day basis and are more keenly attuned to humanity's dependence on the natural world. As such, whether the 19th-century views of farmer virtue can be maintained or not, farmers are harbingers of environmental vulnerability that might well be seen as a contemporary form of valuable consciousness worth of emulation by all.

Plant Production, Food Security, and the Future

The issues noted throughout this volume notwithstanding, plant production systems *have* been able to outpace increases in global food needs due to population growth, at least when measured on a total global productivity basis. This observation is often cited in support of industrial monoculture production systems, and it should not be dismissed lightly. This trend in total productivity has been based on a continuous stream of technological innovations that have consistently increased per acre and per unit of labor yields in plant production systems (though sometimes at the health and environmental cost noted previously). Standards for addressing health and environmental externalities should not lose sight of the need to maintain and, indeed, continue to increase plant production (if we assume no significant decrease in per person needs due to the adoption of vegetarian diets). Three drivers for this are continued human population growth, increases in per-person consumption due to increasing wealth, and declines in the production of existing plant production systems due to climate change.

Nonetheless, lack of secure access to healthy and appropriate foods remains a significant problem for food systems across the globe. To an important extent, these issues are addressed under the heading of public health. A significant part of the problem for food-insecure people in urban areas must be laid on the doorstep of social institutions and economic structures that cannot be tied directly to current methods of plant production. They have to do with income inequalities and the poor's vulnerability to price fluctuations and macroeconomic phenomena (such as inflation). As such, these are not discussed here. However, there are two factors internal to plant production systems that are importantly related to food security. First, as noted more than half (and perhaps up to 75%) of those currently living at or below the World Bank standard for extreme poverty (one euro per day) either are farmers or have incomes closely dependent on the farm economy. Although poor farmers can produce much of what they need to eat, adverse effects on the plant production systems can cause immediate and catastrophic threats to their food security. These threats can take many forms, including losses in productivity of the crops they are growing for their own household consumption and also declines in the prices they receive for that portion of their crops they sell due to increased (and often subsidized) competition from industrial producers in wealthy countries. It should be noted that traditional food aid also depresses their markets, having an ironic and tragic impact on smallholder farms.

The second issue to note is crop selection, also a complex issue. Factors influencing crop selection include farmer knowledge, local climate and soil conditions, and availability of seeds or other inputs. However, government policies also have a significant influence on crop selection either directly, by mandating production of certain cash crops, or (more typically) through subsidies, loan guarantees, and other programs that influence which crops are grown. These policies can create local threats to food security, especially when they encourage production of nonfoods (fiber crops, biofuels) or high-value export crops, such as coffee or tea. More significantly, crop selection steered by government policy can have significant impact on the nutritional quality of diets even in industrialized economies. High consumption of sugars and fats in the United States has been linked to US commodity policies that have made these food items extremely cheap in comparison to healthier fruits and vegetables. Here, the impact on food security may occur less in terms of consumers' access to adequate calories as in the nutritional quality of their diets.

Conclusions

What, then, are we to make of all this? The first point to notice is that however much Jefferson himself may have gone out of favor, we should not give up on the idea that farmers themselves are subjects of moral concern entirely. Nor should we overlook the obvious point that the overall performance of the global food system is dependent on the viability of the farming way of life. As consumption-oriented food ethics has become more engaged with alternative supply chains that mitigate harms to animals, the environment, or workers, it *is* important to bear in mind that the world has to eat. Many food system insiders have the flattery of Jeffersonian rhetoric to occlude their awareness of growing problems. They derive what Robert Zimdahl has called an unwarranted moral confidence in what they do. Their one-dimensional focus on "feeding the world" and the past record of success has made them insensitive to a growing list of problems with the contemporary food system.[6] But advocates of the Choose Food project cannot be seduced into the opposite mistake. It is important to produce enough, and doing so will face new challenges in an era of continued population growth and climate change. Most pertinent to the themes of the present chapter, we will probably need farmers to do that.

And if we are going to have farmers, we will need to treat them fairly. This is not, of course, a new idea, nor is it unknown to the ethical consumption movement. Programs for ensuring that small-scale producers receive a fair rate of return for their products are, in fact, a signature element in ethical consumption programs. This is so much true that one might think that the main thing to do is simply to *add* elements of environmental and animal protection, or public health to the already effective product labels focusing on protecting farm labor and small farmers alike. These poor, numerous, and vulnerable farmers have been the subject of moral concern for successful consumer movements, especially in high-value commodities like coffee.

It is nonetheless important to issue reminders: The success of fair-trade schemes in a few products notwithstanding, these efforts have not penetrated most of the markets in which poor farmers are trying to sell their production on a global basis. What is more, because all these farmers are effectively forced to accept whatever price they are offered—even if it is a fair one—this particular form of ethical consumption has thus far done very little to redress the issues of gender inequality or structural factors that are the legacy of colonialism. Given the uncertainties that come with changes in the earth's climate system, the small farmers that fair-trade schemes seek to protect still face risks that could plunge them into receivership or worse, starvation, on an annual basis. It is not enough simply to assure a fair price. It will be necessary to strengthen farmers' economic position by protecting their land tenure and property rights and to reduce their vulnerability to fluctuations in the weather through technological innovation.

Unfortunately, these are strategies that can and sometimes do run afoul of the other four elements in the Core Ethical Commitments framework developed by the Choose Food project. Strengthening a producer's position can weaken an employee's, and some of the ways we have tried to help farmers have actually turned out to increase environmental vulnerabilities and harm animals. And there is an even more enduring tension between things that benefit the producer and things that lower the cost of food for consumers. The complexity of food systems means that efforts to do one good thing may turn out to do bad things in some other arena. This is not a reason to give up or even to slow down, but bearing in mind the vulnerabilities of the farmer will prove to be a caution that ethical consumption must bear.

REFERENCES
1. Thomas Jefferson and Merrill D. Peterson, *Writings* (New York: Library of America, 1984), 290.
2. Jefferson and Peterson, *Writings,* 818.

3. Roy Graber, "7 Quotes from President Trump to Farm Bureau," WATTAg-Net, January 9, 2018, https://www.wattagnet.com/blogs/27-animal-agribusiness-angle/post/33143-quotes-from-president-trump-to-farm-bureau.

4. Food and Agriculture Organization of the United Nations (FAO), *The State of Food and Agriculture* (Rome: FAO, 2017), http://www.fao.org/3/a-I7658e.pdf.

5. For a more detailed discussion, see Paul B. Thompson, *From Field to Fork: Food Ethics for Everyone* (New York: Oxford University Press, 2015).

6. Robert L. Zimdahl, *Agriculture's Ethical Horizon*, 2nd ed. (Amsterdam: Academic Press, 2012).

FIFTEEN

Ethics over Exploitation

Urgent Moral Issues Associated with Labor
and Communities in the Food System

NICOLE M. CIVITA

Exploitation in Service of Nourishment

Although many aspects of food production have been mechanized since the dawn of the Industrial Revolution, humans have not completely in-novated their way out of contributing the labor of their species to gen-erate sustenance. Human labor remains necessary for a wide range of production activities throughout the food chain. In horticulture, man-ual and machine-assisted and technology-supported labor is employed in cultivating land and preparing other growing media, seeding and planting, and weeding and pruning, as well as harvesting seed, feed, and raw food items. In animal agriculture—which includes livestock raised for not only meat and milk but also fiber and hide; poultry raised for meat and eggs; farmed aquatic animals; and edible and beneficial insects—humans are involved in breeding, tending, feeding and water-ing, milking, housing, maintaining herd or flock health, and slaughter-ing. Wild fisheries use human labor on waterborne vessels for the for-aging of wild fish and seafood. A much smaller but not insignificant amount of land-based food is hunted or foraged by humans. Once pro-duced or collected, humans are involved in the processing of all of these raw products and moving them through markets to consumers.[1] As we face the challenges of sustainably producing and providing access to sufficient food to meet the needs of a rapidly growing human population on a warming planet with an increasingly volatile climate and dwindling natural resource base, human labor, skill, and stewardship become more critical.

Millions of food chain workers involved in the daunting and ceaseless tasks of feeding the global population of humans, livestock, and domesticated animals perform hard physical labor for long hours in the unsheltered outdoors. They work in perilously close proximity to toxic chemicals, powerfully built animals, and dangerous machinery, often performing tasks that are repetitive and may require them to labor in contorted positions that place stress on the musculoskeletal system.[2,3] In the United States, farm work is the most hazardous occupation and commercial fishing is among the deadliest, with a fatality rate 29 times higher than the national average.[4,5] Between exposure to the elements, pesticides, herbicides, fungicides, fertilizers, noise, pathogens (including strains that have developed resistance to medically important antimicrobials), the physically taxing and high-risk nature of the work, the low regard in which their work is held, and impoverished access to health care, it is not surprising that food chain workers have disproportionately poor health outcomes.

For this, most are paid poverty wages and receive no medical benefits or paid sick days.[6] In 2016 in the United States, for example, median earnings for workers in the food system were the third lowest in the national economy at $16,000 per year and lowest in terms of hourly wages—just $10 per hour.[7] Moreover, at the production level, many perform seasonal work and have few opportunities to earn wages for several months of each year; some must migrate long distances in search of temporary work on farms, traveling north as the growing season unfolds.[8]

Because they earn such low wages (and because they often work in remote, rural locales with limited affordable housing inventories), many food chain workers are unable to find and secure access to clean, structurally sound, safe, and reasonably private housing, with running water, electricity, and telecommunications service. These workers often have no choice but to rent space in dilapidated buildings that are crammed full of far more people than legal occupancy levels allow.[9] Migrant workers, in particular, may be required to stay in employer-provided (also known as "grower-owned") housing, made available only at above-market rent and/or board rates.[10]

On top of this, food chain workers may not have access to reliable transportation. Among farmworkers, transportation is often operated by their employers, which makes it challenging to access healthcare and other essential services, shop for affordable food and toiletries, and participate in community activities. Restaurant and retail sector workers, on the other hand, often live far from their workplaces and rely on public transportation, which may provide reduced service at their typical commuting hours. Moreover, cultural and language barriers drive social isolation, which can be especially difficult to combat in the remote, rural areas where food is typically grown and processed.[11]

Few food chain laborers enjoy or are able to exercise rights to collective organization, action, or bargaining.[12] In the United States, farmworkers are expressly excluded from the National Labor Relations Act and enjoy the right to unionize only in states that have explicitly extended such protection. According to the Bureau of Labor Statistics, only 1.3% of the workforce employed in food services and drinking establishments and 2.4% of workers in farming, forestry, and fisheries (combined) were unionized in 2018—far less that the (still low) 10.5% unionization rate for the overall US workforce.[13] Unionization and other tools for increasing worker voice are thought to be critical for improving wages and workplace safety.[14] Organizing and efforts to enhance work voice can also lead to more fair and equitable workplaces, a matter of urgent concern given that food chain workers are subjected to racism, sexism, harassment, assault, and other discriminatory and retaliatory conditions at alarming rates.[15,16,17]

Worse yet, a shocking number of people—more than 3.5 million modern-day slaves—are trafficked, coerced, and forced to contribute hard labor to agriculture and food production. Forced labor is especially prevalent in certain supply chains and regions—for example: cocoa, coffee, nuts, soybeans, sunflowers, and sugarcane produced in Africa and

Latin America; rice produced in Africa and India; palm oil harvested in Asia; cattle raised in Latin America; and poultry produced in Thailand—among many other internationally traded products.[18] Additionally, many fisheries, especially those based in Asia and Africa, maintain their workforce through trafficking of vulnerable migrants and make routine use of forced labor secreted aboard fishing vessels, where isolation of the workplace and tense competition in the industry allow the deplorable practice to fester.[19] But contemporary food-related slavery is not just a developing-world phenomenon. In recent years, deeply disturbing instances of slavery in Florida's tomato fields were revealed and successfully prosecuted.[20] Despite being near universally reviled and condemned for well over a century, slavery—the paradigmatic expression of human exploitation—remains alive and well throughout the food system.[21] Today, thanks to long, globe-traversing supply chains that obscure the vile institution from most consumers' view, slavery is simply less obvious than it once was. Forced labor persists in agriculture precisely because indecent and "disastrous norms" of farm and food chain laborer treatment are all too close to the conditions of enslavement.[22] Moreover, the dramatic asymmetries of power, resources, social capital, and political influence between individual laborers and multinational growers, fishers, and processors enable coercion under relatively good circumstances, exploitation at the hands of less scrupulous players, and abject slavery in the worst cases.

Moreover, child labor is disproportionately prevalent in the food system: 70% of the more than 150 million child laborers around the world work in agriculture. Child labor is especially pernicious because childhood is a special developmental period of unparalleled cognitive, emotional, and physical growth, as well as socialization and discovery. These tender years should be a time for receiving nurturance, playing, cultivating curiosity, and participating in formal education, informal learning, and cultural knowledge transfer. While it is never acceptable to exploit other human beings, children are uniquely vulnerable and deserving of especially protective treatment to increase the likelihood that they are able to mature into healthy, happy, productive, well-socialized adults. That said, not all work by youth in the food system amounts to illicit and unethical child labor. The kinds of enriching family and community-integrated, age-appropriate, nonhazardous work that supports transmission of traditional knowledge and cultural identity are excluded from the definition of child labor and the estimates of the International Labour Organization (ILO). A child's performance of light duties in family enterprises or subsistence settings and time-limited participation in well-supervised, age-appropriate job-training for limited hours can contribute to education and food security. Context and culturally appropriate light duties that directly and meaningfully contribute to a child's security and welfare aside, the ILO estimates that millions of children are laboring in the food system to the benefit of multinational corporations and their own detriment. This is a matter of serious ethical concern that both causes actual harm to youth today and impairs their prospects for thriving and living to their full potential in the future.

Scoping and Characterizing Food Chain Labor

Because the scale, style, and structure of agriculture and food production vary tremendously around the globe, it is difficult to accurately estimate the number of people who labor to produce food. Yet reviewing some labor estimates in various segments of the food chain can provide valuable perspective. Looking at the primary production sector of the food system, the ILO estimates that 1.1 billion people are engaged in agriculture. This estimate includes roughly 300-500 million waged workers, large numbers of casual and temporary workers engaged by small and large growers, and unpaid family members who carry out agricultural work as unrecognized farm labor or to support small-scale family farming, and segments of the rural poor who engage in agriculture for subsistence, but it does not include those who either volunteer in community food production or those who are forced to labor in the food system.[23] Agriculture accounted for 31% of global employment in 2013, down from 45% in 1991.[24] More than 58 million additional people are engaged in the primary sector of capture fisheries and aquaculture.[25] Food and drink processing—which accounted for 4% of world GDP—employs at least another 22 million people.[26] Credible estimates indicate that some 3.5 million people are trafficked or enslaved and compelled to perform agricultural labor (inclusive of fisheries and forestry), with additional forced laborers in food processing.[27]

It is difficult to make useful generalizations about the nature of food chain laborers' experiences, challenges, and vulnerabilities. Attempts to compare the status of a varied people who labor throughout the food chain yields little insight. Consider the likely differences between the experiences of the following food chain workers:

- a second-generation landowner and farm business operator of a large commodity field corn operation in Illinois and his wife;
- a young male Ghanaian smallholder farmer producing cacao for a cooperative;
- a female Mexican migrant farmworker with an H2A visa who is paid a piece-rate for handpicking strawberries in Washington;
- an undocumented dairy worker from Central America who milks cows and manages manure year-round in Northern Vermont;
- a female Somali refugee who breaks down chickens on a poultry processing line in Minnesota;
- a trafficked child forced to work on a forage fish trawler off the coast of Thailand;
- an indigenous Budjiti community practicing regenerative carbon farming in the Paroo River region of Australia; or
- a partnered pair of queer first-generation farmers raising heritage breed sheep and turkeys in the United Kingdom.

Although the labor demands, lived experiences, and legal protections in each situation are widely divergent, their plights connect on our plates. Thus, in a globally interconnected food system, any attempt to inventory and assess the ethical issues associated with labor and communities must make an honest attempt to account for these diverse experiences. To this end, it is helpful to keep the following big-picture principles in mind: ·

- Fundamental Human Rights: The conditions of food chain work must honor the inherent dignity and equal, inalienable rights of all people. Conditions of work should be fully consonant with the Universal Declaration of Human Rights.
- Legal Status and Protections: Legal status or equivalent protections must support human liberty, security, access to justice, and realization of fundamental human rights. Workers must be free to exercise individual and collective voice.
- Working Conditions: Working conditions must be humane, safe, and decent. Workers must have regular access to sufficient food, water, facilities for hygienic needs, and opportunities for respite. Occupational hazards must be reduced whenever possible to minimize both immediate acute injuries and long-term health risks. Training must be provided, and risks must be communicated in ways that are comprehensible to workers across language, literacy, and cultural barriers. Channels for communication and reporting must be open and accessible to all workers without reprisal.
- Compensation and Benefits: Food chain work must be fairly compensated. At a minimum, full-time work must yield sufficient income to maintain an adequate, if modest, standard of living in the region where the work is being performed. Food chain workers must receive equal compensation and benefits, irrespective of nationality, race, color, gender, or other sociodemographic status.
- Standards of Living and Well-Being: Food chain work must not impair the ability of an individual or community to thrive. Food chain workers should not be isolated from each other and from other members of the communities in which they live and work. Isolation is a key risk factor for abuse and trafficking. Integration helps dismantle discrimination. Connection and integration also make the act of consuming the fruits of others' labor more ethical. Food chain workers should have physical, economic, and social access to nutritionally adequate and culturally appropriate foods. Where relevant and appealing, food chain

workers should be able to access the very foods that they help to produce.

- Community Safety and Connectedness: Food production and processing practices must not create negative externalities that degrade the quality of life for workers, their families, and the surrounding communities. Indeed, food chain work should enhance rather than degrade the quality of life, bodily integrity, and mental health of workers and their families. Employment and work practices should facilitate, not impair, access to adequate housing, appropriate education, and community connectedness.

Food-Chain Labor and Consumer Choice

The conditions under which food chain laborers across the globe toil, the economic challenges that these laborers face, and the degree to which their freedoms are curtailed or abrogated call into question the ethics of even the most environmentally sustainable, health-supporting food. Conscientious consumers—those who are particularly deliberative and morally motivated about their food choices—consider values-based factors in addition to the typical biological (hunger, appetite, taste, nutrition), economic (cost, income, availability), physical (education, skills, time), social (culture, family, peers, meal patterns), and psychological (mood, stress, guilt) determinants of food choice.[28] Desires to limit exposure to agrichemical residues, concerns for animal welfare, avoidance of "industrial food," and preferences for buying directly from area farmers and supporting local economies often influence the food choices of conscientious eaters.[29]

Mindful regard for the human beings involved in the production and preparation of food is a far less frequent driver of individual food choices, even among highly conscientious eaters. Though egregious, this oversight is understandable because most of the human labor in food systems is functionally invisible to consumers. The work of farming, ranching, and food production overwhelmingly takes place in remote, rural regions with low populations and minimal tourism. Typically, consumers do not bear witness to the labor of agricultural and food chain workers; nor do they encounter nuanced accounts of their lives. Rather, the imaginations of consumers are often influenced by pastoral agrarian myths and idealized notions of the noble nature of farming or homespun nature of cooking. Moreover, as food moves from one node in the food chain to another on its way to market, the human-powered components of its production are anonymized. Finally, because all but a few jobs in the food chain are low-wage, low-profile endeavors requiring long hours of hard physical labor in the unsheltered outdoors, the types of labor performed by food chain workers rarely appeal to many job-seeking citizens of developed and upwardly mobile nations. In short, consumers rarely have the kinds of relevant personal experiences that would generate empathy, activate concern, and prompt protective advocacy for those who labor to produce food.

Consumers are not alone in their passivity or deliberate incuriosity about the plight of food chain workers. These questions also tend not to receive a level of attention adequate to generate nuanced appreciation and prompt corrective action by upstream actors in the food system, such as suppliers, manufacturers, and retailers. On a very pragmatic level, this lack of action is commercially reasonable: (1) many ethical problems related to food chain labor lack easy, straightforward solutions, and the solutions that do exist can be very expensive to implement; (2) acknowledging such ethical problems may lead to negative publicity and a tarnished brand reputation; and (3) thanks to the logic of markets, if consumers have not expressed a strong interest in worker well-being and are not rejecting products on the basis of their association with or derivation from exploitative labor practices, companies lack their primary incentive to act with urgency. Nevertheless, until widespread, active, or sustained concern for the ethical treatment of food chain laborers is expressed by both a coalition of upstream food system actors (including both companies and consumers) and by political actors, ethically unacceptable conditions for food chain workers will persist.

When it comes to food chain labor, there are many big-picture "infrequently asked questions," that both the agrifood industry and consumers should consider:

- Who produces food that is ultimately brought to market?
- Who controls and manages human food system inputs?
- How is compensation for food chain labor allocated and awarded?
- Who profits from food chain labor and in what proportion?
- Who shoulders negative externalities of food production and food chain work?
- How does the work of food production variously affect owner-operators and food chain workers, as well as their families and their communities?
- How can the agricultural sector's need for a seasonal and mobile workforce be balanced against the needs that workers and families have for permanence, community connectedness, and access to education?
- Who should guard against harm to presently living persons in surrounding communities?
- Who should guard against intergenerational harms? And how?
- How can food chain workers—individually and in community— enjoy liberty, safety, and rights of self-determination?
- Is it ethical for a society and its economy to benefit from the labor of undocumented, unauthorized, potentially stateless workers who lack the basic protections of citizenship or legal status?[30]

Making such inquiries and engaging in thoughtful dialogue on these topics are important first steps. But as we attempt to craft actionable solutions, we must also acknowledge and work to address an array of complicating factors.

Complicating Factors

In developing any information-based governance scheme for food products or businesses that aims to capture the ethical concerns with food chain labor and related community issues, there are numerous complicating factors, which can be grouped into the following concerns.

Assessment of Ethical Performance

Ethical assessment of a particular food product will require aggregation of ethical treatment of laborers throughout the food chain and, in many cases, across the globe. The number of hands involved in the production of food before it arrives on our plates—and the desire to improve working conditions for as many of the implicated food chain laborers as possible—may make assessment in the aggregate quite challenging, especially for products consisting of multiple ingredients, processing aids, and packaging sourced from suppliers around the world. Additionally, given the wide range of human labor that must be performed throughout the food chain, different or supplemental standards or assessment criteria may be needed at various nodes of the food chain to narrow particular opportunities for exploitation or confirm the absence of previously well-documented unethical practices. For example, slaughter workers and meatpackers may need support to deal with the psychological and emotional impact of their inherently violent work to prevent them from becoming insensitive or susceptible to involuntary or coerced participation in acts of animal cruelty.[31] Also, fieldworkers and restaurant workers reliant on discretionary tips, especially female or nonbinary workers in these positions, may require special protection from and especially robust systems for reporting sexual harassment and assault.[32,33] One-size standards will not fit—or adequately protect—all laborers in the food chain.

To accomplish such rigorous and detailed assessment, a high degree of traceability—likely higher than currently practicable—is necessary to credibly assess ethical conduct. This is of particular concern with regard to the conditions of labor along many dimensions. Unlike other domains, information regarding worker, family, or community well-being is not already well documented or publicly available via existing record keeping, labeling, or disclosure requirements.

To deal with the data-paucity concerns, one could simply link ethical assessment to compliance with the labor laws or protections of the jurisdiction where work is performed. But this approach is unavailing and insufficient because: (1) in a trans-jurisdictional food system, the standards will vary tremendously, resulting in uneven and inequitable protections, and (2) the imposition of a single standard may either prompt sinking to a lowest common denominator or make production in certain locations infeasible. Moreover, any compliance-oriented approach to ethical assessment is likely to paint too pretty a picture because many matters of ethical concern are not the subject of any regulation, let alone sufficiently protective regulation. Thus, ethical disagreement can be expected about whether employers should be lauded for basic compliance with existing but often breached and underenforced legal standards that aim to protect workers, even though many such standards afford special treatment to agricultural employers. Additionally, given the well-documented pattern of underenforcing labor protections in many countries (including the United States), lack of a documented violation is not probative evidence of compliance. It may simply mean that a bad actor has not been caught or brought to justice.

Because of the challenges associated with a legalistic approach, it is tempting to look to private governance mechanisms as an assessment tool, relying on third- or first-party certifications, participation in industry self-regulatory efforts, and similar programs to demonstrate more ethical conduct vis-à-vis workers. There will be substantial ethical disagreement about whether employers should be recognized and rewarded for participation in standards and programs that make incremental progress yet do not alter the basic fact that the affordable abundance throughout the globalized food system is often dependent on exploitative labor practices.

Parsing and Protecting Food Chain Worker's Well-Being

Food chain worker health and well-being are difficult to characterize, let alone measure or quantify. Moreover, working conditions are far from the only determinant of food chain laborer health and well-being. Given the complex, dynamic, and interconnected etiology of the well-being of food chain workers, how should we attempt to assess contribution of working conditions to good or ill physical and mental health of diversely constituted populations? This is especially challenging because people may find themselves in the population we aim to protect, at least in part, because of preexisting trauma and vulnerabilities.[34]

There is also a tension between increasing food chain worker, family, and community well-being and protecting the food security of these groups. Adequately addressing unethical labor practices throughout the food chain will almost certainly result in an increase in food prices. Rising food prices are to be expected in an ethical economy that internalizes rather than externalizes the true costs of production. However, we must remember that the laborers throughout the food system already struggle to routinely put food of any kind (let alone health-promoting and ethical food) on their tables.[35] When endeavoring to improve the working and living conditions of food-chain laborers, care must be taken to avoid decreasing their food security, which would undoubtedly cause harm.

As we seek to avoid negative unintended consequences, we must also remain cognizant of the risk that increasing worker protections and raising standards, including compensation and benefits, may push some farms toward further mechanization, eliminating certain categories of jobs (potentially replacing them with fewer jobs that require a different skill set and thus displacing entire categories of workers). Job elimination has the potential to worsen poverty in many parts of the world and may increase the resource intensity and green-house-gas footprint of production.

Parity

Even without moving all the way to a brave new AI-powered food system, new tensions will arise if food chain workers are lifted up. Societies and economies, particularly highly developed societies that enjoy robust economic activity, are dependent on workers "at the bottom." There will be ethical disagreement about what levels of compensation, benefits, and other protections are due to workers in "bottom rung" jobs. Additionally, ethical issues do not disappear when we merely raise wages and improve working conditions for those at the very bottom. Concerns about parity, upward mobility, and attractiveness of midlevel work will emerge after the bottom rung of this proverbial ladder gets raised.

Parity concerns extend beyond the relational dynamics between classes of workers; they also reach the relational dynamics and allocation of benefits as between farmers, ranchers, fishers, or other food system employers and their workers. Many owner/operators of food producing enterprises struggle alongside their workers. Margins are low; their working conditions are extremely rough. To account for this, we must look for ways to make the work of farming and food production more fundamentally fair and humane. Doing so will require careful examination of who is in a position to make the necessary changes and critical assessment of the methods most likely to propel such changes. Here it can be helpful to look at shared value or linked prosperity models, such as the Equitable Food Initiative (see chapter 16).

Relative Hardship

Migrant and seasonal workers may face conditions on farms or in processing plants that seem deplorable to Americans but may be far less perilous or more just than the circumstances they currently face in their countries of origin. This raises critical questions: *Do ethical problems related to particular food-chain labor practices shrink relative to unjust conditions in alternative situations?*

One of the leading drivers of human migration is the search for employment. Countries with robust agricultural and food processing economies and limited citizen interest in jobs within the sector often see large waves of immigration. Thus, we must also ask ourselves: *Is it ethical for a society and its economy to benefit from the labor of undocumented, unauthorized, potentially stateless workers who lack the basic protections of citizenship or legal status?* While others may disagree, this author answers both questions with a resounding "no."

Conclusion

At this point, some readers will feel overwhelmed by the number of ethical problems, the current treatment of laborers in the food system, and the additional challenges that surface when we try to address them.

Others will look at this morass and see an array of opportunities to improve the lives of food chain workers, their families, and their communities. The latter view—if born not just of interest and optimism but also of moral conviction—enables the pursuit of ethical improvement. By considering the interconnected nature of the ethical challenges laid bare in this volume, identifying the circumstances (including powerful cultural notions and prevailing norms) that allow food chain worker mistreatment to persist, centering on our collective dependence on food chain workers, cultivating empathy for these workers, and committing to make change within our respective spheres of influence, we can choose ethics over exploitation.

REFERENCES

1. Food Chain Workers Alliance (FCWA), "The Hands That Feed Us: Challenges and Opportunities for Workers along the Food Chain," June 6, 2012, http://foodchainworkers.org/wp-content/uploads/2012/06/Hands-That-Feed-Us-Report.pdf.

2. Arthur L. Frank et al., "Issues of Agricultural Safety and Health," *Annual Review of Public Health* 25, no. 1 (2004): 225-45.

3. Nicole Civita, "How Should Physicians Help Patients Who Are Ill Because They Work in Agriculture?," *AMA Journal of Ethics* 20, no. 10 (October 2018): E932-40.

4. National Institute for Occupational Safety and Health (NIOSH), "Worker Safety on the Farm," DHHS (NIOSH) Publication No. 2010-137, April 2010, http://www.cdc.gov/niosh/docs/2010-137.

5. National Institute for Occupational Safety and Health (NIOSH), "Commercial Fishing Safety," https://www.cdc.gov/niosh/topics/fishing/.

6. Bon Appétit Management Company Foundation and United Farm Workers (UFW), "Inventory of Farmworker Issues and Protections in the United States," March 2011, http://www.ufw.org/pdf/farmworkerinventory_0401_2011.pdf.

7. Food Chain Workers Alliance (FCWA), "No Piece of the Pie: US Food Workers in 2016," November 2016, http://foodchainworkers.org/wp-content/uploads/2011/05/FCWA_NoPieceOfThePie_P.pdf.

8. Seth Holmes, *Fresh Fruit, Broken Bodies: Migrant Farmworkers in the United States* (Berkeley: University of California Press, 2013).

9. Thomas A. Arcury et al., "Safety, Security, Hygiene and Privacy in Migrant Farmworker Housing," *New Solutions: A Journal of Environmental and Occupational Health Policy* 22, no. 2 (2012): 153-73.

10. National Farmworker Ministry (NFWM), "Farm Worker Issues: Housing," http://nfwm.org/resources/housing/.

11. Holmes, *Fresh Fruit*.

12. Julie Yates Rivchin, "Building Power among Low-Wage Immigrant Workers: Some Legal Considerations for Organizing Structures and Strategies," *New York University Review of Law & Social Change* 28, nos. 3-4 (2004): 397-430.

13. Bureau of Labor Statistics, "News Release: Union Report-2018," January 2019, https://www.bls.gov/news.release/pdf/union2.pdf.

14. Thomas A. Kochan et al., "Worker Voice in America: Is There a Gap between What Workers Expect and What They Experience?," *ILR Review* 72, no. 1 (January 2019): 3-38.

15. Bon Appétit Management Company Foundation and UFW, "Inventory."

16. FCWA, "The Hands That Feed Us."

17. *Rape in the Fields* (PBS Frontline, 2013), https://www.pbs.org/wgbh/frontline/film/rape-in-the-fields/.

18. U.S. Department of Labor, "List of Goods Produced by Child Labor or Forced Labor," https://www.dol.gov/sites/default/files/documents/ilab/ListofGoods.pdf.

19. International Labour Organization (ILO), "Caught at Sea: Forced Labor and Trafficking in Fisheries," 2013, http://www.ilo.org/wcmsp5/groups/public/---ed_norm/---declaration/documents/publication/wcms_214472.pdf.

20. Sean Sellers and Greg Asbed, "The History and Evolution of Forced Labor in Florida Agriculture," *Race/Ethnicity: Multidisciplinary Global Contexts* 5, no. 1 (2011): 29-49.

21. Stefan Gold, Alexander Trautrims, and Zoe Trodd, "Modern Slavery Challenges to Supply Chain Management," *Supply Chain Management: An International Journal* 20, no. 5 (2015): 485-94.

22. Sellers and Asbed, "History and Evolution of Forced Labor."

23. International Labor Office, *Key Indicators of the Labour Market*, 9th ed. (Geneva: International Labour Office, 2016).

24. ILO, *Key Indicators*.

25. FCWA, "The Hands That Feed Us."

26. International Labour Organization, "The Impact of Global Food Chains on Employment in the Food and Drink Sector," 2007, https://www.ilo.org/wcmsp5/groups/public/---ed_dialogue/---sector/documents/meetingdocument/wcms_161663.pdf.

27. International Labour Organization, "ILO Global Estimate of Forced Labour: Results and Methodology" (Geneva: ILO, 2012).

28. European Food Information Council (EUFIC), "The Determinants of Food Choice," https://www.eufic.org/en/healthy-living/article/the-determinants-of-food-choice.

29. Jessica L. Johnston, Jessica C. Fanzo, and Bruce Cogill, "Understanding Sustainable Diets: A Descriptive Analysis of the Determinants and Processes That Influence Diets and Their Impact on Health, Food Security, and Environmental Sustainability," *Advances in Nutrition* 5, no. 4 (July 2014): 418-29.

30. This list a highly abridged sample of the exercise in moral mapping—raising ethical questions about the human dimensions of food production, processing, and provisioning, as well as exploring challenges to assessing ethical performance of particular food system actors or food products—undertaken by this author. For a more detailed and complete list of infrequently asked questions see http://www.bioethicsinstitute.org/wp-content/uploads/2016/11/MoralMapLaborandCommunityIssues.pdf, which articulates and attempts to prioritize morally significant questions pertaining to the fundamental human rights, legal status and protections, working conditions, compensation, standard of living, and well-being of food chain laborers, their families, and their communities.

31. Jennifer Dillard, "A Slaughterhouse Nightmare: Psychological Harm Suffered by Slaughterhouse Employees and the Possibility of Redress through Legal Reform," *Georgetown Journal on Poverty Law & Policy* 15, no. 2 (Summer 2008): 391-408.

32. *Rape in the Fields.*

33. Catrin Einhorn and Rachel Abrams, "The Tipping Equation," *New York Times*, March 12, 2018, https://www.nytimes.com/interactive/2018/03/11/business/tipping-sexual-harassment.html.

34. Holmes, *Fresh Fruit.*

35. Kristen Borre, Luke Ertle, and Mariaelisa Graff, "Working to Eat: Vulnerability, Food Insecurity, and Obesity among Migrant and Seasonal Farmworker Families," *American Journal of Industrial Medicine* 53, no. 4 (2010): 443-62.

SIXTEEN

Equitable Food Initiative

PETER O'DRISCOLL

E QUITABLE FOOD INITIATIVE (EFI) is a nonprofit skill-building and certification organization designed to help farmworkers, growers, and major food buyers collaborate to produce safer food that is ethically grown. As farms comply with rigorous EFI standards to improve working conditions, food safety, and pest management,[1] the initiative creates higher levels of transparency throughout the fresh produce supply chain. EFI is predicated on the idea that standards and verification processes must create measurable value for farmworkers, growers, food companies, and consumers alike.

To support farms' compliance with our standards, EFI created the Leadership Training Program. On each farm we certify, a pair of EFI facilitators trains a "Leadership Team" of workers and managers to identify and address ongoing compliance issues. In addition to learning about the EFI program and standards, all team members gain valuable communication and problem-solving skills, which help them to collaborate in the workplace as well as in their families and communities. Our focus on worker engagement, continuous improvement, labor-management collaboration, and the linkage between food safety and decent working conditions sets EFI apart from other certification processes. EFI's key innovation has been to demonstrate that trained and incentivized farmworkers can address retail, government, and consumer concerns about working conditions, food safety, and pesticide use in the produce industry.

Characteristics of the North American Fresh Produce Industry

The North American fresh produce industry can be considered a microcosm of the broader global food system. The US produce industry employs some 1.6 million farmworkers, of whom up to 70% are undocumented.[2] The median family income is less than $20,000. Fruits and vegetables have been harvested in this country for centuries by abundant but undercompensated labor. The classic response to protect worker rights in the industry has been union organizing. However, over the past few decades there has been a secular decline in union membership across this country for various reasons. Wage demands from farmworkers are also harder to fulfill because growers retain a declining share of the food dollar: 30 years ago, a grower might have kept more than 30 cents of each dollar spent by consumers, but today it's closer to 15 cents.[3] Even if laborers organize to ask for higher wages, growers have less money to meet their demands.

Farmworkers in the United States are aging, and immigration enforcement has also thinned out the agricultural workforce. As a result, there is now major industry investment in robotics and other ways of replacing scarce workers whose children do not want to follow them into agriculture. Farm work is not seen as a career path or sufficiently respected as skilled labor. In the face of a serious labor shortage, growers worried about how to get their crop out of the field are turning increasingly to the H-2A guest worker program, which has tripled in size over the past 10 years.[4] Workers in legal guest worker programs are likely recruited in villages in Mexico, where they often pay thousands of dollars for the privilege of reaching US fields to pay off the debt they incurred to secure the job in the first place.[5] The issues of forced labor and unethical recruitment are a major risk to the produce industry.

Globalization is also shifting the US produce industry: 53% of the fruits and 31% of the vegetables we consume in the United States are now imported, and 45% of total produce imports come from Mexico.[6] The ethics of how farmworkers in produce supply chains are treated has become a more complicated and internationalized issue.

Challenges in the Produce Industry

We should all be eating more fresh produce. Besides having nutritional and disease-prevention benefits, a plant-based diet is more sustainable for the planet. Yet the industry is plagued by two persistent challenges. The first is food safety. According to the Centers for Disease Control and Prevention, fresh produce is responsible for 46% of the foodborne illness outbreaks in this country.[7] This is a huge issue for the retailers facing foregone sales of recalled products, legal settlement costs for those sickened by tainted produce, and brand reputation damage. The industry has been working to improve food safety for years by increasing audits and inspections, and yet the rates of contamination continue at high levels. The second challenge is widespread concern about labor abuse in produce supply chains. The *Los Angeles Times'* "Product of Mexico" series shook the industry in 2014 by shining a bright light on exploitation in Mexican export agriculture.[8]

EFI's Approach

When EFI's multi-stakeholder group came together to try to address both of these challenges, participants came up with an interesting proposition: rather than dismissing farmworkers as expendable factors of production, the industry should instead see them as a significant part of the solution to foodborne illness and labor violations. EFI's premise was that farmworkers who are trained and incentivized can help reduce the risk of food safety violations and labor abuses at the point of production. There are basic things farmworkers can do as they harvest and pack produce to reduce the risk of foodborne illness and create value for the sector. Examples include following basic sanitary practices, identifying and quarantining animal waste in the fields, and allowing workers not to harvest when they are sick. When farmworkers are given voice, agency, and participation in a farm's approach to these challenges, they can also address concerns around labor abuse by verifying for themselves that their rights are respected.

EFI's multi-stakeholder group, which includes retailers like Costco as well as unions like the United Farm Workers, spent three years (2008-11) developing rigorous standards around wage bonuses, working conditions, food safety, and integrated pest management. The core of the program is leadership training, which focuses on building teams on every farm that we certify and teaching them problem-solving, communication, and conflict-resolution skills that they can use to identify and resolve compliance issues with our standards. We then conduct third-party audits that lead to certification and the use of our "Responsibly Grown, Farmworker Assured" label. Most importantly, EFI has worker verification mechanisms between audits for continuous assurance of compliance with our standards. This formula of standards, leadership training, third-party certification, and worker verification creates real value and assurance for an industry that recognizes it has major risks regarding food safety and labor abuse in its supply chains.

EFI started with a common commitment across all stakeholder groups to work together in new ways to achieve a safer and more ethical food supply chain. But turning commitments into practical changes requires the alignment of stakeholder interests to create shared value. In terms of the value for retailers, supply chain assurance is a major focus. In increasingly complex and international supply chains, retailers seek the kind of transparency provided by a worker verification tool that assures retailers that their vendor requirements are being met on a continuous basis. Moreover, as they expand in today's globalizing environment, retailers need trusted suppliers who share their values and who can ensure continuity of quality and supply. Retailers also value opportunities to signal to their customers that they care about consumer safety and worker well-being and are taking concrete steps to satisfy consumer demand for product transparency.

For growers, EFI's value derives in part from building closer customer relationships and achieving "preferred supplier" status. Growers will always work to satisfy the requirements of their best customers. But there is also value in the culture change that happens when EFI creates a mechanism for collaborative workforce engagement. For example, EFI standards include zero tolerance for sexual harassment, which has reached epidemic proportions in agriculture.[9] On a farm we certified in California, the incidence of sexual harassment has gone down markedly, as evidenced by the growing number of women who work on the farm and talk about feeling safe in a way they didn't before. In a very tight labor market, the farm has been able to sustain its labor pool by hiring more women, as male workers bring their wives and family members to work. A culture of collaboration built to raise labor standards can also solve bottom-line business problems when growers invite workers to help solve challenges around productivity, retention, and quality.

Some of EFI's value for farmworkers derives from the skills that they gain. But training on its own is not enough; workers deserve to share in the added value they help create. EFI has developed a program through which participating retailers pay a modest premium—typically one to three cents per pound—for EFI-certified produce. A small part of that premium goes to EFI to help promote our work, but most of it is returned to farmworkers in the form of a wage bonus that rewards their continuous assurance and verification. Transparency in the supply chain goes both ways. EFI wants workers to know for whom they are harvesting, who is paying that premium, and why.

EFI's Impact

EFI is still a relatively new program: we certified our first farm in 2014 and have now certified more than 30 farms in Canada, Mexico, the United States, and Guatemala, with more farms pending. There are more than 30,000 workers employed on farms that are either certified or in the process. We have generated more than $8 million in worker bonuses, and we hope to see that number go up. We are working closely with Costco, Whole Foods, and Bon Appétit Management Company, and we are in discussion with some of the largest retailers in the country about joining our program.

Conclusion

Since that *Los Angeles Times* story about labor abuses on Mexican farms, the produce industry has made two significant moves in response to the exposé. First, the United Fresh Produce Association and Produce Marketing Association released an Ethical Charter on Responsible Labor Practices in 2018,[10] and industry leaders are actively encouraging buyers and growers to abide by it. Second, Mexican growers who export to the United States created a new trade association in Mexico (AHIFORES) that promotes social responsibility in agriculture.[11] Both are important developments, but the key is always going to be verifying meaningful changes in produce supply chains.

EFI's message to the produce industry is that we want to help meet these commitments by inviting workers to verify that suppliers are meeting higher standards for labor practices. Moving from commitments to practical change requires multi-stakeholder dialogue. Bringing everybody—workers, growers, retailers, consumers—to the table is essential. There has to be a focus on stakeholder interests and how those interests align if collaboration is to have impact in the market. For too long, some in the produce industry looked at farmworkers as expendable factors of production. The current labor shortage should be making clear that farmworkers are skilled workers who ought to have career opportunities. EFI is working to help the industry make sure that farmworkers are appropriately valued participants in the produce supply chain for their contributions both to compliance and to improved business performance.

REFERENCES

1. See, Equitable Food Initiative, "EFI Standards," https://equitablefood.org /efi-standards/, for Labor, Food Safety and Pest Management Standards.

2. Farmworker Justice, "Selected Statistics on Farmworkers," 2014, https:// www.farmworkerjustice.org/sites/default/files/NAWS%20data%20factsht%201 -13-15FINAL.pdf.

3. U.S. Department of Agriculture Economic Research Service, "Food Dollar Series," https://www.ers.usda.gov/data-products/food-dollar-series/.

4. Iris Figueroa, "H-2A Program Growing at Unprecedented Rate; Worker Protections at Risk," Farmworker Justice, October 30, 2018, https://www

.farmworkerjustice.org/fj-blog/2018/10/h-2a-program-growing-unprecedented
-rate-worker-protections-risk.

5. Colleen Owens et al., "Understanding the Organization, Operation, and
Victimization Process of Labor Trafficking in the United States," Urban Institute
and Northeastern University, October 2014, https://www.urban.org/sites/default
/files/publication/33821/413249-Understanding-the-Organization-Operation
-and-Victimization-Process-of-Labor-Trafficking-in-the-United-States.PDF.

6. Steven Zahniser, "U.S. Produce Imports from Mexico," October 16,
2018, https://migrationfiles.ucdavis.edu/uploads/farm-labor/2018/11/13
/ZahniserOct15.pdf.

7. John A. Painter et al., "Attribution of Foodborne Illnesses, Hospitaliza-
tions, and Deaths to Food Commodities by Using Outbreak Data, United States,
1998-2008," *Emerging Infectious Diseases* 19, no. 3 (March 2013): 407-15.

8. Richard Marosi, "Hardship on Mexico's Farms, a Bounty for US Tables,"
Los Angeles Times, December 7, 2014, http://graphics.latimes.com/product-of
-mexico-camps/.

9. *Rape in the Fields* (PBS Frontline, 2013), https://www.pbs.org/wgbh
/frontline/film/rape-in-the-fields/.

10. Produce Marketing Association and United Fresh Produce Association,
"Ethical Charter on Responsible Labor Practices," 2018, https://www.ethical
charter.com/.

11. Alianza Hortofrutícola Internacional para el Fomento de la Responsabili-
dad Social (AHIFORES), https://www.ahifores.com/.

SEVENTEEN

How Food Systems Support and Undermine Public Health, Nutrition, and Community Well-Being

Some Ethical Concerns and Controversies

'.ANNE BARNHILL

CONSUMPTION OF FOOD and the ways we produce and market food both support and undermine public health. This chapter gives a brief, broad overview of issues with the food system that are related to public health and nutrition. It discusses some of the ways that dietary patterns, agricultural practices, and food marketing practices affect public health and nutrition and also some of the attendant ethical issues and controversies. While the official topic of this chapter is public health and nutrition, at points it stretches beyond health and nutrition into community well-being more generally, touching on issues such as the quality of life of communities near farms and access to culturally significant foods. This chapter is a companion to the Core Ethical Commitments for Public Health and Community Well-Being.

The Ethical Importance of Health

The premise of this chapter is that public health matters ethically and that positive or negative impacts on public health therefore deserve ethical scrutiny. While this might seem obvious and uncontroversial, it's worth noting the ways in which health has ethical importance.

Health is a central dimension of individual well-being. Good health enables other valuable conditions of life: a life of normal length without excessive pain and suffering, the ability to engage in a wide range of jobs, family and caretaking roles, and other meaningful pursuits. Some might argue that a certain level of health is essential to leading a good life; at the very least, health makes it much easier to lead a good life. Health also has social value. Poor health has economic and social costs, including lost productivity, health care costs, and the costs associated with taking care of the ill, including financial and personal costs on families and communities. Because health has central importance in allowing people to pursue valuable opportunities and lead good lives, some ethicists argue that for a society to be a just society, all people must have meaningful opportunities to be healthy.[1,2]

Though health is clearly ethically important, this does not mean that risks to health are always unethical or should be eliminated. Health is not everything. There can be trade-offs between health and other dimensions of well-being: for example, some unhealthy food practices are nonetheless pleasurable and socially meaningful.[3] There can be trade-offs between health and other social values; for example, regulations and taxes to reduce the consumption of processed food could improve public health while restricting individual freedom to sell, buy, and use products.[4] Thus reducing risks to health is not always ethically desirable given the trade-offs involved, and we should expect stakeholders to disagree about what are ethically acceptable levels of health risk in light of the trade-offs involved. The trade-offs between health and other goods that are considered acceptable may also differ between societies.

Dietary Patterns, Undernutrition, and Overnutrition

The connection between food and health is obvious, of course: food is how we get nutrition and so is essential to health. Lack of nutritious food undermines an individual's health. Globally, 821 million people were undernourished in 2017, meaning they could not access enough food to meet dietary energy requirements.[5] Thus a most basic health-related concern with the food system is undernutrition, which exists at a significant level.

Overnutrition and overweight are also significant public health issues. The food system has changed dramatically during the past few decades, with more food being produced, increased processing of food, improved food distribution, larger portion sizes, pervasive food marketing, and increased consumption of food away from home. The ready availability of convenient, energy-dense foods in our daily lives (e.g., in schools, workplaces, gas stations, and stores) has contributed to overconsumption of these foods relative to energy needs, and rates of overweight and obesity have increased worldwide since the 1980s.[6,7,8] By 2016, 39% of adults were overweight, and 13% were obese worldwide, with significantly higher rates in some countries (e.g., 40% of adults in the United States are obese).[9,10,11] Overweight and obesity are associated with cardiovascular disease, diabetes, kidney disease, and multiple kinds of cancer and contributed to the death of 4 million people globally in 2015.[12]

The public health problem is not only overconsumption of not-so-healthy, high-calorie processed foods but also too *little* consumption of many kinds of healthy food, including fruits, vegetables, and whole grains. This is a result of practices all along the supply chain: fruits and vegetables are less heavily marketed, but also too few fruits and vegetables are grown for everyone to eat recommended amounts.[13] Recent research concludes that in order to achieve good nutritional outcomes globally, we must produce more fruits, vegetables, and other healthy foods.[14] But in addition to producing and eating more of some foods in order to improve public health, we need to produce and eat *less* of other foods—both to improve public health and to reduce the environmental impact of food production. The food system has significant environmental impacts—it is a major source of total greenhouse gas emissions, other forms of pollution, land use, and water use—and animal agriculture, particularly beef production, accounts for a vastly disproportionate share of these impacts. Thus researchers have concluded that to avoid the worst environmental impacts, we should significantly reduce consumption of animal-source food, and in particular red meat, relative to the levels consumed in high-income countries.[15,16,17] Bahadur et al. conclude: "For a growing population, our calculations suggest that the only way to eat a nutritionally balanced diet, save land, and reduce greenhouse gas emissions is to consume and produce more fruits and vegetables as well as transition to diets higher in plant-based protein."[18] Reducing consumption of red meat and animal source foods could improve the health of many populations in high-income countries, if red meat consumption is replaced with healthier (e.g., beans, legumes, or chicken) rather than not-so-healthy foods (e.g., sugary, high-calorie processed food). At the same time, it's important to recognize the value of animal source food for low-income populations at risk of malnutrition and stunting, whose health could be dramatically improved by greater access to animal source food (see chapter 2).

In sum, a most basic public health issue with the food system is producing the right mix of food to support nutritious diets for a growing global population and producing this food in a sustainable way, so that we can keep producing enough of it for successive generations.

Risks to Health and Well-Being from Agricultural Practices

Not just the *consumption* of food matters to public health. What happens elsewhere in the supply chain can support or undermine public health and well-being.

Food system activities are a major contributor to climate change, accounting for 19-33% of all global greenhouse gas emissions, and climate change in turn poses significant risks to public health.[19] As climates get warmer, this may increase vector-borne disease—more ticks carrying Lyme disease, more mosquitos carrying malaria—and climate change is increasing the incidence of heat waves and extreme weather events, which cause injury, illness, and death.[20,21] Climate change may reduce agricultural yields and agricultural productivity, which in turn poses risks to food security and, by extension, nutrition, health, and well-being.[22] Thus food systems pose risks to public health via climate change. Reducing the greenhouse gas emissions associated with the food system to acceptable levels will require, as discussed in the previous section, significant shifts in dietary patterns and agricultural production toward plant-based diets.

Specific agricultural practices can pose health risks for farmers and farmworkers. For example, farm work exposes workers to occupational health risks, including accidents, acute and chronic pesticide poisoning, and respiratory disease from exposure to dust.[23] Agricultural practices can also pose health risks to surrounding communities. For example, confinement animal operations produce large quantities of manure, which, when inadequately treated, can cause runoff and contaminate groundwater, potentially affecting both drinking water and surface water (lakes, streams). This runoff contains antibiotics, hormones, pesticides, heavy metals, fecal bacteria, and pathogens. Confinement operations also produce air emissions containing pollutants—including ammonia, hydrogen sulfide, methane, and particulate matter—which cause respiratory symptoms and disease in people in surrounding communities, potentially including asthma in children.[24,25]

Agricultural practices can reduce community well-being in other ways besides posing health risks. For example, communities surrounding confinement animal operations report a lower quality of life because of noxious smells and air pollution. As one study reports, "CAFO odors can cause severe lifestyle changes for individuals in the surrounding communities and can alter many daily activities. When odors are severe, people may choose to keep their windows closed, even in high temperatures when there is no air conditioning. People also may choose to not let their children play outside and may even keep them home from school. . . . Odor can cause negative mood states, such as tension, depression, or anger, and possibly neuropsychiatric abnormalities, such as impaired balance or memory."[26] At the same time, agriculture can be central to community identity and ways of life, and thus be essentially connected to a community's well-being.

Along with posing health risks to those directly involved in farm work and to surrounding communities, agricultural practices can pose risks to the health of the public at large. A primary example is the routine use of antibiotics in animal agriculture: animals are given antibiotics on a daily basis, even when they are not sick, in order to promote growth and prevent illness. This routine use of antibiotics spurs the creation of antibiotic-resistant bacteria ("super-bugs"), which are a major public health threat globally and in the United States, where two million people develop an antibiotic-resistant infection each year.[27] To give another example, agriculture is a major source of particulate matter in the air: fertilizers and animal waste release nitrogen compounds—for example, ammonia gas—that combine with other kinds of emissions in the air to form solid particles (particulate matter) that, when inhaled by humans, cause cardiovascular and pulmonary disease.[28,29,30] Food safety is another significant public health issue connected to agricultural practices, as consumption of food contaminated with bacteria, viruses, parasites, and chemical substances makes almost 10% of the global population sick each year and kills an estimated 420,000 people.[31] Food can be contaminated during agricultural production (e.g., because contaminated water is used in irrigation) or can be contaminated later in the food supply chain (e.g., during processing or transport).[32]

An additional, somewhat different way that agriculture can undermine public health is that new agricultural practices and forms of farming can displace existing agricultural practices and forms of food provisioning, as when a system of small farms producing a diverse mix of foods is replaced by large farms growing a smaller number of crops for an export market. When existing agricultural practices and food provisioning are displaced, such an outcome can threaten not only livelihoods but also food access and food security, thereby undermining nutrition as well as health and well-being for the affected populations. On the other hand, opening up new markets has the potential to improve livelihoods and increase food security and nutrition, and there can be significant empirical disagreement about specific cases. A case in point is the great quinoa controversy: when quinoa, a plant-based protein "super food," became more popular in the United States, did this help populations in Bolivia and Peru where quinoa was grown, by increasing their income and food security, or did it harm them, by increasing the price of a staple food and thereby reducing food security?[33,34]

Food Marketing

How foods are marketed affects what people consume and how much they pay for it and thus can affect their health and well-being, as a trip down the highway shows.

> Driving down the highway, we see dozens of drive through windows at fast food restaurants, billboards with advertisements for inexpensive snacks, and soft drinks at drugstores, and when we stop for gas, shelf after shelf of high-fat and high-sugar snacks at gas station mini marts. . . . A variety of good tasting snacks and meals are now highly visible and accessible for most Americans, and there is also evidence that since the 1970's, portion sizes have gotten larger, and far exceed federal guidelines. These foods are also extremely convenient compared with home made meals; fast food and packaged foods are easier to obtain and ready to eat immediately, as they require little preparation.[35]

What kinds of marketing are ethically acceptable and which ones cross the line is a matter of intense ethical disagreement. At play are issues of consumer autonomy, consumer well-being (including health and the economic and social dimensions of well-being), the public's interest in protecting public health, and the interests of companies in selling their products.

Truthfulness and Informativeness of Food Labeling

One area of ethical agreement is that food fraud, in which a food is intentionally labeled or marketed as a different food, is an unethical practice. Along with fraud and outright false claims, there is *misleading* marketing: marketing that does not contain a false claim, yet causes consumers to form false beliefs or impressions about the product. For example, research shows that when consumers see "natural" on a food label, they often assume that it is environmentally better, was produced without using synthetic pesticides, or has other attributes or benefits that "natural" does not actually denote.[36,37] Does this mean that use of "natural" on food labels should be more tightly regulated, so that it is used only on products possessing the range of attributes (e.g., not containing genetically engineered ingredients, not being grown with synthetic pesticides), or perhaps that the word "natural" should not be used on food products at all?

Even when marketing does not mislead or misinform consumers, it can still fail to inform them about the important attributes of a product. For instance, labels on food products could contain correct nutritional information but not present that information in a way that helps consumers easily understand the most important nutritional information or rapidly compare products. To improve consumers' access to nutritional information, the US Food and Drug Administration recently redesigned the Nutrition Facts panel, which is required on all packaged food, to include a larger font size for calories, list added sugar, and use serving sizes that reflect the servings people typically consume.[38] Expert groups have also examined front-of-package nutritional labels, and made recommendations for how those labels can clearly communicate nutrition information.[39]

Beyond nutritional information, a range of information about products and their production practices could help consumers make food choices better aligned with their values and preferences. Of all the information that could be useful to different groups of consumers, with their diverse values and preferences, which information should regulators require on food labels? Only information relevant to the health, safety, and economic value of the product? Or should a broader range of information be required, including information on labor, animal welfare, and environmental practices? Beyond the information that regulators require, what information should companies voluntarily include on their labels? An area of ongoing discussion and ethical disagreement is labeling of genetically engineered (GE) food. Opponents of mandatory labeling argue that many consumers falsely believe that GE food is less safe for human consumption and thus labeling of GE food will cause consumers to form the false conclusion that the food is less safe and to needlessly spend more money on non-GE food.[40] Proponents argue that most consumers want to know whether their food is genetically engineered and that this is useful information to many consumers, since they have a range of ethical reasons for preferring non-GE food besides concerns about human health and safety.[41,42]

Beyond misleading or uninformative marketing, various other marketing practices are objected to, for a range of ethical reasons. For example, the marketing of food products to children, and in particular the marketing of unhealthy foods, is objected to as particularly ethically problematic because children do not have the cognitive ability to understand marketing and interpret it correctly and because we have a special ethical responsibility to protect the health and well-being of children.[43,44]

Foundational Ethical Critiques of Food Marketing

Along with these ethical concerns about particular kinds of advertising, labeling, and marketing, there are much more basic objections to the industry formulating and aggressively marketing unhealthy food. A longstanding critique of advertising in general is that it is inherently manipulative; also, because it induces people to buy products they do not need, it thus can cause economic harm.[45,46,47] When the advertised products are consumed in ways that pose health risks—as with some food products—concerns about marketed products causing physical harm are layered on top of concerns about economic harm and manipulation.

What consumers eat is affected by how foods are labeled and advertised but also, of course, by the kinds of products that the food industry creates and offers for sale in the first place. Some object to the basic fact that companies create food products that are both unhealthy (because they are processed, high in calories, high in sugar, or high in sodium) and hard to resist (because they are highly palatable).[48,49] These foods, as well as their marketing, are ubiquitous in our daily environments. Beyond its marketing efforts, the food industry is also ethically critiqued for trying to obscure the health risks of its products, trying to shape public opinion so that the public embraces a free-market ideology and opposes regulation of the industry, and trying to control the policy process.[50,51]

This ubiquity of food and food marketing is a result of food companies' marketing efforts but also the policies adopted by governments, institutions, and retailers. A range of public health efforts aims to change the mix of foods available and how they are marketed. These include fiscal measures (e.g., taxes on sugary drinks), regulations (e.g., bans on the use of trans fat in restaurant food and packaged food, or new nutritional labeling requirements), efforts to increase access to healthier foods (e.g., giving retailers incentives and assistance to offer more fruits and vegetables), and efforts to decrease access to unhealthy foods (e.g., taking sugary drinks out of vending machines in schools).[52,53,54]

Another concern is that food companies are expanding into new markets and undermining public health in an ever widening range of places: if packaged, processed foods and convenience foods are introduced into new markets and heavily marketed, they can displace other ways of cooking and eating and cause increasing rates of overweight, obesity, and diet-related disease.[55,56] The displacement of traditional and local food practices may also diminish access to culturally important foods and participation in culturally important food practices. The ethics of displacement are complicated, however. How should we characterize the cultural impact, positive or negative, of an increase in consumption of packaged food products and a decline of traditional culinary practices? Should this be seen as a cultural loss of ethical concern or just a form of cultural change that is ethically neutral? Should it be characterized as an increase in consumer choice or a loss of communal control over valued cultural practices?

More generally, there is disagreement about how to characterize the marketing of foods that are consumed in ways that worsen public health. When companies engage in this food marketing, are they behaving unethically because this marketing harms consumers (by making them less healthy) and imposes significant social costs (because it worsens public health)? A counterargument is that companies are providing products that consumers want and that have evident value for consumers, health risks notwithstanding. Food is a source of nutrition, of course, but also a source of pleasure, psychological comfort, conviviality, and a way of expressing social identities and personal values.[57,58] When foods are convenient and cheap, this also has real value to consumers. If we recognize that health is not everything and that consumers have legitimate reasons for choosing foods that aren't healthy, what should we conclude about the ethics of marketing these foods? A rejoinder, in turn, is that we shouldn't assume that consumers make food choices that are reasonable and reflect their values. In fact, much eating is uninformed, habitual, and maybe even irrational. What we eat is influenced by environments, social norms, and our own psychology, including cognitive biases that produce irrational behavior.[59] When we eat foods that are not healthy or we adopt overall dietary patterns that increase our risk of poor health, we shouldn't assume that this is a deliberate choice reflecting a careful decision—that this dietary pattern, despite being unhealthy, has the most value for us.

REFERENCES
1. Madison Powers and Ruth R. Faden, *Social Justice: The Moral Foundations of Public Health and Health Policy* (Oxford: New York: Oxford University Press, 2006).
2. Norman Daniels, *Just Health: Meeting Health Needs Fairly* (Cambridge: Cambridge University Press, 2007).
3. Anne Barnhill et al., "The Value of Unhealthy Eating and the Ethics of Healthy Eating Policies," *Kennedy Institute of Ethics Journal* 24, no. 3 (September 2014): 187-217.
4. David Resnik, "Trans Fat Bans and Human Freedom," *American Journal of Bioethics: AJOB* 10, no. 3 (March 2010): 27-32.
5. FAO, ed., *The State of Food Security and Nutrition in the World 2018: Building Climate Resilience for Food Security and Nutrition*, State of Food Security and Nutrition in the World 2018 (Rome: FAO, 2018).
6. Boyd A. Swinburn et al., "The Global Obesity Pandemic: Shaped by Global Drivers and Local Environments," *Lancet* 378, no. 9793 (August 2011): 804-14.
7. Institute of Medicine (IOM) and National Research Council (NRC), *A Framework for Assessing Effects of the Food System* (Washington, DC: National Academies Press, 2015).
8. Anne Barnhill et al., "Grappling with Complex Food Systems to Reduce Obesity: A US Public Health Challenge," *Public Health Reports* 133, no. 1, suppl (2018): 44S–53S.
9. "Prevalence of Overweight among Adults, BMI ≥ 25, Crude Estimates by WHO Region," World Health Organization, September 27, 2017, http://apps .who.int/gho/data/view.main.BMI25CREGv?lang=%20en.
10. "Prevalence of Obesity among Adults, BMI ≥ 30, Crude- Estimates by WHO Region," World Health Organization, September 22, 2017, http://apps .who.int/gho/data/view.main.BMI30CREGv?lang=%20en.

11. Craig M. Hales et al., "Trends in Obesity and Severe Obesity Prevalence in US Youth and Adults by Sex and Age, 2007-2008 to 2015-2016," *JAMA: The Journal of the American Medical Association* 319, no. 16 (April 2018): 1723-25.

12. GBD 2015 Obesity Collaborators, "Health Effects of Overweight and Obesity in 195 Countries over 25 Years," *New England Journal of Medicine* 377, no. 1 (July 2017): 13-27.

13. IOM and NRC, *A Framework*.

14. Krishna Bahadur KC et al., "When Too Much Isn't Enough: Does Current Food Production Meet Global Nutritional Needs?," *Plos One* 13, no. 10 (October 2018): e0205683.

15. J. Poore and T. Nemecek, "Reducing Food's Environmental Impacts through Producers and Consumers," *Science* 360, no. 6392 (June 2018): 987-92.

16. Marco Springmann et al., "Mitigation Potential and Global Health Impacts from Emissions Pricing of Food Commodities," *Nature Climate Change* 7 (November 2016): 69-74.

17. Walter Willett et al., "Food in the Anthropocene: The EAT-Lancet Commission on Healthy Diets from Sustainable Food Systems," *Lancet* 393, no. 10170 (February 2019): 447-92.

18. Bahadur KC et al., "When Too Much Isn't Enough."

19. Sonja J. Vermeulen, Bruce M. Campbell, and John S. I. Ingram, "Climate Change and Food Systems," *Annual Review of Environment and Resources* 37, no. 1 (November 2012): 195-222.

20. National Center for Environmental Health, "Climate Effects on Health," 2014, https://www.cdc.gov/climateandhealth/effects/default.htm.

21. Kristie L. Ebi et al., "Human Health," in *Impacts, Risks, and Adaptation in the United States: Fourth National Climate Assessment*, vol. 2, ed. David R. Reidmiller et al. (Washington, DC: U.S. Global Change Research Program, 2018), 539-71.

22. Prasanna Gowda et al., "Agriculture and Rural Communities," in *Impacts, Risks, and Adaptation in the United States: Fourth National Climate Assessment*, vol. 2, ed. David R. Reidmiller et al. (Washington, DC: U.S. Global Change Research Program, 2018), 391-437.

23. Corinna Hawkes and Marie Ruel, "The Links between Agriculture and Health: An Intersectoral Opportunity to Improve the Health and Livelihoods of the Poor," *Bulletin of the World Health Organization* 84, no. 12 (December 2006): 984-90.

24. Carrie Hribar, "Understanding Concentrated Animal Feeding Operations and Their Impact on Communities" (Bowling Green, OH: National Association of Local Boards of Health, 2010), https://www.cdc.gov/nceh/ehs/docs/under standing_cafos_nalboh.pdf.

25. Pew Commission on Industrial Farm Animal Production, "Putting Meat on the Table: Industrial Farm Animal Production in America," 2008, https:// www.pewtrusts.org/-/media/legacy/uploadedfiles/phg/content_level_pages/reports /pcifapfinalpdf.pdf.

26. Hribar, "Understanding Concentrated Animal Feeding Operations."

27. Centers for Disease Control and Prevention, "Antibiotic/Antimicrobial Resistance (AR/AMR): Biggest Threats and Data," Centers for Disease Control and Prevention, November 26, 2018, https://www.cdc.gov/drugresistance /biggest_threats.html.

28. Susanne E. Bauer, Kostas Tsigaridis, and Ron Miller, "Significant Atmospheric Aerosol Pollution Caused by World Food Cultivation," *Geophysical Research Letters* 43, no. 10 (May 2016): 5394-5400.

29. J. Lelieveld et al., "The Contribution of Outdoor Air Pollution Sources to Premature Mortality on a Global Scale," *Nature* 525, no. 7569 (September 2015): 367-71.

30. "A Major Source of Air Pollution: Farms," Earth Institute, Columbia University, May 16, 2016, https://www.earth.columbia.edu/articles/view/3281.

31. World Health Organization, "WHO Estimates of the Global Burden of Foodborne Diseases: Foodborne Disease Burden Epidemiology Reference Group 2007-2015" (Geneva: World Health Organization, January 2016), https://apps .who.int/iris/bitstream/handle/10665/199350/9789241565165_eng.pdf;jsessionid =33958F0425FF68CB9D401DEBB6100E5E?sequence=1.

32. Hawkes and Ruel, "The Links between Agriculture and Health."

33. Jeremy Cherfas, "Your Quinoa Habit Really Did Help Peru's Poor. But There's Trouble Ahead," *NPR*, March 31, 2016, https://www.npr.org/sections /thesalt/2016/03/31/472453674/your-quinoa-habit-really-did-help-perus-poor -but-theres-trouble-ahead.

34. "Against the Grain," *Economist*, May 21, 2016, https://www.economist .com/finance-and-economics/2016/05/21/against-the-grain.

35. Marlene B. Schwartz and Kelly D. Brownell, "Actions Necessary to Prevent Childhood Obesity: Creating the Climate for Change," *Journal of Law, Medicine & Ethics: A Journal of the American Society of Law, Medicine & Ethics* 35, no. 1 (Spring 2007): 78-89.

36. Consumer Reports National Research Center, "Natural Food Labels Survey," 2015, http://article.images.consumerreports.org/prod/content/dam/cro /magazine-articles/2016/March/Consumer_Reports_Natural_Food_Labels _Survey_2015.pdf.

37. Andrea Rock, "Peeling Back the 'Natural' Food Label," *Consumer Reports*, January 27, 2016, https://www.consumerreports.org/food-safety/peeling-back -the-natural-food-label/.

38. "Changes to the Nutrition Facts Label," US Food and Drug Administration, n.d., https://www.fda.gov/Food/GuidanceRegulation/GuidanceDocuments RegulatoryInformation/LabelingNutrition/ucm385663.htm.

39. Institute of Medicine, *Front-of-Package Nutrition Rating Systems and Symbols: Promoting Healthier Choices* (Washington, DC: National Academies Press, 2012), https://doi.org/10.17226/13221.

40. "Label without a Cause," *Nature Biotechnology* 32, no. 12 (December 2014): 1169, https://doi.org/10.1038/nbt.3094.

41. Robert Streiffer and Alan Rubel. "Democratic Principles and Mandatory Labeling of Genetically Engineered Food," *Public Affairs Quarterly* 18, no. 3 (July 2004): 223-48.

42. Daniel J. Hicks, "Genetically Modified Crops, Inclusion, and Democracy," *Perspectives on Science* 25, no. 4 (2017): 488-520.

43. Mary Story and Simone French, "Food Advertising and Marketing Directed at Children and Adolescents in the US," *International Journal of Behavioral Nutrition and Physical Activity* 1 (February 2004): 3, https://doi.org/10.1186/1479-5868-1-3.

44. Amandine Garde, Elizabeth Handsley, and Mimi Tatlow-Golden, "Children Are far from Protected from Junk Food Ads—Especially on Social Media," *Conversation*, February 27, 2018, http://theconversation.com/children-are-far-from-protected-from-junk-food-ads-especially-on-social-media-92382.

45. Vance Packard, *The Hidden Persuaders* (New York: Pocket Books, 1959).

46. Roger Crisp, "Persuasive Advertising, Autonomy, and the Creation of Desire," *Journal of Business Ethics* 6, no. 5 (1987): 413-18, http://www.jstor.org/stable/25071678.

47. Lynne Eagle and Stephan Dahl, *Marketing Ethics & Society* (London: SAGE, 2015).

48. Michael Moss, *Salt, Sugar, Fat: How the Food Giants Hooked Us* (New York: Random House, 2013).

49. Christina A. Roberto et al., "Patchy Progress on Obesity Prevention: Emerging Examples, Entrenched Barriers, and New Thinking," *Lancet* 385, no. 9985 (June 2015): 2400-2409.

50. Marion Nestle, *Food Politics: How the Food Industry Influences Nutrition and Health* (Berkeley: California: University of California Press, 2007).

51. Kelly D. Brownell and Kenneth E. Warner, "The Perils of Ignoring History: Big Tobacco Played Dirty and Millions Died; How Similar Is Big Food?," *Milbank Quarterly* 87, no. 1 (March 2009): 259-94.

52. Ffion Lloyd-Williams et al., "Smorgasbord or Symphony? Assessing Public Health Nutrition Policies across 30 European Countries Using a Novel Framework," *BMC Public Health* 14 (November 2014): 1195.

53. Belinda Reeve et al., "State and Municipal Innovations in Obesity Policy: Why Localities Remain a Necessary Laboratory for Innovation," *American Journal of Public Health* 105, no. 3 (March 2015): 442-50.

54. Dariush Mozaffarian et al., "Role of Government Policy in Nutrition—Barriers to and Opportunities for Healthier Eating," *BMJ* 361 (2018): k2426.

55. Kenneth Rogoff, "The US Is Exporting Obesity—and Trump Is Making the Problem Worse," *Guardian*, December 4, 2017, http://www.theguardian.com/business/2017/dec/04/us-obesity-trump-processed-foods-health.

56. Andrew Jacobs and Matt Richtel, "How Big Business Got Brazil Hooked on Junk Food," *New York Times*, September 16, 2017, https://www.nytimes.com/interactive/2017/09/16/health/brazil-obesity-nestle.html.

57. Resnik, "Trans Fat Bans."

58. Barnhill et al., "The Value of Unhealthy Eating."

59. Barnhill et al., "The Value of Unhealthy Eating."

EIGHTEEN

Food Safety

HERMAN B. W. M. KOËTER

Background

In the past couple of decades, consumers in developed countries have called for more information about the food they wish to purchase. This increased level of interest is triggered, at least in part, by major food problems such as BSE (bovine spongiform encephalopathy), avian flu and other zoonoses in food-producing bovine animals and poultry, dioxin contamination of dairy products, and food frauds such as the addition of unauthorized chemicals in food and labeling horse meat as beef. In addition, animal health and welfare concerns in food production have become almost a global issue with an increasing demand for food produced as "animal friendly." Furthermore, the introduction of nanoparticles in food, the safety of foods produced from genetically modified organisms (GMOs), and the use of antibiotics as growth promoters in food-producing animals, as well as food security in the coming decades, have become societal issues of great significance and concern with respect to human and environmental safety and sustainability.

Partly in response to these developments and concerns, a new US Food Safety Modernization Act was developed, which came into effect on February 2, 2011. However, the act does not include any new or more stringent food (safety) information requirements. Similarly, in the European Union's new Regulation [(EU)1169/2011] adopted in October 2011, the agreed food (safety) labeling requirements are substantially less informative and descriptive than initially proposed.

Moral and Ethical Issues

Separate from legal requirements, ethical rules and moral principles should be considered when addressing food safety. These rules and principles, listed in no particular order, are addressed here for several aspects that relate to food and food safety.

Access to Food

Accessibility is defined by availability and affordability and, as such, is a first and foremost condition of life. Nonetheless, a substantial part of the world population does not have appropriate access to food. In the list of issues presented here, the moral assumption is that all humans should have access to food.

Food Overproduction and Spillage

Opposite to food shortage is overproduction and subsequent food destruction or food waste dumping. The former will lead to unnecessary use of energy, while the latter is likely to cause substantial health hazards. Alternatively, overproduction may be deliberate to cause "price dumping" (predatory pricing), especially in the context of international trade. It occurs when manufacturers export a product to another country at a price either below the price charged in its home market or below its cost of production. It has been (and probably still is) used as a political and/or strategic action to kill a competitive market. In general, as long as considerable populations suffer from severe food shortage globally and renewable energy is not yet widely available, any form of substantial wasting of quality food is considered unethical.

Food Quality

Although many regulations in developed countries with respect to maximum levels of nutrients, vitamins, minerals, food additives, and food supplements ensure the safety of food, this is not the case for food quality. Examples of poor food quality include injecting water into cooked ham to increase the weight, adding animal proteins from undefined sources in processed meat products, or diluting high-quality olive oil with a lower-quality vegetable oil. Although not necessarily a food safety issue, intentionally misleading consumers for economical gain cannot be stopped by any legislation and is considered a moral breach of trust.

Chemical and Microbiological Food Contamination

Chemical food contamination may occur unintentionally because of a technical failure (e.g., benzene in spring water), accidentally during processing or packaging (e.g., dioxin in potato chips from contaminated water used for washing potatoes), or from unavoidable environmental contamination (e.g., methylmercury in fish). Unfortunately, intentional chemical contamination of food occurs regularly and may result in minor to severe intoxication of the consumer.

Neglect of hygienic practices and lack of adequate hygienic conditions in the food chain, from harvesting through processing, are major sources of microbiological contamination and, consequently, human diseases. Furthermore, poor storage and working conditions, particularly in retail businesses and restaurants, attract insects, rodents, and other animals resulting in serious contamination of the food and, subsequently, infectious diseases in the consumers of this food. Ignorance and cost-saving management practices, including noncompliance with hazard assessment of critical control points (HACCP) are considered unethical as they put workers in the production chain as well as consumers at risk of serious diseases. Such situations frequently occur in but are not limited to small and medium-sized enterprises.

Contamination of any kind is largely an issue of inadequate control and compliance monitoring of the production-transport-retail chain and threatens human and environmental health.

Controversial Food

Controversial food is not necessarily unsafe but is perceived as such or is considered undesirable by a substantial segment of consumers in many countries, most notably in Europe. The segment of food that is considered safe but controversial because of moral principles includes:

- food from cloned animals
- food from genetically modified animals
- food from transgenic animals
- food from animals bred and kept under poor and/or unnatural husbandry conditions
- food containing ingredients derived from any of the animals described above
- irradiated food

A second controversial food group concerns processed food containing undesirable nonessential nutrients or ingredients such as sugar and salt. Although as such not unsafe, the addition of sugar and salt to almost all processed food gradually influences consumers' taste palette toward favoring sweet and salty. This contributes to a diet change having a negative impact on consumers' health (such as obesity and type 2 diabetes) and, as such, is considered unethical.

A third segment is that of herbal food supplements. These are frequently contaminated with unknown or toxic components and claim general health improvement or treatment or improvement of specific body or mind functions. However, the efficacy of any herbal product and other botanicals lacks scientific support or evidence.

Recently, a new food controversy has surfaced, namely, the use of nanoparticles in food. A consumer concern like the not scientifically supported aversion against GMOs is almost unavoidable. Even though the use of nanoparticles as saturated fat replacers is likely to improve the nutritional balance of the food, the food producers remain silent or even deny the use of this technology. The lack of proper communication to society and transparency about the nanotechnology applied will make consumers suspicious when they learn from the product label about the nano-ingredients. This is bound to happen as soon as the revised food safety legislation requires the inclusion of nano-ingredients on the label.

Health and Welfare of Food-Producing Animals

The health and welfare of food-producing animals has been an issue of concern for many years. In Europe, recent legislation on animal welfare is very clear in stating that the animals have an intrinsic value.[1] In practice, this value is generally translated into health and welfare components. Measurable indicators of animal health are available and, hopefully, generally applied. However, the welfare of food-producing animals can be defined only by qualitative indicators, largely extrapolated from the natural conditions and environment of the species of concern. Economic and spatial concerns have always been the limiting factors for welfare. During the preceding 50 to 70 years, a period of exponential growth of intensive farming, the welfare of food-producing animals has been largely neglected. However, to date, consumers are increasingly more concerned about animal welfare and desire more transparency about the husbandry practices used to produce animal-source foods.

Unfortunately, the information provided by producers can be vague and multi-interpretable, with the use of such terms as "free-range," "open air access," "biological," "organic," and "GMO-free"). Criteria to define objectively and scientifically what constitutes welfare, suffering, and "healthy" animals are still largely lacking. Furthermore, while regulations are currently in place that define which sources of animal protein are prohibited for certain animal species, animal feeding practices and other Good Farming Practices are still largely obscure. Many ill-defined labels suggesting animal-friendly food production are currently used. Malpractices in farming that severely affect animal health and welfare are considered highly unethical; misleading or false information about the welfare of farm animals is equally considered highly unethical.

Food Fraud

Unfortunately, food fraud is a widespread phenomenon. The level of severity can be defined in two ways:

- The level of *health risk* resulting from the counterfeit food could be of a negligible hazard such as selling sugar syrup with flavors and colors as genuine maple syrup or selling cheap olive oil from Greece as extra virgin olive oil from Italy. However, it could also be very severe, such as diluting an alcoholic drink with methanol or mixing edible vegetable oil with a dioxin containing mineral oil.
- The *volume* of food involved can be limited, such as the addition of diethylene glycol in white wine, which was limited to one country. But it can also be substantial—for instance, selling horse meat as beef (tons) or a variety of condiments (tons) in a considerable number of countries.

Over the course of four months (November 2015 through February 2016) across 57 countries, a Europol-Interpol operation resulted in the total seizure of 11,000 metric tons of food and 1.5 million liters and 5.5 million units of either counterfeit or substandard food and beverages as a result of checks carried out at shops, markets, airports, seaports, and industrial estates.[2]

Micronutrient Deficiency and Food Fortification

Micronutrient deficiency is not limited to developing countries: in France, there is a rather high incidence of iodine deficiency in children, and in the United Kingdom folic acid deficiency in women was widespread and resulted in relatively high incidence of spina bifida in newborns. Today, in the United Kingdom all bread is fortified with folic acid to ensure adequate exposure to the people at large. This includes men who do not need such fortification and may even show minor adverse effects from it. Hence, fortification of staple food to fight nutrient deficiency that is gender specific unnecessarily exposes the other gender. This is an ethical issue.

In developing countries, micronutrient deficiency is widespread and includes iodine, potassium, iron, magnesium, and folic acid. International organizations such as GAIN (Global Alliance for Improved Nutrition) invest heavily in the fortification of staple foods in these countries by providing food producers with premixes of the deficient micronutrients. However, the producers often add insufficient amounts of the premix or no premix at all, while the assumed fortification level is mentioned on the label of the food. The consequence of this neglect or fraud could be malformations in newborns or other adverse effects, largely in infants. Government reluctance to (co)finance and monitor fortification programs, and a lack of incentives for food producers cause this unnecessary and severe health problem. This situation is considered unethical and intolerable.

Food Certification and Labeling

Dozens of labels suggesting certification are used by industry and NGOs to convey the message that the product carrying the certificate label is "organic," "sustainable," "green," or any other buzz word. However, in the European Union only one logo has legal status. It indicates that the product is qualified as organic because it is in full conformity with the conditions and regulations for the organic farming sector established by the European Union. For processed products, it means that at least 95% of the agricultural ingredients are organic. An international concept and subsequent certificate of animal friendly produced food has not yet been defined. The use of ill-defined, suggestive, or misleading food labels is considered unethical.

Information on processed food packaging is frequently in one way or another misleading in the sense that the label suggests the food contains healthy ingredients (e.g., Kinder Chocolate, which suggests milk is an ingredient in its bars, or "cranberry juice" that is made with only 5% cranberries). Likewise, the label says the product does not contain unhealthy ingredients (e.g., no sugar added in fruit juice with 20+ percent sugar content, or sweets with 98% sugar labeled as "fat free"). Worse are statements such as "biological" or "fair food" without any explanation of what they mean when they appear on products that are neither biological nor fair food. In addition, food labels are generally not consumer friendly and lack relevant information, including country or area of origin of the product. Intentionally misleading information on food labels is immoral.

Food with Expired Best-Before-Date

Food that has passed the "best before" date cannot be sold in Western societies: What can be done with it? Is it ethical to donate such food to charity organizations, such as food banks for distribution to the very poor? Should it be destroyed (as required in the European Union)? Can it be a nutrient source for animal feed? Should it be exported to poor countries? These are all ethical issues that need to be addressed at the international level by regulatory food safety and food management authorities.

REFERENCES

1. European Commission, "Directive 2010/63/EU of the European Parliament and of the Council of 22 September 2010 on the Protection of Animals Used for Scientific Purposes," *Official Journal of the European Union* 276 (2010): 33-79.

2. Europol-Interpol, "Food Fraud: Joint Europol-Interpol Operation Opson V Results Report," news release, October 27, 2016, https://www.europol.europa.eu/newsroom/news/food-fraud-joint-europol-interpol-operation-opson-v-results-report.

NINETEEN

Antibiotic Resistance

LANCE B. PRICE

THE WORLD HEALTH ORGANIZATION (WHO) warns that we are heading toward a post-antibiotic era in medicine, a time when we can no longer count on antibiotics to cure even common infections.[1] The WHO's warning is driven by the fact that some bacteria become resistant to the effects of antibiotics. As this happens, common infections such as urinary tract infections become difficult to treat and perhaps even life-threatening. "Superbugs" are disease-causing bacteria that are resistant to our best antibiotics. While "superbug" may conjure up images from comic books, it is a term that gets the public and the media to pay attention—as they should. According to a report commissioned by the UK government, drug-resistant infections could outpace cancer and other common diseases as the most common cause of death. If left unchecked, by 2050, antimicrobial resistance could kill one person every three seconds.[2] Superbugs are going to change our world. They will affect all of the procedures and treatments that are dependent on antibiotics, such as joint replacements, cesarean sections, prostate biopsies, gastrointestinal surgeries, bone marrow transplants, and cancer therapies. And they will affect large vulnerable populations, such as young children, pregnant women, cancer patients, people over the age of 60, and people living in developing countries that already lack medicines, technologies, clean water, and good sanitation.

Understanding how bacteria become resistant to antibiotics is important. It is really just simple evolution. Bacteria can become resistant just by making an error in their DNA or by picking up little packages of DNA called mobile resistance elements from other bacteria. These random events happen all the time, but in an environment where you have a lot of antibiotic use, bacteria that are susceptible to antibiotics are going to die off and the resistant ones are going to multiply. In a single genetic event, bacteria can pick up the genes necessary to overcome multiple antibiotics. Bacteria grow really quickly. *Escherichia coli* can double every 30 minutes, so we can go from having a single drug-resistant cell to literally billions in 24 hours. This is simple Darwinian evolution but in real-time, and it can take place in a Petri dish, in a test tube, in a person, or in a 100,000-bird factory farm. Each time we use antibiotics, we have to recognize that we are potentially fueling the growth of superbugs.

We most often associate antibiotic use with hospitals. In the United States, we are using far too many antibiotics in human medicine—about 3.4 million kilograms each year.[3] That figure refers to just the active ingredient, not the weight of the pills. Moreover, when staff in hospitals do not wash their hands between patients or sanitize contact surfaces, they become vehicles for drug-resistant bacteria, and hospitals that otherwise look clean can be deemed unsanitary.

Human medicine certainly plays a large role in the emergence of antibiotic-resistant bacteria. But in the United States we actually use more antibiotics in food animal production—about 5.56 million kilograms each year.[4] That figure captures only the classes of antibiotics that are considered important for use in human medicine, so the actual total is larger. We use antibiotics in food animal production for a couple different purposes, which are broadly classified as therapeutic and non-therapeutic. Therapeutic uses are for disease treatment and control (time-limited antibiotic exposure), whereas non-therapeutic uses are for disease prevention and growth promotion (routine antibiotic exposure). Most of the antibiotics used in food animal production are for non-therapeutic purposes. It will come as no surprise that animals raised in confinement share bacteria. Giving them low doses of antibiotics to prevent disease fuels the growth of drug-resistant bacteria, which can spread among these animals very quickly.

Animals pass on resistant bacteria in a few ways. One way is through the environment. Animal waste can contain resistant bacteria or antibiotic residues that can get into water, soil, and air. A second way is through consumption of poorly cooked meat that contains resistant bacteria.[5] From a public health standpoint, we are not as concerned about traces of antibiotics in meat (though it is a concern) as we are about living, infectious microbes on meat that can make people sick if the meat is not properly cooked. A third way is through direct contact between animals and humans.[6] Food animal producers are at much greater risk for picking up drug-resistant bacteria. A study of stool samples from chicken catchers on the Eastern Shore found that these workers had 32 times the risk of carrying gentamicin-resistant *E. coli* as their community peers.[7] Gentamicin is one of the most commonly used drugs in poultry production.

When thinking about the issue of antibiotic use in food animal production, traditionally we have thought about *Salmonella* and *Campylobacter*, the classic foodborne pathogens. Despite all of our food safety messages, these bacteria cause more than two million infections in the United States each year, and about 410,000 of these infections are antibiotic-resistant.[8] This resistance can be traced back to contemporary or historic antibiotic use, mostly in food animal production. That is roughly the population of Minneapolis getting drug-resistant infections each year in the United States from food animal production.

But we need to move beyond just thinking about the classic foodborne pathogens. If you mention "superbug" to infectious-disease doctors, they do not think about *Salmonella* or *Campylobacter*. They think about extraintestinal pathogenic *E. coli*, *Klebsiella pneumoniae*, *Staphylococcus aureus*, and *Clostridium difficile*. These superbugs are also known as colonizing opportunistic pathogens (COPs).[9] COPs can live in the human body indefinitely without causing any symptoms, and they can spread silently from person to person. COPs can cause infections when the host becomes immunologically compromised or visits someone at the hospital who is susceptible. COPs can also have environmental (e.g., air, food, and water) and animal reservoirs. All of these features of COPs make their epidemiology very difficult to understand and can lead to insidious epidemics that spread far and wide before being recognized.

When we finally started looking beyond *Salmonella* and *Campylobacter*, we found that there are a lot of COPs in the food supply. Today we recognize something called livestock-associated methicillin-resistant *Staphylococcus aureus* (LA-MRSA), which was discovered in an infant in the Netherlands in the early 2000s. The infant's family was tested and both parents were colonized with MRSA. It turned out that the family lived on a farm and raised pigs, and most of the pigs were colonized as well.[10,11] This led to a recognition that there was a MRSA strain in pigs that was spreading throughout the pig industry in the Netherlands and then spilling over into the community. It had originated in humans as a nonresistant strain, but once it jumped to pigs it acquired resistance as a result of widespread antibiotic use on farms. Now it jumps back to humans.[12,13] At one point it was causing more than 40% of the MRSA infections in the Netherlands.[14]

Today, we also recognize what we call foodborne urinary tract infections (FUTIs).[15] Researchers had noticed that sometimes UTIs occur in outbreaks, which was a mystery because UTIs had almost always been sporadic infections. They found that these outbreaks were caused by a single strain, and that similar strains could be found in contaminated food.[16] During a recent one-year study in the small, geographically isolated city of Flagstaff, Arizona, we sampled all available brands of chicken, turkey, and pork every two weeks from every grocery store in the city. We collected *E. coli* isolates from more than 2,400 meat products and also partnered with the town's hospital to collect isolates from positive urine and blood cultures. We then used whole genome sequencing to compare the two *E. coli* populations. An estimated 5% to 14% of the UTIs in humans were caused by *E. coli* that originated in food animals. On the basis of this study, it was estimated that a single foodborne *E. coli* strain—ST131-H22—causes more than 30,000 UTIs in the United States each year.[17]

Foodborne UTIs and livestock-associated MRSA infections represent a paradigm shift in terms of what is considered a foodborne infection. No longer just diarrhea and vomiting, it can be a urinary tract infection or a skin and soft tissue infection. This paradigm shift gives new context to the 5.56 million kilograms of antibiotics that we are using in food animal production. These are the same antibiotics that we are using in human medicine. For example, in the United States we have ruined the effectiveness of tetracycline treatment by overusing this class of antibiotics in animals and people.[18] In Sweden, where there is good stewardship of antibiotic use in animals and people, tetracyclines are still functional. To address this travesty, the United States has begun to regulate some of the uses of important antibiotics in food animal production.

However, this regulation does not exist in the developing world, where rapidly developing countries like the BRICS (Brazil, Russia, India, China, and South Africa) are adopting our Western meat-centric diet as well as our means of industrial food animal production, which includes antibiotic use. We are seeing the evolution of resistant bacteria in these countries. For example, food animal producers in China started using the antibiotic colistin in the 1980s. Colistin is not commonly used in human medicine because of its side effects, but it is still an important antibiotic of last resort. Recently colistin has been used to treat multidrug-resistant infections caused by carbapenem-resistant *Enterobacteriaceae* (CRE) like *E. coli* and *Klebsiella pneumoniae*. But because of the routine use of colistin in food animal production, we have seen the evolution of a new mobile resistance element, MCR-1, that codes for resistance to colistin. This resistance gene jumps into different strains of *E. coli* all the time, and it has jumped into CRE strains. As a result, we are seeing the emergence of untreatable CRE strains.[19,20]

There is a lot of counterproductive finger-pointing going on between the human medicine and food animal production communities. Antibiotic resistance is really an ecological problem because antibiotic use in food animals and humans can work synergistically to fuel the emergence of antimicrobial resistant pathogens. The level of synergy depends largely on the proximity and the leakiness of these two systems—with the caveat that it also depends on microbiological factors that we do not yet understand. In other words, it depends on how close food animal production is located to human communities, how water sources are shared, how waste is handled, how animals are housed and fed, and how much direct contact there is between animals and humans. We need to eliminate inappropriate antibiotic use and reduce leakiness in both human and animal systems.

Eliminating antibiotic use in food animal production requires a nuanced, context-specific understanding of why antibiotics are being used. If we look at some US industrial producers who are using antibiotics specifically to make their animals grow faster, it is easy to say that this is an inappropriate use of antibiotics that should be eliminated. But if we look at the developing world, we may find producers who are using antibiotics because they are afraid of losing their livelihoods. Fear of loss, which is perhaps perpetuated by those who sell antibiotics, appears to be a driver for antibiotic use in some subsistence farming communities.[21] In these situations, our best approach may be to try to get the producers to use antibiotics less. Understanding why some producers do not use antibiotics is also insightful. Some producers may not want to lose the added value of being able to label their product as "raised without antibiotics" or "USDA organic." It is sometimes the case that *not* using antibiotics can lead to animal suffering.

We should focus on optimizing rather than reducing antibiotic use in both food animals and humans. We know that while we are overusing antibiotics in the United States, there are people in other parts of the world who are routinely dying of infections that are readily treatable with antibiotics. We need to make sure that those people have access to antibiotics that work. We should use antibiotics in humans when we need them, but we should use them *only* when we need them, and we should try to prevent infections in other ways. The same is true for animals. We have a moral obligation to treat animals when they are sick, but we also need to address the conditions on farms that lead to antibiotic use.

One application of this approach is the Certified Responsible Antibiotic Use (CRAU) standard. CRAU is the first US standard to govern limited antibiotic use in poultry production. It is designed for responsible producers who do all they can to prevent disease without antibiotics. When necessary, antibiotics can be used to treat sick animals or control disease in infected flocks, but this is always done under veterinary oversight. If illnesses persist, producers must work with a veterinarian to develop a written plan to address the problem. If they continue to routinely use antibiotics, they are removed from the program. The US Department of Agriculture's role as a third-party verifier is essential to ensuring the integrity of the standard. Many of the largest poultry producers are CRAU certified. Currently, CRAU-certified products are available only for bulk sale to schools, hospitals, and other institutional buyers, but there is potential for expansion into retail markets as well as for use in other species besides chicken and turkey.[22]

It is important to recognize the value of harm reduction in public health. We can recognize that opioid use is a problem while also supporting needle exchange programs to prevent HIV infection. We can also recognize that commercial sex work is a problem while providing free condoms to those who would otherwise have unprotected sex. This same harm reductionist approach can be applied to industrial agriculture. We need to figure out how to produce food as efficiently as possible while reducing harm and suffering. We have a moral imperative to raise animals in ways that maximize well-being, minimize disease, and obviate routine antibiotic use.

REFERENCES

1. "Antimicrobial Resistance: Global Report on Surveillance," World Health Organization, 2014.

2. "Tackling Drug-Resistant Infections Globally: Final Report and Recommendations," Review on Antimicrobial Resistance, 2016.

3. Brad Spellberg et al., "Antibiotic Resistance in Humans and Animals," NAM Perspectives, 2016, https://nam.edu/antibiotic-resistance-in-humans-and-animals/.

4. "2016 Summary Report on Antimicrobials Sold or Distributed for Use in Food-Producing Animals," US Food and Drug Administration, 2017.

5. "Antimicrobials in Agriculture and the Environment: Reducing Unnecessary Use and Waste," Review on Antimicrobial Resistance, 2015.

6. "Tackling Drug-Resistant Infections."

7. Lance B. Price et al., "Elevated Risk of Carrying Gentamicin-Resistant Escherichia Coli among US Poultry Workers," Environmental Health Perspectives 115, no. 12 (2007): 1738-42.

8. "Antibiotic Resistance Threats in the U.S.," US Centers for Disease Control and Prevention, 2013.

9. Lance B. Price et al., "Colonizing Opportunistic Pathogens (COPs): The Beasts in All of Us," *PLoS Pathogens* 13, no. 8 (August 2017): e1006369.

10. Andreas Voss et al., "Methicillin-Resistant Staphylococcus Aureus in Pig Farming," *Emerging Infectious Diseases* 11, no. 12 (December 2005): 1965-66.

11. Lance B. Price et al., "Staphylococcus Aureus CC398: Host Adaptation and Emergence of Methicillin Resistance in Livestock," *mBio* 3, no. 1 (February 2012), https://doi.org/10.1128/mBio.00305-11.

12. Price et al., "Staphylococcus Aureus."

13. Raphael N. Sieber et al., "Drivers and Dynamics of Methicillin-Resistant Livestock-Associated Staphylococcus Aureus CC398 in Pigs and Humans in Denmark," *mBio* 9, no. 6 (November 2018), https://doi.org/10.1128/mBio.02142-18.

14. Beth J. Feingold et al., "Livestock Density as Risk Factor for Livestock-Associated Methicillin-Resistant Staphylococcus Aureus, the Netherlands," *Emerging Infectious Diseases* 18, no. 11 (November 2012): 1841-49.

15. Lora Nordstrom, Cindy M. Liu, and Lance B. Price, "Foodborne Urinary Tract Infections: A New Paradigm for Antimicrobial-Resistant Foodborne Illness," *Frontiers in Microbiology* 4 (March 2013): 29.

16. Nordstrom, Liu, and Price, "Foodborne Urinary Tract Infections."

17. Cindy M. Liu et al., "Escherichia Coli ST131-H22 as a Foodborne Uropathogen," *mBio* 9, no. 4 (August 2018), https://doi.org/10.1128/mBio.00470-18.

18. "2016 Summary Report."

19. Yang Wang et al., "Prevalence, Risk Factors, Outcomes, and Molecular Epidemiology of Mcr-1-Positive Enterobacteriaceae in Patients and Healthy Adults from China: An Epidemiological and Clinical Study," *Lancet Infectious Diseases* 17, no. 4 (2017): 390-99.

20. Jingjing Quan et al., "Prevalence of Mcr-1 in Escherichia Coli and Klebsiella Pneumoniae Recovered from Bloodstream Infections in China: A Multicentre Longitudinal Study," *Lancet Infectious Diseases* 17, no. 4 (2017): 400-410.

21. Jay P. Graham et al., "Small-Scale Food Animal Production and Antimicrobial Resistance: Mountain, Molehill, or Something In-Between?," *Environmental Health Perspectives* 125, no. 10 (October 2017): 104501.

22. Certified Responsible Antibiotic Use, https://certifiedresponsibleantibioticuse.org/.

TWENTY

Farm Animal Welfare and Human Health

ALAN M. GOLDBERG

IF WE ACCEPT that a diet of the future will include fish and meat (even at a level less than the current Western diet), then the welfare of the animals we eat will continue to be an important moral concern. How *animal welfare* is defined dictates conditions that are and are not morally acceptable.

Worldwide, industrial farm animal food production is approximately 50% of the total food animal production, while in the developed world, this is closer to 90+%.[1,2] Current industrial food animal production is significantly ethically challenged; however, this author believes that animal protein will continue to be a significant part of our future supply of food. It is also recognized that there are movements to eat less meat and fish and thus reduce the amount of animal-based protein in the diet. This chapter will look at the moral issues associated with industrial food animal production and approaches to continue producing industrial farm animal protein in ways that are less ethically challenged (i.e., sustainable intensification).[3] The issues that will be examined are animal welfare, environmental degradation, human health consequences, and cost.

Fraser provides a detailed characterization of the concept of animal welfare and the impact of intensification on animal welfare.[4] Since the 1950s animal welfare has been described as the Five Freedoms (freedom from hunger and thirst; freedom from discomfort; freedom from pain, injury and disease; freedom to express most normal behaviors; and freedom from fear and distress)[5,6] (Brambell report), and most recently Marian Dawkins presented a simplified but informative construct.[7] She describes animal welfare as defining what the animal needs and what the animal wants. Several important activities have informed the animal welfare discussion. These include the 2008 Pew Commission report, "Putting Meat on the Table,"[8] the EU Welfare Quality principles published in 2009,[9] and Nestlé's 2014 animal product sourcing policy.[10]

The Welfare Quality principles,[11] the work of a large group of scientists from Europe and South America, expanded on the Brambell report (as codified by the Federation of Animal Welfare Council) of the Five Freedoms. The Pew Commission study, "Putting Meat on the Table,"[12] examined the impact of intensification on human health, the environment, social justice, and animal welfare. Nestlé, the largest food company worldwide, implemented a policy in 2014 to source animal products (meat, eggs, and dairy) only from animals that have lived their lives according to the Five Freedoms—as a minimum standard.[13] Most recently, many other companies (Panera, Shake Shack, Chipotle, United

---

THE FIVE FREEDOMS

1. Freedom from hunger or thirst: ready access to fresh water and an adequate and nutritious diet
2. Freedom from discomfort: an appropriate environment including shelter and a comfortable resting area
3. Freedom from pain, injury, or disease: including appropriate and timely treatment when necessary
4. Freedom to express (most) normal behavior: sufficient space, proper facilities, and company of the animal's own kind
5. Freedom from fear and distress: ensuring conditions and treatment which avoid mental suffering

Farm Animal Welfare Council, "Farm Animal Welfare Council Press Statement," news release, December 5, 1979, https://webarchive.nationalarchives.gov.uk /20121010012427/http://www.fawc.org.uk/freedoms.htm.

CRITERIA THAT UNDERPIN THE WELFARE QUALITY® ASSESSMENT SYSTEMS

1. Animals should not suffer from prolonged hunger, i.e., they should have a sufficient and appropriate diet.
2. Animals should not suffer from prolonged thirst, i.e., they should have a sufficient and accessible water supply.
3. Animals should have comfortable resting places.
4. Animals should have thermal comfort, i.e., they should neither be too hot nor too cold.
5. Animals should have enough space to be able to move around freely.
6. Animals should be free of physical injuries.
7. Animals should be free of disease, i.e., farmers should maintain high standards of hygiene and care.
8. Animals should not suffer pain induced by inappropriate management, handling, slaughter, or surgical procedures (e.g., castration, dehorning).
9. Animals should be able to express normal, nonharmful, social behaviors, e.g., grooming.
10. Animals should be able to express other normal behaviors, i.e., it should be possible to express species-specific natural behaviors such as foraging.
11. Animals should be handled well in all situations, i.e., handlers should promote good human-animal relationships.
12. Negative emotions such as fear, distress, frustration, or apathy should be avoided whereas positive emotions such as security or contentment should be promoted.

Welfare Quality, "Principles and Criteria of Good Animal Welfare," http://www .welfarequality.net/media/1084/wq___factsheet_10_07_eng2.pdf.

Egg Producers, among others) have also demonstrated concern and established policies toward better farm animal welfare.

In the developed world, almost all farm animals raised for food are produced by intensive operations involving several hundred to thousands of animals confined either in a building or on feedlots (concentrated animal feeding operations).[14] Current intensified practices do not meet even minimal international guidelines of the Five Freedoms and thus are of central moral concern. The issue of sustainable intensification is being addressed by some of the newly developing systems of sustainable intensification that do meet the Five Freedoms and beyond (for a discussion of sustainable intensification, see Godfray et al.).[15]

One consistently raised issue is the cost of food produced with acceptable levels of animal welfare versus industrially produced animal protein. Norwood and Lusk provide an in-depth analysis of the costs of farm animal welfare.[16] Their review in some areas is not critical as they accept some information without the benefit of toxicological evaluation. For example, they state that low levels of hormones, pesticides, and antibiotic residues in meat are of no health concern. This may unfortunately not be accurate, as residues may still induce a biological response; however, this has not been well studied to date. They provide data on the cost of enhanced animal welfare versus traditional industrial production for eggs and pork. Their data confirm what we have learned while working on the Pew Commission, that eggs from caged or cage-free chickens differ by less than a penny an egg, and that pork may be about 50 cents more per pound from sheltered pastured as compared to industrial (about a 15% increase).[17] These findings demonstrate that the current retail price differentials are due to marketing and consumer acceptance. It is important to note that the retail price of industrial animal protein is greatly decreased by subsidies, which do not currently benefit the owner-operated and owner-controlled smaller producers but only industrialized production.[18]

More important are the costs of industrially produced animal protein that are known as externalities. These include the human health consequences, environmental degradation, and the impact on social justice. These have been well described in the Pew Commission report, "Putting Meat on the Table."[19] On all issues of cost, much further independent research is needed to truly evaluate the real costs of industrial, organic, smallholder, and other production approaches.

Current Farm Animal Production

In the United States (and most of the developed world), about 95% of all land-based farm animal production comes from very large production sources.[20] Small farms selling animal products through farmers' markets and farm stands contribute less than 5% of the food supply, although this seems to be increasing over the last few years. Even entities that pledge to raise their own food (mainly crops) are unable to do so completely. For example, Green Mountain College in Vermont is able to provide about 12% of the food for its student body (approximately 825 students), with a target goal of 20% by the end of the decade.

It is possible that over time there will be shifts in dietary habits when less meat is consumed, with increases in consumption of high-protein vegetables, insects as food, or other production methods (tissue culture) that will decrease the consumption of animal protein derived from living animals. However, in the absence of significant changes in dietary consumption, large production sources will continue to be necessary to provide sufficient animal protein to meet dietary preferences. This is particularly important as consumption of animal protein in less developed countries increases and, in some cases, approaches consumption of the developed world. While strategies focused on reducing consumption of animal protein may contribute to the relative reduction of total protein intake that is derived from meat, the absolute amount of animal protein will likely remain high in the next decades. This will be due to the size of the population, rapid changes in dietary patterns in developing countries,[21,22] and the fact that dietary changes require time to make an impact, as it is harder to change dietary habits among middle-aged and older adults, compared to earlier in life.[23] A central question is thus whether there are other approaches to industrial-scale (intensified) production that will allow adequate production of food animals (or food animal protein), preserve the environment, protect or even enhance (e.g., through better nutrition) human health and well-being, and meet acceptable standards of animal welfare. That is, can we ethically produce adequate (what is needed for adequate nutrition and/or what is desired) amounts of farm animals to feed the world of over nine billion people along with their companion animals? The focus of this chapter is on the industrial systems typical of developed countries.

Current practices of intensification, often called concentrated animal feeding operations (CAFOs), contribute to environmental degradation, produce negative consequences to public health, and raise issues of animal welfare.[24] These same methods, however, provide large amounts of what seem to be inexpensive animal protein. Animal protein so produced, however, might not be truly less expensive. After taking into account the many externalized costs (health impacts on consumers and neighboring communities, government subsidies), these intensified practices may be as or even more costly than more agrarian or traditional production methods.

In general, the comments in this chapter refer to industrial large-scale production methods and not small-scale production owner-operated and owner-controlled pasture-based farms. This emphasis should not be interpreted to mean that small-production animal farming raises no moral issues; it does, and some will be identified within the text. However, climate change, non-therapeutic use of antibiotics, and issues of animal welfare—all of which impact human health—are far more pressing considerations in high-intensity production of farm animals than in pasture-based approaches.[25,26]

Regarding the non-therapeutic levels of antibiotics used in farm animal production, the US Food and Drug Administration (FDA) recently (finalized in 2012) proposed voluntary guidelines recommending that sale of antibiotics for growth promotion (a non-therapeutic use) be stopped.[27] It appears that most producers accepted this recommendation. However, the use of non-therapeutic levels of antibiotics for "disease prevention" is still acceptable.[28]

It is noteworthy that the protocol of lifetime dosing using non-therapeutic levels of antibiotics for disease prevention is similar if not identical to the protocol for their use in growth promotion.[29]

Thus, using non-therapeutic levels of antibiotics, which are often the same antibiotics used in the control of human disease, for disease prevention in farm animals still has very negative impacts on human health.[30] It is important to note that short-term low-dose levels of those antibiotics not used for human use can have specific benefits at times of weaning for pigs and shipping of calves.[31,32]

Animal Welfare and CAFOs

After recognizing the need to standardize some aspects of animal welfare practices, the United Kingdom empowered a commission in 1959 to investigate the subject. The commission's report, known as the Brambell report after its chair, Sir Roger Brambell, provided criteria for animal welfare that are known as the Five Freedoms.[33] In 2009, the European Union enlarged the Five Freedoms concept through a series of conferences and workshop and defined a new term, Welfare Quality.[34] In both the Brambell report and the subsequent report, *Welfare Quality*, the ability of an animal to express its natural behavior (experience its innate "animalness"—what Bernard Rollin, following Aristotle, calls its *telos*) is a major criterion that must be included in any practice aimed at providing animal welfare. The intensification of animal production in the United States (and elsewhere) results in conditions that do not allow animals to express their natural behavioral repertoire. A natural behavior of pigs, for example, is to defecate in a designated area separate from their daily living area. When an animal is in a cage with a cement or even slotted floor, it is forced to live on its excrement, causing, at a minimum, distress, but possibly ill health as well. Vertical integration (when a company owns all aspects of production of a food animal, from birth to death, and sometimes including the preparation of table-ready food) and the resulting intensification as found in CAFOs have greatly and negatively modified the welfare of farm animals. While these animals have access to food and water, other aspects of the Five Freedoms are either fully absent or only partially satisfied.

Not all small-scale production meets Welfare Quality standards. Animals on pasture experience large variations in weather, are potentially subjected to predators, and may not receive the same oversight as an animal in a concentrated facility. But the aesthetics of a pastured animal are exceptionally pleasant, and the range of motion considerably enhanced, allowing the animal to express its *telos*, and to have what many understand to be a "good" life for that species. Owner operated/controlled small-scale production is often closer to husbandry, an early acceptance of the obligation to promote and protect animals. Husbandry is taking great pains to put one's animals into the best possible environment to meet their physical and psychological needs, and then augmenting their ability to survive and thrive by providing them with food, protection from predation, water, medical attention, help in birthing, and so on.[35,36]

In most countries, animal welfare is provided and defined by laws and regulations. In the United States, the Animal Welfare Act (AWA) does not define animal welfare. Moreover, the AWA *excludes* farm animals from consideration. US federal regulations only regulate how farm animals are transported and slaughtered. And most recently, there are discussions to increase the possible rate of slaughter, which will impact not only animal welfare but also worker safety. The current rate of slaughter already occurs at dangerous speeds that result in worker injury. Abusing farm animals (cruelty) is not currently against the law, and recently proposed legislation would criminalize the mere *exposing* of abuse of farm animals.[37] An investigative report by Michael Moss in the *New York Times*, on the US Department of Agriculture's Animal Research Facility in Nebraska provides evidence that a lack of oversight resulted in animal abuse and cruelty, none of which is illegal but is immoral.[38]

Although there are no official animal welfare standards in the United States, industrial food animal producers have their own conception of animal welfare. They equate welfare with productivity as measured by the number of eggs laid or weight gain of the animal.[39] Despite numerous debates on the proper understanding of animal welfare,[40,41] it is clear that this reduction of welfare to productivity is incomplete and unacceptable. A few examples of the impact of CAFOs on the welfare of animals can illustrate this point.

Chicken Production

In commercial production, the large companies are vertically integrated. A vertically integrated company owns all aspects of production of a food animal, from birth to death, and sometimes including the preparation of table-ready food. This can include a hatchery, contracts with many farmers to grow chickens under specified conditions, and a plant to process one million or more chickens per week. Each chicken goes from a chick to table-ready in 6 weeks (42 days), and the industry refers to each chicken as a "unit," further distancing itself from the concept of the chicken as a living creature.[42] To provide some indication of the magnitude of production, I quote Nicholas Kristof of the *New York Times*, March 12, 2014: "Tyson, one of the nation's biggest companies, slaughters 135,000 head of cattle a week, along with 391,000 hogs and an astonishing 41 million chickens. Nearly all Americans regularly eat Tyson meat at home, at McDonalds, at a cafeteria, at a nursing home."[43] Tyson is one of the largest producers in the world and among the four major chicken producers in the United States. Some of the negative effects of this intense production methodology, as previously identified, include impacts on animal welfare, the environment, farmers, farm and processing workers, the local community, and human health.

As explained in the next section, antibiotic use at non-therapeutic levels results in the development and spread of antibiotic-resistant bacteria that have significant human health consequences. As a result of genetics and antibiotics, chickens grow so quickly that their bones cannot support their weight, they peck at each other ("give me some room"), and their waste is so concentrated (many chickens, little space per chicken) that the ammonia in the waste is irritating to the eyes and mucous membranes of the animals as well as to humans who happen to be in this environment.[44] As a result of bacterial contamination, a relatively recently introduced practice in chicken preparation includes carefully washing all utensils and surfaces that come in contact with the raw chicken; otherwise, serious contamination and illness can result.[45,46] In a recent incident reported in the US press, eating chicken that had been cooked to 165 °F resulted in illnesses.[47]

Large industrial processors have vertically integrated production. The farmer (often referred to as the grower) is a part of the chain. The grower owns the mortgage on the farm and the animal waste. All else—the chicken, the profits, feed manufacture (feed formulas), and post-slaughter processing—are owned and controlled by the integrator. This same arrangement exists for other land-based industrial production of animal protein.[48] At the present time in the United States, a handful of companies control more than 95% of all animal protein sold. The growers are what is generally called "the family farm," and in the United States, they constitute tens of thousands of households, if not more. These are owner-operated but not owner-controlled; they are controlled by the integrator.

Swine Production

Conditions of confinement for pigs are small group pens or individual stalls.[49] When pigs are at full weight, these pens are very crowded. Both crowded pens and individual stalls prevent the animals from having anything like a species-specific typical life. For example, pigs in individual stalls cannot interact with each other, nor can they turn or sometimes even lie down. All of the issues associated with intensification, including the inability to perform normal behavior and lack of access to the outdoors, are the same in cages or pens. In the case of swine, the quantity of animal waste is huge—about 13 times greater per animal, in fact, than per human. Human waste is always treated in the developed world, whereas swine waste is not treated and either is used as fertilizer or makes its way into runoff and waterways.[50] The resulting contamination has important negative environmental consequences such as contamination of rivers and coastal waterways. Animal waste in pastured animals does not cause the same problems and supports soil health.

Cattle Production

Cattle start their lives on pasture but are moved into feedlots (intensified conditions) where the diet is changed to corn and grain after about 6 months. This diet changes their digestive systems, allows them to grow faster, and changes the quality and quantity of fat to a less healthful variety for humans. Fat from grass-fed animals has higher levels of conjugate linoleic acid and approaches the fat composition of fish.[51] By concentrating these animals in feedlots, they are also forced to live on top of their excrement.

All of these examples converge in demonstrating that CAFOs cannot even approximate the Five Freedoms and fall very far short of Welfare Quality standards. In other words, CAFOs do not allow animals to have what they need or what they want.[52] Land-based industrial animal production, including egg and dairy production, affects all of the issues of moral concern identified in the Global Food Ethics Project's 7 by 5 Agenda for Ethics and Global Food Security.[53]

However, there are research and commercial developments aimed at sustainably intensified approaches that do provide a higher level of animal welfare. These include, for example, the Rondeel system for egg-laying hens and recirculating aquaculture facilities (see later).[54] The Rondeel system meets the Five Freedoms, has a lower environmental impact, meets the need to fit in with the landscape, has greater transparency for the public, and is an economically sustainable enterprise for the farmer.

In January 2015, the National Research Council/National Academy of Science (NRC/NAS) released a report: *Critical Role of Animal Science Research in Food Security and Sustainability.*[55] This report, known as the Goldstein report named after its chairman, Bernard Goldstein, identifies research priorities and recommends government and private-sector support for these activities. The report confirms the finding of the

Pew Commission Report ("Putting Meat on the Table") that research involving farm animals needs to be focused on producing adequate animal-based food products ethically. The report essentially confirms the necessity for greater adherence to the Five Freedoms, with "modified production systems that provide more opportunities to express natural behaviors."[56] This Pew Commission report, "Putting Meat on the Table," is not cited in this newer NAS report, although many of its major conclusions are consistent. The reasons for not referencing the Pew Commission report are unclear.

The Consequences of Intensification on Human Health and the Environment

In all animal species, the non-therapeutic use of antibiotics or antimicrobials is used to prevent diseases that are themselves the result of current intensification procedures.[57] Although many of these diseases are of ancient origin, the intensity and prevalence coincides with the development of CAFOs. There is little question that the use of these drugs, as well as breeding practices and genetics, has changed the rate of growth and feed conversion in these animals. As a consequence, the price of animal products at the retail level has been greatly decreased. However, is this a real decrease in cost or have the costs merely been shifted? How have these practices resulted in troubling human health consequences? What impact have they had on rural communities? Numerous studies have demonstrated that the cost of food is not reflected in the retail price.[58,59,60] Human health issues, environmental degradation, and community impact (social justice) are all part of the cost that each and every person pays. Whether the cost of industrial food is actually higher or lower than that produced by small farms at retail price, as indicated earlier, awaits a true analysis.

The human health consequences of the use of non-therapeutic levels of antibiotics are, however, well researched and significant.[61] There is no question that the use of antibiotics for growth promotion or "disease prevention" has resulted in the spread of antibiotic-resistant infections,

ANTIBIOTICS BY THE NUMBERS (UNITED STATES)

80% of all antibiotics sold in the United States are used in farm animals:
29.9 million pounds for livestock
7.7 million pounds to treat sick people
$21-$34 billion cost to US health system of antibiotic-resistant
infections (2013)
Antibiotic resistance in humans:
2 million illnesses
23,000 deaths
7% of 400 different antibiotics given to animals have been reviewed
by the FDA.

"The Future of Food," special compilation issue, *National Geographic*, 2014.

such as methicillin-resistant *Staphylococcus aureus* (MRSA), in humans. In the United States, 80% of all antibiotics produced are sold for use in farm animals, primarily for non-therapeutic purposes.

Importantly, the therapeutic use of antibiotics to cure diseases in an animal is ethically required. When used in this way, the antibiotic is given at a therapeutic dose only for the period of time needed to effectively treat the disease. By contrast, the non-therapeutic use of low-dose antibiotics for growth promotion or disease prevention requires the drug to be given over the majority of the life of the animal. This low-dose exposure in animals has a significant and negative effect on human well-being.[62]

CAFOs generally find their way into rural and impoverished areas. The impact on the community can be devastating.[63,64] In addition to MRSA, there is always a decrease in property values, impairment of quality-of-life issues, and poor aesthetic. During the Pew Commission hearings, a young girl who lived next to a CAFO testified about the air quality. She stated that when she woke the first morning in her college dorm, she thought she was dead because "there was no smell." While this is a single case report, air pollution studies near CAFOs have supported worsened air quality and adverse respiratory outcomes observed in persons living near CAFOs.[65]

With intensification comes a change in diet for all species. These animals now consume industrially produced crops. Some pesticides that are known to affect human health (e.g., atrazine) are also used on crops to feed animals.[66] An underexplored area is the effect of these pesticide-treated crops on animal health and human health as a contaminant of the animal products. Atrazine, the second most widely used pesticide in the United States, is banned in Europe but allowed in the United States.[67]

It seems that the cost of cheap meat (eggs and dairy included) comes at a very high price.

Aquatic Species

At the present time, some 50-60% of fin and shellfish used for human food is farm raised. Most wild caught aquatic animals are generally *harvested* using large nets, as opposed to being individually line caught. Net harvesting has resulted in depletion of many species, especially cod, and cut productivity of breeding grounds. Overharvesting has been one of the factors resulting in the need for aquatic farms.[68]

There are several different approaches currently in use or development for aquatic farming facilities including small production facilities, open-waterway nets, and technologically advanced water recirculation systems.

Paul Greenberg, in *Four Fishes*, identifies the issues in wild harvested and farmed sea animal products.[69] Although one might think that wild is the best to eat, this may not be correct. Depending on the qualities of the flesh desired, farmed may be a tastier and environmentally better choice. Further, when fish are farmed in some of the recirculating systems, there is considerable sparing of resources, and a very high-quality product results.

Atlantic salmon, a species of fish not necessarily from the Atlantic Ocean, is one of the most abundantly farmed fish and is raised in all types of facilities. Antibiotics are used in some, but not all, systems.[70] In addition, it is possible to use alternative protein-sourced (e.g., grain-based) feeds (although salmon are mainly carnivores) instead of fishmeal-based feeds.[71] Although the fish farming industry has often been criticized for the excessive consumption of wild fish to produce farmed fish, this is becoming less of an issue as feed formulations have improved substantially. In certain life stages, in water recirculation systems, the feed ratio to production can be as low as 0.7 (0.7 units of fish food to produce 1.0 units of fish for human consumption). In some recirculation systems, the waste is used as plant fertilizers or for energy production, resulting in efficient utilization of food resources and great sparing of water.[72]

Several marine species are being farmed in the University of Maryland, Baltimore County research facility in Baltimore, Maryland, and have been taken to a new and incredibly high quality of production. This facility raises multiple species of fish including bass, sea bream, and amberjack. The system is completely recirculating, with the waste filtered and used for the production of energy and the volatile wastes used to grow algae for conversion to biofuels. It is a very green way to intensively grow marine species for consumption.

One interesting species is the oyster. When done well, oyster farming may actually recapture areas for raising better oysters and, at the same time, purify the water for other fish populations.[73]

The animal welfare issues in farmed fishing are more difficult to gauge. Many of the species school, and that is what they are forced to do in the tanks. In properly managed water recirculation facilities, the fish are healthy, show little evidence of body damage, and have low feed conversion ratio. Their density, however, is greater than in the wild. Works by Martins et al. and Huntingford et al. did an excellent job of identifying items that should be considered in any evaluation of fish welfare.[74,75] Welfare Quality has not defined conditions for aquatic species. However, the considerations that are used for land-based animals can be adapted for aquatic species. A recent study has evaluated enrichment (wall colors and shapes) for the marine species sea bream.[76] Fish animal welfare is in need of a thorough study similar to Welfare Quality.

Many issues of fish welfare are under active investigation. At the present time, the slaughter I personally witnessed at the Freshwater Institute was rapid, without any struggling on the part of the fish, and appeared to be humane. The fish were placed on a wet platform and gently fed into a chute. Upon entering the chute an electrical stunning followed by gill displacement terminated the animal's life. There was no indication of stress on the fish, and the speed of the killing was very quick (possibly less than a second). This type of slaughter is currently used commercially, but it is not the only method of killing in the industry.

Moreover, some farming enterprises for aquatic species have negative effects on the fish, the environment, and human health. For example, some shrimp farms are environmentally unsustainable, and many of the aquatic operations are significantly affected by disease.

Other Animal-Based Protein Sources of Food

Important research is currently investigating the potential for insects to serve as a source of protein for humans and animals.[77] Depending on one's view about the value of insect life and the potential of insects to suffer, the production of insects for food will raise fewer concerns about animal welfare than the production of birds, mammals, and aquatic life. Also, in 2013, animal muscle was successfully grown in tissue culture as a proof of concept that cultured "meat" has the potential to be a source of food. This first demonstration involved the production of a "hamburger" from tissue-cultured cow muscle. More research is needed, however, to evaluate the costs (including water and energy) and organoleptic characteristics of cultured meat. If the nutritional content and taste of cultured meat can be well controlled and if the production process successfully scaled up at affordable prices, cultured meat could be an important source of animal protein that will not raise any animal welfare issues. It clearly will be used as animal feed if and when the price becomes competitive.

Conclusions

No one system of food animal production (or for that matter crops) will work for all situations. The local food movement in the developed world, which could be considered as currently affordable only for wealthy sections of the population, entails consumers getting locally produced food from the farm or the farmers' market, if not growing or raising it themselves. This is a remarkable and increasingly popular trend, with farm stores selling not only produce and meat but also dairy products, cured meats, as well as breads, pastas, and other locally made food products. Most recently, many local food vendors are now accepting SNAP benefits and money from food assistance programs.

In most cases, the animal foods produced in owner-operated, owner-controlled small-scale farms and sold in the local food movement context of wealthy countries meet, at an acceptable level, the issues of moral concern identified in the Global Food Ethics Project's 7 by 5 Agenda. In the world of land-based food animals, the small owner-operated, owner-controlled farm has few animals, and the treatment the animals usually receive can be called husbandry. In some areas of the United States, farmers are banding together to raise animals on pasture and then sell them through one or more local stores. In this case, the meat is hormone- and antibiotic-free, respects the environment, and sells at a somewhat higher price (but should not be more than about 20% higher) than meat produced industrially. However, this approach will not produce the quantities of meat produced in intensified facilities.

In the developed world, food animal production at the industrial level requires considerable change to meet any plausible account of ethical acceptability. Intensification and single-species production have significant consequences on the environment, animal welfare, and human health and use resources at unsustainable levels.

The issue of animal welfare is central if we are to feed the world ethically. The lack of adequate animal welfare practices for industrially raised animals is unacceptable. The Pew Commission report described industrial practices as "inhumane" but did not use the word *cruel* as some of us would have liked. In addition to strategies aiming at reducing animal protein consumption and increasing vegetable protein consumption, intensified practices will likely be needed to provide sufficient animal protein to meet the nutritional needs of over nine billion people. These practices, however, will have to be modified significantly from our current practices if they are to be sustainable and resilient, incorporate good animal welfare, and protect human health and the environment. Animal welfare approaching the EU Welfare Quality standards,[78] with the Five Freedoms as a minimum, must become incorporated into the developing framework for feeding the world of nine billion-plus people ethically.

This chapter is reprinted with minor editorial changes by permission from Springer Nature: Alan M. Goldberg, "Farm Animal Welfare and Human Health," *Current Environmental Health Reports* 3, no. 3 (September 2016): 313-21, https://doi.org/10.1007/s40572-016-0097-9.

REFERENCES
1. "The Future of Food," special compilation issue, *National Geographic*, 2014.
2. Caroline Ash et al., "Food Security. Feeding the Future. Introduction," *Science* 327, no. 5967 (February 2010): 797-833.
3. Since this chapter's original publishing in 2016, many, including this author, prefer the term "regenerative agriculture" over "sustainable intensifica-tion" due to the food industry's frequent co-opting of the latter term to promote industrial agricultural practices as "sustainable."
4. David Fraser, *Understanding Animal Welfare: The Science in Its Cultural Context* (Oxford: Wiley-Blackwell, 2008).
5. Farm Animal Welfare Council, "Farm Animal Welfare Council Press Statement," news release, December 5, 1979, https://webarchive.nationalarchives .gov.uk/20121010012427/http://www.fawc.org.uk/freedoms.htm.
6. Brambell Committee, "Report of the Technical Committee to Enquire into the Welfare of Animals Kept under Intensive Livestock Husbandry Systems," London: Her Majesty's Stationery Office, 1965.
7. Marian Stamp Dawkins, *Why Animals Matter: Animal Consciousness, Animal Welfare, and Human Well-Being* (Oxford: Oxford University Press, 2012).
8. Pew Commission on Industrial Farm Animal Production, "Putting Meat on the Table: Industrial Farm Animal Production in America," 2008, https:// www.pewtrusts.org/-/media/legacy/uploadedfiles/phg/content_level_pages /reports/pcifapfinalpdf.pdf.
9. Welfare Quality, "Principles and Criteria of Good Animal Welfare," http://www.welfarequality.net/media/1084/wq___factsheet_10_07_eng2.pdf.
10. Nestlé, "Nestlé Announces Farm Animal Welfare Commitment," news release, August 21, 2014, http://web.archive.org/web/20150104231012 /http://www.nestle.com/media/newsandfeatures/nestle-animal-welfare -commitment.
11. Welfare Quality, "Principles."

12. Pew Commission on Industrial Farm Animal Production, "Putting Meat on the Table."

13. Nestlé, "Nestlé Announces Farm Animal Welfare Commitment."

14. "The Future of Food."

15. H. Charles J. Godfray et al., "Food Security: The Challenge of Feeding 9 Billion People," *Science* 327, no. 5967 (February 2010): 812-18.

16. F. Bailey Norwood and Jayson L. Lusk, *Compassion, by the Pound: The Economics of Farm Animal Welfare* (Oxford: Oxford University Press, 2011).

17. Norwood and Lusk, *Compassion*.

18. Pew Commission on Industrial Farm Animal Production, "Putting Meat on the Table."

19. Pew Commission on Industrial Farm Animal Production, "Putting Meat on the Table."

20. "The Future of Food."

21. Christopher L. Delgado, "Rising Consumption of Meat and Milk in Developing Countries Has Created a New Food Revolution," *Journal of Nutrition* 133, no. 11, suppl. 2 (November 2003): 3907S–10S.

22. Barry M. Popkin, Linda S. Adair, and Shu Wen Ng, "Global Nutrition Transition and the Pandemic of Obesity in Developing Countries," *Nutrition Reviews* 70, no. 1 (January 2012): 3-21.

23. Ronni Chernoff, "Nutrition and Health Promotion in Older Adults," *Journals of Gerontology: Series A, Biological Sciences and Medical Sciences* 56, spec. no. 2 (October 2001): 47-53.

24. Pew Commission on Industrial Farm Animal Production, "Putting Meat on the Table."

25. "The Future of Food."

26. Pew Commission on Industrial Farm Animal Production, "Putting Meat on the Table."

27. US Food and Drug Administration, "FDA Announces Voluntary Withdrawal of 16 Antimicrobials for Use in Food-Producing Animals," news release, April 9, 2014, http://web.archive.org/web/20140413020111/https://www.fda.gov/AnimalVeterinary/NewsEvents/CVMUpdates/ucm392461.htm.

28. Keeve E. Nachman, Tyler J. S. Smith, and Robert P. Martin, "Antibiotics: Call for Real Change," *Science* 343, no. 6167 (January 2014): 136.

29. US Department of Agriculture, Animal and Plant Health Inspection Service, "Questions and Answers: Judicious Use of Antimicrobials in Food-Producing Animals," April 2014.

30. Pew Commission on Industrial Farm Animal Production, "Putting Meat on the Table."

31. David Fraser, personal communication, 2016.

32. South Dakota State University, "Beef Procedures: Antibiotic Use," http://web.archive.org/web/20160306034406/http://www.sdstate.edu/vs/extension/beef-procedures-antibiotics.cfm.

33. Brambell Committee, "Report of the Technical Committee to Enquire into the Welfare of Animals Kept under Intensive Livestock Husbandry Systems," 1965.

34. Welfare Quality, "Principles."

35. Bernard Rollin, *Putting the Horse before Descartes: My Life's Work on Behalf of Animals* (Philadelphia: Temple University Press, 2011).

36. Alan Goldberg and Bernard Rollin, "Husbandry and Industry: Animal Agriculture, Animal Welfare, and Human Health," in *Introduction to the US Food System: Public Health, Environment, and Equity*, ed. Roni A. Neff (San Francisco: Wiley-Jossey Bass, 2014), 294-99.

37. Kay Henderson, "Iowa Governor Signs Law Penalizing Animal Rights Activists," Reuters, March 5, 2012, https://www.reuters.com/article/usa-iowa -agriculture-idUSL2E8E605920120306.

38. Michael Moss, "U.S. Research Lab Lets Livestock Suffer in Quest for Profit," *New York Times*, January 19, 2015, https://www.nytimes.com/2015/01 /20/dining/animal-welfare-at-risk-in-experiments-for-meat-industry.html.

39. United Egg Producers, "Animal Husbandry Guidelines for U.S. Egg Laying Flocks: 2016 Edition," 2016, https://web.archive.org/web/20160803235428 /https://unitedegg.com/information/pdf/UEP-Animal-Welfare-Guidelines2016 .pdf.

40. Fraser, *Understanding Animal Welfare.*

41. David Fraser, "Could Animal Production Become a Profession?," *Livestock Science* 169 (November 2014): 155-62.

42. Pew Commission on Industrial Farm Animal Production, "Putting Meat on the Table."

43. Nicholas Kristof, "The Unhealthy Meat Market," *New York Times*, March 12, 2014, https://www.nytimes.com/2014/03/13/opinion/kristof-the -unhealthy-meat-market.html?_r=0.

44. Pew Commission on Industrial Farm Animal Production, "Putting Meat on the Table."

45. Consumer Reports, "The High Cost of Cheap Chicken," January 2014, https://www.consumerreports.org/cro/magazine/2014/02/the-high-cost-of-cheap -chicken/index.htm.

46. US Department of Agriculture, Food Safety and Inspection Service, "Chicken from Farm to Table," https://www.fsis.usda.gov/wps/portal/fsis/topics /food-safety-education/get-answers/food-safety-fact-sheets/poultry-preparation /chicken-from-farm-to-table/ct_index.

47. David Pierson, "Costco Unsure How Cooked Chicken Was Tainted in Salmonella Outbreak," *Los Angeles Times*, October 14, 2013, https://www .latimes.com/business/la-xpm-2013-oct-14-la-fi-mo-costco-recall-20131014 -story.html.

48. Pew Commission on Industrial Farm Animal Production, "Putting Meat on the Table."

49. Pew Commission on Industrial Farm Animal Production, "Putting Meat on the Table."

50. Pew Commission on Industrial Farm Animal Production, "Putting Meat on the Table."

51. Liesbeth A. Smit, Ana Baylin, and Hannia Campos, "Conjugated Linoleic Acid in Adipose Tissue and Risk of Myocardial Infarction," *American Journal of Clinical Nutrition* 92, no. 1 (July 2010): 34-40.

52. Stamp Dawkins, *Why Animals Matter.*

53. Johns Hopkins Berman Institute of Bioethics, Global Food Ethics Project, "7 by 5 Agenda for Ethics and Global Food Security," http://www.bioethicsinstitute.org/globalfoodethics/the-7-by-5-agenda-for-ethics-and-global-food-security?doing_wp_cron=1576852583.0286719799041748046875.

54. Rondeel, http://www.rondeeleieren.nl.

55. National Research Council, *Critical Role of Animal Science Research in Food Security and Sustainability* (Washington DC: National Academies Press, 2015).

56. National Research Council, *Critical Role.*

57. Rollin, *Putting the Horse before Descartes.*

58. Erin M. Tegtmeier and Michael D. Duffy, "External Costs of Agricultural Production in the United States," *International Journal of Agricultural Sustainability* 2, no. 1 (January 2004): 1-20.

59. Kathleen Delate et al., "An Economic Comparison of Organic and Conventional Grain Crops in a Long-Term Agroecological Research (LTAR) Site in Iowa," *American Journal of Alternative Agriculture* 18, no. 2 (June 2003): 59-69.

60. Daniel Imhoff, "Overhauling the Farm Bill: The Real Beneficiaries of Subsidies," *Atlantic*, March 21, 2012, https://www.theatlantic.com/health/archive/2012/03/overhauling-the-farm-bill-the-real-beneficiaries-of-subsidies/254422/.

61. Margaret Carrel et al., "Residential Proximity to Large Numbers of Swine in Feeding Operations Is Associated with Increased Risk of Methicillin-Resistant Staphylococcus Aureus Colonization at Time of Hospital Admission in Rural Iowa Veterans," *Infection Control & Hospital Epidemiology* 35, no. 2 (February 2014): 190-92.

62. Ellen K. Silbergeld, Jay Graham, and Lance B. Price, "Industrial Food Animal Production, Antimicrobial Resistance, and Human Health," *Annual Review of Public Health* 29 (April 2008): 151-69.

63. Pew Commission on Industrial Farm Animal Production, "Putting Meat on the Table."

64. Leah Schinasi et al., "Air Pollution, Lung Function, and Physical Symptoms in Communities near Concentrated Swine Feeding Operations," *Epidemiology* 22, no. 2 (March 2011): 208-15.

65. Joan A. Casey et al., "Industrial Food Animal Production and Community Health," *Current Environmental Health Reports* 2, no. 3 (September 2015): 259-71.

66. Silbergeld, Graham, and Price, "Industrial Food Animal Production."

67. Tyrone Hayes, "What Is Atrazine? And Why Do We Love It?," http://web.archive.org/web/20160310164428/http://www.atrazinelovers.com/m1.html.

68. Paul Greenberg, *Four fish: The Future of the Last Wild Food* (New York: Penguin Press, 2010).

69. Greenberg, *Four Fish.*

70. Greenberg, *Four Fish.*

71. John H. Tibbetts, "In Booming Aquaculture Industry, a Move to Plant-Based Food for Fish, *Yale Environment 360*, September 3, 2015, https://e360 .yale.edu/digest/in_booming_aquaculture_industry_a_move_to_plant-based _food_for_fish.

72. Katie McCollow, "Aquaponics Revives an Ancient Farming Technique to Feed the World," *Newsweek*, May 15, 2014, https://www.newsweek.com/2014 /05/23/aquaponics-revives-ancient-farming-technique-feed-world-251020.html.

73. National Centers for Coastal Ocean Science, "Measuring Parasites and Disease in U.S. Oysters and Mussels," February 5, 2015, https://coastalscience .noaa.gov/news/measuring-parasites-disease-u-s-oysters-mussels/.

74. Catarina I. M. Martins et al., "Behavioural Indicators of Welfare in Farmed Fish," *Fish Physiology and Biochemistry* 38, no. 1 (February 2012): 17-41.

75. F. A. Huntingford et al., "Current Issues in Fish Welfare," *Journal of Fish Biology* 68, no. 2 (February 2006): 332-72.

76. Alkisti Batzina et al., "Environmental Enrichment Induces Changes in Brain Monoamine Levels in Gilthead Seabream Sparus Aurata," *Physiology & Behavior* 130 (May 2014): 85-90.

77. Jessica Fanzo, "Ethical Issues for Human Nutrition in the Context of Global Food Security and Sustainable Development," *Global Food Security* 7 (December 2015): 15-23.

78. Welfare Quality, "Principles."

TWENTY-ONE

Animal Welfare

BERNARD ROLLIN

Husbandry as the Historical Basis for Agriculture

Domestication of animals began more than 12,000 years ago and was a plausible and rational successor to an earlier period of hunting and gathering, which was inherently unpredictable, dependent on the vagaries of weather, animal reproductive success, and forage. The need to constantly follow the food supply in turn created instability in communities. Such a situation erected a roadblock to the predictability presuppositional to the development of culture and civilization.

Thus, animals congenial to the company of humans created a state of symbiotic mutual benefit for humans as well as for the animals possessed of these traits. As Darwin pointed out, this arrangement was gradually augmented by artificial selection, further refining the traits of animals amenable by nature to domestication.

As domesticated animal agriculture grew more rational, its basis in *good husbandry* became firmly established. "Husbandry" is derived from the Old Norse phrase "*hus bond*," meaning "bonded to the household." Husbandry has been termed "the ancient contract with animals," where, as in any fair contract, both parties benefit from the relationship. Virtually until the 20th century, husbandry was the key concept in animal agriculture.

The essence of husbandry was *care*. Humans put animals into the most optimal environment congenial to the animals not only surviving but thriving, the environment for which they had evolved and been selected. The better the animals did, the better farmers did. Sanctioned by their own self-interest, humans provided farm animals with sustenance, water, shelter, protection from predation, such medical attention as was available, help in birthing, food during famine, water during drought, safe surroundings, and comfortable appointments. The Noah story is emblematic of this "ancient contract." In the Noah story, we learn that even as God preserves humans, humans preserve animals. In the Psalm 23, the Psalmist points out that God is to humans as the shepherd is to sheep.

The singular beauty of husbandry is that it was at once an ethical and prudential doctrine. It was prudential in that failure to observe husbandry inexorably led to ruination of the person keeping animals. Not feeding, not watering, not protecting from predators, not respecting the animals' physical, biological, and physiological needs and natures, what Aristotle called their *telos*—the "cowness of the cow," the "sheepness of the sheep"—meant your animals did not survive and thrive, and thus neither did you. No formally articulated animal ethic was needed.

The Decline of Husbandry

Not only was traditional husbandry agriculture largely ethical in terms of animal treatment; it also met what has become a major concern today, in that it was *sustainable*—that is, it was "a balanced aquarium" requiring very minimal additional inputs. Pasture fed the animals; the animals also ate the weeds, thereby minimizing the need for herbicides; animal manure nourished the ground, with no petrochemical material incorporated into the soil.

We have thus argued that the development of animal agriculture based in husbandry is presuppositional to the development of Western civilization and culture, which is itself presuppositional to the development of industry and technology. And in this surely resides one of the most profound ironies in human history. For it is the very fact of husbandry undergirding civilization that created the possibility of the undoing of husbandry-based agriculture.

The 18th century witnessed an industrial revolution in both plant and animal agriculture that greatly increased productivity.[1] The animal welfare that was assured by the need to put square pegs in square holes and round pegs in round holes was rendered obsolete by newly emerging "technological sanders" that allowed producers to force square pegs into round holes and round pegs into square holes—animals into environments congenial to profit, but radically inimical to the animals' biological natures.

In essence, new technology radically severed the connection traditionally observed between productivity and animal welfare. Under technological agriculture, animals were ripped from the pastoral environments they were evolved to live in and crowded into abrasive and alien confinement situations where they were totally unable to express their *telos*—that is, their inherent psychological and biological natures. If husbandry-era producers had attempted to raise, for example, hundreds of thousands of chickens in cages for egg production, the animals would be dead within months, the flocks decimated by disease that could take hold and spread like wildfire. Under an agriculture based in husbandry animals were slaughtered, processed, and consumed within a relatively short distance of where they were reared. Today, animals are shipped hundreds and even thousands of miles under conditions highly erosive of their health and well-being, where they are sold to consumers oblivious to how they came to be.

One of the most prominent "sanders" is the prolific use of antimicrobials both to promote growth and to enable the animals to survive and be productive under the previously mentioned unnatural and pathogenic conditions. Antibiotic use for any purpose other than treating disease was predicted in the 1940s, by Darwinian principles, to lead inexorably to antibiotic resistance. *To put it simply, excessive antibiotic use is a foundational linchpin for industrial agriculture.* It is a growth promotant; it smooths over the pathogenic effects of disease-causing systems; it allows us to keep animals under conditions where they are very likely get sick and die; and the animals continue to create large profits despite their being miserable.[2]

The industry contends that limiting antibiotics will greatly raise the price of animal products. But estimates of this effect say that it would raise the price of food insignificantly; perhaps a maximum of $10 a year per consumer, according to the National Research Council. In my experience, very few consumers would balk at paying somewhat extra so that the animals could live decently. And *no* parents would cavil at spending more money to assure that their children—or for that matter, they themselves—did not develop an infection resistant to common antibiotics.[3]

Current Welfare Issues in Confinement Agriculture

The key to success in husbandry agriculture and in assuring good animal welfare has been putting square pegs into square holes, round pegs into round holes, while creating as little friction as possible in doing so. As noted, the use of "technological sanders" has allowed us to ignore this pattern, and, as a result, animal welfare is no longer respected, yet animals remain productive. These "sanders" include antibiotics, bacterins, air handling systems, and vaccines without which the animals would, in addition to being miserable, sicken and die and fail to produce. Surgical mutilations, performed without anesthesia or analgesia, are ubiquitous in confinement agriculture—for example, castration, dehorning, beak-trimming, and, most recently, tail-docking of dairy cattle.

Given the fact that husbandry was the dominant approach to agriculture in the West for more than 12,000 years, it is remarkable how quickly it was supplanted by industry. By the mid-20th century, virtually all of agriculture, with the exception of the extensive beef and sheep industries, became industrialized with virtually no concern for animal well-being. For example, the egg industry crowds enormous numbers of chickens into cages, with the animals unable to express any of their natural behaviors or meet any of the needs dictated by their *telos*. Meat chickens, though not caged, are terribly crowded in indoor barns and also unable to express natural behaviors.

One encounters the same dismal situation for animals in all areas of industrialized animal agriculture. Consider, for example, the dairy industry, once viewed as the paradigm case of bucolic, sustainable animal agriculture, with animals grazing on pasture giving milk and fertilizing the soil for continued pasture with their manure. Though the industry wishes consumers to believe that this situation still exists—the California dairy industry ran advertisements proclaiming that California cheese comes from "happy cows," with depictions of cows grazing on pastures—the truth is radically different. Most California dairy cattle spend their lives on dirt and concrete, and in fact never see a blade of pasture grass, let alone consume it. So outrageous is this duplicity that the association was sued for false advertising, and a friend of mine, a dairy practitioner for 35+ years, railed against such an "outrageous lie."

In actual fact, the life of dairy cattle is not a pleasant one. In a problem ubiquitous across contemporary agriculture, animals have been single-mindedly bred for productivity—in the case of dairy cattle, for milk production. Today's dairy cow produces three to four times more milk than she did sixty years ago. In 1957, the average dairy cow produced between 500 and 600 pounds of milk per lactation. Fifty years later, it is close to 20,000 pounds.[4,5] From 1995 to 2004 alone, milk production per cow increased 16%. The result is a milk bag on legs, and unstable legs at that. A high percentage of the US dairy herd is chronically lame (some estimates range as high as 30 percent),[6] and these cows suffer serious reproductive problems.

Whereas in traditional agriculture a milk cow could remain productive for 10 and even 15 years, today's cow lasts slightly longer than two lactations, a result of metabolic burnout and the quest for ever-increasingly productive animals, hastened in the United States by the use of bovine somatotropin (BST) to further increase production. Such unnaturally productive animals suffer from mastitis, and the industry's response to mastitis in some areas of the country has created a new welfare problem in the form of docking cow tails without anesthesia in a futile effort to minimize teat contamination by manure. Still practiced, this procedure has been definitively demonstrated not to be relevant to mastitis control.[7] (In my view, the stress and pain of tail amputation, coupled with the concomitant inability to chase away flies, may well dispose to *more* mastitis.) Calves are removed from mothers shortly after birth, before receiving colostrum, creating significant distress in both mothers and infants. Bull calves may be shipped to slaughter or a feedlot immediately after birth, generating stress and fear.

The intensive swine industry, which through a handful of companies is responsible for 85% of the pork produced in the United States, is also responsible for significant suffering that did not affect husbandry-reared swine. Certainly the most egregious practice in the confinement swine industry and possibly, given the intelligence of pigs, in all of animal agriculture is the housing of pregnant sows in gestation crates or stalls—essentially small cages. The *recommended* size for such stalls, in which the sow spends almost her entire productive life of about four years, is according to the industry 3 feet high by 2 feet wide by 7 feet long—this for an animal that may weigh 600 or more pounds. (In reality many stalls are smaller.) The sow cannot stand up, turn around, walk, or even scratch her rump. In the case of large sows, she cannot even lie flat but must remain arched. The only exception to such confinement is the period of farrowing—approximately three weeks—when she is transferred to a "farrowing crate" to give birth and nurse her piglets. The space for her is no greater, but there is a "creep rail" surrounding her so the piglets can nurse without being crushed by her postural adjustments.

Under extensive conditions, a sow will build a nest on a hillside so excrement runs off, forage an area covering a mile a day, and take turns with other sows watching piglets and allowing all sows to forage.[8] With the animal's nature thus aborted, she goes mad and often exhibits bizarre and deviant behavior, such as compulsively chewing on the bars of the cage; she also endures foot and leg problems and develops lesions from lying on concrete in her own excrement. Baby piglets are castrated, their tails cut short without anesthesia or analgesia to prevent tail biting (which can in turn engender infections), and their teeth clipped. Tail biting, like cannibalism in chickens, is not a problem under extensive conditions where animals can avoid more aggressive animals. To the great credit of Smithfield Farms, I was able to convince them in 2007 to phase out gestation crates,[9] a process that was completed in 2018 at all of its US company-owned sow farms.[10]

Poultry were the earliest animals raised in confinement. This includes both egg-laying hens and broilers utilized for meat production. This is partly a result of the very small size of chickens as compared with such animals as cattle and swine. As a result of high confinement in the meat chicken industry, chicken has gone from a luxury food served only on special occasions, to the cheapest of meats, the lowest price today hovering at about $1.00 per pound or less in the US markets.

It is arguable that chickens suffer the most extreme welfare abuses of any animals raised in confinement in the United States, certainly in terms of numbers. In 2016, 305 million laying hens were raised, 95% of them in cages, and almost 9 million broiler chickens were grown.[11]

Laying hens suffer from every sort of welfare insult possible, from total violation of their *telos* to painful surgical mutilations. With up to six birds kept in each battery cage, and sometimes even more, each hen is allotted a ridiculous 67 square inches. In some operations I have seen, one chicken literally lives on the backs of the others—this for an animal evolved to live in open spaces! Contrary to industry propaganda, chickens are not mindless, simple automata but are in fact behaviorally complex, highly social animals showing a good deal of intelligence and learning ability. Anyone who has raised barnyard chickens under open conditions knows that they have very distinct personalities and often bond with people.

Given that the nature of chickens is to live in plenty of space, packing them into cages diminishes their productivity of eggs per chicken but maximizes productivity per cage. Cages are expensive; chickens are cheap. Crowding leads to feather-pecking and cannibalism, since the animals lack the space necessary for escape. To rectify the situation, the industry "debeaks" or trims the beak of the animals with a hot blade. Though the industry would have the public believe that the beak-trimming causes no suffering, analogous to humans cutting their nails, this is patently false. The beaks are innervated and trimming them leads to both acute and chronic pain. After trimming, nerves develop into extensive neuromas, conclusively shown to be painful. With unconscious but bitter irony, the egg industry refers to cannibalism as a "vice," as if the chickens are morally reprehensible for engaging in behavior created by the abnormal conditions in which they must live. Trimming of toes is also practiced to prevent related claw injury.

Virtually every behavioral need of chickens is thwarted in battery cages. This includes inability to engage in exercise, wing flapping, leg stretching, and preening. Caged birds have significant incidents of lameness, bone brittleness, osteoporosis, and muscle weakness. Roughly 30% of hens go to slaughter with fractures. Air quality, particularly ammonia levels, is extremely poor in battery cages, and infectious disease spreads rapidly.

Not surprisingly, nest building and dust bathing represent powerful needs determined by the chickens' natures, yet are totally unachievable in battery cages. Obviously, all social needs are thwarted as well. Recently, the public has moved beyond lack of concern for poultry—"they are just chickens"—and numerous states have abolished battery cage systems. Since male chickens are of no use to the egg industry, they are killed as soon as they are hatched, either by being suffocated in garbage bags or being macerated. Withholding of food and water from laying hens in order to increase the frequency of laying cycles, commonly known as "forced moulting," represents an additional and ubiquitous welfare issue.

Broiler chickens are not raised in cages; rather they are raised in huge barns, lacking in proper air quality and sunlight and resulting in significant crowding and easy spread of disease. In addition, today's broiler chickens have been genetically bred and are fed to reach market weight in seven weeks, a reduction of nearly two-thirds from the time it took the traditional broiler, leading to musculoskeletal injuries and very large amounts of bone breakage and bruising. With tens of thousands of chickens per building and a very small labor force, it is impossible to inspect the animals for disease, injury, or other kinds of suffering.

Because broiler breeders have been bred for fast growth rate and great appetite, problems of obesity are created, particularly with chickens used for breeding. As a result, these animals are placed under severe food restriction. Because food is a primordial inelastic demand, it is extremely likely that these animals suffer.

Finally, as is the case with virtually all animals raised in confinement, loading of the animals onto trucks, transport, and slaughter raise major welfare issues. The animals being transported are not only buffeted around in the trucks but also suffer from extremes of heat and cold, crowding, noise, and odor. Pre-slaughter stunning ranges from trauma induced by a captive bolt pistol in the beef and sheep industries, to CO_2 asphyxiation in swine, to electrical stunning effected in poultry that are fitted to the birds' heads while they are hanging upside down. Electrical stunning, I have been told by slaughterhouse workers, fails more than half the time in poultry. The result is that conscious birds are eviscerated by machines and then immediately immersed in scalding water. The poultry industry is currently considering alternatives to electrical stunning.

Fish Welfare in Confinement

With the world population increasing exponentially, there is a pressing demand for affordable protein. Fish seems to represent the most plausible answer to this problem. Whereas it takes six pounds of grain to produce one pound of beef, fish is very close to a one-to-one ratio, thereby creating a level of production efficiency unmatched in any other area of protein production. Inevitably, aquaculture, not only of fish but also of crustaceans, particularly shrimp and mollusks, has proliferated around the world.

It would be a huge and grievous error to underestimate the degree of potential public concern for the welfare of aquatic animals. In the 1990s, in Great Britain, there was a precipitous drop in the sale of live lobsters in supermarkets, as housewives were reluctant to take the animals home and boil them alive. The industry was forced to develop a stunner that would render the lobsters unconscious in the store. Two recent books, entitled *Do Fish Feel Pain?* and *What a Fish Knows*,[12,13] authored respectively by Victoria Braithwaite and Jonathan Balcombe, have helped to thrust fish sentience into public awareness. Two Disney studio feature films, *Finding Nemo* and *Finding Dory*, have done for sea creatures what, generations earlier, *Bambi* did for forest animals.

Behavioral, neurophysiological, and biochemical data clearly indicate that fish feel pain and fear as well. In addition, cephalopods have demonstrated in experiments their ability to solve complex problems. It is also well known that under conditions of crowded intensive production, massive die-offs and significant epidemics of disease run rife. Fish are probably more susceptible to stress than any other animals.

These examples suffice to illustrate the absence of good welfare in confinement. Rest assured that a long litany of issues could be addressed. In general, all animals in confinement agriculture (with the exception of beef cattle who live most of their lives on pasture, and are "finished" on grain in dirt feedlots, where they can actualize much but not all of their nature) suffer from the same generic set of affronts to their welfare absent in husbandry agriculture. The fate of beef cattle in feedlots is problematic in its own way. Feedlots developed after World War II as the "green revolution" created a vast oversupply of grain, and producers reasoned that putting that grain through cattle considerably enhanced the value of the grain, which is in effect converted to beef.

What Is Animal Welfare?

The US agriculture community has been far behind societal concern. When one discusses farm animal welfare with industry groups, one finds the same response—animal welfare is solely a matter of "sound science."

In fact, questions of animal welfare are at least partly "ought" questions, questions of ethical obligation. The concept of animal welfare is an ethical concept to which, *once understood, science brings relevant data. When we ask about an animal's welfare, or about a person's welfare, we are asking about what we owe the animal, and to what extent.* A document called the CAST (Council for Agricultural Science and Technology) report, first published by US agricultural scientists in the early 1980s, discussed animal welfare and affirmed that the necessary and sufficient conditions for attributing positive welfare to an animal were represented by the animals' productivity. A productive animal enjoyed positive welfare; a nonproductive animal enjoyed poor welfare.[14]

This notion was fraught with many difficulties. First of all, productivity is an economic notion predicated of a whole operation; welfare is predicated of individual animals. An operation, such as caged laying hens, may be quite profitable if the cages are severely overcrowded, yet the individual hens do not enjoy good welfare. Second, as we shall see, equating productivity and welfare is, to some significant extent, legitimate under husbandry conditions, where the producer does well if and only if the animals do well, and square pegs, as it were, are fitted into square holes with as little friction as possible. Under industrial conditions, however, animals do not naturally fit in the niche or environment in which they are kept and are subjected to "technological sanders" that allow for producers to force square pegs into round holes—antibiotics, feed additives, hormones, air handling systems—so the animals do not die and thus produce more and more kilograms of meat or milk. Without these technologies, the animals could not be productive.

Even if the CAST Report definition of animal welfare did not suffer from the difficulties we outlined, it is still an ethical concept. It essentially says, "What we owe animals and to what extent are simply what it takes to get them to create profit." This in turn would imply that the animals are well-off if they have only food, water, and shelter, something the industry has sometimes asserted. Even in the early 1980s, however, there were animal advocates and others who would take a very different ethical stance on what we owe farm animals. Indeed, the famous Five Freedoms articulated in Britain by the Farm Animal Welfare Council during the 1970s represents quite a different ethical view of what we owe animals, when it affirms that:

> The welfare of an animal includes its physical and mental state and we consider that good animal welfare implies both fitness and a sense of well-being. Any animal kept by man must at least be protected from unnecessary suffering.

We believe that an animal's welfare, whether on farm, in transit, at market or at a place of slaughter should be considered in terms of "five freedoms."

1. Freedom from Hunger and Thirst—by ready access to fresh water and a diet to maintain full health and vigor.

2. Freedom from Discomfort—by providing an appropriate environment including shelter and a comfortable resting area.

3. Freedom from Pain, Injury or Disease—by prevention or rapid diagnosis and treatment.

4. Freedom to Express Normal Behavior—by providing sufficient space, proper facilities and company of the animal's own kind.

5. Freedom from Fear and Distress—by ensuring conditions and treatment which avoid mental suffering.[15]

Clearly, the two definitions contain very different notions of our moral obligation to animals (and there is an indefinite number of other definitions). Which is correct, of course, cannot be decided by gathering facts or doing experiments—indeed, which ethical framework one adopts will in fact determine the shape of science studying animal welfare. Thus, sound science does not determine your concept of welfare; rather, your concept of welfare determines what counts as sound science.

The failure to recognize the inescapable ethical component in the concept of animal welfare leads inexorably to those holding different ethical views talking past each other. Thus, producers ignore questions of animal pain, fear, distress, confinement, truncated mobility, bad air quality, social isolation, and impoverished environment unless any of these factors impact negatively on the "bottom line." Animal advocates, on the other hand, give such factors primacy and are totally unimpressed with how efficient or productive the system may be.

What Notion of Animal Welfare Is Likely to Prevail?

A major question obviously arises here. If the notion of animal welfare is inseparable from ethical components, and people's ethical stances on obligations to farm animals differ markedly across a highly diverse spectrum, whose ethic is to predominate and define, in law or regulation, what counts as "animal welfare"? It is to this issue we now turn. The answer is patently the animal ethic of society in general.

What is the nature of the emerging new ethical thinking that underlies and informs the dramatic social changes in level of social concern for animal treatment? Although society has always had an articulated ethic regarding animal treatment, that ethic has been very minimalistic, leaving most of the issue of animal treatment to people's personal ethic, rather than to the social ethic. That limited social ethic has forbidden deliberate, willful, sadistic, deviant, purposeless, and unnecessary infliction of pain and suffering on animals, or outrageous neglect, such as not feeding or watering. Beginning in the early nineteenth century, this set of prohibitions was articulated in the anticruelty statutes of the laws in all civilized societies.

For the overwhelming majority of human history, until some four decades ago, the anticruelty ethic served as the only socially articulated moral principle for animal treatment. Except for a few sporadic voices following in the wake of Darwin's articulation of human-animal continuity, no one spoke of animals' rights, nor did society have moral concepts for animal treatment that went "beyond cruelty." The obvious question that presents itself is this: What has occurred during the past half century which led to social disaffection with the venerable ethic of anticruelty and to strengthening of the anticruelty laws, which now make cruelty a felony in more than 40 US states?

In a study commissioned by USDA to answer this question, I distinguished a variety of social and conceptual reasons:[16]

1. Changing demographics has prompted *consequent* changes in the paradigm for animals: Whereas at the turn of the century, more than half the population was engaged in producing food for the rest, today only some 1.5% of the US public is engaged in production agriculture.[17] One hundred years ago, if one were to ask a person in the street, urban or rural, to state the words that come to mind when one says "animal," the answer would doubtless have been "horse," "cow," "food," "work," etc. Today,

however, for the majority of the population, the answer is "dog," "cat," "pet." Repeated studies show that most of the pet-owning population views their animals as "members of the family."[18] Divorce lawyers note that custody of the dog can be as thorny an issue as custody of the children.

2. We have lived through a long period of ethical soul-searching: For almost 50 years society has turned its "ethical searchlight" on humans traditionally ignored or even oppressed by the consensus ethic—people of color, women, the handicapped, other minorities. The same ethical imperative has focused attention on our treatment of the nonhuman world—the environment and animals. Many leaders of the activist animal movement in fact have roots in earlier movements—civil rights, feminism, homosexual rights, children's rights, labor.

3. The media have discovered that "animals sell papers": One cannot channel-surf across normal television service without being bombarded with animal stories, real and fictional. (A *New York Times* reporter told me that more time on cable TV in New York City is devoted to animals than to any other subject.) Recall, for example, the extensive media coverage of some whales trapped in an ice floe and freed by a Russian icebreaker. This was hardly an overflowing of Russian compassion—an oxymoronic notion applied to a people who gave us pogroms, the Gulag, and Stalinism. Rather, someone in the Kremlin was bright enough to realize that liberating the whales was an extremely cheap way to score points with US public opinion.

4. Strong and visible arguments have been advanced in favor of raising the status of animals by philosophers, scientists, and celebrities.

5. Changes in the nature of animal use demanded new moral categories.

While all of the reasons listed here are relevant, they are nowhere nearly as important as the precipitous and dramatic changes in animal use that occurred after World War II. These changes were, first of all, huge conceptual changes in the nature of agriculture from husbandry to industry, and, second, the rise of significant amounts of animal research and testing, the latter exemplified by the formation of the National Institutes of Health, whose current budget is well over $37 billion. Neither of these major changes were the result of cruelty but were rather attempts to provide enough food for the burgeoning population and to improve biomedical research and product safety. That means the old ethic of cruelty did not apply, and a new ethic was needed to mitigate animal suffering.

Society eventually became aware that new kinds of suffering were engendered by research and modern agriculture. Once again, producers could not be categorized as cruel, yet they were responsible for new types of animal suffering on at least four fronts:

1. Production diseases arise from the new ways the animals are produced. The idea of a method of production creating diseases that were "acceptable" would be anathema to a husbandry agriculturalist.

2. The huge scale of industrialized agricultural operations and the small profit margin per animal militate against the sort of individual attention that typified much of traditional agriculture.

3. Another new source of suffering in industrialized agriculture results from physical and psychological deprivation for animals in confinement: lack of space, lack of companionship for social animals, inability to move freely, boredom, austerity of environments, and so on. Because the animals evolved for adaptation to extensive environments but are now placed in truncated environments, such deprivation is inevitable.

4. In confinement systems, workers may not be "animal smart"; the "intelligence," such as it is, is in the mechanized system. Instead of husbandmen, workers in swine factories are minimum wage, often animal-ignorant labor. So there is often no empathy with or concern for the animals.

Where, then, does the necessary new ethic come from? Plato taught us a very valuable lesson about effecting ethical change. If one wishes to change another person's—or society's—ethical beliefs, it is much better to *remind* than to *teach* or, in my martial arts metaphor, to use *judo* rather than *sumo*. In other words, if you and I disagree ethically on some matter, it is far better for me to show you that what I am trying to convince you of is already implicit—albeit unnoticed—in what you already believe. These points are well-exemplified in 20th-century US history. Prohibition was *sumo*, not *judo*—an attempt to forcefully impose a new ethic about drinking on the majority by the minority. As such, it was doomed to fail, and in fact people drank *more* during Prohibition. Contrast this with Lyndon Johnson's civil rights legislation. Johnson, himself a Southerner, realized that even Southerners would acquiesce to the following two propositions: all humans should be treated equally, and black people were human—they just had never bothered to draw the relevant conclusion.

If Johnson had been wrong about this point, if "writing this large" in the law had not "reminded" people, civil rights would have been as ineffective as Prohibition. At the same time, recall that Western society has gone through almost 50 years of extending its moral categories for *humans* to people who were morally ignored or invisible—women, minorities, the handicapped, children, citizens of the third world. So a plausible and obvious move is for society to continue in its tendency and *attempt to extend the moral machinery it has developed for dealing with people, appropriately modified, to animals.*

What aspect of our ethic for people is being so extended? One that is, in fact, quite applicable to animal use, is the fundamental problem of weighing the interests of the individual against those of the general welfare. Different societies have provided different answers to this problem. Totalitarian societies opt to devote little concern to the individual, favoring instead the state, or whatever their version of the general welfare may be. At the other extreme, anarchical groups such as communes give primacy to the individual and very little concern to the group— hence, they tend to enjoy only transient existence. In our society, however, a balance is struck. Although most of our decisions are made to the benefit of the general welfare, fences are built around individuals to protect their fundamental interests from being sacrificed to the majority. Thus we protect individuals from being silenced even if the majority disapproves of what they say; we protect individuals from having their property seized without recompense even if such seizure benefits the general welfare; we protect individuals from torture even if they have planted a bomb in an elementary school and refuse to divulge its location. We protect those interests of the individual that we consider essential to being human, to *human nature*, from being submerged, even by the common good. Those moral/legal fences that so protect the individual human are called *rights* and are based on plausible assumptions regarding what is essential to being human.

It is this notion to which society in general is looking in order to generate the new moral notions necessary to talk about the treatment of animals in today's world, where cruelty is not the major problem but where such laudable, general human welfare goals as efficiency, productivity, knowledge, medical progress, and product safety are responsible for the vast majority of animal suffering. People in society are seeking to "build fences" around animals to protect the animals and their interests and natures from being totally submerged for the sake of the human purpose. Although, as legally property, animals cannot be directly granted rights, an equivalent to rights can be achieved by limiting property rights over animals.

In the case of farm animals, people wish to see their basic needs and nature, *teloi*, respected in the systems that they are raised. Because this no longer occurs naturally as it did in husbandry, it must be imposed by legislation or regulation. A Gallup poll conducted in 2003 shows that more than 60% of the public want strict laws concerning the treatment of farm animals.[19] By 2012, the number had risen to 94%. In 2004, 2,100 pieces of legislation pertaining to animal welfare were floated across the United States. Legal codification of rules of animal care respecting animal *telos* is thus the form animal welfare takes where husbandry has been abandoned. This, in essence, constitutes what I have called "animal rights as a mainstream phenomenon."

REFERENCES

1. Mark Overton, *Agricultural Revolution in England: The Transformation of the Agrarian Economy, 1500-1850* (Cambridge: Cambridge University Press, 2010).

2. Bernard E. Rollin, "Antibiotic Use and the Demise of Husbandry," *Journal of Ethics* 22, no. 1 (March 2018): 45-57.

3. Rollin, "Antibiotic Use."

4. Colorado Dairy Industry, *Quick Facts Based on 2005 Production*, provided by Bill Waites, 2005.

5. US Department of Agriculture, National Agricultural Statistics Service, "Milk Production and Milk Cows," https://www.nass.usda.gov/Charts_and _Maps/Milk_Production_and_Milk_Cows/index.php.

6. Kenneth V. Nordlund, Nigel B. Cook, and Garrett R. Oetzel, "Investigation Strategies for Laminitis Problem Herds," *Journal of Dairy Science* 87 (2004): E27-35, doi:10.3168/jds.s0022-0302(04)70058-2.

7. Clell V. Bagley, "Tail Docking of Dairy Cattle," 2003, http://extension.usu .edu/dairy/files/taildock.

8. Bernard E. Rollin, *Farm Animal Welfare: Social, Bioethical, and Research Issues* (Ames: Iowa State University Press, 1995).

9. Smithfield Foods, "Smithfield Foods Makes Landmark Decision Regarding Animal Management," news release, January 25, 2007, https://www.smithfield foods.com/newsroom/press-releases-and-news/smithfield-foods-makes-landmark -decision-regarding-animal-management.

10. Smithfield Foods, "Smithfield Foods Achieves Industry-Leading Animal Care Commitment, Unveils New Virtual Reality Video of Its Group Housing Systems," news release, January 8, 2018, https://www.smithfieldfoods.com/newsroom/press -releases-and-news/smithfield-foods-achieves-industry-leading-animal-care -commitment-unveils-new-virtual-reality-video-of-its-group-housing-systems.

11. US Department of Agriculture, National Agricultural Statistics Service, "Chickens and Eggs," 2017, https://www.nass.usda.gov/Charts_and_Maps/Milk _Production_and_Milk_Cows/index.php.

12. Victoria Braithwaite, *Do Fish Feel Pain?* (Oxford: Oxford University Press, 2010).

13. Jonathan Balcombe, *What a Fish Knows: The Inner Lives of Our Underwater Cousins* (New York: Scientific American / Farrar, Straus and Giroux, 2016).

14. Council for Agricultural Science and Technology, *Scientific Aspects of the Welfare of Food Animals*, Report #91, 1981.

15. Farm Animal Welfare Council, "Farm Animal Welfare Council Press Statement," news release, December 5, 1979, https://webarchive.nationalarchives .gov.uk/20121010012427/http://www.fawc.org.uk/freedoms.htm.

16. Rollin, *Farm Animal Welfare.*

17. Agricultural Machinery Conference, 18th Agricultural Machinery Conference, Cedar Rapids, IA, May 5-7, 2003.

18. "Survey Says Pets Are Members of the Family," *Acorn*, January 31, 2002, https://web.archive.org/web/20050118115936/; http://www.theacorn.com/News /2002/0131/Pets/036.html.

19. Gallup, "Public Lukewarm on Animal Rights," May 21, 2003, https:// news.gallup.com/poll/8461/public-lukewarm-animal-rights.aspx.

TWENTY-TWO

Biotechnology and Animal Well-Being

KEVIN ESVELT

WHAT DO INVENTORS and society owe animals? Most new advances are developed to benefit humans, but the rise of biotechnology demands careful consideration of what might be done to benefit the many other creatures with whom we share the planet.

When it comes to moral responsibility, powerful new technologies are worse than swords without hilts: even when we decline to grasp them, we are cut. Few would argue that developing and using a new advance make us responsible for the consequences, both accidental and intended. But when we decline to solve a problem newly within our capabilities, the problem continues because of our choice. That makes us increasingly responsible not only for the continued suffering of our pets and our livestock but also for wild species.

Six years ago, no one even imagined that individual researchers might be able to edit wild organisms. Today, we can use CRISPR genome editing to build self-propagating gene drive systems predicted to spread over generations to every population connected by gene flow.[1,2] Insert a DNA sequence that encodes the desired change—the new phenotype that we want the organism to display—into the genome of an organism, along with the CRISPR genome editing machinery responsible for making that change. Now the organism can repeat that genome editing step without further human intervention. When it mates with a wild-type organism, the CRISPR components are produced in the reproductive cells of the offspring, which carry one edited and one original copy. The enzyme finds the targeted original site in the genome, cuts it, and copies the edited DNA sequence in its place. When the organism mates, most or all of its offspring—not just half, as is normal—will inherit the engineered copy. Repeat the process every generation, with the new version replacing the old. With the correct design and enough generations, models suggest that every member of the species could potentially be edited.[3,4,5,6] With the right alteration—say, ensuring that all organisms who inherit are born male—we can also suppress populations.[7,8]

To be clear, we don't know for sure that CRISPR-based gene drive systems will work in the wild. But the evidence points that way, and if they do, the moral implications are substantial. Although much has been written on the moral quandaries of using gene drive to prevent malaria transmission in Africa, giving even marginal moral weight to the well-being of animals renders the ethical implications of using gene drive to reduce animal suffering equally formidable.

A Human-Made Ecological Problem: Animal Suffering from Anticoagulant Poisons

Somewhat unbelievably, the animals that we raise for food greatly out-mass all wild terrestrial vertebrates.[9] Yet most of us determine the moral weight of an elephant to be greater not because of its considerable mass but due to its cognitive sophistication. If not quite so bright, rats are also quite intelligent animals; indeed, their cunning is part of why we consider them pests. There's no question that rodents are the source of a great deal of harm; black and brown rats together are the number one cause of extinctions on islands, and they inflict more than $19 billion in economic damages every year in the United States alone.[10,11] But there's also no question that they suffer. Our preferred way of mitigating damage caused by rodents is to kill them with poison, usually an anticoagulant rodenticide that causes them to bleed out and die over the course of 72 hours. Thanks to intense migraines from cerebral hemorrhaging, it's a fairly agonizing death, one that we gift to perhaps as many as five billion rodents every year; Australia alone kills more than a billion mice in agriculture with rodenticides annually.[12] That is a great deal of animal suffering for which we humans are directly responsible. And it is suffering that might be eliminated by using biotechnology to ensure that fewer rodents are born.

There are many reasons we should think carefully before considering the use of a self-propagating CRISPR gene drive to suppress rat populations everywhere, because rats may be doing something important ecologically in their native Eurasian habitat. Fortunately, there are several ways we could alter local but not global populations. The trick is to separate the components of the gene drive system. Rather than having everything in one place where it can copy itself, we separate the CRISPR elements and scatter them throughout the genome but arrange them in a daisy chain such that each element copies the next in the chain. Imagine that elements C, B, and A are on separate chromosomes but are arranged in a linear daisy chain. Element C causes element B to be copied, and element B causes element A to be copied. Element A, for example, might have the CRISPR nuclease and the male-determining trait that we want to spread. The result is that the local population gets distorted in favor of males, so you don't have very many females, and thus they don't reproduce.

How does this play out in a family tree? When a daisy drive rat is released into the wild population and mates with a wild-type rat, all of the offspring will inherit elements A and B because element C is present, but because element C isn't copied, only half of the offspring will inherit it. Natural selection eventually eliminates element C from the population. Once it's gone, element B loses its advantage and disappears, followed by element A, until finally there are no engineered offspring left. The spread of the desired trait is controlled by the number of organisms released and the number of elements in the daisy chain, which serve as a form of genetic fuel.[13]

A Natural Ecological Problem: Animal Suffering Due to Wild Parasites

Most people believe that livestock should be raised outdoors. It's intuitively plausible that the well-being of chickens, pigs, goats, sheep, and cows might be greater when they can see the sky, although this assumption deserves more rigorous empirical testing than has been reported to date. But what if raising livestock outdoors means that some will quite literally be devoured alive by flesh-eating maggots? In South America, that is reality. The New World screwworm fly (*Cochliomyia hominivorax*) is a particularly horrifying parasite because it lays its eggs in open wounds as small as a tick bite, and once the maggots hatch, they don't just consume dead and dying flesh—they burrow into and devour healthy living tissue. The smell of bacteria from the wound attracts new gravid females that continue the macabre cycle. Animals often die if left untreated. We know that it's agonizingly painful because the species infests humans too; *hominivorax* is Latin for "man-devourer." Patients often receive morphine just so they can bear the pain when doctors examine the wound. But most victims are either wild animals or livestock in poor rural communities least able to afford the loss. Back-of-the-envelope calculations based on mark-recapture estimates and habitat suitability models suggest that more than a billion animals are devoured alive every single year.[14,15]

We could avert this suffering by deliberately eliminating *Cochliomyia hominivorax* from the wild. Indeed, we've done so before across an entire continent. One of the most significant human projects to benefit animal well-being in history involved the elimination of this particular species from all of North America using the sterile insect technique.[16] Starting in the 1950s, the US Department of Agriculture (USDA) bred screwworm flies in factories on dead meat slurry, irradiated them, and released them into the wild in huge numbers, enough that the wild flies couldn't find one another to reproduce.[17] Over decades, the technique drove them all the way down to Panama, where the USDA now releases 10 million sterile screwworm flies each week, creating a living wall preventing re-invasion by South American screwworms.

Screwworm was not eradicated from North America because it caused tremendous animal suffering; as a society, we seldom take action just to help animals. Rather, screwworm was eliminated due to the estimated $750 million in economic damages it inflicted in the United States each year. In South America, where the species is more entrenched, it causes about $3.5 billion in economic damage annually.[18] Biotechnology could make complete removal feasible, even without the use of a self-propagating gene drive. Even though the elimination from South America will likely be undertaken primarily for reasons other than to reduce animal suffering, that does not in any way diminish the magnitude of the benefit to animal well-being.

How Should the Research Be Conducted, and Who Decides Whether and Where the Technologies Are Used?

Developing ecological engineering technologies is fundamentally different from inventing products used by individuals. If a laboratory develops a new drug and your doctor recommends it to you, you can always decline. But if a technology we develop for editing the shared environment is used in your area, it will affect you and your community. No one can opt out.[19,20] That makes it more like infrastructure development, which history has shown benefits from community guidance from the earliest stages. Shared-impact projects just work out better if everyone affected has the opportunity to have a voice from the earliest stages, enabling them to help decide what form the project takes and how it will affect their community.

The problem is that science isn't set up to encourage dialogue and participation—in fact, quite the opposite. Changing incentives is absolutely essential if we want to overcome the biggest hurdle to preventing use of beneficial technologies: public rejection due to factors other than values, costs, and benefits.

If we want to make rational decisions about whether we should move forward with a given technology, we need to do everything possible to keep politics out of it. GMOs are a clear example of what not to do; indeed, when in doubt, we should look at that example and default to the opposite approach. That means developing early applications that are obviously beneficial to the typical person, not just a tiny minority. It means reaching out to potentially interested early adopter communities before research begins, ensuring the technology is openly developed with local guidance. It means actively inviting criticism, listening, and responding, because many locals know things about their local environment that no scientist does. And it means ensuring the technology isn't captured by major economic interests early on. That last point, though particularly important for agriculture, is generally good advice: if there is funding for development by nonprofit institutions, all early applications should steer clear of the profit motive—not that there's anything wrong with it, but because it's been shown to reduce public trust and acceptance. Today, there may be no surer way to condemn a technology to widespread public opposition than to have it be pioneered by Big Ag.

So which potential early adopter communities should guide research on daisy drives in rodents? My research group has been engaging with the Māori communities of Aotearoa New Zealand, who are particularly interested in finding a way of removing invasive rodents that does not involve poisons. Because New Zealand's government has committed to eliminating invasive rats by 2050, there is likely to be strong pressure to apply in Aotearoa any suppression drive system developed elsewhere. Since we view Māori support to be ethically and legally vital to any such use, and their cultural and ecological knowledge may be critical to determining whether local use is ecologically advisable, it would be foolish to proceed without their guidance.

What about removing the New World screwworm from the wild? This decision is primarily up to the citizens of South American nations, because they are the ones who may be affected by any unintended ecological effects. No such effects were observed following eradication in North America, but that doesn't mean there wouldn't be any in South America, which has different ecosystems. We have consequently been discussing the possibility of biotech control measures with potential South American early adopter communities.

Of course, people who do not live alongside the target species can also have a voice in these decisions, especially because ecosystems might be connected in ways we don't understand. In addition, some individuals genuinely revere nature and arguably suffer when they perceive it to be damaged or contaminated, no matter where that occurs. Their beliefs should be respected. But in these examples, neither rodents nor screwworm would be permanently altered or driven to extinction: unaffected rodents would remain in Eurasia, and screwworm flies could be maintained indefinitely in captivity on dead meat slurry, or even frozen as larvae for resurrection later on. As such, it seems appropriate for potential early adopter communities to guide research on both projects.

A Human-Created Agricultural Problem: Livestock Well-Being

The suffering of wild animals is a tremendous problem, whether or not humans are responsible; however, biotechnology could do more for domesticated animals. The reason is that we control most of the selective pressures facing domesticated animals, allowing us to breed or engineer traits that could never be maintained in the wild. One such trait is enhanced well-being. This raises an important question: Is there some point at which we should stop, or is more animal well-being always better?

Domesticated vertebrate mammals may greatly out-mass wild ones, in some cases approaching parity in numbers. There is now reportedly one chicken for every five wild birds in the world.[21] If we're interested in improving animal well-being, improving the well-being of chickens matters a great deal. Most people would agree that a wild bird has greater well-being than a factory-farmed chicken. Should we aim to make that chicken's well-being comparable to that of the wild bird? Or should we do more? Is a "natural" level of well-being acceptable, or do we have a moral obligation to do better than nature? People of different philosophical positions may disagree on this issue, but we need to begin discussions, for relevant discoveries and new technologies enabling this type of intervention are likely to proceed even absent a concerted effort by researchers aiming to improve the well-being of domesticated animals.

Well-being reflects neurochemistry, and neurochemistry is primarily determined by genetics. Should we use our increased knowledge of genetics to breed happier domesticated animals? To date, we have been doing the exact opposite—that is, breeding animals with phenotypes that are economically advantageous but result in animal suffering. It's possible that we have indirectly selected for greater acclimation to at least growth in captivity and life in captivity, but sufficiently few generations have passed since the onset of factory farming that it's fairly unlikely we have selected for psychological adaptation to the uniquely confined conditions.

Improving farm animal well-being through traditional selective breeding in a timely manner would be difficult because many generations and large populations are typically required. The benefit is that such interventions would likely be viewed as not just acceptable but desirable by most consumers. In contrast, genome engineering could be accomplished considerably more quickly but is viewed as undesirable in important markets.

Crucially, either method could improve well-being beyond natural levels. Evolution by natural selection does not care about the well-being of chickens, cows, or pigs. We should, of course, improve the conditions in which factory farmed animals are kept, but doing just that will result only in the maximum level of well-being permitted by their genetics, as determined by, first, natural selection and, more recently, human selection. And we know that natural selection favors a hedonic treadmill: an animal that basks too long in the glow of finding food or mating is less likely to pass on its genes than one that quickly comes down from the opiate high and strives for the next opportunity.

From an engineering perspective, that means there's great deal of room for improvement to be found in breaking the hedonic treadmill. It's very hard to beat natural selection at its own game, but if natural selection has been actively selecting against continued bliss, there's potentially a lot of low-hanging fruit. Could we breed or engineer a chicken whose baseline well-being, instead of being 0 on a scale of -10 to +10, is +2, +20, or +200? Whatever level we chose, it would surely be substantially better than that of a wild animal.

The question we will increasingly face is whether we are morally obligated to (1) ensure that the animals for which we are responsible enjoy lives as much as natural genetics permit or (2) work toward gifting them with as much subjective happiness as is physically possible. The disparity is likely to be dramatic. And with the potential to extend these benefits to as many as 100 billion farm animals per year, the moral burden of a wrong decision will be heavy indeed.

REFERENCES

1. Kevin M. Esvelt et al., "Emerging Technology: Concerning RNA-Guided Gene Drives for the Alteration of Wild Populations," *eLife* 3 (2014): e03401.

2. Kenneth A. Oye et al., "Regulating Gene Drives," *Science* 345, no. 6197 (August 2014): 626-28.

3. Charleston Noble et al., "Evolutionary Dynamics of CRISPR Gene Drives," *Science Advances* 3, no. 4 (April 2017): e1601964.

4. John M. Marshall et al., "Overcoming Evolved Resistance to Population-Suppressing Homing-Based Gene Drives," *Scientific Reports* 7, no. 1 (June 2017): 3776.

5. Thomas A. A. Prowse et al., "Dodging Silver Bullets: Good CRISPR Gene-Drive Design Is Critical for Eradicating Exotic Vertebrates," *Proceedings. Biological Sciences/The Royal Society* 284, no. 1860 (August 2017): 20170799.

6. Charleston Noble et al., "Current CRISPR Gene Drive Systems Are Likely to Be Highly Invasive in Wild Populations," *eLife* 7 (June 2018): e33423.

7. Austin Burt, "Site-Specific Selfish Genes as Tools for the Control and Genetic Engineering of Natural Populations," *Proceedings. Biological Sciences/The Royal Society* 270, no. 1518 (May 2003): 921-28.

8. Kyros Kyrou et al., "A CRISPR-Cas9 Gene Drive Targeting Doublesex Causes Complete Population Suppression in Caged Anopheles Gambiae Mosquitoes," *Nature Biotechnology* 36 (September 2018): 1062-66.

9. Yinon M. Bar-On, Rob Phillips, and Ron Milo, "The Biomass Distribution on Earth," *Proceedings of the National Academy of Sciences of the United States of America* 115, no. 25 (June 2018): 6506-11.

10. Tim S. Doherty et al., "Invasive Predators and Global Biodiversity Loss," *Proceedings of the National Academy of Sciences of the United States of America* 113, no. 40 (October 2016): 11261-65.

11. David Pimentel, Rodolfo Zuniga, and Doug Morrison, "Update on the Environmental and Economic Costs Associated with Alien-Invasive Species in the United States," *Ecological Economics* 52, no. 3 (2005): 273-88.

12. Owain Edwards, CSIRO, personal communication to author, 2018.

13. Charleston Noble et al., "Daisy-Chain Gene Drives for the Alteration of Local Populations," *Proceedings of the National Academy of Sciences of the United States of America* 116, no. 17 (April 2019): 8275-82.

14. Robert B. Matlock Jr. and Steven R. Skoda, "Mark-Recapture Estimates of Recruitment, Survivorship and Population Growth Rate for the Screwworm

Fly, Cochliomyia Hominivorax," *Medical and Veterinary Entomology* 23 (2009): 111-25.

15. Pablo Fresia, Ana Maria L. Azeredo-Espin, and Mariana L. Lyra, "The Phylogeographic History of the New World Screwworm Fly, Inferred by Approximate Bayesian Computation Analysis," *PloS One* 8, no. 10 (October 2013): e76168.

16. M. Vargas-Terán, H. C. Hofmann, and N. E. Tweddle, "Impact of Screwworm Eradication Programmes Using the Sterile Insect Technique," in *Sterile Insect Technique: Principles and Practice in Area-Wide Integrated Pest Management*, ed. V. A. Dyck, J. Hendrichs, and A. S. Robinson (Dordrecht: Springer Netherlands, 2005), 629-50.

17. J. H. Wyss, "Screwworm Eradication in the Americas," *Annals of the New York Academy of Sciences* 916 (2000): 186-93.

18. Vargas-Terán, Hofmann, and Tweddle, "Impact of Screwworm Eradication Programmes."

19. Kevin Esvelt, "Gene Editing Can Drive Science to Openness," *Nature* 534, no. 7606 (June 2016): 153.

20. National Academies of Sciences, Engineering, and Medicine et al., *Gene Drives on the Horizon: Advancing Science, Navigating Uncertainty, and Aligning Research with Public Values* (Washington, DC: National Academies Press, 2016).

21. Bar-On, Phillips, and Milo, "The Biomass Distribution on Earth."

TWENTY-THREE

Certified Humane

ADELE DOUGLASS

Humane Farm Animal Care (HFAC) is an international non-profit organization dedicated to improving the lives of farm animals in food production from birth through slaughter. We operate a certification and labeling program, Certified Humane®,[1] for meat, poultry, egg, and dairy products that come from facilities that meet our precise and objective animal care standards.

Our Standards

Our standards address feed and water, environment, management, health, transportation, and slaughter. Animals must have fresh water and quality feed free of animal by-products, antibiotics, and hormones. Antibiotics can only be used therapeutically (for disease treatment) as directed by a veterinarian. The environment in which animals are kept must consider their welfare needs, be designed to protect them from physical and thermal discomfort, fear, and distress, and allow them to perform their natural behaviors. Animals are never kept in cages, crates, or tie stalls, and all animals have minimum space requirements that are specific to their species.

The Standard-Setting Process

Our standards were written by a 40-member scientific committee composed of animal scientists and veterinarians from the United States, Canada, Europe, and South America. Our standards are based on research into the actual needs of farm animals. We continually update our standards as new science-based information becomes available. The updating process starts with the species subcommittee preparing a draft, which then goes to the full scientific committee for comments. All of the relevant producers in our program also receive copies of the draft standard. Producer comments are important because raising animals on a university farm can be different from actual production. The standard then goes to the standards committee for approval. If the standard is approved, it goes to the HFAC board of directors for a vote.

The Application Process for Certification

Once HFAC receives an application, the certification staff conducts an initial review. HFAC then arranges an inspection of the applicant's operation, and the certification staff reviews the inspector's report. If the report finds no nonconformances, the applicant receives a certificate valid for one year. If the report finds a nonconformance that does not affect animal welfare (in most cases, a record-keeping problem), the applicant has 30 days to correct the problem. If a nonconformance affects animal welfare, the applicant must correct the problem and then reapply. Operations must reapply annually to renew their certification.

Inspector Qualifications

Our inspectors must have a master's degree or PhD in animal science or be a veterinarian. In addition, they must have expertise in a specific species. They also go through extensive HFAC training led by our existing inspectors. In addition to our species specialists for farm inspections, we also have specialists for slaughterhouse inspections and traceability audits.

Producer Benefits

HFAC provides valuable marketing assistance. With producers' help, we maintain a consumer-friendly app (free to download on Apple and Google) that tells shoppers where to find Certified Humane® products. We issue press releases to the general and trade press whenever a producer joins the program. We write "farm stories," which are posted on our website and made available to the press. We work with producers to help transmit good news about their business to important press outlets.

Consumer Outreach

We communicate directly with consumers through the "Take Action" page on our website, directing them to retailers who feature Certified Humane® products. We have sample letters that consumers can use to thank retailers for carrying Certified Humane® products or request that retailers add them. Without consumers driving the demand for humanely raised food, our program cannot be successful.

Our Progress

The number of animals raised under Certified Humane® standards has increased from 143,000 in 2003 to more than 197 million in 2018. We have a presence in the United States, Canada, Brazil, Argentina, Chile, Hong Kong, Peru, Uruguay, Australia, and New Zealand. Certified Humane® products can be found in more than 52,000 supermarkets worldwide.

Transparency is very important to us. We want every member of the public to know how HFAC operates. Our standards, policy manuals, staff members, scientific committee members, board of directors, certified producers, and additional information are available on our website: www.certifiedhumane.org.

REFERENCES

1. HFAC is not called Certified Humane because a certification name can be used only on a certified product.

This section describes some of the approaches that food companies and nonprofit organizations are using to address ethical challenges in the food system. Specifically, it covers pork and fish production, plant-forward menu design, and sourcing practices in food service and retail. The organizations featured in this section did not provide funding to the Choose Food project; their selection was based on a general recognition that they, among many others, have developed and expressed an awareness of ethical concerns in food production and consumption.

TWENTY-FOUR

Niman Ranch

PAUL WILLIS

I STARTED RAISING PIGS in the mid-1970s after moving back home to the family farm in Thornton, Iowa. I bought a sow with five piglets, and in a few years I was raising about 3,000 pigs a year. Business was doing well until concentrated animal feeding operations (CAFOs)—factory farms—started moving in on us in the 1990s. They were housing pigs in buildings with slatted floors over liquid manure pits. I had a chance to go inside one or two of these buildings and knew I never wanted to raise pigs like that. I continued raising my pigs on pasture, but factory farms were squeezing us out of the market. I was getting paid less for my pigs because they were too fat and yielded less meat. Pigs raised outdoors have larger bodies and larger hearts and lungs because they use them for running around and other natural behaviors. The leaner pork produced on factory farms was fetching a better price.

I visited California during this time and saw a woman at a supermarket buying chicken that was labeled as free-range. I asked her why she was willing to pay twice as much for the free-range chicken. Her answer: it tasted better. That's when I started to think there might be a market for free-range pork. I knew there was no market in Iowa, so I had to go to where the food culture was on the West Coast. I met Bill Niman in 1994, and he arranged to have chefs in San Francisco sample some of my pork. They loved it, and in February 1995 we shipped 30 pigs to the Bay Area. That number kept increasing on a fairly regular basis, so eventually I had to look for more farmers. In 1998, Niman Ranch Pork Company, LLC was formed with about 30 farmers.

One of my goals at the time, and to this day, was to differentiate ourselves as much as possible from the commodity market. We were raising our pigs outdoors or in deeply bedded pens with plenty of room, but we also eventually decided to never use antibiotics or hormones and to feed the pigs only a vegetarian diet. We brought in farm animal husbandry experts like Diane and Marlene Halverson and Temple Grandin, who helped us write our pig husbandry protocols. In 2016 we became Certified Humane® by the Humane Farm Animal Care program. We have continued utilizing heritage breeds for better flavor and quality of the meat. We have done a lot of testing for eating quality because it is very critical that we provide a good eating experience. Niman Ranch is also different because we have fair pricing for our farmers. We have always paid our farmers a premium in addition to a guaranteed price floor to protect them against market lows. We never wanted to lose a farmer due to financial strife.

Supporting our farmers and their local communities has always been a priority for Niman Ranch. Building off our foundation of fair pricing, we now offer many benefit programs for our farmers to thank them for their partnership and help bring on the next generation of sustainable farmers. These benefits include scholarships for the children of our farmers, free gilts, zero-interest loans, and covering the costs of third-party animal welfare certification. I have heard countless times, "I wouldn't be farming if it weren't for Niman Ranch."

We created a business structure that would benefit our farmers, but one of the early challenges was how we would raise operating capital. We started out with a loan for $80,000 from the Iowa Department of Economic Development, which would become forgivable when we bought 300 pigs per week for three consecutive weeks. Because we were already paying our 30+ farmers a premium at the time, we decided that each time a farmer made a sale, we would retain a capital contribution, which was $0.01 per pound or roughly $2.50 per head. This contribution was put into the LLC in the farmer's name along with a matching contribution from Niman Ranch, Inc. Niman Ranch Pork Company was 50% owned by the farmers and 50% owned by Niman Ranch Inc., and we continued to raise capital in this way. The farmer's share was always redeemable by request if the farmer decided to leave the company or retire. The money was in the company and that was considered the price of being part of the Niman Ranch system.

One of the big moves we made was to start selling to Whole Foods. Our supply had gone up—one week we jumped from 300 to 800 pigs—and we had more pigs than customers, who were mostly high-level chefs at the time. We were facing a problem because we feared we could not buy all the pigs from our farmers. Once we started selling to Whole Foods, we again exceeded our market of hogs and could continue the growth. Marketing to Whole Foods created some problems, though. The store only wanted the loins, which meant that we had a lot of parts—shoulders, legs, and bellies—that ended up being dumped into the commodity market for a lower price. This was not sustainable, but luckily right around this time, Chipotle came along and started buying our pork shoulders. This was a big boost for us and really helped balance the carcass in terms of profitability. Our system has always been a true nose-to-tail program. We don't buy parts and pieces but the whole animal.

In 20 years we have gone from having one market—San Francisco—to having customers nationwide. Our network of independent hog farmers has grown from about 30 to 620. We sold more than 5,000 pigs per week in 2018 compared to just 500 per month in 1998. But to put that number in perspective, 400,000 pigs are slaughtered in the United States every day. We are still relatively small, but we have made a significant contribution to rural economic development. Many small independent family farms have been pushed out by large-scale corporate operations, so we are supporting the back-to-the-land movement. We have returned millions of dollars in capital contributions to farmers as they have retired. Since Perdue Farms purchased us in 2015, we have not had to worry about raising more capital, so by 2018 we fully paid out the contributions to farmers. The total amount paid to farmers in the last 20 years is $470 million. This is money that has not gone to outside companies; it has gone to farmers who live and spend their money in their small towns.

Our way of raising pigs is better for the animals. It is better for the environment because the farmers are replenishing the land they farm naturally. And it is better for farmers because the premium they receive makes it economically viable for generations of family farmers to stay on the land and in the local community.

TWENTY-FIVE

Menus of Change

ANNE E. MCBRIDE

Menus of Change is a joint project of The Culinary Institute of America (CIA) and the Harvard T. H. Chan School of Public Health. It is designed to give guidance on menu design and food choices at the intersection of nutrition, sustainability, food ethics, business insight, and culinary strategy for chefs and business leaders in the $800 billion foodservice sector. The project is especially active in working to advance a protein shift in the restaurant and foodservice sector, moving away from an overreliance on animal-based protein and toward an elevation of plant-forward menus. Efforts to drive a heightened sense of priority around ethics in animal agriculture can be supported and accelerated by the culinary menu and food experience strategies that the CIA is incubating with the Menus of Change initiative.

The CIA was founded in 1946 as a not-for-profit college. Its current enrollment is 3,000 students, about 2,000 of whom study at the main campus in Hyde Park, New York. Its 50,000 alumni work in all sectors of the food industry, in the United States and around the world. The CIA has a big contingent of alumni in Latin America, Singapore (where the college has a campus), and Korea; that international component is ever growing. The second CIA campus opened about 25 years ago in St. Helena, California. The newest one is the CIA at Copia in Napa,

California, where a lot of the college's thought leadership programs take place.

Everything at the CIA centers around the idea that chefs are thought leaders and very often function as the trusted intermediary between food production and consumption. As chefs' profiles have risen in the past 20 years, consumers and diners tend evermore to trust chefs to have done research and made the right choices so that what is on the plate is good and/or good for them. This means that chefs need to keep learning about the issues that matter to their customers. The CIA's industry leadership conferences present information to the foodservice industry in a way that is easily translatable and actionable. Worlds of Flavor, which celebrated its 20th anniversary in 2018, is the first of such conferences. It focuses on cultures, traditions, authenticity, and innovation and typically features about 80 presenters from all over the world. For 15 years, we have also been working with the Harvard T. H. Chan School of Public Health on a number of health and wellness initiatives, including Worlds of Healthy Flavors, the Healthy Menus R&D Collaborative, Healthy Kitchens, Healthy Lives, and Menus of Change.

Menus of Change is designed to provide evidence-based guidance to the restaurant and foodservice industry about the business of healthy, sustainable, and delicious food choices. The initiative's vision is for food to be nutritious and healthy, socially responsible and ethical, delicious, and environmentally sustainable. But how does one turn these four points into a business model and strategies? It's one thing to want to cook plant-forward food, for example, or reduce consumption of processed products or animal products. But the foodservice industry needs to know how to make that work from a business perspective. That is exactly the challenge that Menus of Change takes up in both strategic and pragmatic ways. Its Scientific and Technical Advisory Council provides the most current evidence base as a foundation for the work of the initiative, while the Business Leadership Council suggests approaches for translating this evidence into action and real industry change and highlighting the already considerable innovation that is underway.

Another effort, the Menus of Change University Research Collaborative, launched three years ago. It marks the first time that senior university administrators, academics, dining directors, chefs, nutritionists, and sustainability managers are coming together with a research agenda, as well as an agenda of advancing the Menus of Change principles in dining halls and throughout food practices on campuses. College students are tomorrow's consumers, and by meeting their concerns heads-on, college dining is the perfect terrain for sustainability innovation.

Menus of Change advances 24 principles for healthy, sustainable menus, with a specific focus on the concept of "plant forward." Plant forward is a style of cooking and eating that emphasizes and celebrates, but is not limited to, plant-based foods—including fruits and vegetables; whole grains; beans, other legumes, and soy foods; nuts and seeds; plant oils; and herbs and spices—and that reflects evidence-based principles of health and sustainability.

The core of the CIA's message is that plant forward is about health, sustainability, *and* deliciousness. It includes, of course, vegetarian and vegan diners, menus, and menu research and development, but is ultimately all-inclusive in order to maximize the ways in which chefs can effectuate menu transformation through a wide portfolio of approaches. CIA has identified 10 key interconnected strategies, challenges, and levers of change for reducing reliance on animal agriculture and increasing the role of plant proteins in menu design:

1. Less meat, better meat: If, as an industry, we're able to make and market smaller portions of meats but charge a higher price per ounce, for what many have called better meats, this will create economic incentives for animal agriculture that avoids or is less reliant on antibiotics, promotes less crowding, and eliminates other animal agriculture practices that today's consumers are increasingly rejecting.

2. Value for values on our plates: In order for chefs and operators to sell "less meat, better meat" to their customers, we have to tackle the issue of the premium, or the value that most diners place on food from animal sources versus food from plant sources. How do we disrupt the age-old perception that a large portion of meat equals real value worthy of a higher check, while other elements of the plate do not?

3. Will I be hungry in an hour?: Chefs need to develop strategies and skills that utilize slow metabolizing plant-based ingredients, from nuts and legumes to whole grains and plant-based oils, and we need to avoid false choices between chicken on one hand and a plate of steamed vegetables on the other. Satiety is a real concern for most people, especially when they are dining out and want to make sure that what they have paid for will keep them full.

4. Isn't vegetable protein "low quality" in terms of long-term health?: There's ample evidence to indicate that a reasonably diverse whole food plant-forward diet yields more than enough of all the amino acids we need to live long and healthful lives. Chefs, but also all of us, need to stop referring to meat and other animal protein as "high-quality" protein, as it is misleading at best and, in the case of red meat, mostly wrong in the impression it creates.

5. Visual cues in plant-forward and serving contexts: CIA asked the research firm Datassential to conduct a survey of what consumers thought, in the abstract, was an optimum serving of animal-based protein. The typical answer was six to seven ounces. Then they showed the same group of consumers a picture of a grain and vegetable bowl—what you see on menus everywhere now—with two to three ounces of meat or chicken on top of the bowl. On average, these consumers commented that this seemed like an "appropriate" amount of meat. Strategies around presentation context and perception are important in terms of changing behavior.

6. What chefs promote in new pathways to deliciousness: Historically in the United States and Northern Europe, chefs have looked to meat and meat flavors as a principal strategy to achieve deliciousness. With the plant-forward movement underway across the country, chefs are bringing previously peripheral flavor development strategies and techniques to the fore, such as roasting vegetables, using spice blends, leveraging plant-based sources of umami, and working with plant breeders to prioritize flavor.

7. The package leading to cultural discovery: Much of what we're doing in terms of plant-based flavor development techniques has its roots in various plant-forward food cultures from the Mediterranean to Asia and Latin America. Tapping those cultural resources has the added benefit of packaging dishes that are either vegetarian, vegan, or plant-rich but with small quantities of meat as a ticket to cultural discovery. Will diners really miss the meat when they are spending the night immersed in the flavors of Turkey, Mexico, Senegal, Italy, Thailand, or South India?

8. Pioneer a new menu category, beyond "regular" and "unleaded": Part of the challenge in adding to menus dishes that feature just one or two ounces of meat is that chefs often don't know what to label or call them. Many of diners' expectations around menus fall under either the "regular" category, which includes a large portion of animal protein, or an "unleaded" category, which includes vegan or vegetarian options. However, more and more chefs are starting to use strategies such as listing meats as sides, or reframing the order in which they list the components of a dish, starting with more plant-forward elements rather than positioning the animal protein as the first and thus presumably the most important and/or valuable ingredient. These strategies set diners' expectations differently in terms of what they might see on their plate. Another category change that the CIA's Healthy Menus R&D Collaborative has long been working on is the Blended Burger, where 30% or more of the beef is replaced with ground mushrooms without compromising the textural juiciness and umami components that people love so much about a burger.

9. Rethink customer engagement and communications: The World Resources Institute recently conducted research in London that showed that when we drop descriptors like vegetarian and instead use language that communicates high flavor, seasonality, global cultural roots, or specific farm sources, sales of these items go up.[1] Most consumers don't love to be told what to do.

It's about transforming the dining experience for them and having menu items and language that support objectives like plant forward but do not bury consumers in information.

10. Leverage the move toward integrated nutrition and sustainability targets for dietary guidance by leaders in the international scientific community: As mentioned earlier, the CIA does a lot of practical translation work. We are especially looking forward to translating for food professionals the findings of the EAT-Lancet Commission on Food, Planet, and Health. The EAT-Lancet report was published in January 2019 and was the result of a two-year study that set specific per capita numerical dietary guidance targets that are optimal from a nutrition and a chronic disease prevention standpoint and fit within evidence-based planetary boundaries tied to current and projected patterns of population growth, climate change, and resource depletion.[2]

The scientific case for a shift toward plant-forward diets is well established. As an ever-greater proportion of the food consumed in the United States is prepared by professionals—whether in restaurants or in retail operations—the foodservice industry has a key role to play in moving its customers toward diets that are healthier for them and for the planet. The industry cannot be expected to bear that responsibility without help. What is needed, and what Menus of Change, along with related CIA initiatives, aims to provide, is more translation of scientific evidence into actionable strategies for every meal.

REFERENCES

1. Jonathan Wise, Daniel Vennard, and Linda Bacon, "How Language Can Advance Sustainable Diets: A Summary of Expert Perspectives on How Research into the Language of Plant-Based Food Can Change Consumption," World Resources Institute, June 2018, https://www.wri.org/publication/how -language-can-advance-sustainable-diets.

2. Walter Willett et al., "Food in the Anthropocene: The EAT-Lancet Commission on Healthy Diets from Sustainable Food Systems," *Lancet* 393, no. 10170 (February 2, 2019): 447-92.

TWENTY-SIX

Bon Appétit Management Company

MAISIE GANZLER

B ON APPÉTIT MANAGEMENT COMPANY is a foodservice provider to colleges and universities, corporations, restaurants, and specialty venues in 33 states across the country. We serve more than 250 million meals every year in over 1,000 cafés. We serve real food, prepared from scratch using authentic ingredients. We call this a revolutionary act because food service hasn't always been known for serving real food. Our dream is to be the premier on-site restaurant company known for its culinary expertise and commitment to socially responsible practices. To us, food service for a sustainable future means flavorful food that's healthy and economically viable for all, produced through practices that respect farmers, workers, and animals; nourish the community; and re-plenish our shared natural resources for future generations.

Since our founding in 1987, we have launched several sustainability initiatives. This chapter examines two of these initiatives, Farm to Fork and The Last Straw, through an ethical lens.

Farm to Fork

Farm to Fork, which launched in 1999, is our commitment to buying locally. We require our chefs to purchase at least 20% of their ingredients from small ($5 million or less in sales), owner-operated farms and ranches located within 150 miles of their kitchens. In developing the criteria, we wanted the program to capture scale, not just distance. We spent a lot of time thinking about how far a farmer could realistically drive back and forth in a day, and we came up with 150 miles. It's not a perfect number, but it blazed a trail in 1999 and since then has become quite standard for local sourcing. We settled on $5 million or less in sales because, even though the US Department of Agriculture defines small farms as farms with $250,000 or less in sales, to us that seemed like hobby farming and not small business. The $5 million figure was more realistic. We also set the ownership requirement because we believe that on owner-operated farms and ranches, there is a different level of care for the land, animals, and workers.

Within the Farm to Fork program, there has been an ethical evolution around animal production. Several years in, it became clear that $5 million or less in sales for a ranch is a really small ranch. There was also the problem of "Ag in the Middle"—we had to be sure that the ranchers in our program were raising animals in a way that was appreciably different from Big Ag. We came up with a new midsize guideline that permits sourcing from ranchers with less than 1% of industry leaders' sales volume for each species cultivated. Currently, this ranges from $15 million for turkey to $132 million for beef. These ranchers also are required to have a credible third-party humane certification, such as Humane Farm Animal Care, Animal Welfare Approved, Global Animal Partnership, or Food Alliance. This new guideline was our way of carving out a special niche and providing market access to ranchers who are too big to sell directly to consumers through farmer's markets or local restaurants but who have not had access to large foodservice providers.

Antibiotic use is another issue that arose in the program. Our policy for poultry—chicken and turkey, specifically—has long been that we are committed to using animals raised without the routine, non-therapeutic use of medically important antibiotics. For beef, we had a policy of no antibiotic use under any circumstances. Why the different policies? It was really a reflection of what was available in the marketplace. There was no middle ground for beef. It was either no-antibiotics-ever or all-the-antibiotics-you-want. That is why we used only certified humane beef from cows that had never, ever been given antibiotics. We were really proud of this policy until we received a letter from a Farm to Fork rancher whose calves had pinkeye. He wanted to treat them with antibiotics, but that would mean he could no longer sell them to us. We created the Farm to Fork program to give market access to small producers, so to have a rule that automatically either knocks them out of contention or incentivizes them not to treat sick animals was not a consequence that we wanted. For this reason, we consulted extensively with the Johns Hopkins Center for a Livable Future to rewrite and streamline our antibiotics policy. The revised policy came out in January 2019 and states that we will strive to buy only meat, poultry, and seafood raised without the use of antimicrobials, except where necessary to treat sick animals in the documented presence of disease in the flock, herd, or fish population as verified by a veterinarian.

The Last Straw

We were the first foodservice company in the United States to ban the use of plastic straws in 2018. We have been on a journey with this since then. At first, we received great recognition. We took a stand and committed to doing something that was probably going to cost us more money (paper straws are really expensive!). Other companies started following, including Starbucks, Royal Caribbean Cruises, and Disney. We were feeling really good about ourselves because we had started this wave of plastic straw bans.

Then we learned that some people need plastic straws. People with certain disabilities need a flexible straw that they can bite on. Because paper straws tend to become mushy when wet, manufacturers have started making them harder and more inflexible. It certainly was not our intention to put an additional burden on people with disabilities, but that is what we had done. We had to adjust the policy, and I'm not sure that we have the right one yet. We will still have plastic straws available, and there are all sorts of supply chain ramifications to that. With an outright ban, we could take away our managers' ability to buy plastic straws. Now that they can buy some plastic straws to have available, we have no way to monitor that only people with disabilities are taking them. How do you do that without putting an additional burden on people with disabilities to identify themselves as having a disability? This was an unintended consequence of a very well-intended policy, and we are still trying to figure it out.

Conclusion

Food service for a sustainable future is not a discrete destination, but rather a journey where the vision can change from day to day. Sustainability initiatives in practice often involve ethical trade-offs. The two initiatives discussed in this chapter demonstrate that even within our own definition of sustainability, there were factors that were at odds with each other, like respect for farmers, the environment, animals, and the community. It is important to understand the nuances of what seem to be, on their face, rather simple decisions but are actually very complex.

TWENTY-SEVEN

Wegmans

GILLIAN KELLEHER

What We Believe

At Wegmans, we believe that good people working toward a common goal can accomplish anything they set out to do. In this spirit, we set our goal to be the very best at serving the needs of our customers. Every action we take should be made with our customers in mind. We also believe that we can achieve this goal only if we fulfill the needs of our own people. To our customers and our people, we pledge continuous improvement, and we make the commitment: "Every Day You Get Our Best."

Our Values

We care about the well-being and success of every person. High standards are a way of life. We pursue excellence in everything we do. We make a difference in every community we serve. We respect and listen to our people. We empower our people to make decisions that improve their work and benefit our customers and our company.

Consumer Affairs

Our Consumer Affairs Department is the voice of the customer. It focuses on two-way communication and active listening. The voice of the customer comes to us every day through employees at our stores, phone calls, e-mails, and social media. That feedback loop helps us deliver on our pledge to continuous improvement. We're always tracking what our customers are concerned about, and when a concern is elevated to a stage where we want to take a closer look, we set up an Emerging Issues work group. The Consumer Affairs Department is all about being transparent and building trust with our customers over time. That trust is precious to us, and we never want to lose it.

A recent example of how we listen to our customers is the introduction of visual assistance technology in our stores. When our blind and low-vision customers told us that they needed help shopping in our stores, we partnered with a company called Aira to offer remote visual assistance for free.

Food Safety

At Wegmans, food safety is not a competitive issue. We approach food safety strategically through external and internal partnerships. Externally, we partner with the Food Marketing Institute, our trade association located in Washington, DC. We also partner internationally with the Consumer Goods Forum, which houses the Global Food Safety Initiative (GFSI). We're actively engaged in trade associations and groups. Internally, we take that partnership to all sectors of our business—stores, internal manufacturing, warehouses, distribution, our private label program, and our partner-growers.

Wegmans is a huge supporter of GFSI, a multi-stakeholder network whose mission is safe food for consumers everywhere. GFSI was started by a group of food retailers and manufacturers concerned by consumers' lack of confidence and suppliers' audit fatigue. GFSI harmonizes and raises the standards of food safety certification programs worldwide by building food safety capacity. GFSI offers free tools for any small supplier anywhere in the world that wants to start producing food safely.

Sustainability at Wegmans

Our Zero Waste program started in 2016 as a pilot at our Canandaigua, New York store. The goal was to increase the recycling rate from 63% to 80% percent by year's end; by December, the store had surpassed its goal by 3%. In 2018 Wegmans recycled more than 200 million pounds of material. Our front-end plastic bags contain 40% postconsumer recycled content, which is generated by customers returning their plastic bags to the store. In 2018, our recycling rate for plastic bags averaged around 50%. Wegmans participates in the How2Recycle label program, which encourages customers to recycle bags (not just shopping bags but some packaging bags as well) at the store.

Along with the Zero Waste program, Wegmans is a member of the EPA's US Food Loss and Waste 2030 Champions, which is for businesses and organizations that have pledged to cut their food waste in half by 2030. Our first aim is to reduce the volume of food waste that is generated. Next, we donate food to food banks, soup kitchens, and shelters. Then, we divert food scraps to animal feed in local livestock operations. We then provide waste oils for rendering and fuel conversion and food scraps for anaerobic digestion to recover energy or for composting. The last resort for disposal is landfilling/incineration.

We strive to offer sustainable choices to our customers. We offer more than 4,000 different organic products throughout our store. We operate our own organic farm and orchard to develop and share innovative growing practices with our partner-growers. Whenever possible, we work with producers and growers located near our stores. For fresh produce, we work with more than 500 local growers who deliver fresh fruits and vegetables to our stores. We're also transparent and provide customers with information about how our products are sourced, raised/grown, and manufactured.

Conclusion

Wegmans is clearly on the right path—and, most importantly, our employees and customers seem to agree. Our philosophy and values underpin this success. Doing the right thing is a never-ending effort on our part. We operate with a mindset of continuous improvement and strive to meet our commitment to our customers that "Every Day You Get Our Best."

TWENTY-EIGHT

US Foods

SYLVIA WULF

US Foods is the conduit between the producer and the chef. As the nation's second-largest foodservice distributor, we have more than 60 distribution centers, 5,000 trucks on the road, 25,000 employees, and $24 billion in annual revenue. We are in a position to make a difference when it comes to sustainability and transparency.

Industry Trends

Local and sustainable products are key drivers shaping the restaurant industry today, and transparency is a priority. Recent industry research shows that 80% of consumers want to know more about their food source; 75% are drawn to foods that are natural, authentic, premium, and locally sourced; 75% strongly agree that restaurants should be more transparent about where they get ingredients; and 67% have a better impression of restaurants that offer sustainable foods.[1,2]

Diners and operators now expect a certain level of transparency and product provenance. The Hartman Group reports that 69% of consumers would like companies' sustainability practices to be more publicly visible. According to its CEO, "consumers associate transparency with how authentically committed a company is to ethical action."[3]

Recent focus groups conducted by US Foods reveal that operators continue to increase purchases of proteins that meet high animal welfare standards. Operators value transparency when selecting meat products and are receptive to third-party certifications. They directly connect animal welfare to serving higher-quality meat in their operation, which in turn connects to the reputation of the operation.

Our research also suggests that 77% of operators purchase local foods, particularly produce. Many of them purchase locally sourced foods because it supports the economic viability of their local communities.

Leveraging US Foods's Position in the Supply Chain

US Foods purchases billions of dollars' worth of meat, seafood, and produce every year, so we believe that we can make a difference in the supply chain. We utilize our position to facilitate dialogue and information sharing between our vendors and our operator customers so that they understand the capabilities that our supply chain needs to build to meet the evolving need for local and sustainable products.

We used four key principles as we began to frame our sustainability position. First, we want our vendors to understand the issues. Second, we want them to think about sustainability as a long-term investment. Third, we need to collaborate with other stakeholders. Lastly, we need to share our stories.

Serve Good

Our Serve Good program features products that are responsibly sourced or contribute to waste reduction. To be included in the Serve Good program, a product requires two attributes. First, it must come with a claim of responsible sourcing or contribution to waste reduction. Product claims fall into one of several categories that include organic, non-GMO, sustainable seafood, animal care, responsible disposables, and reduction of waste. Second, it must meet strict packaging standards that are designed to reduce waste, prioritize the use of recycled materials, and help minimize our ecological footprint. We launched Serve Good in 2016 with 26 products, and to date we offer more than 300 products that meet the program's requirements.

Progress Check

We take a long-term approach to sustainability, and seafood is a perfect example of that. Our Progress Check program recognizes seafood products and vendors that have made significant progress toward meeting the requirements of the Serve Good program. The program incentivizes vendors to use Best Aquaculture Practices, which has a four-star system. Achieving four-star status requires time and capital investment. The Progress Check program gives our seafood vendors a starting point in their sustainability journey as well as specific benchmarks and timelines that we expect them to meet along that journey.

Currently, 80% of our Harbor Banks Exclusive Brand seafood meets either Progress Check or Serve Good requirements, and we are committed to making that number 100% by the end of 2020. We also put in place an action plan in 2019 for all of our other Exclusive Brand seafood products to meet those requirements.

Serve Local

In 2018, we launched Serve Local in select markets as a pilot program for locally sourced produce. Products offered through Serve Local are sourced within 400 miles of one of our distribution centers. We know that there is seasonality in produce, and we want to give our customers choices. The program is about letting our customers know where and how their produce is grown and connecting them with their local farmers.

Conclusion

Conversations about local sustainable products continue to take place within our company and across the foodservice industry. We believe that, as an intermediary, we can catalyze change because we know what the supply chain needs are, we know what our vendors are capable of, and we can incentivize change. Our Serve Good, Progress Check, and Serve Local initiatives ensure that we can continue providing choice and transparency to our customers and their patrons.

REFERENCES

1. US Foods, "US Foods Expands Sustainable Products with Spring Scoop™ 2018," news release, February 26, 2018, https://ir.usfoods.com/investors/stock -information-news/press-release-details/2018/US-Foods-Expands-Sustainable -Products-with-Spring-Scoop-2018/default.aspx.

2. Aaron Jourden, "Technomic's Take: 2018 Global Megatrends," Technomic, April 6, 2018, https://www.technomic.com/newsroom/technomics-take-2018 -global-megatrends.

3. Hartman Group, "Who's Walking the Talk? Consumers Name Top 10 'Transparent' Companies—Hartman Group Report," news release, November 6, 2017, https://www.hartman-group.com/press-releases/2112427415/who-s-walking -the-talk-consumers-name-top-10-transparent-companies-hartman-group-report.

TWENTY-NINE

Water Recirculating Aquaculture Systems and the Future for Land-Based, Closed-Containment Salmon Production

CHRISTOPHER GOOD

L AND-BASED WATER recirculation aquaculture systems (RAS) have the potential to be a viable and sustainable method for salmon industry expansion. In traditional salmon farming, salmon are cultured on land, beginning as fertilized eggs derived from broodstock, hatched and raised as fry and parr, and then transferred to sea cages following smoltification—the physiological process that prepares salmon for the transition from freshwater to saltwater. While public demand for salmon products continues to grow, there are relatively few areas in the world with the appropriate maritime climate for raising salmon in open sea cages. The Freshwater Institute, which is a program under the Conservation Fund, focuses on assisting the aquaculture industry to grow in a sustainable manner. With major funding from the USDA Agricultural Research Service, we have spent several decades developing and refining technologies for land-based salmonid production. Since 2011, we have raised Atlantic salmon entirely on land, in freshwater, without the need for moving salmon to the ocean for growout. These efforts are aimed at supporting the salmon farming industry through pioneering new methods for sustainable industry expansion.

Currently, the Atlantic salmon industry is in transition. RAS technologies are being increasingly utilized to produce smolts and post-smolts, and several companies around the world are now focused on entirely land-based salmon production. For example, the Atlantic Sapphire Bluehouse™ is currently under construction just outside of Miami, Florida. This will be a very large land-based recirculation facility to raise harvest-sized Atlantic salmon, with an anticipated production capacity of about 90,000 metric tons per year.[1]

Land-based, closed-containment aquaculture provides farmers with the opportunity for environmental optimization to promote fish health, welfare, and performance, and from a biosecurity perspective, closed containment provides much lower risk than an open net pen system. With a closed system, you reduce the possible avenues for obligate pathogens (bacteria, viruses, or parasites that require an animal host to replicate) to enter the facility and infect fish populations. An entirely pathogen-free system, however, is virtually impossible, and therefore there will always be opportunistic pathogens to consider as potential risks, regardless of the facility type. Traditional avenues of obligate pathogen entry into a fish farm include fish introductions, infected eggs, personnel, feed, birds, animals, and water source. As such, land-based, closed-containment systems enclosed in biosecure buildings, using deep groundwater, supplied with specific pathogen-free eggs, and operated with effective biosecurity protocols, will have a relatively low risk for obligate pathogen entry, unlike traditional open sea cage operations.

In the Freshwater Institute's semi-commercial-scale growout system, we raise Atlantic salmon up to a harvest size of four kilograms in approximately 24 months post-hatch (figure 29.1). We utilize the "Cornell-style" dual-drain tanks (i.e., water exits from both a bottom center drain and a side drain), wherein water is injected from a sidewall inlet manifold to create both a rotational water flow, which the fish can swim against (this is important for Atlantic salmon production because salmonids, which are active, athletic fish, thrive in environments that provide exercise), and a secondary radial flow that flushes solids out a bottom center drain. This system maintains good water quality; when a fish releases a fecal pellet, it is only in the water column for a short period of time before it is flushed out the bottom drain. Fish waste, therefore, has very little time to solubilize, and it can be captured very quickly.

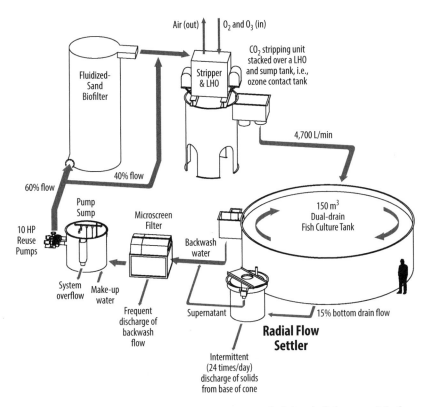

Air (out) ↑ | O₂ and O₃ (in)

CO₂ stripping unit
stacked over a LHO
and sump tank, i.e.,
ozone contact tank

Stripper
& LHO

Fluidized-
Sand
Biofilter

4,700 L/min

40% flow

60% flow

150 m³
Dual-drain
Fish Culture Tank

Pump
Sump

Microscreen
Filter

10 HP
Reuse
Pumps

Backwash
water

System
overflow

Make-up
water

Frequent
discharge of
backwash
flow

Supernatant

15% bottom drain flow

**Radial Flow
Settler**

Intermittent
(24 times/day)
discharge of solids
from base of cone

Figure 29.1. RAS Schematic for Bringing Post-Smolt Atlantic Salmon to Market Size.
Source: John Davidson, Travis May, Christopher Good, Thomas Waldrop, Brett Kenney, Bendik Fyhn Terjesen, and Steven Summerfelt, "Production of Market-Size North American Strain Atlantic Salmon Salmo Salar in a Land-Based Recirculation Aquaculture System Using Freshwater," *Aquacultural Engineering* 74 (September 1, 2016): 1-16, doi: 10.1016/j.aquaeng.2016.04.007. This figure is reproduced here under the terms of the Creative Commons 4.0 license.

Because of the hydrodynamics, water exiting the tank bottom is solids-heavy relative to water exiting the side drain, and we can concentrate those solids in a radial flow settler while reclaiming some of that water for reuse. The flows from both the bottom and side drains are then combined and pass through a microscreen drum filter for fine particle removal. In addition to solids, fish produce ammonia and carbon dioxide as waste products, and these can accumulate and cause health problems as water is reused; therefore, it is necessary to treat the water with biofiltration and gas conditioning, respectively. Following microscreen filtration, water is pumped up through a biofilter that converts ammonia to nitrate, which is relatively nontoxic to fish, and then moves down through a gas conditioning unit via gravity to reduce carbon dioxide and add pure oxygen to ultimately maintain culture vessel levels at 100% oxygen saturation.

Fish coming out of a RAS must be "purged" (i.e., moved to a different, disinfected system and kept off-feed for, in our case, six days) to rid the flesh of off-flavor compounds, which are derived from microbial biofilms and produce an earthy or musty flavor in unpurged fish. These biofilms produce two compounds, geosmin and 2-methylisoborneol (MIB), which are taken up through the gills and accumulate in muscle tissue. Until an efficacious solution is developed to eliminate off-flavor production in RAS, the fish have to go through a purge system prior to harvest, processing, and delivery to market.

Reclaiming the Nutrients from RAS

All aquaculture produces wastes; however, RAS production provides a better opportunity to capture the wastes and potentially turn these into sellable products to offset some of the production expenses. Solids can be composted or processed through anaerobic digestion to produce biogas. Nutrients can be utilized to fertilize plants in aquaponics, which is the marriage of fish farming and crop production.

RAS Addresses Market Needs

Indoor RAS-produced Atlantic salmon has been ranked by Monterey Bay Aquarium's Seafood Watch program as a "best choice" for seafood.[2] The product can be additionally marketed as local, fresh, and sustainable. Production is consistent and highly traceable, and at the Freshwater Institute we do not need to vaccinate our fish or use antibiotics, which are typically necessary procedures in the traditional industry. Therefore, operational cost is reduced as well as stress on the fish.

At present, there are about a dozen facilities around the world that are raising Atlantic salmon to market size on land. For example, Superior Fresh (Wisconsin) is the world's first land-based Atlantic salmon and leafy green aquaponics facility, and the first US commercial operation to successfully raise Atlantic salmon to market size in RAS.

Atlantic Salmon Growout Trials

The Freshwater Institute has had several important funders—mainly the USDA Agricultural Research Service, as well as various environmental organizations and foundations—to assess the feasibility of RAS as a means of growing fish on land. In each of the growout trials that we have carried out, we try to tweak a variable and see how the fish respond. These variables include photoperiod (how much light vs. dark they get over the course of a day), diet, density, strain, and early rearing conditions.

When comparing the growth curves from all of our growout trials, it is interesting to note that once the fish reach approximately 500 grams, the growth rate moving forward is consistent (i.e., 400 grams per month) regardless of any variables being assessed in a given trial. Optimizing growth performance during the pre-500-gram phase appears to be critical and can shave off a month or two in harvest timing.

Economic Viability of RAS

If this technology has been proved, why is it not being adopted at a more rapid pace? The reason is the enormous amount of capital expense that is required up front to establish a land-based closed containment RAS salmon facility. At present, it is most often viewed as cost-prohibitive for the traditional industry to adopt, given the cost of a facility site with good water quality, RAS infrastructure, buildings, feeding systems, and permits. In terms of the operating expenses, the biggest component by far is feed, but there is also oxygen, power, and labor representing significant expenses. We have compared costs of land-based and traditional sea cage operations, in collaboration with Norwegian researchers, with 3,300 metric tons of salmon production at each conceptual site. When you compare the capital expenses for the same tonnage of fish, it comes to about $54 million for the land-based facility versus about $30 million for the net-pen system. If you break it down, probably the biggest expense when it comes to the land-based system is the up-front capital cost, and the biggest expense for the net-pens is the licensing fees, which are enormous in Norway. If you break down the total production cost for a head-on gutted fish—in other words, the wholesale cost of a fish—then the two systems are comparable. The cost comes to $5.60/kg for RAS versus $5.08/kg for the net pen system.[3] RAS is therefore more expensive on the whole, but one reason people are starting to consider it an economically viable route is that you can locate these facilities very close to your market. Much of the cost of Norwegian fish, for example, is product shipment to the United States. Another reason is that it sets your product apart if you are local and sustainable, and labeled as such. We produce 20 metric tons a year, which is a very modest amount, but we send our product to local high-end grocery stores where we are able to achieve a premium price. Our salmon, local in the Washington, DC area, at one time was selling for $12.99/lb. versus $8.99/lb. for traditional salmon. It is interesting to note that the basis for the premium of land-based salmon appears to be different in different markets. In Washington, DC, the basis for premium pricing was that the salmon were "local," whereas we found that in the Vancouver area the key to premium pricing was the "sustainable" labeling, which differentiated it from sea cage systems.

Other Challenges

There is more than just capital expense involved with the slow growth of the land-based salmon industry. An additional, significant bottleneck is the scarce availability of skilled labor. To run these high-tech facilities effectively requires highly trained personnel who must also have knowledge of fish husbandry and production techniques. Another issue is that environmental conditions for optimized salmon production have not been entirely established. For example, some facilities are using full-strength seawater, while others use water that is brackish or even fresh. Seawater systems mimic the natural environment of post-smolt Atlantic salmon; however, oxygen saturation in seawater is 20% less than freshwater, and carbon dioxide removal becomes a lot less efficient. Ozone, normally employed to improve water quality, can create toxic bromine in seawater systems. More recently, Norwegian seawater RAS producing smolts and post-smolts have experienced major fish health problems likely related to the production of hydrogen sulfide gas in stagnant areas of the systems. Finally, seawater systems require more expensive materials to prevent corrosion.

At the Freshwater Institute, "grilsing" has been our most significant problem when raising Atlantic salmon to market size. Grilse are sexually mature Atlantic salmon, which are predominantly males in mixed-sex diploid populations. These fish present a range of problems for farmers. Grilse can become more aggressive, and they often have a lower fillet yield compared to immature fish. Probably the biggest problem, however, is that as the gonad is developed at the expense of fillet growth, pigment is extracted from the muscle, leading to a pale fillet that consumers generally will not purchase if pink fillets are also available. Thus, precocious maturation results in a downgraded product. Initially, we observed about 80% of male salmon maturing by harvest size, and for a farmer this would result in an unacceptable economic loss. We carried out a growout trial utilizing an all-female germplasm, but unfortunately 70-80% of those females matured for unknown reasons. The issue in trying to solve this problem is that with Atlantic salmon, sexual maturation is part of their evolutionary biology. They are opportunists in this way, and there are many different variables—for example, photoperiod, water temperature, salinity, genetics—that can influence maturation either on their own or through interaction with other variables. As we can focus on only one or possibly two environmental variables during each growout trial, it has been a slow process in trying to prevent early maturation. Presently, we have a cohort of all-female diploids and all-female triploids, and at 1.5 kg we are seeing no maturation in either of those groups, which is promising.

As mentioned, keeping out pathogens, particularly obligate pathogens, is a huge benefit of closed containment aquaculture. But we should never claim that this production approach is "disease-free," because that is simply not the case. Pathogens will evolve in novel environments like these systems, and we therefore need to be ready to deal with the unexpected. Anecdotally, we have seen a few "mystery diseases" pop up at the Freshwater Institute. In one of our studies, we identified a novel bacterium called *Flectobacillus roseus* that was able to intermittently colonize our systems;[4] it seemed to bloom, disappear, and then bloom again. During peak blooms, we were counting more than 100 million colony-forming units per milliliter of RAS water. Thankfully, the organism turned out to be nonpathogenic, but it presented other problems such as clouding of the water (and hence a reduction in feeding efficiency) as well as very high total suspended solids, which likely had indirect impacts on fish production. Complete system disinfection appeared to remediate the issue. Overall, this episode countered our view that the microbially mature RAS water does not allow for opportunists to significantly proliferate.

Another unexpected issue was the occurrence of a novel pathogen, *Serratia liquefaciens*, in our growout system. We started seeing about one or two mortalities a day over the course of a week or two, which was highly unusual because once we move fish into the growout system, we rarely see any mortalities. After some investigation, it was determined that the affected fish were becoming septicemic with this particular pathogen. We theorize that the diet was causing enteritis, which in turn provided access for this bacterium to cause systemic infection. We managed the situation without any antibiotics by culling the occasional fish, dropping the water temperature, and adding low-level salt to reduce stress.

Lastly, we also had a chronic wasting condition appear in one of our growout cohorts, the pathology of which was characterized as systemic granuloma. At harvest time we estimated that about 20% of the fish were affected in one way or another with this particular pathology. The fillets were very thin, and the granulomas could be seen in all tissues examined, including the viscera, fillets, and brains.[5] Again, recirculating aquaculture is a novel environment. Pathogens, or potential pathogens, might be able to evolve in it. We have been trying to optimize the environment for smolt and post-smolt production in land-based recirculation systems since 2011, and it is an ongoing process, but the results have been quite optimistic. RAS has the potential to be the future of fish farming, but there will be issues to deal with along the way.

REFERENCES

1. Cliff White, "Atlantic Sapphire Building USD 350 Million Land-Based Salmon Farm in Miami," Seafood Source, March 19, 2017, https://www .seafoodsource.com/news/aquaculture/atlantic-sapphire-building-usd-350 -million-land-based-salmon-farm-in-miami.

2. "Salmon Recommendations from the Seafood Watch Program," Monterey Bay Aquarium Seafood Watch, https://www.seafoodwatch.org/seafood -recommendations/groups/salmon.

3. Yajie Liu et al., "Comparative Economic Performance and Carbon Footprint of Two Farming Models for Producing Atlantic Salmon (*Salmo Salar*): Land-Based Closed Containment System in Freshwater and Open Net Pen in Seawater," *Aquacultural Engineering* 71 (March 2016): 1-12.

4. John Davidson et al., "Evaluating the Effects of Prolonged Peracetic Acid Dosing on Water Quality and Rainbow Trout *Oncorhynchus Mykiss* Performance in Recirculation Aquaculture Systems," *Aquacultural Engineering* 84 (February 2019): 117-27.

5. Christopher Good et al., "Systemic Granuloma Observed in Atlantic Salmon *Salmo Salar* Raised to Market Size in a Freshwater Recirculation Aquaculture System," *Aquaculture Research* 47, no. 11 (May 2015): 3679-83.

PART V THE CORE ETHICAL COMMITMENTS

A Framework for Ethical Food Systems

THIRTY

The Ethical Basis for Choose Food

ANNE BARNHILL, NICOLE M. CIVITA, AND RUTH FADEN

THIS CHAPTER describes the Core Ethical Commitments (CECs),[1] a set of 47 statements that capture ethically important outcomes, practices, and features of the food value chain and food products. The CECs can be found in the next chapter. This chapter begins with a discussion of what the CECs are and how they might be used. We then address what they are not, including the limited role they are intended to play in analyzing the overall ethics of the global food system. Next we discuss how they were developed and spell out the underlying assumptions about the food system that informed their identification. Lastly, we discuss the five areas that the CECs cover—environment and resources; food chain labor; farmers, ranchers, and fishers; public health and community well-being; and animal welfare—and consider why each is a proper object of moral concern.

What the Core Ethical Commitments Are and How They Might Be Used

The 47 commitments provide parameters for ethical conduct. They set goals for actors along the food chain who have the power to make ethical improvements to their practices and products. They also provide guidance to consumers who prefer to buy foods that cohere with their values.

Each CEC has been selected both because it is ethically important and because it is amenable to market-based change in the near term.

We also believe that the CECs reflect areas of reasonable concern among the consuming public. We view all the CECs as important to a range of values-driven consumers, as well as to the producers that seek to earn their business.

Not all values-driven producers and consumers will embrace all of the CECs. Consumers and companies will not care equally about each CEC or each area of moral concern. For example, some will be far more motivated by environmental sustainability than animal welfare or public health. Some will prioritize ethical treatment of laborers above all else. Others will strive for a balance of performance across all areas of concern, expecting perfection or even high performance in none.

The Core Ethical Commitments Identify Ethical Imperatives

All the commitments are ethical imperatives on which society should make collective progress—they highlight aspects of food that are worthy of concerted attention. A few of the commitments are absolute rules applicable to all actors in the food chain at all times. Because violation of these absolute commitments is indisputably unethical, these commitments require immediate and rigorous fulfillment. For example, it is always unethical to use slave, trafficked, or forced human labor. When these absolute rules are not followed, an ethical violation has occurred. From an ethics perspective, producers have no discretion as to whether or when they meet these absolute rules. Companies should take care not to violate these absolute rules and to make sure that downstream players in their supply chain also do not do so. Likewise, when consumers are aware that a product violates an absolute rule, they should consider not purchasing the product in order to avoid complicity with an unethical practice.

Most of the commitments, however, are not absolute rules prohibiting specific production practices but instead identify important goals that may be realized in various ways. While these commitments generally accommodate progress over time, aspects of some are especially urgent.

The CECs cover five areas of moral concern (environment and resources; food chain labor; farmers, ranchers, and fishers; public health and community well-being; and animal welfare), and we encourage consumers and other food system actors to use them in ways that align with their values. For example, companies with a particular commitment to one area of concern might prioritize their effort there, and consumers who place high moral value on one area of concern might prioritize products and companies that are leaders in that area.

In practice, it will not be uncommon for tensions between CECs to surface. For example, some measures to address greenhouse gas (GHG) emissions may have negative consequences for land use or biodiversity. Moreover, it is possible that some pro-environmental actions may negatively affect nonenvironmental areas of concern, such as workers' well-being or animal welfare, amplifying the need to acknowledge trade-offs and balance interests. Different actors will reach different conclusions about which commitments to emphasize on the basis of their underlying values and goals. Moreover, the Choose Food project appreciates that collective progress in a system as vast, complex, and multifarious as the global food system depends on different food chain actors focusing more and earlier effort on some commitments rather than others.

It should be noted that most commitments apply to all products and producers. Some, however, apply only to a subset—for example, a commitment about the use of antibiotics in livestock animals would not apply to the producer of a wholly plant-based product, and a commitment to avoid inappropriate marketing practices targeting children would not be relevant to foods that experts in child health are encouraging children to consume in greater quantities.

The Core Ethical Commitments as an Ethics Tool and Backbone of Future Tools

We envision the CECs being used to create various ethics tools for market-based change of the food system. The CECs will form the backbone of these future tools. We also see the CECs as an ethics tool in and of themselves.

Ethics tools are practical tools designed to improve decision making and outcomes by systematically incorporating ethical considerations and structuring ethical reflection. Ethics tools have been developed for multiple sectors to facilitate decision making by policy makers and professionals (physicians, public health practitioners), to register the opinions of the public to inform decision making, and to help communicate about the ethical dimensions of decisions. These tools include ethics frameworks to help identify important considerations and structure reflection, checklists of concerns that can be used to assess specific decisions, and methods for structuring discussion among groups of stakeholders, including methods for reaching consensus decisions.[2]

The CECs are an ethics framework for market-based change to the food system—that is, change that occurs in and through markets as a result of economic signals. Various tools for market-based change could be built around the CECs. The CECs could be used by producers and processors to assess their production practices and guide improvement. The CECs could also form the foundation of guidance for investors, to help them direct investment toward companies engaged in ethically preferable practices. Advocacy groups could also use the CECs as a framework to help them clarify their priorities and to assess the progress being made by producers and companies.

The Cultural Context of the Core Ethical Commitments

Many contemporary commercial food transactions are multinational in structure, creating a web of ethically significant connections that span the globe. Ideally, a set of ethical commitments would be equally at home anywhere in the world. We cannot claim that to be the case with this set of CECs. While we hope that some if not most of the commitments are universally endorsable, the experience, worldviews, and subject matter expertise of our academic team and key advisors and of the stakeholders consulted are skewed predominantly toward North America and, to a lesser degree, Europe.

Additionally, because legal regimes and regulatory standards differ so significantly across international boundaries, acting in accordance with some CECs may be a relatively straightforward matter of legal obligation and compliance in one region but may conflict with prevailing policy imperatives in another. Thus, while we aimed to create broadly applicable CECs, we also wanted the statements to be straightforward and minimally burdened by the kinds of caveats that would be necessary to capture the nuances of different national and political-economic contexts.

Thus, at this point the CECs are most readily applicable to the US context. By this, we mean that they work best when used to guide decision making by actors operating in, designing products for or selling products to consumers in the United States. Similarly, the CECs may serve as a more useful framework for consumers in the United States than in other parts of the world. Nevertheless, we anticipate that the CECs may also prove to be a useful tool in other national and regional contexts, especially if refined through a process of stakeholder engagement featuring a diverse group of context-relevant stakeholders.

What the Core Ethical Commitments Are Not

For the CECs to be effectively used, it is important to clarify not only what they are but also what they are not. While the CECs identify ethically important features of food and supply chains, they do not provide a blueprint for designing a perfectly or even completely ethical food system.

Core Ethical Commitments Are a First Step, Not the Final Word

The CECs are not meant to be comprehensive. Many ethically important aspects of food production and consumption were not included. Our only claim here is that each of the CECs we have enumerated is an important component of an ethical food system that is amenable to change in the near term. We view this list of CECs both as evolving over time and as open to expansion by others. We hope that it will inspire a more inclusive and sophisticated dialogue about food ethics, which will inform subsequent iterations of the CECs as they evolve.

Core Ethical Commitments Are a Tool for Market-Based Change, Not a Recipe for Resolving All Food System Problems

One reason why the CECs are not a comprehensive blueprint for an ethical food system is that they were developed primarily as a tool for participants in markets: a tool for consumers to decide which products to buy, a tool for producers and processors to use in assessing their production practices, and a tool for distributors and retailers to inform sourcing and stocking standards in ethically desirable ways. Because regulation by states and global trade agreements help to shape markets, this tool may also be effectively used to inform or reform regulations and the enforcement discretion of regulators.

However, while we hope that this tool will be useful in accelerating market-based change of the food system, this does not mean that we think market-based change alone can solve many of the ethical problems associated with the food system. Indeed, this tool should not be interpreted as an endorsement of the presently dominant system of food production and provisioning.

We recognize that the contemporary food system, which involves substantial trade across globalized markets, is at once an extraordinarily productive triumph and a source of staggering harms. Since 1961, the world population has doubled. This rate of growth, unprecedented in human history, features prominently in the narrative of the modern industrialized food system and gives rise to legitimate concern about how best to feed such a sizable human population. As we grapple with the population problem, its long shadow often eclipses an even more staggering upward trend: the growth of international food commerce. Over the same period, the tonnage of food shipped between nations has increased fourfold, and the value of international trade in food has more than tripled.

For those living in high-income countries, this long-distance food system offers the reassurance of well-stocked shelves and the delight that comes with an abundance of options regardless of the season. But the force of the global food system often displaces local economies, traditions, cuisines, varieties, and forms of agriculture. All too often, farmers producing for export sacrifice the use of their land to feed an insatiable global craving for more and varied foods, from staple commodities to sudden superfoods. At the same time, rising numbers of low-income urban dwellers in both developing and advanced economies live in undercapitalized neighborhoods that are unable to provide the kinds of margins that supermarkets have come to rely on, sharply limiting access to diverse and healthy food options. The global food market has undoubtedly succeeded in providing affordable abundance to many, but its successes have come with costs and have carved gaps of substantial ethical concern. Only some of these concerns can be addressed through market-based action, and even then only in part.

Thus, we acknowledge that the CECs do not form a blueprint for comprehensive change or reform of the global food system. Comprehensive reform requires policy change at the national and international level and, arguably, reorientation of some economic goals. Ethical improvement of the food system also hinges on participatory and direct-action strategies, community engagement, and multi-stakeholder dialogue about the ethically important features of the food system and its significant impacts. In the opinion of some, including several of the experts who consulted or worked on this project, radical change to the structure of markets and political systems, including international governance, is also essential.

Although this tool is primarily designed to accelerate market-based shifts toward a more ethical food system, organizations and individuals focused on driving more sweeping forms of change—including those who favor community-based, sovereignty-oriented, and extra-market measures for satisfying human food needs—may also find it valuable. This tool can and should also be usable by proponents of place-based, human-scale, and sovereignty-oriented food systems to assess the ethics of the alternatives they are working to create, to guard against harms, and to catalyze consideration of ethical dilemmas inherent in the task of equitably and sustainably feeding a growing global population.

Assumptions Underlying the Core Ethical Commitments

The CECs are premised on the notion that, in the near term, the food system will continue to be largely moved by the logic of capitalism in a globalized economy and will feature substantial international trade of goods and exchange of knowledge. We neither endorse nor oppose this state of affairs. We assume that certain basic features of the global agrifood system will not change dramatically over the next few decades. Specifically, we assume that:

- There will continue to be global markets in agricultural inputs and products, food, and associated technology.
- Multinational institutions and governance will not radically change or disband.
- Animal agriculture will continue to be a part of the food system; both the flesh and the products of livestock and certain wild species will continue to be part of human diets.
- Commodity markets and futures trading in food will continue to exist.
- Nations with substantial roles in and influence over the global food system (including the United States) will continue to have largely market-based economies and will, to varying degrees, embrace free markets in food and agriculture.
- Globalized, regional, and localized food systems will coexist.

Although the CECs were developed with these assumptions in the background, the tool does not destabilize if there are some shifts. For example, if, in line with many recommendations for more sustainable diets, the consumption of animal-source foods is reduced (but not eliminated), the CECs regarding animal welfare remain relevant; they would simply apply to a smaller number of products and may be pertinent to fewer consumers. Likewise, even if the rates of local food consumption rise dramatically, displacing some internationally traded foods in the diets of consumers, most of the CECs remain applicable to local producers.

CECs from the Consumer's Point of View

The CECs are written, first and foremost, with the aim of guiding food sector actors in thinking through, prioritizing, and establishing a distinctive set of ethical commitments to guide their practices. The CECs can also be used by consumers in developing and actualizing their values related to food. We recommend that consumers reading through the CECs "flip" the obligation. For example, consumers are rarely in a position to determine or directly influence whether the "use of inputs, such as fertilizers and pesticides, is appropriate and judicious." However, consumers can seek out foods produced by companies that provide information—directly or through participation in credible third-party certification programs—about the type and extent of inputs used. In their purchasing, consumers can favor products and producers that both offer transparency about inputs and demonstrate a commitment to judicious use.

Using the CECs to Assess Dietary Patterns

We also recommend that consumers consider how different types of foods and different overall dietary patterns align with the CECs of most concern to them. Broadly speaking, plant-based foods will generally fare better on many of the "Environment and Resources" CECs, as compared to animal-source foods—and, of course, they will also fare better on the "Animal Welfare" CECs. Thus, consumers who wish to better align their overall dietary pattern with those CECs could consider reducing consumption of animal-source foods in favor of plant-based foods.

Consistent with the broad generalization that production of plant-based foods has fewer negative environmental impacts than animal-source foods, there are significant differences between types of plant-based food. For example, production of almonds uses approximately 4 times more water than the production of pistachios and 17 times more water than production of peanuts.[3] There are also differences between types of animal-source food. The emissions from a serving of red meat are, for example, 5.25 times higher than from a serving of chicken.[4]

Thus, consumers could also consider shifting consumption from some types of plant-based foods to others and from some types of animal-source foods to others.

In addition, for a given food (i.e., beef or almonds), typically there are significant differences in environmental impact (along various dimensions) between the best-performing and worst-performing producers.[5] Accordingly, consumers who wish to shape their dietary patterns to optimize performance related to a particular set of CECs may wish to favor or avoid certain categories of food altogether and to select from other categories only when they are able to determine that certain production practices are used or eschewed.

Development of the Core Ethical Commitments and Next Steps

The CECs were developed over a two-year period. Seven academic researchers from the United States and Europe were commissioned to write white papers laying out significant ethical concerns with food production and consumption in their area of expertise (e.g., environment, public health, animal welfare, labor, crops and horticulture, water, and food safety). Drawing on the content of these white papers, and through discussion over a two-day meeting in March 2017, the project team and content area experts identified a preliminary set of concerns, or Core Ethical Commitments. Over the ensuing year, these preliminary CECs were further refined through continued analysis and discussion, as well as in response to initial feedback from attendees at one small workshop and one public symposium.

The next step in the development of the CECs is for a broadly inclusive set of stakeholders to assess the CECs as a tool for market-based change. This process was begun at the Choose Food Symposium in November 2018 but should be expanded to include diverse food system actors (farmworkers, farmers, distributors, investors, consumers, etc.) who represent a range of demographics and identities. Subjecting the CECs to an inclusive process of thorough vetting by diverse stakeholders will help ensure that subsequent versions of the CECs accommodate different value systems and serve as a useful tool for a wider range of food system actors.

Another further step in the development of the CECs is having each commitment explicated by subject matter experts in more detail. These explications will involve several elements: defining key concepts used in the commitment; clarifying exceptions to the commitment; identifying practices that do and do not satisfy the commitment; and listing additional resources of use when thinking about and implementing that commitment, such as links to relevant important empirical work and relevant laws, voluntary agreements, and guidance documents. The CECs are intentionally expansive, and while they can be used in their current form to guide thinking, they will become increasingly actionable and valuable across a range of applications as they are explicated by a range of experts with deep subject matter expertise in each topic.

In addition to being presented in the next chapter of this volume, the CECs are published with supporting material and resources at https:// bioethics.jhu.edu/choose-food.

The Areas of Moral Concern
Environment and Resources

Human beings have always extracted plants, animals, fungi, and minerals from the earth to meet their needs and advance their civilizations. However, the pace and scale of resource extraction has escalated in modern times, depleting and degrading the earth's resources, emitting greenhouse gases, and disrupting the biogeochemical cycles upon which all life depends. As a result, we now face a climate crisis of our own making—a crisis that threatens the persistence of the life-supporting atmosphere that has made the earth uniquely congenial to human flourishing.

Contemporary food systems have a very significant, and generally very negative, impact on our climate and environment. The way we currently produce and consume food gives rise to some 20-30% of global climate changing greenhouse gas emissions. Livestock production accounts for an estimated 14.5% of global GHG emissions from human activities.[6]

Food and associated human activities are also responsible for tremendous consumption and pollution of natural resources. For example, food production and consumption accounts for around 70% of freshwater use and acts as a major source of water pollution.[7] Occupying nearly 40% of the earth's land surface, agriculture has long been the main driver of land use changes (including deforestation); it is also directly and indirectly responsible for about 80% of associated biodiversity loss.[8,9] Moving from land to sea, unsustainable fishing practices in combination with water pollution, often from terrestrial agriculture, have led to the collapse of many fish stocks. Approximately 90% of fish stocks are now overexploited or fully exploited, or depleted, and there have been major attendant disruptions to marine and freshwater ecosystems.[10] Agriculture is also the major global user of land and natural resources, both finite and renewable.

The environmental and climate-related impacts of food systems are determined in large part by the kinds of foods that are produced as well as how they are produced and distributed. Also important is how much food is produced and what portion of production is ultimately consumed by humans, as opposed to being fed to animals, turned into biofuels, or wasted. By 2050, without substantive changes, food production is expected to exhaust the emissions budget we must maintain to limit warming to 2 degrees Celsius.[11] Research indicates that a 50% reduction in wastage of food and a substantial shift toward consumption of more plant-based foods can actually *reduce* the GHG footprint of global food production by 50% over the same period.[12] Additionally, shifts toward more regenerative, soil-building, and perennial agricultural practices create opportunities for substantial carbon-sequestration, allowing us to return to the ground the climate-destabilizing compounds that we have sent skyward.[13] These are just a few indicators of how the aggregated effects of environmentally astute choices by both producers and consumers can transform food production from a source of tremendous harms into an effective tool for positive change.

The mounting natural challenges to food production, such as extreme weather events, drought, coastal flooding, mudslides, and impaired water supplies, demonstrate the connectedness of human and planetary well-being. As the human population continues to swell, food demand will increase, and the challenge is to conserve land and natural resources while meeting this demand.

Limiting the environmental impacts of the food system and restoring ecosystem health is ethically important for at least four clusters of reasons. First, the food system's negative impacts on the natural world affect the well-being of current generations. Both secular and religious moralities acknowledge that we have ethical responsibilities toward other living people—extending beyond our own families and communities. These responsibilities may be based in justice concerns, in moral imperatives to avoid harming others and to enhance the well-being of others, and in recognition of fundamental human rights.

Environmental degradation threatens the physical and mental well-being of living humans (i.e., current generations) in multiple ways: from pollution, heat stress, and an increased spread of diseases into new regions of the world; from an increased incidence and severity of extreme weather events; from dwindling resource availability, which diminishes prospects for economic development; from reduced stability and increased volatility of habitats and livelihoods; and from diminished ability to experience and integrate meaning and purpose in life through a connectedness with the natural world.[14] More specific to food, environmental degradation also triggers challenges to food security, impairs access to adequate nutrition,[15] and reduces the nutrient content of food grown in poor soils or amid elevated CO_2 levels.[16]

Second, environmental degradation negatively affects the well-being of future generations. Both secular and religious moralities acknowledge that we have ethical responsibilities toward future generations of human beings, including responsibilities not to impose a risk of significant harm on future generations, and responsibilities to ensure that future generations have natural resources and opportunities that are equivalent to those that our generation had. Some believe that we owe ethical duties to future generations because it is our reproductive behavior that brings about their existence. More basically, insofar as we are invested in the continued persistence, thriving, and evolution of the human race, we should care about promoting the well-being of future generations.

We cannot be certain precisely how dramatic an impact environmental damage will have on future people or what roles technology and innovation may play in mitigating the consequences of ecosystem disruption, resource exhaustion, climate change, and related harms. We can be reasonably certain that we are bequeathing a less natural resource-rich and less resilient planet to future generations than that which those of us living today experience. This is bound to negatively affect the well-being of future generations. At best, we are impairing the prospects for future generations to enjoy a quality of life commensurate with that enjoyed by their recent ancestors. At worst, we are seriously degrading the habitability of the only planet known to support human life and jeopardizing the existence of our successors.

Third, environmental degradation also has negative consequences for living organisms of other species besides humans. Some believe that humans have ethical duties to avoid directly or indirectly harming other species and, in particular, other species of sentient animals. Ethical duties to animals may be based on a conceptualization of animals as beings who are objects of moral concern in their own right. Alternatively, some religious doctrines conceive of human beings as caretakers of all creatures, giving rise to obligations both to limit harm to animals and to meet their needs in connection with meeting our own.

Human-caused environmental damage threatens the well-being and existence of nonhuman animals in multiple ways, including through destruction and fragmentation of habitats, intensified competition for scarce resources, human-catalyzed extinctions, and resulting disruptions in food webs.

Fourth, reductions in biodiversity and ecosystem integrity matter in and of themselves, according to some ethical views. Some people think the natural environment, inclusive of the variety and variability of life-forms on earth, has intrinsic value. Those who emphasize intrinsic value—the value of nature and its variety in and for itself—assert that the natural diversity of organisms and species, the complexity of ecological systems, and the resilience created by evolutionary processes are objects of moral concern. This ecocentric philosophy, central to conservation biology and deep ecology, holds that maintaining and restoring biological diversity are individual and collective responsibilities of humans. In the view of *biospheric egalitarians*, we must demonstrate care for the environment and practice resource conservation not only because a failure to do so prevents human and animal flourishing but also because earth's varied terrains, ecosystems, and biodiversity have high intrinsic value. Others, including *environmental humanists*, emphasize that acknowledgment of inherent value provides secondary benefits to humans. On this theory, by recognizing and respecting the inherent value of our planet, its natural systems, and its other inhabitants, we are able to enjoy a deeper connection to the natural world and more fully realize humanity's inherent dignity and exceptional capacity for empathy.

Food Chain Labor

Although the Industrial and Digital Revolutions have dramatically changed the way food is produced, humans have not completely innovated their way out of working for their food. Advancements in agricultural and food-related technology have relieved most people from the obligation to perform land-based and food-producing work, allowing ever more of us to move to cities and pursue nonagricultural careers, advancing innovation, expression, and progress in countless other fields, generating wealth, and enabling leisure pursuits. Modern humans who enjoy the freedoms that flow from the ready availability of sufficient food owe much of their liberty and available time to the labor of over a billion people who continue to perform essential work producing food throughout the food chain.

From farm and sea to market, human labor remains necessary for a wide range of production activities. In horticulture, manual, machine-assisted, and technology-supported human labor is employed in cultivating land and preparing other growing media, seeding and planting, weeding and pruning, and harvesting seed, feed, and raw food items. In animal agriculture (which encompasses the husbandry of livestock raised for meat, milk, fiber, and hide, poultry raised for meat and eggs, farmed aquatic animals, and edible and beneficial insects), humans are involved in breeding, tending, feeding and watering, milking, housing, maintaining herd or flock health, and slaughtering. Additionally, wild fisheries use human labor on waterborne vessels for the foraging of wild fish and seafood. A much smaller but not insignificant amount of land-based food is hunted or foraged by humans.

Owing to the use of heavy machinery, sharp implements, and toxic chemicals, as well as proximity to large animals and exposure to the elements, agriculture and fishing are among the three most dangerous job sectors in terms of work-related fatalities, nonfatal accidents, and occupational diseases. Slaughterhouse work is similarly dangerous and taxing, with workers required to spend long hours in hot and humid kill rooms or frigid meatpacking areas while performing difficult, fast-paced, repetitive manual tasks with very sharp implements.

Humans are also involved in the processing of raw products into safe comestibles, moving food through markets to consumers, and preparing and serving food for consumption. As we face the challenges of sustainably producing and providing access to sufficient food to meet the needs of a rapidly growing human population on a warming planet with an increasingly volatile climate and dwindling natural resource base, human labor, skill, ingenuity, and stewardship only become more critical.

The ability to meet our food needs through relatively little labor of our own is a great and often undervalued privilege. It would be reasonable to expect that food chain workers, given the importance of their labor to so many, would be honored for the work that they do and be well compensated and protected. To the contrary, the conditions under which food laborers across the globe toil—and the economic challenges that they face—call into question the ethics of even the most environmentally sustainable, animal welfare-centric, and nutritious food. Food chain workers perform hard physical labor for long hours, often in unsheltered outdoors or in sheltered but dangerous facilities. They work in perilously close proximity to dangerous machinery, toxic chemicals, or powerfully built animals. Despite these conditions and risks, most earn poverty wages, receive no medical benefits or paid sick days, enjoy little job security, and have minimal opportunity for advancement.

Farm workers, who must live in close proximity to productive lands, often have no choice but to rent a small sliver of space in crowded and dilapidated houses or to sleep in makeshift shelters. They rarely have access to reliable transportation; when they do, that transportation is often operated by their employers. Few farm and food-processing workers enjoy or are able to exercise rights to collective organization, action, or bargaining.

Because food chain labor is often performed by people living in diaspora, cultural and language differences form barriers and lead to social isolation, which can be especially difficult to combat in the remote, rural areas where food is typically grown and processed.[17] Many perform seasonal work and have few opportunities to earn wages for several months of each year; some must migrate long distances in search of temporary work on farms, traveling as the growing season unfolds.[18] Food chain workers are subjected to racism, sexism, harassment, assault, and unsafe working conditions at alarming rates.[19,20] Worse yet, an indeterminate but not insubstantial portion of the estimated 20.9 million victims of human trafficking worldwide, including children, are forced to work in agriculture, fisheries, and food processing.[21]

We have already noted that there is a range of reasons why people owe general ethical duties to the other humans with whom we share a planet and era. There are also some specific reasons why we owe duties to those who produce our food and help bring it to market, regardless of where they may work or live. The food we need to sustain our health and enjoy our lives is the result of the labor of others in a global web of interdependent connections between food producers, consumers, and countless food chain workers. These connections give rise to specific duties toward the workers who contribute their labor to the enterprise and the sustenance, welfare, and livelihoods of others.

The commitments under the Food Chain Labor area of concern aspire to ensure that decent, safe work and sustainable livelihoods are available to those who labor in the food system regardless of job classification or location. Generally speaking, it is ethically important that conditions of work live up to the International Labour Organization's conception of "decent work," which is defined as productive work for women and men in conditions of freedom, equity, security, and human dignity. Decent work involves opportunities for work that is productive and delivers a fair income; provides security in the workplace and social protection for workers and their families; offers prospects for personal development and encourages social integration; gives people the freedom to express their concerns, to organize, and to participate in decisions that affect their lives; and guarantees equal opportunities and equal treatment for all.[22]

Farmers, Ranchers, and Fishers

Both practically and ethically, farmers, ranchers, and fishers have much in common with other food chain laborers. For example, while running their operations, farmers, ranchers, and fishers also dedicate their time and contribute their labor to enterprises that produce food to satisfy the irreducible needs of other humans.[23] Additionally, farmers, ranchers, and fishers are often exposed to some of the same risks and harms as other food chain laborers because they work in similar spaces, sometimes side by side. Nevertheless, there are key distinctions between farmers, ranchers, and fishers and other food chain laborers that should not be overlooked—differences of power, authority, autonomy, recognition, voice, and cultural position. Farmers, ranchers, and fishers are often held in the collective imagination as hardworking, honorable contributors to society possessing a laudable entrepreneurial spirit. By contrast, other food chain workers are more readily dismissed or overlooked. While farmers, ranchers, and fishers have a long history of organizing for and obtaining government protection of their interests, others who work as food chain laborers are often discouraged or barred from such organizing and have seen less success in achieving public recognition of their plight.

But to say that some farmers, ranchers, and fishers may hold a privileged position relative to many food chain laborers is to tell only part of the story. If, instead, we compare farmers, ranchers, and fishers to other food system business owners and corporate interest groups, their stature diminishes. This is, in part, because farmers, ranchers, and fishers are a large but fairly disparate group. There are more than 570 million farms and ranches globally, about 500 million of which are family-run or smallholder farms operating on two hectares or less.[24] These small farms exist alongside much larger operations with access to more sophisticated technologies and abilities to leverage the benefits of economies of scale. A similar dualism exists in the marine fisheries context where small-scale or artisanal fisheries forage in the same waters as large-scale or industrial fisheries, creating real disparities in types of technology used, degree of capital intensity, opportunities to hire help, and challenges to maintaining ownership.[25]

Concentration in the food industry is intense. In almost every sector, the differential in economic power between the top four firms and smaller players like most farmers, ranchers, and fishers is enormous.[26] Oligopolistic levels of consolidation have been observed in many sectors of the food system including, for example, input providers, commodities brokers, food processors, distributors, and retailers. By comparison, the primary production portion of the food system is far more diverse and diffuse and wields less cohesive political power and far less economic power. Differential power of this magnitude puts smaller players in a position of substantial disadvantage and makes it easier for larger players to engage in business practices that pose significant threats to the viability of smaller-scale players. Moreover, because of this asymmetry, farmers, ranchers, and fishers are often "price-takers" with little ability to negotiate the value they receive for what they produce or the terms upon which they contract with buyers of their products. Moreover, they may find themselves at greater risk of unfair business practices. Because of these dynamics, farmers, ranchers, and fishers are worthy of distinctive moral concern.

Farmers, ranchers, and fishers are in a special ethical position. How they run their operations has ethical implications for workers, animals, public health, and the natural environment. Yet, in addition to being moral agents capable of bringing about good or harm for others, they are also subjects of moral concern. The livelihoods of farmers, ranchers, and fishers and their ability to conduct their enterprises in ethically appropriate ways are heavily influenced by the actions of upstream players in the food system, ethical conduct in markets, and just systems of regulation. When we think about the interests and ethical claims of farmers, ranchers, and fishers, five interrelated sets of issues arise.

First, large players in the agrifood system sometimes engage in practices that are unfair and exploitative of smaller players and that threaten their livelihoods. This conduct is enabled by the disproportionate size and economic and political power of multinational corporations, multidivisional companies, conglomerates, and trade groups. For example, as food supply chains have been restructured through horizontal and vertical integration, some integrators have outsourced the most risky and low margin segments of their business to growers under contract terms that many analysts have critiqued as fundamentally unfair. A prime example here is outsourcing the raising of live animals to slaughter weight. Similarly, some processors who buy from independent growers now compete with growers by raising their own "captive supply" of animals that can be slaughtered when market prices rise above what the processors want to pay.[27,28]

Second, even when unfair and exploitative practices are *not* used, small players can still be driven out of business by large players with greater power to dominate markets, influence political processes, benefit from economies of scale, and gain a competitive edge through the aggregation and use of "big ag data."[29] For example, widespread and rapid consolidation across the agrifood industry has left farmers with a scant selection of both input suppliers and potential purchasers of their products. The lack of competition on both sides of their business squeezes their incomes and limits their choices about what to grow, how to grow it, and for whom.

Both the first and the second set of issues result in conditions that combine to create a third, instrumental reason why the interests of small and midsized producers are ethically important. These conditions make it difficult for small producers to act ethically with respect to workers, animals, public health, and the natural environment without jeopardizing their livelihoods and the viability of their own businesses. Thus, small and midsized producers must sometimes choose between ethically preferable conduct (i.e., using practices that are more sustainable or respectful of labor) and financial viability. Unfair arrangements for small and midsized producers not only are thus problematic from the standpoint of the interests of small producers but can also result in harm to other things we care about with respect to food.

Fourth, and relatedly, smaller players, especially those who truly own and operate as family enterprises and have tangible connections to the places in which food is grown or captured, may be more likely than large operators to emphasize relationships in ways that yield ethically desirable conditions. A relational, rather than extractive, approach to farming lends itself to reciprocity with and care for the land and other species on which farmers, ranchers, and fishers depend. Such an approach also emphasizes community well-being and sharing of resources. Relatedly, smaller players may be more apt to favor practices that are ethical, conservation-driven, and welfare promoting. Additionally, if smaller producers tend to have more diversified operations, they would be more likely to produce food that can be readily consumed by humans without conversion by animals (as feed) and without intensive processing. For these reasons, some view the work of these farmers as more directly responsive and essential to meeting human needs.

Fifth, some consider small farms, farming and fishing communities, and the rural heritage they embody, to possess a combination of cultural, historical, and inherent values that makes them worth preserving. The values that these land- and sea-based enterprises serve and instantiate are seen as reasons to protect and promote the distinctive lifeways and communities that dominate and define many interior and coastal rural places.

Whether or to what extent small producers should be protected from economic losses, and their ways of life preserved, is a matter of debate. There is significant disagreement about the bounds of appropriate conduct in markets and the degree to which any particular business is obligated to restrain itself or limit its opportunities for profit in service of the welfare of smaller operators and the value they bring to neighboring communities and ways of life. There is also foundational disagreement about how markets ought to be structured. Some activists and scholars of food systems object to the globalization of the food system, object to it functioning as a relatively free market (or, alternatively, object to the use of free-market rhetoric in the face of subsidies and protectionist practices), and even object to food being treated as a commodity at all. Others argue that the best way to help small farmers is to make food and agricultural markets freer—for example, by reducing tariffs. Thus, the CECs in this section might be criticized as going too far by asking too much of larger business enterprises and also as not going nearly far enough by failing to lodge important, foundational ethical critiques of how markets are structured.

Whatever one's views on these foundational issues, there exists a core set of problems that we hope all can recognize and be concerned about, including: when free markets fail to function as intended, and some actors engage in unfair, exploitative, or anticompetitive behavior, either by design or by lack of enforcement; when otherwise fair conduct within a well-functioning market nonetheless disincentivizes ethical conduct by other actors; and when otherwise fair conduct undermines people's ability to meet their basic needs by threatening their livelihood or food security.

Public Health and Community Well-Being

One job of societies is to protect and promote human well-being, including importantly, human health. Food consumption patterns, agricultural practices, and other food system practices matter morally because they are simultaneously essential to the realization of health and well-being and a threat to them.

Food consumption can be a source of health and well-being, providing good nutrition, pleasure, psychological comfort, and social goods for individuals, families, and communities. Food is a locus of our social lives and a way of expressing personal and group identities, including religious and cultural identities, and expressing personal values. But food consumption can also undermine health and well-being. Consumption of food contaminated with bacteria, viruses, parasites, and chemical substances makes 10% of the global population ill each year and kills an estimated 420,000 people.[30] Food consumption patterns are also the main cause of the increasing rates of overweight and obesity in recent decades. These high rates of overweight and obesity have significant consequences for public health, increasing risk for diet-related disease and causing an estimated 4 million deaths worldwide in 2015.[31] Significant rates of undernutrition exist alongside overnutrition: globally, 821 million people were undernourished in 2017, meaning they could not access enough food to meet dietary energy requirements.[32] Thus, a most basic health-related concern with the food system is malnutrition in all its forms.

Some agricultural practices pose occupational health risks to farmers and farmworkers, such as health risks from exposure to pesticides.[33] Agricultural practices can pose health risks to surrounding communities or reduce their quality of life. For example, improper handling of manure on animal operations can lead to groundwater pollution and noxious smells that affect surrounding communities. Agricultural practices can also pose risks to the health of the public at large. For example, the routine use of antibiotics in animal agriculture spurs the creation of antibiotic-resistant bacteria, a significant threat to public health. At the same time, agriculture can be central to community identity and ways of life and thus be essentially connected to a community's well-being.

Health has clear ethical importance, given its value to individuals, families, communities, and societies. Health is a central dimension of individual well-being. Good health enables other valuable conditions of life: a life of normal length, without excessive pain and suffering, with gainful employment, family and caretaking relationships, and other meaningful pursuits. Some would argue that a certain level of health is essential to leading a good life; at the very least, health makes it much easier to pursue valuable opportunities and lead good lives. Health also has social value. Poor health has economic and social costs, such as lost productivity, health care costs, and the financial and personal costs of caretaking.

Given the personal and social value of health, some argue that for a society to be a just society, all people must have meaningful opportunities to be healthy.[34] There is disagreement, however, about which opportunities to be healthy societies ought to provide and about the ways in which societies are required to support public health.[35] Thus, although there might be broad agreement that we owe it to each other to collectively protect public health, and we owe it to future generations of people to bequeath to them a society and natural world that can sustain their health, there will be disagreement about what more precisely this requires.

Because the value of health is so significant, food production practices that threaten health raise ethical concerns. It is not feasible, however, for production practices to be risk-free. Nor is this always ethically desirable, because there can be trade-offs between reducing health risks from production and other goals, such as profits for producers or wages for workers. Stakeholders may disagree about what are acceptable levels of risk, given the trade-offs involved in reducing risk. Societies may differ in the trade-offs between health and other goods that are considered acceptable, as well as the level of risk to public health that is acceptable.

Nonetheless, some production-side practices exceed an acceptable level of risk to the health of workers, communities, and the public. Similarly, risks of foodborne illness that exceed certain thresholds are unacceptable—though, again, what counts as an acceptable level of risk will depend on the trade-offs and values particular to a society.

It is not only production practices but also practices along the food value chain that can affect public health and community well-being. For example, how foods are marketed affects what people consume and why they consume it. Various marketing practices raise ethical concerns because of how they affect consumer autonomy and public health and well-being. A general concern is that the food industry formulates and markets foods in ways that both diminish consumers' health and undermine their autonomy—by formulating foods that are hard to resist even when consumers wish to eat less of them, by labeling foods in ways that are misleading or uninformative, and by marketing foods in ways that prompt overconsumption, such as packaging foods in large serving sizes. As food companies expand into new markets, newly introduced and heavily marketed packaged foods, processed foods, and convenience foods can displace other ways of cooking and eating, causing an increase in overweight, obesity, and diet-related disease.[36] At the same time, the wide consumption of these foods suggests that they have perceived value for consumers, health risks notwithstanding.

Animal Welfare

Most animals raised for food in the United States (as well as many around the world) live in confinement systems, colloquially called "factory farms." As judged by widely accepted standards of animal welfare, many animals raised under conditions of confinement do not have good lives. This includes swine, egg-laying chickens, meat chickens, dairy cows, and, to a lesser extent, beef cattle raised in feedlots and some farmed fish. These animals may be biologically productive in the sense that they grow quickly and reproduce abundantly, but biological productivity and animal welfare are not the same thing.

In confinement systems, animals typically live in cages, pens, or stalls, or in open areas with a high density of animals. In these conditions, they cannot express certain species-typical behavior, such as pecking in chickens, rooting in pigs, or migrating in fish.[37] Animals have been bred to put on weight more quickly, which has resulted in high rates of physical abnormalities in some species—for example, a high rate of poor locomotion and poor leg health in broiler chickens.[38] Animals' bodies are altered, in some cases without relief of the pain these alterations likely cause: for example, chickens' beaks are trimmed and pigs' tails are docked in order to prevent potentially harmful behaviors such as pecking and tail biting that arise when these animals are raised in crowded conditions. Pasture-based systems, in which animals spend much of their time outdoors, at lower density, have inherent welfare advantages over confinement systems, though pasture-based systems also have some vulnerabilities for animals because of increased exposure to the elements and to predators.

Views about how humans should relate to animals and what is a good life for animals vary widely within and across societies and over time, and they are rooted in religious and secular beliefs. Some people attribute moral rights to animals and consider many of our uses of animals—for food, clothing, research, companionship—contrary to these moral rights and thus morally wrong. Others believe that it can be ethical for humans to use animals, but this use comes with a responsibility to take care of the animals, perhaps as a result of an "implicit contract" with animals: they give us food, clothing, and other goods, and in exchange we care for them and give them good lives.

In animal agriculture, this responsibility historically manifested as husbandry. The essence of husbandry was good care. Humans put animals into the most optimal environment congenial to the animals not only surviving but also thriving. The better off the animals were, the better off humans were. Humans provided farm animals with sustenance, water, shelter, protection from predation, such medical attention as was available, help in birthing, food during famine, water during drought, safe surroundings, and comfortable appointments. Because husbandry was grounded in human self-interest, very few additional ethical rules or laws for animal treatment were required.

Industrial-scale production departs from the practices and values of husbandry in morally important ways. Despite underlying diversity of values and worldviews about the moral status of nonhuman animals and our obligations to them, there is increasing concern among the public for the welfare of farm animals in many countries. In addition, laws prohibiting cruelty to animals, traditionally the only social consensus ethic pertaining to animals, have been elevated to felony status in most US states.

There is debate about how animal welfare should be understood, including what it means for an animal to have a good life or to have a sufficient level of well-being. Animal welfare expert David Fraser charts the historical development of conceptions of animal welfare:

> In summary, then, as people formulated and debated various proposals
> about what constitutes a satisfactory life for animals in human care,
> three main concerns emerged: (1) that animals should feel well by being
> spared negative affect (pain, fear, hunger etc.) as much as possible, and
> by experiencing positive affect in the form of contentment and normal
> pleasures; (2) that animals should be able to lead reasonably natural lives

by being able to perform important types of normal behavior and by having some natural elements in their environment such as fresh air and the ability to socialize with other animals in normal ways; and (3) that animals should function well in the sense of good health, normal growth and development, and normal functioning of the body.[39]

Fraser identifies three concerns, which ground three components of animal welfare: animals' subjective experience, animals' biological health, and animals' ability to engage in normal/natural behaviors.

As Fraser notes, some who embrace natural behaviors and natural lives as a component of animal welfare do so because they believe this is inherently good for animals. The idea here is that for an animal to have a good life, it must be able to engage in behaviors typical of its species—a good life for a chicken requires ample and regular opportunity to do chicken-like things. We might also think of this as the ability of the animal to express its innate animalness. For example, Bernard Rollin uses the philosophical concept of "telos" to capture this—the telos of an animal is "the set of interests constitutive of its unique form of life—the 'pigness' of the pig, the 'dogness' of the dog." Rollin argues that violations of telos may be more significantly harmful to animals than physical pain.[40] Others who embrace natural behaviors as a component of animal welfare do so for a different reason: because they believe the ability to engage in natural behaviors improves the animals' subjective experience. That is, it reduces animals' negative affect and causes positive affect.

All three components—biological health, subjective experience, and the ability to express some normal/natural behaviors—are included in the Five Freedoms, which is perhaps the most widely accepted conception of animal welfare. The Five Freedoms was first developed in 1965 in the United Kingdom, by a committee of veterinarians, biologists, and animal scientists tasked to examine the welfare of farm animals. Underlying the Five Freedoms is a conception of animal welfare according to which: "The welfare of an animal includes its physical and mental state and we consider that good animal welfare implies both fitness and a sense of well-being. Any animal kept by man must, at least, be protected from unnecessary suffering." According to its conception, "an animal's welfare, whether on farm, in transit, at market or at a place of slaughter should be considered in terms of 'five freedoms.'" These freedoms are:

1. Freedom from Hunger and Thirst—by ready access to fresh water and a diet to maintain full health and vigor
2. Freedom from Discomfort—by providing an appropriate environment including shelter and a comfortable resting area
3. Freedom from Pain, Injury or Disease—by prevention or rapid diagnosis and treatment
4. Freedom to Express Normal Behavior—by providing sufficient space, proper facilities and company of the animal's own kind
5. Freedom from Fear and Distress—by ensuring conditions and treatment which avoid mental suffering.[41]

The Core Ethical Commitments in this section assume that the conception of animal welfare expressed in the Five Freedoms is substantially correct. These commitments are also consonant with existing guidance on how animal production systems can meet the Five Freedoms.

REFERENCES

1. The Core Ethical Commitments were collectively authored with contributions from Anne Barnhill, Nicole M. Civita, Claire Davis, Shauna Downs, Ruth Faden, Sara Glass, Alan M. Goldberg, Herman B. W. M. Koëter, Bernard Rollin, Paul B. Thompson, Kees van Leeuwen, and Suzanne McMillan. They were developed over the life of the project by those who participated in workshop discussions and those who worked on them directly until they were presented at the symposium.

2. See, for example, Ben Mepham, "A Framework for the Ethical Analysis of Novel Foods: The Ethical Matrix," *Journal of Agricultural & Environmental Ethics* 12, no. 2 (January 2000): 165-76; Nancy E. Kass, "An Ethics Framework for Public Health," *American Journal of Public Health* 91, no. 11 (November 2001): 1776-82; Volkert Beekman et al., "Ethical Bio-Technology Assessment Tools for Agriculture and Food Production: Final Report Ethical Bio-TA Tools (QLG6-CT-2002-02594)," LEI, The Hague, February 2006; Volkert Beekman and Frans W. A. Brom, "Ethical Tools to Support Systematic Public Deliberations about the Ethical Aspects of Agricultural Biotechnologies," *Journal of Agricultural & Environmental Ethics* 20, no. 1 (February 2007): 3-12; Ruth Faden and Madison Powers, "A Social Justice Framework for Health and Science Policy," *Cambridge Quarterly of Healthcare Ethics* 20, no. 4 (October 2011): 596-604;

Lisa M. Lee, "Public Health Ethics Theory: Review and Path to Convergence," *Journal of Law, Medicine & Ethics* 40, no. 1 (Spring 2012): 85-98; Ben Mepham, "Agricultural Ethics," in *Encyclopedia of Applied Ethics*, ed. Ruth Chadwick, Daniel Callahan, and Peter Singer (London: Academic Press (Elsevier), 2012), 86-96; Ruth R. Faden et al., "An Ethics Framework for a Learning Health Care System: A Departure from Traditional Research Ethics and Clinical Ethics," *Hastings Center Report* 43, no. s1 (January–February 2013): S16-27; and Scott Bremer et al., "Inclusive Governance of Aquaculture Value-Chains: Co-producing Sustainability Standards for Bangladeshi Shrimp and Prawns," *Ocean & Coastal Management* 131 (November 2016): 13-24.

3. M. M. Mekonnen and A. Y. Hoekstra, "The Green, Blue and Grey Water Footprint of Crops and Derived Crop Products," *Hydrology and Earth System Sciences* 15, no. 5 (May 2011): 1577-1600.

4. Martin C. Heller and Gregory A. Keoleian, "Greenhouse Gas Emission Estimates of US Dietary Choices and Food Loss," *Journal of Industrial Ecology* 19, no. 3 (2015): 391-401.

5. J. Poore and T. Nemecek, "Reducing Food's Environmental Impacts through Producers and Consumers," *Science* 360, no. 6392 (June 2018): 987-92.

6. Tara Garnett et al., "Food Systems and Greenhouse Gas Emissions" (Foodsource: chapters), Food Climate Research Network, University of Oxford, 2016.

7. Food and Agriculture Organization of the United Nations, *Water for Sustainable Food and Agriculture: A Report Produced for the G20 Presidency of Germany* (Rome: FAO, 2017).

8. Jonathan A. Foley et al., "Global Consequences of Land Use," *Science* 309, no. 5734 (July 2005): 570-74.

9. Gabrielle Kissinger, M. Herold, and Veronique De Sy, *Drivers of Deforestation and Forest Degradation: A Synthesis Report for REDD+ Policymakers* (Vancouver: Lexeme Consulting, 2012).

10. Mukhisa Kituyi and Peter Thomson, "Nearly 90% of Fish Stocks Are in the Red—Fisheries Subsidies Must Stop," World Economic Forum, July 13, 2018, https://www.weforum.org/agenda/2018/07/fish-stocks-are-used-up -fisheries-subsidies-must-stop.

11. Brent Kim et al., "The Importance of Reducing Animal Product Consumption and Wasted Food in Mitigating Catastrophic Climate Change," Johns Hopkins Center for a Livable Future, 2015.

12. Brian Lipinski et al., "Reducing Food Loss and Waste. Working Paper, Installment 2 of Creating a Sustainable Food Future" (Washington, DC: World Resources Institute, 2013).

13. Eric Toensmeier, *The Carbon Farming Solution: A Global Toolkit of Perennial Crops and Regenerative Agriculture Practices for Climate Change Mitigation and Food Security* (White River Junction, VT: Chelsea Green Publishing, 2016).

14. Prasanna Gowda et al., "Agriculture and Rural Communities," in *Impacts, Risks, and Adaptation in the United States: Fourth National Climate*

Assessment, vol. 2, ed. David R. Reidmiller et al. (Washington, DC: U.S. Global Change Research Program, 2018), 391-437.

15. Marco Springmann et al., "Options for Keeping the Food System within Environmental Limits," *Nature* 562, no. 7728 (October 2018): 519-25.

16. See Irakli Loladze, "Rising Atmospheric CO_2 and Human Nutrition: Toward Globally Imbalanced Plant Stoichiometry?," *Trends in Ecology & Evolution* 17, no. 10 (October 2002): 457-61; Samuel S. Myers et al., "Increasing CO_2 Threatens Human Nutrition," *Nature* 510 (June 2014): 139-42; Samuel S. Myers et al., "Effect of Increased Concentrations of Atmospheric Carbon Dioxide on the Global Threat of Zinc Deficiency: A Modelling Study," *Lancet. Global Health* 3, no. 10 (October 2015): e639-45; and Danielle E. Medek, Joel Schwartz, and Samuel S. Myers, "Estimated Effects of Future Atmospheric CO_2 Concentrations on Protein Intake and the Risk of Protein Deficiency by Country and Region," *Environmental Health Perspectives* 125, no. 8 (2017): 087002.

17. See Bon Appétit Management Company Foundation and United Farm Workers (UFW), "Inventory of Farmworker Issues and Protections in the United States," March 2011, http://www.ufw.org/pdf/farmworkerinventory_0401_2011 .pdf.

18. Seth Holmes, *Fresh Fruit, Broken Bodies: Migrant Farmworkers in the United States* (Berkeley: University of California Press, 2013).

19. Southern Poverty Law Center, "Sexual Violence against Farmworkers: A Guidebook for Criminal Justice Professionals," 2008, https://www.splcenter.org /sites/default/files/d6_legacy_files/downloads/publication/OVW_CriminalJustice .pdf.

20. Mary Bauer and Mónica Ramírez, "Injustice on Our Plates," Southern Poverty Law Center, November 8, 2010, https://www.splcenter.org/20101107 /injustice-our-plates.

21. International Labour Organization, "Global Estimates of Modern Slavery: Forced Labour and Forced Marriage" (Geneva: ILO, 2017).

22. International Labour Organization, "Toolkit for Mainstreaming Employment and Decent Work" (Geneva: ILO, 2008).

23. Because the CECs are primarily a tool for market-based change of the food system, the CECs in this section place particular emphasis on farmers, ranchers, and fishers who intend that at least some of their land- and water-derived products will be sold in local or international markets. Yet not all people who coax food from the land and seascape neatly fit the common understanding of farmers, ranchers, and fishers. Some are more accurately described as foragers and hunters, who may market their products or use their food provisioning skills for personal, familial, or close community subsistence. Foragers and hunters may participate in the global food system but do so in ways that differ substantially from commercial farmers, ranchers, and fishers. While the interests of foragers and hunters are certainly worthy of moral consideration, because they do not substantially engage with the market they are not a primary focus of most of the commitments in this section. Foragers

and hunters do figure prominently in CEC #23, however, which addresses access to and use of land, water, and associated resources.

24. Sarah K. Lowder, Jakob Skoet, and Terri Raney, "The Number, Size, and Distribution of Farms, Smallholder Farms, and Family Farms Worldwide," *World Development* 87 (November 2016): 16-29.

25. Theodore Panayotou, *Management Concepts for Small-Scale Fisheries: Economic and Social Aspects* (Rome: FAO, 1982).

26. IPES-Food, "Too Big to Feed: Exploring the Impacts of Mega-Mergers, Consolidation and Concentration of Power in the Agri-Food Sector," 2017, http://www.ipes-food.org/_img/upload/files/Concentration_FullReport.pdf.

27. Angela Huffman, Joe Maxwell, and Andres Salerno, "Consolidation, Globalization, and the American Family Farm," Organization for Competitive Markets, August 2017, https://competitivemarkets.com/wp-content/uploads/2017/08/Consolidation-Globalization-and-the-American-Family-Farm.pdf.

28. Organization for Competitive Markets, "Distorted Incentives: The Simple Arithmetic of Captive Supply," November 2016, https://competitivemarkets.com/wp-content/uploads/2016/11/Distorted-Incentives.pdf.

29. IPES-Food, "Too Big to Feed."

30. World Health Organization, "WHO Estimates of the Global Burden of Foodborne Diseases: Foodborne Disease Burden Epidemiology Reference Group, 2007-2015" (Geneva: World Health Organization, 2015).

31. GBD 2015 Obesity Collaborators, "Health Effects of Overweight and Obesity in 195 Countries over 25 Years," *New England Journal of Medicine* 377, no. 1 (July 2017): 13-27.

32. Food and Agriculture Organization of the United Nations et al., *The State of Food Security and Nutrition in the World: Building Resilience for Peace and Food Security* (Rome: FAO, 2017).

33. Corinna Hawkes and Marie Ruel, "The Links between Agriculture and Health: An Intersectoral Opportunity to Improve the Health and Livelihoods of the Poor," *Bulletin of the World Health Organization* 84, no. 12 (December 2006): 984-90.

34. Madison Powers and Ruth Faden, *Social Justice: The Moral Foundations of Public Health and Health Policy* (Oxford: Oxford University Press, 2006).

35. James Wilson, "Health Inequities," in *Public Health Ethics: Key Concepts and Issues in Policy and Practice*, ed. Angus Dawson (Cambridge: Cambridge University Press, 2011).

36. Andrew Jacobs and Matt Richtel, "How Big Business Got Brazil Hooked on Junk Food," *New York Times*, September 16, 2017, https://www.nytimes.com/interactive/2017/09/16/health/brazil-obesity-nestle.html.

37. Food and Agriculture Organization of the United Nations, *Rural Structures in the Tropics: Design and Development* (Rome: FAO, 2011), 225-98, http://www.fao.org/3/i2433e/i2433e.pdf.

38. Toby G. Knowles et al., "Leg Disorders in Broiler Chickens: Prevalence, Risk Factors and Prevention," *PloS One* 3, no. 2 (February 2008): e1545.

39. David Fraser, *Understanding Animal Welfare: The Science in Its Cultural Context* (Hoboken, NJ: Wiley-Blackwell, 2008).

40. Bernard E. Rollin, "Telos," in *Veterinary & Animal Ethics*, ed. Christopher M. Wathes et al., vol. 25 (Oxford: Blackwell Publishing, 2012), 75-83.

41. Farm Animal Welfare Council, "Farm Animal Welfare Council Press Statement," news release, December 5, 1979, https://webarchive.nationalarchives.gov.uk/20121010012427/http://www.fawc.org.uk/freedoms.htm.

THIRTY-ONE

The Core Ethical Commitments

ANNE BARNHILL, NICOLE M. CIVITA, CLAIRE DAVIS, SHAUNA DOWNS,
RUTH FADEN, SARA GLASS, ALAN M. GOLDBERG, HERMAN B. W. M. KOËTER,
BERNARD ROLLIN, PAUL B. THOMPSON, KEES VAN LEEUWEN, AND
SUZANNE MCMILLAN

Environment and Resources

Climate

1. Production, distribution, and waste management methods minimize greenhouse gas emissions, sequester carbon, and/or offset climate impacts.

Conservation and Regeneration

2. Practices are in place to conserve natural resources.

Soil Quality

3. Practices are in place to improve soil quality and management.

Water, Water Footprint, and Stress

4. Practices are in place to manage and conserve water and to prevent water pollution, especially under conditions of water stress and scarcity.

Air Quality

5. Practices are in place to avoid contributing to air pollution through food production, processing, and distribution activities.

Environmental Degradation and Agricultural Inputs

6. Use of inputs, such as fertilizers and pesticides, is appropriate and judicious.

Waste

7. Practices are in place to ensure optimal nutrient cycling within the agrifood system and to prevent waste from polluting or leaching into surrounding ecosystems.

Biodiversity

8. Practices are in place to enhance biodiversity of species and genetics, both wild and cultivated.

Food Chain Labor
Legal Status, Human Rights, and Protections

9. Conditions of work honor the inherent dignity and equal, inalienable rights of all people, consonant with the Universal Declaration of Human Rights.
10. Workers are afforded legal status in the jurisdictions where they live and work adequate for the exercise of fundamental rights and access to justice. Where this is not practicable, protections that support human liberty, security, access to justice, and realization of fundamental human rights are provided, including provisions for communication about these protections in the worker's native language.

11. Workers have the right to organize and the ability to assert their interests individually or collectively to influence the conditions under which they work without being subjected to retaliation.
12. Forced labor, including enslaved and involuntarily trafficked individuals of all ages, is never employed, and robust systems are in place to screen for and protect against its use.
13. Child labor is not employed, and robust systems are in place to screen for and protect against its use.
14. Workers are protected not only against marginalization, harassment, assault, violations of bodily integrity, and traumatization but also from the increased incidence of crime and victimization that flows from such conditions.

Working Conditions

15. Workers have safe working conditions. These conditions include regular access to sufficient food, water, and facilities for hygienic needs; open, accessible channels for communication and reporting; attention to occupational health and safety; and protection against exposure to chemicals, pathogens, and the elements.

Compensation and Benefits

16. Workers are ensured just compensation and benefits, regardless of nationality, race, color, gender, religion, sexual orientation, and gender identity.

Standards of Living and Well-Being

17. Work duties and conditions of employment, as well as the production and processing of food, do not compromise the well-being of workers and their families. Employment and work practices provide opportunities for housing, education, and community.

18. Workers have access to health care that is equivalent to comparable labor in other industries and in adjacent communities and that is commensurate with occupational hazards.

Farmers, Ranchers, and Fishers ·
Producer Viability

19. The long-term economic viability of farming, ranching, and fishing enterprises is not unfairly threatened by vertically related players in the food system with significantly greater power.
20. Contractual relations between farmers, ranchers, and fishers and integrators are fundamentally fair, involve equitable sharing of risk, and support the preservation of agricultural land, water, and seedstocks.
21. Owner-operators are not compelled or required by downstream players in the food system to use unethical business, land management, production, labor, and husbandry practices.
22. To prevent upstream players from having to choose between ethical conduct and long-term economic viability, downstream players in the food system favor more ethical products or producers.

Land Access and Tenure

23. Independent, smallholder, peasant, and qualified beginning producers have fair and adequate access to land and land tenure.

Public Health and Community Well-Being
Health Risks from Consumption

24. Foods do not pose unacceptable risks to public health, given population-level dietary patterns and individual health needs.
25. Practices are in place to ensure acceptable risk levels for chemical and microbiological food contamination. Adequate hygienic conditions are ensured through each step of the value chain.

26. Food packaging enhances food safety and does not pose unacceptable risks to public health.

Food Fraud and Economic Adulteration

27. Food is not adulterated for economic reasons, and traceability of ingredients is sufficient to guard against adulteration.

Product Information and Marketing

28. Labels are truthful, informative, transparent, easy to understand, and not misleading.
29. Food marketing provides consumers with information about the food product, storage conditions, and shelf life in ways that increase the likelihood that consumers can have an accurate understanding of the food, including its ingredients, nutritional properties, health and environmental impact, and production, labor, and animal welfare practices.
30. Inappropriate marketing practices, especially those targeting children or containing misleading messaging, are absent.

Animal Production and Waste Management

31. To minimize the risk of novel pathogens (including antibiotic-resistant bacteria) to public health, antibiotics and antimicrobials are used only to treat disease at therapeutic levels for the time necessary to treat the animal, with few exceptions. Antibiotics are not routinely used at subtherapeutic levels.
32. Practices are in place to minimize the spread of antibiotic-resistant bacteria and other pathogens, on and off farm.
33. Waste products from animal production are handled in ways that minimize the likelihood that the health and well-being of adjacent communities will be affected.

Excess Food, Waste, and Disposal

34. Excess food is directed and used in ways that conserve embedded resources, always cycling nutrients, water, and energy back into the food system.

Health Effects

35. Practices are in place to minimize negative health effects for animals (domesticated and wild) and humans that might occur as a result of crop and animal production (including the use of agricultural inputs) and distribution (including concentrated pollution around distribution hubs).

Access to Nutritionally and Culturally Important Foods

36. The product is produced, distributed, marketed, and sold in ways that do not threaten access to and the continued availability of nutritionally and culturally important foods.

Corporate Practices

37. Corporate practices are designed to improve public health and the well-being of workers, producers, and communities.

Animal Welfare
Biological and Psychological Nature

38. Animals are free to express behaviors that are normal and typical for their species and sufficient to reduce stress and enable coping.
39. Breeding and genetics do not adversely affect the animal's well-being and, where possible, improve it.
40. Living environments are respectful of the animal's health and well-being.
41. Feed is appropriate in quantity and type.

Pain and Distress

42. Pain and distress are avoided. Where possible, animals are free of discomfort.

43. Surgical procedures are designed to minimize pain and to support animal welfare.

44. The conditions and practices of animal transfers are designed to minimize pain and fear. Transport and transition conditions are humane and conducive to coping.

45. Animal injury and disease are minimized. If injury or disease occurs, prompt, effective, humane, and judicious treatment is administered.

46. The conditions and practices of slaughter function to minimize pain and distress.

47. Workers interact with and handle animals in ways that minimize pain and fear and support coping.

quinoa, 215
Quorn, 172

recycling, 161, 163–64, 311, 314
regenerative agriculture, 340. *See also*
  agroecology
rodenticides, 281–82
Ruhl, J. B., 58

Schusky, Ernest, 52–53
slaughtering: animal welfare and, 242,
  247, 254–55, 270, 273, 291, 356,
  367; worker health and safety, 39,
  196, 247, 344
slavery. *See* food chain labor
Smithfield Foods, 49–50, 268
soil health, 52–55, 70, 133–35, 141,
  250, 263, 340–41, 361
Sprengel, Carl, 53
staple foods, 10–11, 23–24, 102, 109,
  215, 230
Steiner, Rudolf, 54
stunting, 14, 22–25, 213
sugar-sweetened beverages, 9–10, 24,
  91–93, 219
Sustainable Development Goals (SDGs),
  16, 21, 112
sustainable intensification, 129–30, 132,
  141, 240, 243, 340
swine. *See* pigs

trade-offs, 16, 69, 128, 131, 134, 136,
  142–44, 211, 306–8, 352
Tyson Foods, 248

urbanization, 12, 14–15, 32–33, 104–5,
  142, 146–47, 151, 335
US Department of Agriculture (USDA),
  33–34, 39–40, 79–82, 84–85, 164,
  177, 238, 247, 283, 306, 317, 321

veganism and vegetarianism. *See*
  plant-based diets
vertical integration, 34, 36, 246–49, 348,
  364

water footprint, 11, 13, 47–48, 58–59,
  68–69, 127, 147–51, 160, 170, 214,
  337, 340, 361
Western diets, 38, 65, 99, 105, 117, 236,
  240
Whole Foods, 207, 297
World Food Programme, 22, 24
World Health Organization (WHO), 23,
  149, 232
World War II, 53, 271, 275–76

xenobiotics. *See* antibiotics; fertilizers;
  pesticides

zoonoses, 39–40, 224, 235, 251–52